For Brilliant Ben,
With high hopes and
full confidence in you
as the next pioneer — indeed
EXPLORER — in the land
of SCHOLARSHIP THAT MATTERS

You have all that it takes..''
the courage, intellect, and
tenacity to speak truth
to power, Thank you for finding
me! Always by your side,
Bev

PROGRESS IN POSTWAR
INTERNATIONAL RELATIONS

THE POLITICAL ECONOMY OF INTERNATIONAL CHANGE
John Gerard Ruggie, Helen Milner, General Editors

THE POLITICAL ECONOMY OF INTERNATIONAL CHANGE
John Gerard Ruggie, Helen Milner, General Editors

PROGRESS IN POSTWAR INTERNATIONAL RELATIONS

EDITED BY
**EMANUEL ADLER
AND BEVERLY CRAWFORD**

Columbia University Press
New York

Columbia University Press
New York   Oxford
Copyright © 1991 Columbia University Press
All rights reserved

Library of Congress Cataloging-in-Publication Data

Progress in postwar international relations / edited by Emanuel
Adler
   and Beverly Crawford.
   p. cm. — (The Political economy of international change.)
   Includes bibliographical references (p.   ) and index.
   ISBN 0–231–07278–3
   1. International relations. I. Adler, Emanuel. II. Crawford,
Beverly. III. Series.
JX1391.P77 1991
327′.09′045—dc20   90-2617
                                                           CIP

CONTENTS

FOREWORD
Kenneth N. Waltz

Ernst B. Haas has been studying, teaching, and writing about international relations for more than forty years.* His students populate the faculties of our colleges and universities and through their own publications have in turn become our teachers. He has written about the meanings of balance of power, the processes of economic and political integration, all sorts of international organizations, nationalist movements around the world, and many other topics. Moreover, as his students and colleagues know, he can comfortably and discerningly discuss an astonishing range of subjects, both near to and far from his areas of primary interest. Haas' combination of breadth of interest and mastery of detail has become all too rare among today's political scientists.

Over the years, Haas has followed a consistent approach and maintained a steady theoretical orientation. Continuity does not imply lack of change but rather a measured progression. More than most scholars, Haas has been willing to reconsider conclusions while amending the methods that produced them. In his early work on European integration, he developed what has since been known as neofunctionalism. He relied on two central ideas. The first is that scientific and technological changes produce incentives and pressures for international institutional innovation. The second is that the processes of institutional evolution lead to redefinitions and expanded notions about appropriate means for international coopera-

*I am grateful to James Fearon for his insightful review of Haas' work.

tion. In short, political leaders, national bureaucracies, and international organizations can "learn."

In *The Uniting of Europe*, published in 1958, and in *Beyond the Nation State*, published in 1964, spill-over is the process that is to lead to institutional innovation. In practice, however, spill-over did not increase the range of tasks passing from national governments to international organizations. The failure of practice to support theory led Haas to look beyond integration to more general questions of interdependence and the formation and functioning of intenational regimes. In doing so, he began to give still greater emphasis to the role of ideas and of "consensual knowlege," asking, for example, how groups of experts may influence the course of international affairs. From the middle 1970s, recognizing that earlier work on integration placed too much reliance on incremental changes rooted in the routine processes of economic and political life, he began to pay more attention to the role of political leaders, or as he put it, to the "goals considered by politicians."

In the categories into which students of international relations are often placed—structural–behavioral and realist–idealist—Haas falls in the second one of both pairs. He favors process over structure, believing that if structural constraints interfere with the achievement of desired ends, purposeful actors can find ways of breaking the bonds. Moreover, he has always rejected the assumption of a national interest defined by a unitary actor, even as a simplifying assumption. He believes that those who make policy can redirect the course their country follows and therefore emphasizes the autonomous role that consensual knowledge can play in changing the texture of international relations. In that sense, although not in the philosophic sense, he is an idealist. Reacting to the pressures of increasing interdependence, capitalizing on advances in scientific knowledge, and responding to the complexities of modernization, political leaders are pressed to move from national to transnational and international remedies. That is the hope, but Haas has always been a most realistic idealist. People can figure out what needs to be done in order to rescue an endangered planet. While believing that, he also understands the difficulties that stand in the way and frankly confronts the possibility of failure.

This volume is a well-deserved tribute to a career that is by no means over. The contributions from some of Ernie's colleagues, and from many of his students, give some idea of the esteem in which he is held. Some of the essays examine parts of his work; others represent applications of it. Some of the essays explore themes that he introduced; others sum up and interpret his work. Taken together, they illustrate the variety of directions that follow from a single body of work. This volume is but the latest evidence of the breadth of his influence. His own volume, *When Knowledge Is Power: Three Models of Change in International Organizations,* attests to his continuing creativity. Having had the pleasure of serving in the same department with Ernie for two decades, I am deeply aware of how much he has contributed to the development of the field and to the intellectual growth of his students and associates. I am especially pleased therefore to have the opportunity to write this brief note of appreciation.

Acknowledgments

With gratitude we acknowledge the institutions that made this project possible: the Davis Institute of International Relations and the Truman Institute of the Hebrew University of Jerusalem; the Graduate School of Public and International Affairs at the University of Pittsburgh; the Center for Science and International Affairs, Harvard University; the Institute of International Studies and its former Director, Carl Rosberg, and the Institute on Global Conflict and Cooperation at the University of California. We also thank Albert Fishlow, Dean, International and Area Studies at the University of California at Berkeley.

Many people read all or parts of this manuscript and offered helpful comments and criticism as well as support and encouragement. It is a pleasure to acknowledge the help we received from Hayward Alker, Don Babai, Michael Brecher, William Dunn, Bahman Fozouni, Robert Gilpin, Robert Gromoll, Ronnie Gruhn, Stanley Hoffman, Peter Katzenstein, Robert Keohane, Tim McKeown, Andrew Moravscik, Joseph Nye, John Ruggie, and William Soroos. We would especially like to acknowledge the contribution of Craig Murphy to the intellectual content of this project. The idea of the "roads to progress" is his. All of the contributors to this volume had a profound impact on the evolution of our ideas about progress, and working with them made this project enjoyable as well as intellectually rewarding. We would like to express both our respect and our affection for all of them. Ernst Haas provided the original intellectual inspiration for this project, and this book is for him.

We would also like to thank Bodine Brown, Florence Myer, Sally Fifer, and the entire staff at IIS for their help and support with the preparation of the manuscript. Kate Wittenberg's editorial expertise pushed this project along at every stage, and we are grateful. Finally and most importantly we thank our respective families. Sylvia was involved in this project from its inception, and we leave this book on Progress as a legacy to our children, Erin, Shirli, Nadav, and Jonathan.

INTRODUCTION
Robert O. Keohane

During the last forty years, students of international politics have been reluctant to speak about "progress," an idea associated with the utopianism of Enlightenment thinkers such as Condorcet, Turgot, and the Abbé de Saint-Pierre, or with the expectations of imminent world peace held by many American Progressives before World War I. Advances in technical knowledge and power over nature manifestly did not lead, during the first half of this century, to better realization of humane values; and idealistic views of international relations, relying on the improved moral quality of national decisions, seemed cruelly falsified. Furthermore, the extensive development of highly technical economic theory and the positivistic orientation of the behavioral revolution in politics led aspiring social scientists to be cautious about explicitly discussing the values they sought, through their analysis, to promote. To declare an interest in "progress in international relations" would have been both to expose one's own naiveté and to make one's work seem less scientific than that of one's apparently more objective peers.

Against this intellectual tradition, to publish a volume on *Progress in Postwar International Relations* is a bold action, worthy of notice. What Emanuel Adler, Beverly Crawford, and their collaborators have done is to be explicit about the values and concerns that many students of international relations have—and in being explicit, they help think more carefully about these issues. They are pioneers, moving to a frontier worthy of further cultivation.

Like the pioneers of the American West, however, Adler, Crawford, and their contemporaries did not chart the initial path. Explorers come first; pioneers, bold as they may be, follow. The early explorer of progress in international relations has been Ernst Haas, the teacher of most contributors to this volume and the valued colleague and friend of others. For over thirty years, Haas has been interested in how elites, with some influence over state policy, redefine their interests; and how this process of interest redefinition changes the focus of loyalties and the patterns of transnational and international politics. Recently, he has been reformulating his views in terms of "progress."

The editors of this volume provide a sophisticated analytical definition of progress in international relations, which is consistent with the view that states act to promote their perceived self-interests. That is, progress occurs not principally because governments pursue policies of what Arnold Wolfers once called "self-abnegation," but because they redefine their interests and therefore develop policies that "reduce conflict or increase cooperation so as to further security, welfare or human rights."* Furthermore, the advancement of scientific knowledge is neither a necessary nor a sufficient condition for progress, which depends principally on the "political selection, retention, and diffusion of values and expectations that tend to enhance human interests across borders" (opening paper, this volume). That is, in the view of Adler, Crawford, and their colleagues, progress is more the result of a highly political process than of a scientific one.

With this conception of progress and how it occurs in international politics, the "key question is what causes expectations and values that enhance human interests across national borders to be politically selected, maintained, and spread at domestic and international levels" (Adler, paper 2, this volume). That is, under what conditions will progress become possible? In her conclusion, Beverly Crawford argues that the opportunity for progress to occur is provided in contemporary international relations by a framework of international norms based on mutual respect for sovereignty; and by increased interdependence, which may create interests in cooperation or even create shared values and senses of obligation, restraint, or even empathy. "Interdependence can modify the calculations by which

---

*Arnold Wolfers, *Discord and Collaboration: Essays on International Politics* (Baltimore: Johns Hopkins University Press, 1962), p. 91; opening paper, this volume, p. 9).

states choose to exercise their power and under conditions of complex interdependence, power can be exercised to promote human interests" (paper 12, this volume). Adler emphasizes that for interdependence to lead to progress, it must generate changes in "collective understandings," which lead to a "reevaluation process that causes old interests to veer away from war, poverty and human rights violations because they have suddenly become dysfunctional" (paper 2, this volume). Scientists, linked together in "epistemic communities," may be able to play "an instrumental role in producing shared understandings that can lead to progressive changes."

The Adler–Crawford argument is plausible. Students of world politics know that national interests are not objective, but depend on shared understandings—on values and expectations. Views of how international relations should be organized differ from one culture to another, and they have changed within Western society over time. Changes in attitudes toward war have been evident for over a century; the two world wars of this century and the invention of nuclear weapons have, for the first time, rendered widespread the conception that war is dangerous and obsolete as a method of problem solving. Multilateral institutions are now accepted as valuable instruments for state policy in a variety of issue areas: arenas for the pursuit of redefined self-interest by governments rather than the impractical fantasies of dreamers about world federalism. To speak of global interests in environmental quality, human rights, or health no longer invites ridicule, even in high policy circles.

But to make a plausible case that progress could occur is not to demonstrate that it has taken place, much less that its underpinnings are secure. To do so would require establishing, for a variety of issue areas, that

1. Progress as defined in this volume has been taking place; that is, changes in state policies have promoted security, welfare, and human rights.
2. Progress has occurred through the redefinition of elite interests rather than as the result of mere conjunctures of interests or reversible structural change.*

*Emanuel Adler, in "Seasons of Peace," argues that substantive progress in international security can be achieved through structural transformation, political settlement, or changes in values and expectations of war. However, as he points out, structural changes can be reversed and political settlements are only temporary in the absence of changes in values.

3. Progressive redefinition of elite interests has been made possible by norms of sovereignty and by interdependence and has been fostered by epistemic communities of scientists.

Six of the essays in this volume discuss specific issue areas in which postwar progress could have taken place. The evidence with respect to the propositions listed earlier is decidedly mixed. In two cases (security and environment) substantial progress seems to have taken place, as a result to some extent of the redefinition of interests by elites. In each case, increased interdependence—coupled with higher costs of failure to manage interdependence successfully—prompted changes in interests, whether toward war or environmental pollution. In two other cases (human rights and the U.S.–Canada Free Trade Agreement), a more questionable argument could be made for progress. The area of human rights, as Jack Donnelly points out, is characterized by weak international regimes of a declaratory or promotional nature, based on a rather diffuse sense of moral interdependence. The U.S.–Canada Free Trade Agreement can be considered "progress" on the basis of a set of values stressing individualistic and materialistic well-being; from the standpoint of Canadian autonomy it is retrogressive. And in any case, it depends less on a redefinition of values than on a narrower recalculation of interests by various firms and groups in Canada. Finally, in the Palestinian issue and in the issue of nuclear proliferation there is little evidence of progress defined as changes in state policies that have promoted security, welfare, and human rights. UNRWA may well have prevented worse disaster, and superpower policies may have slowed down nuclear proliferation; but there is little evidence in either case of value-change leading to long-term improvement in security, welfare, or human rights.

This volume shows that it is far from foolish to raise the question of progress in contemporary international relations. It does not demonstrate that such progress has, on balance, taken place. Focusing on other issue areas would presumably point in different directions. One could make a case that there has been substantial progress in economic development where conditions and state policies have been appropriate (as in the newly industrialized countries of Asia); in moving away from statist authoritarian forms of rule in both Eastern Europe and Latin America; and in promoting an open international economic order among capitalist countries. On the other hand, there seems to have been little progress in economic development in Africa and much of Latin America; in institutionalizing income transfers from rich to poor (countries or individuals); or in establishing multilateral peacekeeping techniques on more than an *ad hoc* basis. International macroeconomic policy coordination, management of international indebtedness, and the control of terrorism may be ambiguous cases, where the cases for progress could be made, but contested.

Sometimes progress seems to take place through major changes in values and expectations, as exemplified by changes in views of war (discussed by Adler). Other instances of progress may reflect much more modest redefinitions of interest—as in the outward orientation of formerly parochial Canadian business-people, faced with changes in economics of scale and transborder capital movements. Progress can be more or less value-laden; we have not sorted out the conditions under which it occurs through extension of existing self-interests as opposed to those where a major reevaluation takes place.

All the case studies seem to agree that interdependence promotes redefinition of interests and at least makes progress possible, although hardly assuring progressive change. Yet although Crawford lists sovereignty as promoting progress by securing the state, it also restrains progress—as Donnelly points out for human rights. Fears for Canadian sovereignty were a source of opposition to the Free Trade Agreement. And surely the weakness of multilateral institutions has something to do with the sovereignty norm at the heart of those organizations. Finally, except in the environmental area—where scientists were involved as lobbyists and power-holders as well as experts—epistemic communities do not seem very important in the stories told in this volume. Scientists are not the driving forces of contemporary world politics.

A great merit of this volume is that it raises more questions than it answers. We need to think about progress in international relations —its incidence, its forms, and the conditions under which it takes place. Our knowledge of these issues is slim. Yet if we are to develop the sort of understanding of world politics that we need—a realistic but humane and value-laden perspective on our world—we should seek to continue cultivating this promising terrain that Ernst Haas has explored and that Adler, Crawford, and their associates have pioneered.

PROGRESS IN POSTWAR
INTERNATIONAL RELATIONS

1

DEFINING AND CONCEPTUALIZING PROGRESS IN INTERNATIONAL RELATIONS

Emanuel Adler
Beverly Crawford
Jack Donnelly

Progress consist (sic) swapping old troubles for new.
—Chinese fortune

Is progress possible in international relations? Have we been able to observe progressive change in international politics in the post–World War II period? National policy agendas and the programs of international organizations are guided by an implicit belief in international progress. They are filled with references to the goals of development, equality, human survival, "quality of life," and foreign policy programs that would bring about cooperation, stability, economic growth, and social justice in relations among nations. But what is progress in international relations? What are the international conditions under which "progressive change" takes place?

It is the purpose of this volume to explore these questions. We raise the question of progress because we wish to discover the dynamics and assess the direction of international change.[1] Both the analysis of change and an underlying concern with progress have been central themes in Ernst B. Haas' work and have influenced his intellectual contribution to the study of international relations.[2] We build on this contribution, aiming to focus our analysis of changes in postwar international relations on the question of progress.

But an examination of progress is more than an analysis of change. Webster defines progress as an "advance or movement toward an objective or toward a goal" or the "action or process of advancing or improving by marked stages or degrees." Progress involves not merely directed change, but change in a direction or toward an end that is positively valued; as Francisco Ayala has defined it, "directional change toward the better."[3] Both progress itself and the end by which progress is measured may be either intrinsically or instrumentally valued. Our discussion of progress—both of the ends and of the means by which it is (or is not) achieved—is therefore inescapably normative. Of course value-neutral discourse on progress is possible, but unless we also engage in evaluative discourse, we can only consider part of the subject; if values are entirely eliminated, we cannot discuss progress. At the outset, then, we must carefully specify and defend the standards by which we will define, measure, and explain progress in international relations. This chapter is devoted to these three tasks.

DEFINING PROGRESS

We begin with our working definition of progress: Progress in international relations implies changes in the pursuit of states' national interests in ways that further human interests. Human interests are defined here as security, welfare, and human rights for individuals. Because we recognize the definitional controversy that can arise when scholars think about international progress, a defense of this definition is in order.

Statist vs. Systemic Perspectives

We can begin by outlining two basic approaches to the specification of progress in international relations, which we can call "statist" (or "national") and "systemic" (or "international") perspectives. The statist approach would view progress as whatever furthers the realization of the objectives or interests of a particular state. "Progress in international relations" thus would become the realization of the goals or national interest of state x in or as a result of its international activities. The systemic approach, by contrast, would view international relations as a collective endeavor with goals in addition to (or arising out of the interplay of) the particular purposes of separate states. "Progress in international relations" in this conception would involve movement toward ends that cannot simply be reduced to the goals or interests of a particular state or group of states. Within the systemic approach, the goals, standards, and values are derived from an examination of those consensual values espoused by the international community.

The statist approach makes all evaluation essentially "subjective," specific to a single subject. Therefore, evaluations of the "same" changes may differ radically from subject (in this case, state) to subject (state): A may claim that x is progressive; B, that x is regressive; and C, that x is neutral—and all three may very well be right. "Progress" thus is reduced to something very much like "what I want" or the realization of a narrowly defined "national interest" in a state's international relations. As such it is hardly worth serious investigation, even if it should prove to be the case that states do in fact adopt essentially statist definitions of progress in their international relations. Therefore, our approach must be systemic. This brings us back to the problem of selecting and defending particular goals for measuring progress in international relations.

We suggest that security, welfare, and human rights should be singled out as providing the consensual standard or definition of those goals. Consider the United Nations Charter, as good a place as any to discover the higher aspirations of the international community from which a systemic definition of progress in international relations might be distilled. Despite the U.N.'s problems, there is still significant international consensus on these goals as embodying the higher aspirations of the international community. The Preamble lists four purposes of the organization: "to save succeeding generations from the scourge of war"; "to reaffirm faith in fundamental human rights, (and) in the dignity and worth of the human person"; "to establish conditions under which justice and respect for . . . international law can be maintained"; and "to promote social progress and better standards of life in larger freedom." A very similar list is provided in Article 1: "to maintain international peace and security"; "to develop friendly relations among nations"; "to achieve international cooperation in solving international problems of an economic, social, cultural or humanitarian character, and in promoting and encouraging respect for human rights and fundamental freedoms";

and "to be a center for harmonizing the actions of nations." The Charter, then, provides an intersubjective measure of progress in international relations. It fits our conception of progress as involving change toward greater security, economic and social welfare, and human rights.

We come to a similar conclusion if we consider the goods we expect from domestic politics. Most people, in most countries, expect or desire that the state provide law and order (domestic peace and tranquility or "security") and foster the economic and social development and welfare of the community. Furthermore, it is widely expected or desired that domestic security and welfare be pursued with respect for human rights and, more generally, that justice be established as the norm in social relations. Fully recognizing the differences between domestic and international politics—between political and anarchic societies—it nonetheless does seem plausible to extend the values sought in national politics to international politics, however different the means and institutions through which they are pursued.

Such arguments, which can be easily multiplied, suggest that security, welfare, and human rights represent plausible standards for progress in international relations that are at least no more controversial than any others. As such, we will adopt them. We refer to these goals as "human interests" to distinguish our systemic approach from a statist one that would focus only on a narrow conception of the "national interest" with regard to progress in international relations. We will discuss the relationship between "human interests" and "national interests" in more detail later.[4]

The contributors to this volume focus on one or more of these goals as the standard for measuring progress in a number of issue areas. Philippe Schmitter focuses on both welfare and security as he analyzes the impact of democratization on economic interdependence and political cooperation among states. Emanuel Adler, in his analysis of changing expectations of the outcomes of war and cooperation, assesses progress according to standards of increased security. Peter Haas, in his analysis of international environmental issues; John Ruggie, in his analysis of change in international economic regimes; and Robert Kudrle and Stefanie Lenway, in their analysis of the U.S.–Canada Free Trade Agreement focus on welfare. Haas associates welfare gains with a cleaner environment, Ruggie associates these gains with the stability of international regimes that protect national welfare as well as liberalize trade, and Kudrle and Lenway examine the welfare gains associated with free trade in "rich" countries. Jack Donnelly examines progress in international human rights, and Ben Schiff examines the progress achieved in both human rights and welfare for Palestinian refugees.

Minimalist vs. Maximalist Conceptions

Next, we need to distinguish "minimalist" (or "negative") from "maximalist" (or "positive") views of security, welfare, and human rights. The minimalist, in exploring progress in international relations, is concerned primarily with reducing the level and intensity of violent conflict, exploitation, misery, and injustice: for example, changes in the number, duration, or intensity of wars; in the number or proportion of people in mass poverty, or the extent of their suffering; in instances of peaceful settlement of conflicts according to principles of law, justice, or equity; or in the incidence of gross, systematic, and persistent violations of basic human rights. In other words, for the minimalist, progress is achieved when human interests are represented and promoted as states continue to pursue their national interests, and that progress will usually amount only to less war, less misery, and less injustice.

The maximalist, however, would count such changes as involving only the most preliminary progress. "Real" progress, for the maximalist, would require substantial positive movement toward the attainment of "real" security (not merely a reduction in war), "real" welfare (not merely a reduction in misery), and "real" human rights (not merely a reduction in the grossest sorts of injustices). For the maximalist, progress is achieved only when pursuit of "human interests" comes to replace pursuit of the "national interest" in international politics.[5]

The nature of contemporary international politics suggests choosing a minimalist approach, or at least emphasizing progress negatively defined in an approach that combines minimalist and maximalist elements. For better or worse, anarchy, in the strict sense of absence of rule, remains the dominant feature of contemporary international relations. However much we emphasize the rise of interdependence, transnational and transgovernmental relations, and international organizations and regimes in this volume, national sovereignty—that is, the absence of international authority—remains the central organizing principle of the international system, in theory and in practice. Whether we bemoan or revel in the fact, the "Westphalian" system of autonomous nation-states not only persists but seems remarkably vigorous. Whatever disagreements there may be about the pace of change, the direction of trends, or the desirability of the status quo, this description of international relations is almost universally accepted by serious students of the subject.

Anarchy may not exactly breed violent conflict, but it does provide an environment in which it flowers freely; in the absence of legitimate authority, power and force readily become the rule by which disputes are resolved. Sovereignty may not exactly create misery, but it does contribute greatly to lower levels of welfare—for example, by protecting national and international inequality, impeding welfare-enhancing cooperation, or requiring expenditures for guns at the expense of butter. Likewise, sovereignty may not be a fundamental cause of human rights violations, but it is often used to cloak or protect the depredations of ruling elites, both at home and abroad. In other words, international anarchy makes it difficult even to achieve substantial reductions of war, misery, and human rights violations. Therefore, a minimalist conception of progress seems more consonant with the nature of contemporary international politics and problems than a maximalist conception.

Notice that we are not arguing that the nation-state is the source or root of international problems. We are not even arguing that weakening or eliminating states would guarantee progress; for example, a tyrannical world government might easily produce greater human rights violations, more misery, and even more violence than the state system of the last three or four centuries.

Indeed, classical realists have argued that the rise of the state system in the seventeenth century was a "progressive" moment in the history of international relations. Gradually, as territorial boundaries became more stable, a rational calculation of the national interest largely (although not entirely) came to replace ideology or religion as the basis for policy. Thus, enlightened statesmen could create orderly relations with others, because their demands on others would be limited by security interests.[6]

As Crawford's essay suggests, the triumph of the sovereignty norm in the late nineteenth century can also be viewed as a progressive moment in diplomatic history. As the rules of diplomacy shifted from great power primacy to the juridical equality of all states, great and small, states came to accept some limits on "maximizing" their power. Territorial boundaries may even minimize violence between those whose ultimate goals conflict. Craig Murphy has argued that boundaries of nations with more progressive social and political standards have helped protect the social progress achieved by democratic forces.[7]

Despite the fact that these developments may be considered "progressive" in relation to what preceded them, the pursuit of the "national interest" (however broadly defined to include goals other than political survival) rather than "human interests" remains the driving force behind most of the behavior of states in international relations. The contemporary system of sovereign states suggests that human interests are unlikely to replace the national interest soon and that only progress defined in largely negative, minimalist terms is likely in the foreseeable future—if that. Therefore, we should concentrate on exploring movement toward the minimal goals of reducing (national, and especially international) violence, misery, and human rights violations.

Most of the contributors to this volume adopt this focus. As a whole, we are modest about the kinds of changes we expect, if not about the changes we would like to see. For example, rather than focusing on the broad task of eliminating environmental degradation, Peter Haas has focused his analysis on the narrow problem of collective action to reduce cross-border pollution. Reagan and Gorbachev took a maximalist approach to security when they advocated the elimination of all nuclear weapons. In this volume, however, Adler takes the minimalist road. In his analysis, progress in international relations between the superpowers is best evaluated by looking at the political conditions that make the use of nuclear weapons less likely. Jack Donnelly looks at international conditions under which gross human rights violations within states can be reduced, a very minimalist approach to progress in this issue area. Ben Schiff takes a minimalist approach to progress in his analysis of the Palestinian refugee problem in the Middle East. He does not demand sweeping solutions to the refugee problem or peace in the region as the test of progress; rather, he looks at the role of one international organization in improving individual welfare and rights of the Palestinian refugees. Philippe Schmitter, however, is more demanding here; for him, economic and social progress for individuals involves increasing democratization within states, a view that goes beyond minimalism. In fact, Schmitter's essay draws its inspiration from Kant's maximalist view that only a system of republics would be able to evolve into a system of "perpetual peace."[8] Finally, John Ruggie and Robert Kudrle and Stefanie Lenway take a minimalist approach to progress in international economic relations. For Ruggie, "embedded liberalism" as the central assumption guiding international trade represents incremental progress toward general welfare when compared to the economic orders of laissez faire and closure that preceded World War II. Similarly, in their analysis of bilateral U.S.– Canadian free trade negotiations, Kudrle and Lenway define progress as simply the creation of a bilateral dispute settlement mechanism to resolve conflicts sparked by independent national economic policies.

Instrumental and Substantive Progress

Recent literature on international cooperation and international "regimes" has implicitly suggested that more cooperation in international relations is an indicator of progress.[9] In this volume, we both build on this literature and move a step beyond it. We make a distinction between "instrumental" and "substantive" progress. Substantive progress refers to the goals or ends by which progress is measured. We have identified these goals as security, welfare, and human rights, however minimal the achievement of these goals might be. If at least one of these values is enhanced over time across national borders without creating unbearable harm to other values and human interests, progress is achieved. Instrumental progress, on the other hand, involves the "means" by which substantive progress comes about. These "means" include but are not limited to international cooperation. Other instruments of progress might be unilateral policy changes, or the activities of International Non-Governmental Organizations (INGOs). We do not consider these instruments progressive unless they lead to the promotion of human interests in international relations. For example, international cooperation may indeed lead to progress as we define it. But it is not the *only* instrument by which progress is achieved, nor is it *necessarily* progressive. We will provide more concrete indicators of instrumental progress in a moment, when we discuss how progress can be measured.

Assuming both a systemic perspective, a minimalist conception, and a distinction between instrumental and substantive progress, progress in international relations can now be defined succinctly: progress will involve changes in the policies and relations of states that reduce conflict or increase cooperation so as to further security, welfare, or human rights, understood as a reduction in violence, misery, or human rights violations. In other words, progress in international relations implies the pursuit of the national interests of states in ways that further human interests. This does not mean that actors must relinquish their national interests or their power. Rather, it implies that actors apply their power differently from the way they used it in the past, and invest time and resources in finding solutions to problems from which individuals across borders suffer.

There still will be considerable definitional controversy about the meaning or substance of war, and especially about misery and human rights violations. In addition, the practical implications of a commitment to reduce war, misery, and violations of human rights —however they may be defined in detail—will also be controversial, even within—let alone across—values. Nonetheless, the ideas of war, misery, and human right violations are sufficiently clear in their broad outlines to serve our purposes here.

This approach also seems to be at least loosely compatible with most standard "schools" in the study of international relations. Most realists could easily live with this conception of progress, although they would stress order and the reduction of violence in international relations and would probably hold out little hope for major progress even here. World order theorists and other contemporary "idealists" would chafe at the minimalism of our conception and would stress the importance in any analysis of the ultimate introduction of a maximalist conception of positive peace, welfare, and justice. Nonetheless, they probably could tolerate it. Liberal internationalists and interdependence theorists should feel very much at home with this formulation. But so should most Marxists, neo-Marxists, and dependency theorists, however different their accounts of the causes of war, misery, and human rights violations might be. Therefore, the definition of progress as forms of international interaction (instrumental progress) that reduce violence, misery, or human rights violations (substantive progress) is perhaps the closest we can come to a widely acceptable working definition.

Nonetheless, we should not forget security, welfare, and human rights conceived in more positive terms, however far away they seem and however slow our progress toward them may be. A minimalist conception of progress in international relations may be imposed on us by the depth and scope of the problems we face and the painfully slow and costly pace of our progress toward the goals of security, welfare, and human rights. A minimalist conception allows us to measure and analyze better what progress we are able to see today. But it remains a weak and thin conception. Therefore, while we focus on how far we have (or haven't) come, defined minimally, we must keep in the back of our minds how far we have to go, defined maximally. A maximalist conception of progress cannot be the principal standard used in our analysis, but it must ultimately enter into our account.

Priorities and Beneficiaries

Security, welfare, and human rights, however, are often incompatible goals. For example, greater human rights may require the resort to violence and even war, as in the case of the Tanzanian invasion to overthrow Idi Amin. Peaceful coexistence, during the four decades of the Cold War, from the perspective of East and West alike, was probably a classic example of the sacrifice of human rights, and perhaps even welfare, in the name of peace.

Was peaceful coexistence an indicator of progress in international relations? It clearly was progressive when compared to the patterns of international interaction that gave us two world wars. But it can easily be argued that human rights violations and misery were intensified in Eastern Europe and other countries (or, from the Soviet perspective, in Western Europe and the Third World). The Cold War also increased defense spending on both sides at the expense of welfare. On balance, the reduction in international violence during the Cold War period was probably more important. But progress in this case looks a lot like one step forward and two smaller steps back. And if we question, as Adler does in the conclusion to his essay on

security, the long-run stability of the nuclear balance of terror, even this much is not clear. Philippe Schmitter argues that states' human rights policies internally and their external economic exchanges and political cooperation with others are all mutually reinforcing. More internal democratization leads to increased international economic development and security. Revolutionary developments toward de-mocratization in Eastern Europe reinforce his conclusions.

This "virtuous circle" of democracy, welfare, and peace notwith-standing, there may indeed be some injustices that are worth fighting a war over—for example, to prevent a recurrence of the Holocaust. Others, however, such as the injustices of guest worker programs in Germany, may not be worth a resort to violence. When the mass of a country's population is starving or seriously malnourished, unjust means and even war may be justified to achieve significant reduc-tions in misery. In many other circumstances, even major improve-ments in welfare are not worth significant increases in violence or human rights violations.

All three values are important; in fact, each is of paramount impor-tance. Nonetheless, in many instances they conflict. And even when they conflict, progress can still be achieved. In such cases, the best we can do is to weigh one against another, roughly, in the particular circumstances in question. The trade-offs we are forced to make among these goals are ultimately dependent upon particular histori-cal conditions and upon our own good judgment. The complications that arise in assessing progress are undoubtedly serious. They are, however, just as assuredly unavoidable, because here as elsewhere, the simple fact is that the values to which we are committed are all too often incompatible in particular cases.

Finally, to conclude this definitional discussion, we stress that although we are talking about progress in or as a result of interna-tional relations, the benefits of that progress are likely to be national and even individual. By reducing international conflict or increasing international cooperation so as to reduce violence, misery, or injus-tice, states (and other relevant international actors) are almost certain to benefit themselves and (at least some of) their nationals directly and the ultimate beneficiaries of a world with less war, misery, or injustice are the individuals who live in that world.

Therefore, adopting a systemic rather than a statist perspective of progress does not mean ignoring either states or individuals. Quit

the contrary, as we discuss in more detail later, the focus of the papers in this volume is on the *actions* and *interactions* of states and how they contribute to or retard progress in international relations. From the perspective of progress in international relations, the relations of states are of interest primarily insofar as they provide individuals with more peaceful, more just, more pleasant, and better-developed life. We thus take the view that individuals, not states, are the "subjects" of progress. That is, individuals, though not the unit of analysis here, provide the source of value, and they are the main standard by which to assess the quality of outcomes in international relations.

MEASURING PROGRESS

Where do we look for progress in international relations? And how do we know when it has or has not been achieved? Recall that we argue that progress is achieved when states pursue their national interests in ways that further human interests. As indicators of progress, then, the contributors to this volume have traced changes in the *ways* states have defined and pursued their national interests and solved their problems throughout the postwar period (instrumental progress) to enhance international security, welfare, and human rights (substantive progress).[10]

This "tracing" is done in four ways: (1) assessments of international institutional change, (2) analysis of changing interactions among states, (3) exploration of the formulation and implementation of national and international policy, and (4) assessments of changes in values, expectations, and attitudes, both at the elite and popular levels. Several authors who argue that progress in their issue area is achieved through international collaboration trace the actual development of international institutions, looking for increasing institutional strength or institutional maintenance. Careful measures of increasing institutional strength can provide a good indicator of change in the way these institutions' members pursue their national interests. Other contributors trace processes of interaction *among* states as they negotiate with one another either tacitly or explicitly, as they build and develop international institutions, and as they intensify cooperative diplomatic and economic efforts. Here, shifting preference orderings and bargaining positions provide a second indicator

of change in the way negotiators represent and pursue their national interests. Still other authors have examined how states pursue their national interests by tracing the policy process and policy outcomes both *within* states and *within* international organizations and regimes as they face changing international problems. Finally, others believe that measures of value, and attitude change provide a good indicator of whether human interests are incorporated into conceptions of the "national interest." All the authors trace the changes they believe to be relevant with an eye to whether our minimalist definition of progress is achieved.

Institutional Development

Stronger international institutions whose norms, rules, and procedures constrain international violence, provide incentives for welfare-oriented policies, or protect human rights are indicators of a "progressive" definition of the national interest of their members. A discussion of institutional development is not, however, an examination of deliberate plans for the design of better institutions. It is rather an examination of the actual historical process of institutional change and the impact of international institutions on developments within their member nations.

John Ruggie's analysis of postwar international economic regimes for trade and money provides the broadest examination of change in postwar international institutions. He traces the evolution of members' commitment to the institutions and alienation from them, as well as institutional flexibility in meeting members' economic needs as indicators of institutional capabilities to promote progress in international economic relations.

Both authors who explore the issue area of human rights focus on the development of human rights regimes as indicators of progress. Jack Donnelly surveys the growth of the regime as a whole. He measures progress by examining whether the human rights regime has become "stronger" over time. To establish regime strength, he differentiates among types of regimes according to their norms and decision-making activities. The more authoritative and binding the international norms governing human rights activity and the more authoritative the international decision making and monitoring procedures are, the stronger the regimes and the more progress we are able to observe in the issue area. Ben Schiff focuses his analysis on the development of one specific human rights organization, the United Nations Relief and Works Agency for Palestine Refugees (UNRWA) as a measure of international commitment to refugee rights. By tracing the organization's development and establishing measures for its success in wending its way through the minefields of Middle East politics, he is able to assess progress in one "hard case" of international human rights and welfare activity. Finally, Adler measures progress in both security and welfare by analyzing the effects of arms controls agreements. For example, the Partial Test Ban Treaty and the treaties on Antarctica and Space link security issues with issues of environmental quality.

Changing International Interactions

Analyses of the negotiating process among states also permits us to trace whether definitions of the national interest or the means by which states pursue their interests have changed over time. Within international negotiations, decision makers often discover what they want by finding out what they can get and by learning the impact of their preferences on others. The revelation of one state's preferences provides information to the others. Thus, negotiations can become a channel by which, according to Adler's notion of "cognitive evolution," ideas that originate in one nation are "diffused" to others. As states gain additional information and new ideas of any kind, they reevaluate the net benefits attached to the pursuit of alternative policies. Thus, their policy preferences may shift in the negotiating process itself.[11]

Note here that it is not necessary for interests per se to change for progress to be achieved. It is necessary only that the ways by which states pursue their interests change in a manner that leads to less violent conflict among states, less poverty, and fewer human rights violations. For example, by tracing the negotiating process that led to the Med Plan, Peter Haas shows that, although fundamental interests of the negotiators did not change, their initial bargaining positions shifted during the period of negotiations as they learned about the negative consequences of their previous policies. Participants actually changed their positions to expand the scope of international control over pollution. They also increased the amount they were willing to pay in order to achieve more pollution control. Adler argues here that the negotiation of arms control agreements helped to dispel beliefs in both the United States and the Soviet Union about the inevitability of war and built confidence in the efficacy of cooperative means to avoid nuclear war.

Philippe Schmitter takes the broadest approach here to changing interactions among states. As indicators of progress in welfare and security, in quite different areas of the world, he examines changes in the volume and variety of economic exchanges between countries and the scope and intensity of their political and cultural contacts.

The Policy Process: Changing Problems and Changing Solutions

Many problems are never "solved" once and for all, but as our Chinese fortune reminds us, "progress consists of swapping old troubles for new." Progress is achieved if today's policy problems are preferable to—that is, less harmful than—those of the past.[12] Therefore, it is useful to examine how policy problems are redefined over time. The definition of a problem is usually characterized by a hypothesis about cause–effect relationships. If we increasingly know more about causes, or if the cause is ameliorated but the problem persists, the conditions are ripe for a redefinition of the problem. For example, international food problems were once largely defined by their technical causes and the Malthusian problem of food supply. As technical solutions were found to increase food supply, and as more information about malnutrition filtered into the policy process, problems of food distribution and "entitlement" came to replace problems of supply. International food problems are now largely defined by their social, rather than their technical, causes.

This does not mean, however, that actual policy solutions do not provide a good measure of progress as we defined it earlier. The "green revolution" was a durable and progressive solution to some international food problems, despite its obvious unintended negative consequences. If present policies seem to be less coercive, less exploitative, and more respectful of human rights, progress is achieved. An examination of changes in actual *policy solutions* over time allows us to discover whether states' definitions of interests have changed.

Peter Haas' chapter here serves to illustrate. He asks whether states are increasingly able to solve their problems of industrial development in ways that will protect the environment and contribute to the welfare of both their own citizens and the citizens of other states. He identifies progress in environmental protection by looking at how states have begun to incorporate consideration of cross-border environmental consequences of their actions in foreign and development policies.

Of course this process of redefining problems and solutions as a measure of progress is not confined to the policy process within states. It is equally important to look at how this process unfolds within international organizations or within international "regimes." Schiff, for example, shows how UNRWA achieved progress by redefining refugee problems to match politically manageable solutions.

Changing Values

Adler argues that when new values emerge and old values are redefined to advance human interests across national borders, we can indeed claim that progress in international relations is achieved. Thus, one of the reasons for the arrival of a "progressive season" in international security after World War II was a change in values wherein some nations, taking everything else into consideration, came to prefer peace more than war. Likewise, he argues, a change in expectations regarding the outcomes of war can also spell progress.

Crawford's essay examines progressive changes in valuing the means by which the national interest is pursued. She suggests that if states come to value "restraint," "obligation," and "empathy" as principles guiding the definition and pursuit of the national interest, an important measure of progress can be identified. States may place an increasing value on *restraint* when fear of retaliation enters the policy calculation. If conflict is reduced, progress may be achieved. Likewise, new *obligations* to others may arise as a basis for policy decision, when decision makers begin to value their interdependent relationships. When obligations guide decisions, we can say that the concept of "self-interest" is expanded to include an interest in the welfare of foreigners. Finally, a sense of human solidarity and awareness of connections between people can lead decision makers to place a higher value on *empathy* in their foreign policy calculations.

These value changes are indicators of progress if they promote human interests across borders.

In short, only Philippe Schmitter's essay measures progress by looking at overall increases in political cooperation and economic exchanges among states and decreasing human rights violations within states. Other authors focus specifically on indicators of change in how states define and pursue their national interest in discrete issue areas. These changes can best be measured by changing policy problems and policy solutions, changing bargaining positions, changing international institutions, and changing social values. If the definition and pursuit of the national interest grow to include "human interests" as we have defined them here, progress is achieved.

MAKING PROGRESS

What causes states to build stronger progressive institutions, change their preferences in negotiations, and formulate national policies to protect human interests? Why would state interests—or the way states pursue their interests—ever change? Just as surely as we believed that there is more than one measure for progress, we also believe that there is more than one explanation for and one path to "progressive" change in international relations.

We begin by arguing that rapid scientific and technological advance, on the one hand, and rising international interdependence, on the other, are the central changes that provide the context for progress in postwar international relations. We then examine two promising roads to progress and an explanation for why actors might choose to travel along them. Finally, we caution against taking these or any arguments for progress as "blueprints" for progressive change. To reinforce this point we discuss the limitations of our argument in some detail.

Scientific and Technological Advance

Rapid advances in science and technology in the twentieth century have triggered unprecedented global economic growth and increasing connectedness among nations. The application of science to agriculture and industrial production has substantially enhanced the material welfare of the global population. Rapid growth in the technology of transportation and communication has increased the impact societies have upon one another and provided ample opportunities for international cooperation. For example, progress toward solutions to the problem of worldwide famine has been achieved by technological advances in agriculture and transportation.

From the functionalist perspective pioneered by David Mitrany,[13] these advances could lead to a "maximalist" vision of progress by virtue of the fact that informed publics within states would pressure their governments to remove their national restrictions inhibiting the creation of economies of scale. At the same time, intergovernmental agencies would be created to regulate the new technologies over much larger regions. Technological progress would thus increase the number of activities regulated by world government, leading to the demise of the state system as we know it.

Indeed, as the research conducted by some of the authors here suggests, technological changes have led to the creation of many new intergovernmental organizations. Yet these multilateral agencies have hardly transformed the state system, as the functionalist vision of progress had promised. The changes leading to 1992 in Europe notwithstanding, there is little reason to believe that informed publics will demand that governing responsibilities be handed over to a larger body simply because technology creates economies of scale. There is also little evidence that such a process is perceived as "rational." Further, there is little reason to believe that such changes would be progressive. As we discussed earlier, world government may be no more and even less progressive than the present state system. Likewise, international "regimes" may or may not be progressive. Just as technological changes can be a boon to welfare and global connectedness, they can make war far more destructive, lead to environmental degradation, and make torture and repression more efficient. Reliance on scientific and technological "solutions" to social problems can lead to entrapment in an ideology of success that blocks recognition of negative consequences and the search for new solutions.[14] As we will see, Adler argues that dependence on technological solutions to the nuclear dilemma for greater national security has led to greater insecurity in the long run. Technological advance is certainly not a sufficient condition for international progress.

This is not to say that scientific and technological advance cannot provide important conditions for progress in international relations.

As discussed earlier, these advances can lead, albeit in a dialectical way, to "better problems" and a search for new solutions. Technological advances can cause problems among states providing incentives to cooperate in the search for joint problem resolution. They can thus create new opportunities for international collaboration. As such, they can be a means toward progress, but not ends in themselves. For example, the problem of cross-border pollution can trigger a process of international cooperation to manage the negative environmental effects of industrial technologies. And the same pollution can trigger escalating conflict among the affected states. There is no way that we can determine at the outset that progressive change results from advances in science and technology. Nonetheless, these advances can facilitate the changes we believe will enhance human interests.

International Interdependence

If scientific and technological change do not directly bring about progress in international relations, what about the role of international interdependence? Interdependence implies states' reliance on common technologies and common resources, and thus more connectedness among nations, measured by the development of a new international division of labor and increasing international flows of people, ideas, technology, money, and trade. Interdependence creates shared constraints and shared opportunities. Common constraints impose an "authority" over states that set limits on unilateral action. Mutual dependence creates common interests and even common values. Interdependence thus creates incentives for self-interested actors, including states, to seek new, nonconflictual or more cooperative forms of interaction. Under conditions of interdependence, a state wants something that can only be achieved with the cooperation—formal or informal, express or tacit, ad hoc or institutionalized—of another state. Thus, they are likely to seek out cooperative arrangements with other states, or arrangements that minimize conflict. This is especially evident in Kudrle and Lenway's discussion of U.S.–Canadian free trade negotiations. The motivation for both to negotiate a free-trade area stems in part from the magnitude of bilateral trade between the two countries.

Like scientific and technological innovation, however, international interdependence and its incentives for cooperation do not automatically lead to progress. There is no reason to believe that simply because states are more connected or because societies increasingly affect one another, that violence, poverty, and human rights violations will be minimized. Two interdependent states may decide to cooperate in such a way that one or more other states are exploited. Conversely, an overwhelmingly dominant power—that is, a state that is largely independent rather than interdependent— may choose to act fairly or benevolently rather than exploitively. And interdependence may create tension, friction, or conflict and thus actually impede progress or even lead to regressive forms of interaction.

Take, for example, the "strategic interdependence" of the two superpowers. Robert Jervis has observed that nuclear weapons have made the two principal actors increasingly dependent on each other's military strategies.[15] This mutual dependence leads to mutual vulnerability, which implies that the two nations can no longer rely upon their defensive forces for security. Each must rely for its own survival upon the other's policies of restraint; a unilateral decision to use nuclear weapons would mean self-destruction. Unilateral decisions are thus constrained because payoffs for acting in the "common interest" of avoiding nuclear war are increased.

This interdependence, however, does not reliably lead to cooperation that would increase international security. The shared common interest of avoiding all-out war can be competitively exploited because achieving this goal requires that only one side make concessions. The very strength of the shared value—to avoid all-out nuclear war—can permit one side to shift the burden of avoiding mutual destruction to the other. Of course, one change that could fundamentally alter this outcome would be the development of an effective ballistic missile defense. The technological innovations leading to an effective defense create an incentive to strike first and thus actually increase the odds of conflict. Any realization of common interests that might result from the condition of strategic interdependence could be prevented by technological changes that appeared to give nuclear weapons defensive or warfighting capabilities. Thus, as Adler argues, only when the superpowers come to realize that they cannot shift the burden of avoiding mutual destruction to the other side does the awareness of security interdependence set in, and with it the opportunity for progress.

To be sure, then, there is no way that we can determine, on abstract theoretical grounds, the relative overall impact of dependence, independence, and interdependence on progress in international relations. Nevertheless, it provides a context in which insecurity, misery, and injustice can be reduced. We thus argue that interdependence—in particular, complex interdependence—is a permissive condition for progress in international relations.

Complex Interdependence

It is commonplace to note that, as a rule, states choose an interdependent relationship with other states only when separate national action proves unsuccessful or prohibitively expensive. Therefore, the presence of international interdependence usually implies the failure of national action in the particular issue area in which unilateral policy is insufficient. Successful management of this interdependence thus implies that the capacity of states to achieve their objectives is enhanced, even if they must relinquish some unilateral control in the process. If this increased political capacity is used so as to reduce war, misery, or injustice, progress will result.

This is especially true in an environment of "complex interdependence,"[16] Keohane and Nye's model of an international system characterized by multiple channels of interaction, the absence of a hierarchy of issues on the policy agendas of states, and the relatively infrequent use of force, even by the strong, in most issue areas. An environment of complex interdependence is conducive to progress in international relations both because it may contribute to managing the (ordinary) interdependence discussed earlier and because it may even foster the emergence of more interdependence.

Complex interdependence rests on at least relatively stable international political relations that succeed in holding the security dilemma in abeyance. Security is the paramount international objective of nearly all states, at nearly all times; beyond all the constraints on the pursuit of any political objective, objectives other than security— and all states have many—will be pursued only to the extent that they do not appear to interfere with their security. Security preempts other values in almost all cases of conflict. And perceived insecurity is likely to impede cooperation in managing interdependence even in many instances where an outside observer would find no conflict with national security.

An international system dominated by an active concern for security cannot be a system of complex interdependence. Under the prevailing concept of national security, there exists a hierarchy of issues, at least for individual states, and almost certainly at the international level: security takes priority, as in the old terminology of "high" and "low" politics. The priority of security fosters centralization: central foreign policy decision makers do not readily tolerate multiple channels of interaction. And with the stakes perceived in terms of security or even survival, the resort to force is likely to be relatively frequent, and the reservation of the right to war of relatively great practical importance.

Therefore, simply ameliorating the security dilemma will allow states to pursue a broader range of objectives—and it is quite likely that at least some of these objectives will engender or amount to progress. In addition, the pursuit of multiple objectives is likely to lead to the emergence of new objectives, especially new objectives that are instrumental to the achievement of better-established goals. Furthermore, and perhaps most important, each of the distinguishing features of complex interdependence is in itself quite conducive to progress.

A reduction in the resort to force in most issue areas is, obviously, in itself progressive—it implies reducing war. The erosion of the old issue hierarchy, with security not merely preeminent but preemptive, allows (although certainly does not guarantee) the emergence to prominence of issues of welfare and human rights. The increasing use and importance of transgovernmental and transnational channels of communication and interaction increases the number of issues states are able to pursue and alters the bargaining environment in ways that are likely to increase opportunities for cooperation (e.g., by increasing the influence of INGOs and by a greater use of bureaucratic experts in international negotiations). More generally, complex interdependence makes international relations much more fragmented and increasingly issue-specific, thus increasing the opportunities for progress in some issue areas by providing more manageable problems and a bargaining environment more conducive to success.

It is thus our contention here that interdependence is a progressive force when it triggers a change in the way decision makers pursue their national interests. Perceptions of interdependence can lead to more cooperation, the creation of shared values, and a deepening in importance of the reciprocity norm. One cannot fail to notice, for example, that Gorbachev has justified his revolutionary thinking and actions—which led to the end of the Cold War and to a large degree of international cooperation—on the basis of an unprecedented condition of security, economic, and environmental interdependence.

Of course, none of this means that progress is any more inevitable with complex interdependence than with scientific and technological advance. Furthermore, no account at this level of generality can provide even hints of the pace of progress. And progress certainly is possible in other environments. Nonetheless, complex interdependence does seem to be an environment in which progress is relatively likely, a conclusion that is especially interesting because complex interdependence is a model that is widely acknowledged to provide a fairly accurate account of large portions of contemporary international relations.

Power and Interdependence

The one element that is missing in the discussion sketched so far is power, which often, perhaps even usually, is the decisive determinant of international outcomes.

The account of progress we are trying to present seeks to explain progress, and especially the lack of progress, principally in terms of the actions of states. Despite our "systemic" and evaluative perspective on progress, the explanation of progress in any particular instance will be made primarily in terms of power and national interests. For example, Crawford's discussion suggests that complex interdependence contributes to progress in large measure by altering the ways in which states tend to exercise their power.

If states are to manage interdependence, they must choose—decide that it is in their interest—not to exercise their power so as to frustrate the desires of the power(s) with whom they are interdependent or choose to exercise their power in ways that will maximize joint gains from an interdependent relationship. Such decisions in turn are likely to be influenced primarily by the state's own power and interests. Progress thus will involve not the transcendence of national power and interests, but their coordination or conciliation in mutually beneficial ways. Progress requires a particular type of conception of the national interest in the area in question, as well as a particular type of exercise of national power—but nothing more.

In other words, there is nothing "idealistic" or moralistic in the account of progress presented here. Quite the contrary. No matter how much we emphasize interdependence, whether ordinary or complex, it is not an alternative to power but a framework within which national power is exercised. Jack Donnelly provides a good example of the relationship between power and progress in his analysis of the growth of the American human rights regime. He argues that in the context of what he calls "moral interdependence," the exercise of American power was crucial to the development of a concern with human rights in the Americas and the promotion of that concern through the construction of an international regime.

It is hardly worth extended commentary on the ways in which power can be exercised so as to frustrate or retard progress, or cause regress in international relations. Even (complex) interdependence only provides an environment that is merely more conducive to progress; for example, states often decide that the loss of autonomy required is not worth the gains to be achieved from cooperatively managing interdependence. Nonetheless, our concern here is with the possibility that power can be exercised progressively.

The Roads to Progress

To this point we have argued that scientific and technological advance can be a means to achieve progressive change and can trigger a redefinition of states' interests in international relations. We have argued that international interdependence provides incentives for states to discover and pursue common interests and goals at a maximum, or exercise restraint to reduce their dangerous and potentially violent conflicts of interest at a minimum. We can now take the argument one step further by suggesting that at least two patterns of progress exist in international relations: progress is achieved when actors either solve their problems affecting security, welfare, and human rights by collaborating with others to achieve common goals or, recognizing that goals conflict, approach unilateral solutions in mutually acceptable ways.[17]

Terry Nardin's distinction between "purposive" and "practical" association catches the essence of the two roads to progress described here. According to Nardin, purposive association is a "relationship among those who cooperate for the purpose of securing certain shared beliefs, values, and interests, who adopt certain practices as a means to that end, and who regard such practices as worthy of respect only to the extent that they are useful instruments of the common purpose."[18] Thus, in issue areas where actors share common interests, the purposive road is traveled. Progress is the result of the increasingly rational pursuit of the shared ends. When based on common goals, progress can be achieved through the sorts of techniques that functionalists, such as David Mitrany, emphasized.[19]

First, actors must place limits on the scope of problems before progress can occur. This first pattern of progress is predicated upon the rational isolation of particular problems from one another so that each could be consciously understood. A thorough understanding of cause–effect relationships cannot be achieved and a technically rational solution cannot be applied unless issues are "bounded." Second, progress occurs when state officials come to see particular social problems as so threatening to their own political power that they are happy to distance themselves from the issue and hand it over to the study of experts or bureaucrats in an international organization.[20]

Ernst Haas' neofunctionalist theory also leads us along this road. He argued that cooperation in intergovernmental organizations where issues were bounded would lead to "spillover" from one issue to another and to more complex decision making among states. This would be an evolutionary process in which international organizations would gradually take over the responsibilities of states in an increasing number of functional areas. Within this process the authority of experts and bureaucrats in the multilateral organizations would increase as they solved problems for member states. Thus, decision-making authority would gradually transfer from the state to the intergovernmental organization.[21]

This pattern of progress should not be confused with attainment of the maximal goals described earlier. Although the positive attainment of peace, welfare, and justice might indeed be the outcome of a process in which responsibility for security, economic, and social issues is gradually handed over to an international authority, it is not necessarily linked to this process. A minimalist outcome is indeed most likely, in which states, agreeing on minimal goals and interests, build institutions that facilitate the reduction of conflict and human rights violations and welfare improvements among members. If minimalist goals are met through this process, progress is achieved.

The second road to progress was pioneered by Hans Morgenthau and is based on an "agreement to disagree" on goals and a joint search for mutually acceptable ways to pursue those goals.[22] It is consistent with Nardin's concept of practical association, a "relationship among those who are engaged in the pursuit of different and possible incompatible purposes, but who are associated with one another . . . only in respecting certain restrictions on how each may pursue his own purposes."[23] The choice of this road is based on elite recognition that because states exist in an interdependent relationship, conflict over goals can be too dangerous, damaging, and counterproductive to the national interest. Along this road, states are drawn to find cooperative solutions to their problems because they converge on the recognition of what has to be prevented, rather than on what has to be mutually achieved; each side constrains itself in order to constrain the other. Cognitive evolution is a necessary condition, however, because states have to arrive at common meanings as to how to translate their prudence into agreed normative behavior.

Thus, there are issues of international relations that cannot be made subjects of successful functionalist cooperation or "technical rationality." These issues involve conflicting national goals, as defined by statesmen, and progress involves agreement upon prudential means to meet their goals and deal with each other in nonviolent ways to serve them. A clear example of prudential action is the use of traditional diplomacy and customary international law. If this prudential action—in which the national interest is defined to include obligation or restraint—reduces violence, misery, and human rights violations, progress is achieved.[24]

Finally, we must not confuse the two patterns. Throughout the post-war period, U.S.–Soviet relations were not guided by common security goals. Thus, progress in arms control followed the pattern of traditional diplomacy. As long as goals conflicted and the superpower security dilemma persisted, joint "technical" solutions were the exception. In other words, the functionalist logic couldn't be considered progressive when applied to problems of superpower national security.

Even then, however, successful efforts to separate negotiations over medium-range missiles in Europe from discussions of space-based antimissile systems provide a good example of "bounding issues" along the second road to achieve progress in arms control, showing that the two "roads" are ideal types and many features of each are common to both. Thus, even when the superpowers shared goals, interests, and values, they did not necessarily agree to follow the functionalist process to achieve those goals. Often they disagreed over the most rational means to pursue those goals; it is hardly worth mentioning that bargaining over those means is evident in most intergovernmental organizations. Today, after the revolutionary changes in the Soviet Union and Central and Eastern Europe, the superpowers' growing mutual interest in building a new European order through peaceful change may have created a fertile ground for progressive actions predicted in a combination of prudential diplomatic means with functional technical cooperation. It would be a mistake to limit ourselves to the belief that progress is achieved either one way or the other. Progress along both roads is possible, but they are ideal types and should be kept analytically distinct.

Therefore, we are not arguing that actors come to share their goals and interests or find mutually acceptable ways to minimize their conflicts automatically or easily. The bulk of the analysis here suggests that for progress to be achieved under conditions of complex interdependence, state elites must recognize that, at a minimum, national interests cannot be achieved at the expense of others, and at a maximum, their own interests depend on the realization of others' interests. We are thus interested in discovering the process by which that recognition occurs.

This section summarizes the essays in this volume that explore these arguments. Emanuel Adler's theoretical contribution describes a process of cognitive change that permits actors to travel along those roads. In addition, he examines how that change has happened in international security. Peter Haas, Jack Donnelly, Ben Schiff, John Ruggie, Robert Kudrle, and Stefanie Lenway put to work the arguments for progress advanced here in the issue areas of environmental protection, human rights, and international economic relations. Philippe Schmitter provides the most ambitious treatment of the issues of trade, political cooperation, and democratization by linking them together in a causal argument.

Neofunctionalism, Learning, and Cognitive Evolution

How do actors come to recognize their common interests and values, which drive them along the first road, or the need for restraint and pragmatism, which drives them along the second? Answers to these questions are suggested by Ernst B. Haas' neofunctionalist logic. The "failure" of previous policies, which leads to disappointment, uncertainty about the consequences of a given action, and intense disagreement among would-be collaborators, can trigger a search for new knowledge as a guide to policy. Linking scientific knowledge to social purpose can help international actors share meanings and therefore view problems similarly.

Haas defines a shared meaning as a "consensus among the relevant national elites that a problem exists, that this problem can be defined and circumscribed in terms of agreed criteria, and that 'solutions' requiring international collaboration can be devised which meet the criteria, while also expressing the political values of the participants. . . . Shared meanings are an indicator of how the consequences of interdependence are actually perceived by decision-makers."[25] In short, the key to progress along both roads described above lies in the realm of cognitive change or learning, which can result from the increasing use of knowledge in the policy process. For Haas, the real test of progress is whether disagreement among actors (over goals or means) is bridged with the help of more new knowledge and shared meanings and whether actors come to a more complex understanding of the issues as a result.

Drawing directly on Haas' work and using insights from evolutionary epistemology, Emanuel Adler's theoretical contribution develops the concept of "cognitive evolution." Cognitive evolution describes the process of intellectual innovation and political selection that occurs within and between institutional settings, that becomes the collective descriptive and normative set of understandings of what it takes to advance the nation's power, influence, and wealth. Cognitive evolution suggests that because those understandings are based on ideas, they are subject to change as political forces drive the selection of new ideas at the domestic political level. A cognitive evolutionary approach requires the externalization of domestic practices and paradigms. It further requires that political stakes be created, which political groups and institutions and other interest groups may then help to maintain through the use of power.

From this perspective, progress in international relations depends less on the advancement of scientific knowledge per se, or on the cunning of reason, than on the political selection, retention, and diffusion of values that tend to enhance human interests across borders. The political selection and international diffusion of arms-control ideas in the 1960s, and of economic ideas about an international economic order after World War II, and their instrumental effects in enhancing human interests across national borders make this case well.

Cognitive evolution may have become progressive, because interdependence, rising to the level of political collective consciousness, helped to break old ideas and beliefs about the autonomy of political actors in the international arena. Further, interdependence may have led to the recognition that old interests that depended on war or trade wars may have become dysfunctional. In turn, this recognition could trigger a reevaluation process that ends up in new definitions of interests and the way they are pursued.

Cognitive evolution is thus progressive when an awareness of interdependence engenders a further awareness of limits and obligations. This awareness can be triggered by negotiations in which actors learn about preferences and expectations of others or by crises in which shared experience can quickly lead to shared problem definitions, shared disappointments, and a search for solutions.

Disappointment, then, can be the first step in this process of increasing awareness. To be sure, disappointment with previous or expected outcomes does not automatically lead to cognitive evolution. It can lead to frustration and inaction. For disappointment to be a progressive force, it must lead to the reassessment of preferences, priorities and problems, a reordering of goals, and the search for new solutions.

Security

Defining security as a systemic freedom from, or low threat of, major nuclear or conventional war, Adler argues that progress in international security results from a reduction of the expected utility from war. This preference for peace over war has its roots in changes in values and expectations of war. To measure progress, Adler develops a scale of increasingly progressive states or "seasons" of peace. Beginning at the most minimal state of security, these are the following: general stability by way of common security, concert, a pluralist security community, and Kantian Peace. He grades each "season" according to the stability of expectations of peace, the degree of mutual predictability of behavior, the extent of communication and diplomatic interaction, and the degree of information exchange and security integration.

One of the most important changes in the late twentieth century has been the emergence of a season of general stability. Since the end of World War II, substantive progress in international security has occurred because the great powers have reevaluated their national interests and have eschewed the initiation of nuclear hostilities. They have also avoided the use of conventional forces in ways that might have led to nuclear war, and they have increasingly eluded international crises that could increase the danger of unpremeditated or accidental war. This learning and reevaluation process is linked to value change. Value change, in turn, is due to modernization processes and to the unacceptable economic, political, and human costs of large wars. It is also due to changes in expectations of cooperation and of the outcome and efficacy of war, which followed the introduction of nuclear weapons to the world scene. In the nuclear age, winners and losers in the international system must be selected by peaceful means.

Equating instrumental progress in international security with the setting of security regimes, Adler shows that partial arms control regimes of the postwar era have helped to institutionalize common understandings of the nuclear predicament and rules of reciprocity. They have limited competition and helped to transfer not just information but also the philosophical understandings that are necessary to keep cooperation going. The main importance of arms control agreements, however, lies in their provision of proof to the actors that they are making progress by achieving intermediate goals.

Finally, Adler offers an important caveat: progress in security is minimalist to the extreme and fully reversible. Rivalries and power conflicts have not decreased; inadvertent and unpremeditated nuclear war can still occur; nuclear, chemical, and biological weapons proliferation looms on the horizon; and many Third World countries have not given up their preference for war over peace. Furthermore, progress in international security is constantly constrained and imperiled by technological developments, domestic politics, cultural differences, unresolved nationalism, modernization, and border problems.

The Environment

Peter Haas shows how cognitive evolution helped bring about progress in the area of environmental protection. He analyzes negotiations leading to the Mediterranean Action Plan, an evolving collaborative agreement consisting of regional treaties, coordinated research and monitoring, integrated planning, and administrative and budgetary support to protect the Mediterranean Sea from marine pollution. Haas argues that progress occurred because national leaders recognized environmental interdependence. They conceptualized this interdependence as a group of interlinked environmental problems that were caused by unregulated industrial policies and impinged on the realization of those same industrial policy goals. They also recognized that the solutions to these problems demanded joint action, and collectively, they pursued more comprehensive policies.

What triggered the process of cognitive evolution? Global environmental disasters helped generate concern about the issue of pollution; marine scientists established transnational networks of experts to lobby their respective governments. Throughout the process of negotiation, officials needed to draw upon their expertise; the demand for their expertise enhanced their standing in the negotiating process. They were thus able to convince their governments of the legitimacy of the linkages they had discovered and guide their countries toward more convergent policies in the Mediterranean region.

But the pattern of instrumental action is not the only pattern of progress at work here. Haas also describes areas of negotiation whose outcome depended not on expert pressure and technical knowledge, but on traditional bargaining behavior (i.e., side payments to LDCs for their cooperation and compromises among all negotiating parties). Here it was not knowledge but actually a "fudging of the issue," leadership, and mediation that were key to the final agreement. Thus, Haas describes how both roads to progress were traveled on the way to the creation of the Med Plan.

Human Rights

Jack Donnelly's explanation for progress in human rights also involves a process of cognitive evolution, beginning with a consensus on values and leading to the establishment of new international institutions. The human rights crisis set off by Hitler triggered frustration, guilt, and unease among statesmen after World War II about their obligations to protect the rights of individuals across borders. Shared meanings about the universality of human rights led to a general consensus that they must be protected by international and regional organizations. Donnelly conceptualizes that consensus as a recognition of "moral interdependence," which led to a demand for human rights regimes and undercut the power and legitimacy of those who would oppose them.

The limitations on this pattern of progress in human rights are imposed by the equally strong consensus on sovereignty among states. In the American regime, for example, ideological hegemony of human rights values was tied to U.S. power; that power was crucial to the creation of the regime, but it was not sufficient to build a strong regime. Donnelly's argument asserts that state sovereignty prevents the growth of human rights regimes beyond the level at which human rights are simply "promoted." Nonetheless, the effects of sovereignty can be muted by a homogeneous cultural community that permits a consensus on human rights obligations and allows statesmen to construct a stronger regime.

Ben Schiff's study of UNRWA, however, demonstrates that progress in human rights can be achieved even under the most adverse international conditions. UNRWA operates in an area where ideological and cultural communities clash and where sovereign states are at war with one another. Nonetheless, the existence of the organization itself demonstrates international commitment to protecting the rights of refugees, and UNRWA has evolved over time in ways that have successfully protected those rights. Schiff shows how the organization has learned what kinds of objectives it can attain and what kind of objectives it should avoid. He further shows how the organization has expanded programs in areas of success, avoiding fruitless activities. Thus, he demonstrates that a shared commitment to protecting refugee rights can lead to progress, despite the existence of deeper disagreements and even military conflict.

Economic Relations

John Ruggie shows how cognitive evolution as indicated by norm-governed change helped bring about progress in international trade and monetary regimes in the postwar period. His analysis is grounded in an exploration of changing assumptions governing those regimes and how changing norms were clearly promoted or rejected according to changing power relationships in the international system. His essay shows how ideas can shape institutions and how these ideas can change as political forces drive the selection of new ideas in both the domestic and international political arenas.

Ruggie argues that the pre–World War I gold standard was grounded on the idea that the state should step aside to allow market equilibrium to adjust the balance of payments, changes in gold reserves, and domestic credit supply. These unbridled market forces, however, ultimately resulted in economic ruin. In the interwar years, a new set of ideas took hold, pushed ahead by the consequences of the Depression: States must mediate between the market and society and must not sacrifice social stability to the vagaries of the market. As a result, market ties between states that bound them together in interdependent relationships were severed, thus deepening the Depression. The economic assumptions of the postwar period, which Ruggie calls "embedded liberalism," were rooted in the belief that, to promote economic welfare, neither laissez faire nor absolute state control and closure could dominate policy. International interdependence, to be progressive, must be "managed" by multilateral institutions built upon a belief in the necessity of domestic interventionism. In this case, cognitive evolution was triggered by crisis, and the norm of embedded liberalism was clearly promoted by the United States, the most powerful actor in the system.

Kudrle and Lenway show that in U.S.–Canadian trade, increasing recognition of interdependence led to an evolutionary change in beliefs about autonomy and control and increasing recognition that the national interests of the two countries were no longer served by outmoded trade barriers. The new trade agreement, they argue, represents a new definition of interests that enhances aggregate welfare in the two countries. Both sides' continued insistence on national control, however, limits the possibilities for economic integration; nevertheless, the successful negotiation of a dispute settlement mechanism indicates that each is willing to give up some sovereignty in exchange for economic benefits.

Linking Issues: The Role of Internal Political Change

Philippe Schmitter's essay argues that progress in international economic and political cooperation can be explained by increasing internal democratization. Kant argued persuasively that "republics" would eventually—after some crises and a good deal of learning—interact "in perpetual peace." Whether they would also have a propensity to increase their reciprocal economic and social exchanges more than those between democracies and nondemocracies or nondemocracies among themselves has been less subjected to speculation. Nonetheless, the underlying *"doux commerce"* thesis suggests a positive relation over time and a changing conception of the national interest to embrace human interests.

Schmitter explores this triad of conditions. He uses recent cases of democratization—Argentina, Brazil, and Uruguay—to examine whether the advent of political democracy was associated with a significant increase in economic exchanges and/or efforts at political cooperation, compared to their previous level under authoritarian rule.

The Limits to Progress

None of the contributions here prescribe a panacea for progress. We have been careful to qualify our argument by stating its limitations at each step: scientific and technological change and international interdependence can facilitate increased conflict, violence, exploitation, and repression. Disappointments and failures can lead to alienation and conflict. But until we know the pitfalls of our arguments they cannot be repaired to reflect more realistically the sources and process of progressive change.

Perhaps the greatest pitfall to progress lies at the cognitive level. There is nothing inevitable about the process of cognitive evolution described here; cognitive closure leading to policy rigidity and regress is just as likely as cognitive progress. Such closure might even be facilitated by an "ideology" of progress or a closed belief system that contains a blueprint for progress or overreliance on a single solution to problems. Indeed, scientific and technological advance has fostered a misguided belief that a "technological or organizational fix" can solve a wide range of military, economic, and social problems. From the so-called green revolution, which produced a plethora of unintended and undesirable outcomes, to the so-called Star Wars solution to the nuclear predicament, cognitive closure to an investigation of possible negative unintended consequences of scientific development has been part of the problem.

Michael Brenner's essay warns us that an ideology of progress as a guide to policy can have serious unintended consequences. His critique focuses on U.S. nonproliferation policy. He argues that central decision makers, guided by the Enlightenment idea of progress, believed that they could design a peaceful nuclear future by creating effective international institutions to regulate the diffusion of nuclear technology. They thus pushed for a technological "fix" to problems of Third World development and an organizational "fix" to international security, both embodied in the international nonproliferation regime.

The solutions (as conceived by the United States) were bound to fail, he argues, because they did not take into account the realities of an essentially competitive international system. The Atoms for Peace program was the first "blueprint" for progress. It offered to "open to the world the wondrous, bountiful beneficence of the peaceful atom." International cooperation to regulate nuclear technology would both hold in check the atom's destructive capabilities and facilitate the international diffusion of nuclear capability for peaceful purposes. Underlying U.S. strategies in promoting Atoms for Peace and participating in the nonproliferation regime was the view that international cooperation could remove the motivations of security and pride that moved states to build nuclear arms.

U.S. decision makers acted on the belief that an open but partially regulated transfer of nuclear technology was a step toward internationalizing the norm of collective responsibility. These men encouraged a vision of the nuclear future that included the recycling of plutonium as a standard feature. It took the Indian nuclear blast in

1974 to shake that vision. Given competing goals among states, limited knowledge, and continual change in the nuclear environment, Brenner argues, a blueprint for progress in the form of technological and organizational innovation is bound to fail.

For Brenner, the way out of this dilemma lies in breaking out of the cognitive closure that, in American political culture, is expressed in the faith that aspiration can be reified through enlightened acts of will—regardless of circumstance. A heavy dose of disappointment has led to some learning and accommodation of deep-seated liberal precepts to practical reality. Cognitive evolution would be indicated by what Brenner calls a more "mature" policy characterized by tolerance for ambiguity and contradiction, a capacity for deferred gratification, a readiness to acknowledge the multicausal basis of most occurrences, and a willingness to accept responsibility without immediate reward.

All the preceding notwithstanding, Brenner's essay shows that minimalist progress (i.e., a reduction of the rate and degree of proliferation and the successful blocking of the widespread commercial transfer and use of plutonium) has occurred. This is because success was rooted not in the maximalist expectations of American architects of regimes, but in the superpowers' deployment of national power, in their increasing conviction that a global structure of peace was valuable, and in economic circumstances that militated against expansion of civilian nuclear energy. Brenner's essay reminds us that progress may occur not as a result of international institutions transforming the "nature of political intercourse in world affairs," but when those institutions are supported by the instrumental action of national political power or a change in national values and convictions that tend to enhance human interests.

Our argument, then, is clearly indeterminate. Reliance on scientific and technological advance or international interdependence to bring the changes we prefer can bring the opposite results. International collaboration to manage the diffusion of science and technology does not necessarily lead to progressive changes in definitions and pursuit of the national interest. We cannot design our future because our information is imperfect and incomplete. Blueprints for progress are unreliable. Expectations placed on a particular solution cannot be so high that failure brings about disappointments too deep to trigger constructive change.

We do not advance a blueprint for progress here; rather, as Adler's essay emphasizes, an important part of our argument is that progress is indeterminate and reversible. The limitations discussed here only reinforce this point.

Progress in Our Thinking

Stephen Haggard's paper assesses progress in international relations theory. His critical assessment permits us to reflect on both the strengths and limitations of our own attempts to theorize about progress in the real world of international relations. His essay begins by analyzing current research programs that share a structural and systemic approach. These are neorealism, the international economic structures literature, and the reflectivist approach. He argues that progress in the discipline demands that new theories demonstrate their competence against competing alternatives by accounting for new empirical data. His conclusion is that although these programs have been broadly progressive in forcing the consideration of variables that previous analyses neglected, they do not do well in predicting both state action and systemic change.

Haggard blames the weakness of structuralist approaches to international change on their metatheoretical proclivites and their neglect of "second image" variables. Thus, the theories generate broad claims, but an uncertain "fit" between structural conditions and outcomes. Likewise, the literature on economic structures and world politics—such as the world systems approach—predicts actor preferences on the basis of economic position in an international division of labor. Here the gap they leave is between preferences and outcomes.

The reflectivist literature, however, views situational constraints as looser. This literature focuses on structural variables as "possibilistic" rather than causal. But in so doing it neglects the fact that human action is correlated not only with normative, but also with material constraints.

This third approach to change has been mainly advanced by Haas and his neofunctionalist followers, including many in this volume. Although Haggard is persuaded that this approach may indeed be theoretically "progressive," with its emphasis on cognitive rather than structural variables, he argues that shifting the research focus to a much broader and ambitious program based on an "evolutionary epistemology" will create problems. For example, the reflectivist approach deals inadequately with the political processes through which the selection of ideas takes place, and it fails to clearly conceptualize the relationship between knowledge and power.

On the basis of his analysis, Haggard contends that there are two alternatives open for further progress in the theory of international relations: First, scholars can continue with the structuralist program by refining the concept of structure, to yield more powerful explanations. Second, they can stress nonstructural variables.

This volume suggests that a bridge can be constructed that will link the two approaches. This linkage would broaden the conventional discourse in international relations theory and provide a lens that would allow us to identify progress when it appears. Beverly Crawford begins to refine the concept of structure by dissecting the notion of anarchy into three component parts: anarchy as a self-help system, anarchy as a system where there are no common values, and anarchy as a system in which unequal power relationships determine outcomes. Each of these attributes of anarchy, she contends, obstructs progress in international relations as we have defined it. And our willingness to believe that progress in international relations is possible has been blocked by our acceptance of these effects.

International interdependence, however, has muted each of these effects of anarchy. Perceptions of interdependence can change decision makers' calculations about the usefulness of unilateral action in states' international relations. It can trigger the creation of shared values, meanings, rights, and obligations. And it can modify the calculations by which states choose to exercise their power. Within the anarchic condition, then, interdependence can pave the way for a redefinition of states' interests in ways that can embrace human interests. A theoretical focus on interdependence and actor response can link structural and reflectivist arguments.

Interdependence and the resulting interest redefinition, however, are only the necessary conditions for international progress. The sufficient conditions are actor learning and the incorporation of restraint, obligation, and empathy into policy choice. If "better problems" are the result—that is, if problems are created whose solution does not require violence, is more respectful of the environment and of peoples' economic and social rights, than we know that progress is achieved.

CONCLUSION

Despite our skepticism about how much progress can actually be achieved, and the methodological limitations of our approach, we believe that an attempt to think about progress systematically can add an important dimension to our understanding of international phenomena. A normative perspective forces investigators to think about and provide answers to such questions as, "Can the welfare of individuals across national borders be advanced by changing state interests?" "Can interdependence produce unintended consequences, some of which may induce nation-states to cooperate?" "Can peaceful change be promoted in the light of the security dilemma?"

A normative perspective means not only that we study the phenomena out there, but that we care for global welfare, peace, and human rights. This is the case even if we know, as political realists, that it is utopian to think that they could be achieved at this stage. This is the Haas legacy. By systematically showing what changes we can consider to be "better" or "worse" from a systemic, though minimalist perspective, we can shed some light on the intimate relationship that exists between politically relevant research and the "reality" out there. Our volume takes up Robert Keohane's challenge to scholars when he wrote:

> We think about world politics not because it is aesthetically beautiful, because we believe that it is governed by simple, knowable laws, or because it provides rich, easily accessible data for testing of empirical hypotheses. Were these concerns paramount, we would look elsewhere. We study world politics because we think it will determine the fate of the earth. Realism makes us aware of the odds against us. What we need to do now is to understand peaceful changes by combining multi-dimensional scholarly analysis with more visionary ways of seeing the future.[26]

ENDNOTES

1. In the last decade scholarship on change in international relations has been growing. See, for example, E. Antela, "Theories of Peaceful Change: An Excursion to the study of Change in International Relations in the 1930's," *Cooperation and Conflict* (1984), 19:235–250; Barry Buzan and R. J. Barry Jones, eds., *Change and the Study of International Relations: The Evaded Dimension* (London: Pinter, 1981); Robert Gilpin, *War and Change*

in World Politics (Cambridge: Cambridge University Press, 1981); Ole R. Holsti, Randolph M. Siverson, and Alexander L. George, eds., *Change in the International System* (Boulder, Colo.: Westview, 1980); Richard L. Merritt, "On the Transformation of Systems," *International Political Science Review* (1980), 1:13–22; George Modelski, "The Long Cycle of Global Politics and the Nation-State," *Comparative Studies in Society and History,* 20:214–238; James N. Rosenau, "Micro Sources of Macro Global Change," Institute for Transnational Studies, University of Southern California (mimeo, May 1986); J. G. Ruggie, "Continuity and Transformation in World Polity: Toward a Neorealist Synthesis," *World Politics* (1983), 35(2):261–285; R. B. J. Walker, "Realism, Change, and International Political Theory," *International Studies Quarterly* (1987), 31:65–86. For a critique of some of the theories of change in international relations see: R. J. Vincent, "Change and International Relations," *Review of International Studies* (1983), 9:63–70. K. J. Holsti has related the study of change to the question of progress. See "The Horsemen of the Apocalypse: At the Gate, Detoured, or Retreating?" *International Studies Quarterly* (1986), 30(4):355–372.

2. See, for example, the following:

   The Uniting of Europe: Political, Social and Economic Forces 1950–1957 (Stanford, Calif.: Stanford University Press, 1959).
   Beyond the Nation State (Stanford, Calif: Stanford University Press, 1964).
   "Why Collaborate: Issue Linkage and International Regimes," *World Politics* (1980), 32 (2):357–405.
   "Words Can Hurt You or, Who Said What to Whom About Regimes," in Stephen D. Krasner, ed., *International Regimes* (Ithaca, N.Y.: Cornell University Press, 1983), pp. 23–60.
   "What Is Progress in the Study of International Organization" (mimeo n.d.) Published in Japanese in *Kokusai Seiji* (1984), pp. 11–46.
   "What Is Nationalism and Why Should We Study It?" *International Organization* (1986), 40(3):707–744.
   "War, Interdependence and Functionalism," in Raimo Vayryhen, ed., *The Quest for Peace* (London: Sage, 1987).

3. Francisco J. Ayala, "The Evolutionary Concept of Progress," in Gabriel A. Almond, Mervin Chodorow, and Roy Harvey Pearce, eds., *Progress and Its Discontents* (Berkeley: University of California Press, 1977), p. 109.
4. For a somewhat different use of the concept of "human interests" in international relations see Richard Ashley, "Political Realism and Human Interests," *International Studies Quarterly* (1981), 25(2):204–236.
5. See Richard Falk, *A Study of Future Worlds* (Princeton, N.J.: Princeton University Press, 1975).
6. See Hans Morgenthau, *Politics Among Nations* (New York: Alfred A. Knopf, 1973).

7. See Craig Murphy, "Color It Mitrany: The Activities of Global Intergovernmental Agencies, and Progress in International Relations" (Wellesley, Mass.: 1986), mimeo. Ernst Haas has argued that war, "once considered the normal and legitimate method for settling intractable disputes among states," is no longer considered a legitimate way to assert the national interest. Thus, today, when states go to war they must go to great lengths to justify their actions.

8. See Immanuel Kant, *Perpetual Peace and Other Essays on Politics, History and Morals* (Indianapolis: Hackett, reprinted 1983).

9. Robert Keohane in *After Hegemony* provides an important exception when he discusses the moral value of international cooperation. He explicitly separates the morality of "means" from the morality of "ends." In his introductory chapter he states: "I seek to increase our understanding of cooperation, in the belief that increased understanding can help to improve political amity and economic welfare . . . (t)o inquire about the moral value of cooperation is partly to ask about the ends for which it is pursued. Along with many others, I would disapprove of cooperation among the governments of wealthy, powerful states to exploit poorer, weaker countries." See *After Hegemony: Cooperation and Discord in the World Political Economy* (Princeton, N.J.: Princeton University Press, 1984), p. 10 and ch. 11.

10. The "tracing" approach was suggested by Alexander L. George, "Case Studies and Theory Development: The Method of Structured, Focused Comparison" in Paul Gordon Lauren, ed., *Diplomacy: New Approaches in History, Theory, and Policy* (New York: Free Press, 1979).

11. Beverly Crawford and Stefanie Lenway, "Decision Modes and International Regime Change: Western Collaboration on East–West Trade," *World Politics* (1985), 37(3):375–402.

12. Aaron Wildavsky, "Progress and Public Policy," in Almond et al., eds., *Progress and Its Discontents*, p. 373.

13. David Mitrany, *A Working Peace System* (Chicago: Quadrangle Books, 1966).

14. On this point see Harvey Brooks, "Can Technology Assure Unending Material Progress?" in Almond et al., eds., *Progress and Its Discontents*, p. 299.

15. Robert Jervis, *The Illogic of American Nuclear Strategy* (Ithaca, N.Y.: Cornell University Press, 1984), pp. 47–51.

16. See Robert O. Keohane and Joseph S. Nye, Jr., *Power and Interdependence: World Politics in Transition* (Boston: Little, Brown, 1977).

17. We owe this insight to Murphy, "Color It Mitrany."

18. Terry Nardin, *Law, Morality, and the Relations of States* (Princeton, N.J.: Princeton University Press, 1984), p. 14.

19. See Mitrany, *A Working Peace System,* and Murphy, "Color It Mitrany."

20. Murphy, "Color It Mitrany."

21. Haas, *The Uniting of Europe.*

22. The best contemporary examples of this perspective are Hedley Bull, *The*

Anarchical Society: A Study of Order in World Politics (New York: Columbia University Press, 1977) and Terry Nardin, *Law, Morality, and the Relations of States.*

23. Nardin, *Law, Morality, and the Relations of States*, p. 9.
24. Murphy, "Color It Mitrany."
25. Haas, "War, Interdependence and Functionalism," p. 113.
26. Robert O. Keohane, "Theory of World Politics: Structural Realism and Beyond" in Ada W. Finifter, ed., *Political Science: The State of the Discipline* (Washington, D.C.: American Political Science Association, 1983), p. 533.

2

COGNITIVE EVOLUTION: A DYNAMIC APPROACH FOR THE STUDY OF INTERNATIONAL RELATIONS AND THEIR PROGRESS

Emanuel Adler

BEING AND BECOMING

A hunter sees a living duck. He makes a "rational" prediction of its speed and movement, wind speed, and other physical conditions; aims at the point where he figures it will be when his shot reaches it; shoots . . . and misses. But the same hunter aiming at a duck in a shooting gallery at a county fair will most likely "kill." The difference lies in the fact that live ducks can suddenly turn to the right, to the left; they can back or tumble; they can move in undeterministic and unpredictable ways. Ducks have reflexes and they can surprise us.

The contrast between the target duck and the live duck can illustrate the difference between "being" and "becoming." "Being" is a prevalent notion that sees everything in nature and society as being static and mechanistic, including change. The idea of "becoming" considers everything to be in flux, as a permanent process of change and evolution, even that which appears to be static.

Galileo, Descartes, and Newton can be mentioned as "intellectual parents" of being. In their concepts of nature (and philosophy), "space and time were absolute, in the sense of existing objectively and of being completely independent of any physical content. Matter, to be sure, occupied, and moved in, space, but space itself remained . . . 'always similar and immovable.'"[1] Since then, science and the arts have evolved considerably from being to becoming, over a period of several centuries. For example, Voltaire, Rousseau, Kant, and Hegel can be seen as links in this chain of the transformation of ideas. But becoming grew stronger as we approached the twentieth century. The most important transformation occurred in the second half of the nineteenth century and the beginning of the twentieth because of the work of Charles Darwin, Herbert Spencer, Henri Bergson, and Albert Einstein, among others. The philosophical ideas about becoming promoted developments in physics, which at the same time influenced the former. The formulation of quantum theory by Max Planck and the theory of relativity by Einstein fueled philosophical ideas of becoming.[2]

International relations theories, mainly of the realist and neorealist strands, are still based on the image of being.[3] International systems and their components have been perceived as Newtonian elements, "suspended in space"; time has little to do with them, and movement and change are linear, just like the ducks in the shooting gallery. This kind of theory studies international relations and international phenomena according to the metaphors of equilibrium and balance of power: It looks for the recurrent, for "stability," and tries to predict the future from past events. International relations theory thereby fails to grasp the nature of the phenomena it tries to describe and explain, which are in flux and evolution. It therefore has been and still is basically shooting at live ducks as if they were the predictable ones that rhythmically move along the gallery track.

Kenneth Waltz's *Theory of International Politics* and Robert Gilpin's *War and Change in World Politics*[4] are among the best illustrations of being. Waltz's theory deals with structural continuity,[5] yet continuity here means change within a similar pattern, rather than the absence of change itself. (Without any change there would be no reason for theories.) However, to catch the essence of change within a pattern —wherein anarchy and the stratification of power determine "broad expectations about the quality of international-political life"—Waltz has portrayed an international system and a concept of change that strikingly resemble Newton's astronomical universe.[6] He has taken space and time—indeed the international system itself—as absolute, in the sense of existing objectively and of being independent of the content of units and their attributes. Waltz has therefore portrayed a predictable and static balance of power system, in which movement is linear and change automatic.[7] Emphasizing equilibrium, he has looked for the recurrent, and stressing material power alone, he has overlooked the capacity of humans to change the meaning and understanding of power with a change in expectations and values, which occurs at the unit level—the "ultimate source of systemic change."[8] The crux of the matter, however, is that expectations, whether general or specific, are not "readily amenable to cause-and-effect 'clocklike' models or metaphors. . . . The actors in politics have memories; they learn from experience. They have goals, aspirations, calculative strategies. Memory, learning, goal seeking, and problem solving intervene between 'cause' and 'effect,' between independent and dependent variable."[9]

Gilpin's *War and Change* proposes an elegant and provocative theory of change. Change to Gilpin, however, means only the rearrangement of things:

> In every international system there are continual occurrences of political, economic and technological changes that promise gains or threaten losses for one or another actor. . . . As a consequence of the changing interests of individual states, and especially because of the differential growth in power among states, the international system moves from a condition of equilibrium to one of disequilibrium.[10]

Equilibrium must be restored because a disjunction has been created between the existing, basically unchanged, social system—the hierarchy of prestige, the division of territory, the international division of labor, and the rules of the system—and the redistribution of power, which now favors those actors that would benefit most from a change in the system, and that disjunction has weakened the foundations of the existing system. Although the resolution and restoration of equilibrium may happen peacefully, the "principal mechanism of change throughout history has been war."[11] Change in world politics, therefore, turns out to be the perpetual rise and decline of hegemons; political, economic, and social changes are important only insofar as they fuel the differential growth process that leads to mechanistic alterations in the positions of things; and war is mostly determined in the "celestial" mechanics by which the system rearranges itself.

Because states move deterministically like the ducks in the shooting gallery, caught as it were in the equilibrium–disequilibrium–equilibrium movements caused by differential growth, their interests, as well as their motivations, are predetermined, and changes in the nature and quality of things are ruled out unless and until we "learn to develop an effective mechanism of peaceful change."[12] But Gilpin's approach does not provide us with the tools and incentives to inquire how, why, and when an effective mechanism of peaceful change may develop. Thus, for example, his theory cannot show under what conditions great powers will choose peaceful change, even when there are structural opportunities to win a hegemonic war.

My critique is not based on a radical historicist and reflectivist view of international relations,[13] for it "is far from clear on what grounds history and historicism can provide an adequate alternative to the structuralist turn."[14] The alternative, therefore, is to look at international relations as partly determinate or "*intermediate* in character between perfect chance and perfect determinism—something intermediate between perfect clouds and perfect clocks,"[15] and to adopt a becoming epistemology that would be able to catch both *historical* and *structural* forces, explaining change in a dynamic way. This epistemology would have to bridge an ontology based upon a strong element of intersubjectivity and an epistemology that has circumvented the actors and looked for explanations exclusively at the structural level.[16]

Following and trying to build on the work of Ernst Haas, I claim that the bridge can be built with the aid of an epistemology that Donald T. Campbell called evolutionary,[17] which, consistent with a contemporary interpretation of science[18] and evoking what Campbell called "epistemic humility,"[19] makes the intersubjective level of analysis more "real" or "objective" and more amenable to generalization, and our epistemological assumptions less cast iron and more dynamic.

To Haas, an evolutionary epistemology has meant that politics is a historical process that changes with physical changes and with the evolution of meanings. When applying evolutionary thinking to the study of international regimes, Haas argued that emphasis should be placed on learning and on the collective understandings of political choices, which depend on how we think about nature and culture.[20] Learning thus is a creative process by which individuals and organizations reevaluate cause–effect relationships and arrive at new interpretations of the social world; these interpretations are then ejected back into the historical process, where they affect political action and events.[21]

EVOLUTIONARY EPISTEMOLOGY

The evolutionary epistemology Haas is using to grasp the dynamic nature of international relations can be traced back to Popper's understanding of the process by which knowledge grows,[22] and to a group of philosophers and psychologists who have followed Popper's insights. This is true with Campbell's ideas on cognitive evolution, Thomas Kuhn's insight about paradigms and their evolution, and Stephen Toulmin's idea of the evolution of concepts and disciplines.[23] These ideas, paradigms, or concepts have something in common: They constitute interpretative practices and collective meanings and understandings, neither valid nor true a priori, that evolve into the collective expression of human understanding at a particular time and place, after being selected by authoritative processes.

What the group mentioned earlier has found in the realm of scientific growth and human behavior to be similar or compatible (but not isomorphic) to natural selection processes, I find it useful to describe and explain as the evolution of common understandings in international relations, which I see as a condition for change and for progress. The main insight that I carry over from natural selection processes to international relations, by way of the philosophical understanding of scientific growth, is that at any point in time and place of a historical process, international actors, mainly nation-states, may be affected by politically relevant collective sets of understandings of the physical and the social world that are subject to political selection processes and thus to evolutionary change.

Popper's evolutionary epistemology can be summarized as taking a succession of theories in science as similar to the process of selective elimination in nature. According to Popper, the highest creative thought, like animal adaptation, is the product of "blind variation" and "selective retention," or to use his own terminology, a product of trial and error, or of conjectures and refutations.[24] This means that science is never free from assumptions, and at every instant it presupposes a horizon of expectations or a frame of reference that precedes and confers meanings or significance on our experience, actions, and observations. As hypotheses are falsified and replaced by others, so are the meanings we confer on experience, on action, and on observations. From this point of view, therefore, science is a "shot in the dark," a bold guess that goes far beyond evidence and to which justification is less important than the viability of the mutation. The problem of whether a theory is "true" or not is resolved by exposing the "mutations" to the processes of selection, or attempted criticism and refutation. Survival in this process does not justify the survivor, either; a species that has survived for thousands of years may nevertheless become extinct. A theory that has survived for generations may eventually be refuted.[25]

To show that his theory of "conjectures and refutations" does not turn science into a subjective and relativist enterprise, Popper introduced the notion of "World 3," which, in contrast to "World 1" (the physical universe) and to "World 2" (the subjective experience of individuals), encompasses the products of the human mind, such as art, scientific theories, technologies, institutions, plans, stories, and myths. These may be autonomous of any knowing subject, once they are communicated, that is, once they have become part of a collective understanding or culture.[26] World 3 thus is the world of the logical content of books, computers, and institutions; it is "real" because, once communicated to and shared by other individuals, it can affect the physical environment through all manner of intended and unintended consequences.[27]

Following Popper, one can turn the understanding of international relations into a problem of control, that is, the "control of behavior and other aspects of the physical world by human ideas."[28] In contrast to the cast iron control one gets from a deterministic and mechanistic epistemology, an evolutionary epistemology offers the alternative of "plastic control," which by combining notions of freedom and control enhances our understanding of how such nonphysical things as plans, decisions, theories, intentions, and values can play a part in bringing about physical changes in the physical world.[29]

Kuhn's concepts of "paradigms" and "scientific revolutions" help explain the organizing effect of World 3 "products" that transcend the subjective minds of particular individuals and thus highlight the effect of shared understanding in international relations and their evolution. Kuhn has shown that in any type of scientific discipline a

collectively agreed-upon set of concepts and epistemological understandings creates the framework for research by structuring the activities of science and scientists. The bulk of "normal" science, according to this view, consists of solving problems within the paradigm,
which indicates what "makes sense," what phenomena are important, what questions to ask, and what inferences to draw. Most
important for our purposes, the paradigm leads scientists to reject
flatly evidence that is fundamentally out of line with the expectations
it generates.[30] It follows, then, that scientific communities give meaning to data and evidence in accordance with the paradigms that
govern periods of "normal" science. During scientific revolutions—
those critical moments when belief about scientific phenomena
changes, not unlike changes in belief about religion, political and
aesthetic interpretative communities—however, one paradigm replaces another, and a new period of normal science commences.[31]

The notion that scientific paradigms structure the development of
scientific concepts and make nature intelligible is not alien to Toulmin, for whom science progresses not by recognizing the truth of
new observations but by making sense of them.[32] Taking evolution
as a shift in the composition of a gene pool shared by a population,
rather than specified in an individual, Toulmin creates an explicit
analogy between population genetics and the evolution of concepts
that I find congenial with Popper's interpretation of the evolution of
science and with Kuhn's concept of paradigmatic change. Substitut-
ing competing intellectual variants for genes, and indicating the *collectivity* of scientists as being the carriers of selective variants, Toulmin explains that through processes of selective diffusion and retention
some intellectual variants eventually become predominant, others
are completely eliminated, and still others do not remain viable but
do not disappear and may come back as circumstances change.[33]
Science progresses—and social processes evolve—through intellectual innovation and authoritative selection; what survives is collective understandings as embedded in institutions.

Like Toulmin, Campbell uses the evolutionary metaphor and re-
lies on processes of innovation and selection for explaining how
ideas, beliefs, and behavior change, but he goes farther than the
authors previously mentioned in explaining learning and creative
learning, which he conceptualizes as cognitive evolution. The three
requirements for evolution are (1) mechanisms for replication or re-

production, (2) variety in whatever is reproduced, and (3) mechanisms for selection that consistently favor one type of variation over others. In cognitive evolution, learning provides the mechanisms for replication. Our ideas, beliefs, and behavior are learned from other people. When variation is introduced into this learning process, creativity results.[34]

COGNITIVE EVOLUTION

I will present here a theory of collective learning in international relations that follows my evolutionary epistemological principles. The theory interprets foreign policy as a process by which intellectual innovations are carried by domestic institutions and selected by political processes to become the descriptive and normative set of understandings of what it takes to advance the nation's power, influence, and wealth. Likewise, the theory interprets international politics as a process of diffusion of domestic initiatives and innovations through agenda setting, strategic interaction, negotiation, and intersubjective processes involving socialization and learning. My argument is that we can find the sources of collective learning in international relations at the national level—more precisely, in processes of intellectual innovation and political selection—and that with increasing interdependence and diplomatic, political, economic, and cultural contacts, nations transmit to each other the political innovations that have been selectively retained at the national level. Power plays a crucial role in both domestic selection and international diffusion processes. I also argue that once values and expectations that affect concepts and understandings in international relations are shared, they help to condition or structure international relations. The latter part of my theory builds on a concept developed by James Rosenau that he called "aggregative processes," a dynamic or set of dynamics whereby individual actions are summed and thereby converted into collectivities and then at subsequent points of time converted over and over again into more or less encompassing collectivities.[35]

Robert Putnam describes international politics as a "two-level game." He suggests that at the "national level, domestic groups pursue their interests by pressuring the government to adopt favorable policies, and politicians seek power by constructing coalitions among those groups. At the international level, national governments seek to

maximize their own ability to satisfy domestic pressures, while minimizing the adverse consequences of foreign developments."[36] I argue, in addition, that the two-level games are not only about fixed
interests and power, but about the selection, retention, and spread
of expectations and values at national and international levels. The
domestic game therefore refers to how expectations and values enter
into the political process through the active participation of political
groups with a stake in them, and how through the political process
(e.g., coalition building) these ideas help to define the national interest, which then becomes a conceptual and normative input to the
international game. In the international game, governments not only
act out of concern for the domestic political environment, but also
are motivated by solutions—whether through conflict or cooperation
—to problems, solutions whose interpretations and meanings are
embedded in the national interest. As part of this game, governments transmit expectations and values that compete to become the
basis of international behavior.

I operationalize this theory by showing how national interests are
born, how they become part of a general *domestic* political understanding that helps create political agendas, policy options, and bargaining positions, and how such understanding can have both interactive and structural effects at the international level. My approach
therefore captures the essence of creativity in international relations,
when new alternatives are generated and when suddenly political
actors become aware of something new. Understanding how change
in international relations occurs, therefore, entails grasping how national interests are created and how their essence is transmitted to
other nations.

Thus, a structural theory of international relations calls equally for
a theory of cognitive and institutional change as its natural complement. We need to learn how cognitive and institutional variants
make their appearance in the first place, how they show their merits
as solutions to outstanding international problems, and how they
succeed—given favorable conditions—in spreading and establishing
themselves more widely. We therefore must pay attention not only
to the distribution of power and to the structural–functional aspects
of institutions, but also to the historical processes by which political
innovations demonstrate their validity as solutions to domestic and
international problems.[37]

The Searchlight Theory of Learning

Realists view learning as a response to structural changes in the environment or, in game theory terms, adjustment of state behavior to changes in the pay-off matrix.[38] But game-theoretical approaches, as well as others that deal with cooperation from a realist perspective,[39] say very little about the sources of preferences, how interests are created in one area and not in another and why at a certain time and not before or later, and whether there is creative learning.

I define learning as the adoption by policymakers of new interpretations of reality, as they are created and introduced to the political system by individuals and institutions. This implies that national policymakers are subject to absorbing new meanings and interpretations of reality, as generated in intellectual, bureaucratic, and political circles, and therefore are subject to changing their interests and ability and/or willingness to consider new courses of action. Seen in this light, learning increases the capacity and motivation to understand competing alternatives to a currently entertained inference and becomes a creative process by which alternatives and preferences or "interests" are generated. The capacity to generate new cognitions is related not only to the acquisition of new information about the environment but also to new and innovative ways of drawing linkages between causes and effects and between means and ends.

This last point is crucial if we are to understand international relations from an evolutionary epistemology perspective. Most of the notions of learning used in the literature do not lend themselves to such study because they are informed by what Popper called the "bucket theory of science." According to this theory, most, if not all, of what we learn is by the entry of experience into our sense openings, so that all knowledge consists of information received by experience. Our mind is a "bucket," originally more or less empty, into which material enters, accumulates, and becomes digested.[40]

Popper believes this theory is wrong. Instead, he offers a "searchlight theory of science," wherein experience or observations are secondary to the theories or hypotheses people already have in their minds. These theories color, inform, and even determine the kind of observations and anticipations we make.[41] For learning to occur, therefore, we need to change not only our "knowledge" base but also our underlying theories. In any social context, consensus over these theories is also necessary. Thus, without an assessment of the theories and hypotheses and of the ideological barriers that impede transideological communication, "lessons" from experience may have very little impact, falling, as it were, in the "bucket."

The theories or hypotheses people have in their minds we call "expectations." Human knowledge consists of linguistically formulated expectations that are continually submitted to critical assessment and reality tests.[42] Thus, an expectation can be described as an image of the future bounded by what is physically, humanly, and socially possible. To expect is to imagine situations and events that seem possible, given a certain act. Popper's theory of learning therefore assumes that learning consists in the modification or rejection of expectations. He backs his arguments with a logical exercise: expectations could not arise just from experience because experience presupposes repetition; repetition presupposes similarity, and similarity presupposes a theory or an expectation. Thus, any observation is always preceded by a question, a problem, something theoretical, that carries expectations.[43]

In this sense all knowledge, including scientific knowledge, is subject to bias[44]; therefore, regardless of the content of knowledge, the difference between facts and hypotheses is assumed to be one of subjective confidence rather than of objective truth.[45] It follows, then, that, depending on the conditional "if–then" linkages (major premises) that individuals happen to form, several conclusions or inferences can be deduced from a piece of "evidence," and in this sense any conclusion or inference inevitably goes "beyond the information given."[46]

When we apply this interpretation to international relations, it follows that (1) the environment does not "instruct" policymakers, it challenges them; and (2) scientific knowledge is not a sufficient condition for international learning because it can be subject to bias, sometimes as much as nonscientific knowledge. The capacity of institutions in different countries to learn and to generate similar interests, therefore, will depend not only on the acquisition of new information, but on the political selection of similar cause–effect premises. The political importance of these premises lies not in their being "true," but in their being shared across institutions and nation-states. Learning in international relations takes place as biases or collective understandings (as World 3 phenomena) become selected, anchored,[47] established, and spread across institutions in different nation-states. I will show that this approach may have profound implications for how we think about progress in international relations: If the key to change lies in the sharing of "biases" or expectations that need not be a priori valid or "true," then scientists, *their values,* and the institutions they help to build or in which they participate may play a political role in the process of change equal to or even greater than knowledge itself.

Cognitive Evolution

Cognitive evolution is the process of innovation and political selection, occurring mainly within and between institutional settings, that creates the "objective" collective understanding that informs the interests of governments. A cognitive evolutionary approach requires that new or changed ideas be communicated and diffused and that political stakes be created that political groups and institutions and other interest groups may then help to maintain through the use of power. To be politically relevant, cognitive evolution must be backed by enough power to invalidate and make people set aside competing expectations and values.

Cognitive evolution is politically relevant because it replaces cause–effect and end–means relationships that collectivities accept as true, thus leading to new political, military, and economic strategies and to the channeling of action in new and different directions. This in turn will most likely lead to the creation of new interests, institutions, and interest and pressure groups, which will further create new paths and alternatives. As each new path is taken, others will be abandoned, and the world out there will never be the same. For once

> a critical choice has been made it cannot be taken back . . . once a path is taken it canalizes future developments. Sidney Verba has referred to this conceptualization as the branching tree model of sequential development. A critical choice forecloses other options in part because the "choice to set up a program in relation to a particular problem area may lead almost inevitably to the maintenance and even expansion of the program because of the vested interests it creates."[48]

Cognitive evolution and branching tree models may imply some kind of historical irreversibility, but what is really irreversible? A revolution may topple a democratic regime, but democracy may be restored. Nations go to war, but they later make peace; progress is reversible, and so is regress. Cognitive evolution is irreversible only in the sense that it adds new meanings and understandings to collective experience.[49]

Crises may play an important role in cognitive evolution because change in political processes tends to be episodic. "The importance of crises," says John Ikenberry, "stems from the intransigence of political institutions and relations. Politicians and administrators are continuously engaged in coping with socio-economic challenges; responses are channeled through existing institutions. At particular moments, however, these challenges call into question existing rules of the game and the repertories of state action."[50] Thus, dramatic events such as war, depression, acute hunger, or a large environmental accident such as Chernobyl may have the effect of a "cognitive punch," making apparent to political actors that existing institutions and types of political behavior have become dysfunctional and can no longer deal with the situation in the old ways. A crisis is thus an environmental incentive to hasten the process of reevaluation and change from one set of collective understandings or "paradigms" to another. It helps to show, in fact, that policies based on old analogies to the past are likely to have deleterious consequences.[51]

Cognitive evolution therefore is a useful corrective to institutional approaches that have used a branching-tree model but disregarded the cognitive factor. Although historical circumstances and institutional realities may tend to limit, delay, and even prevent institutional change,[52] the latter does sometimes take place. And when it does, it is most likely to be the result of a dynamic process of change in collective understandings.

Cognitive evolution involves three processes:

1. *Innovation*—the creation of new expectations and values that become collective within institutions.
2. *Selection*—political processes that determine which policies are effectively adopted and therefore which expectations and values are selected to be tested in politics, in both national and international arenas. Political selection then determines which expectations and values become at least temporarily perpetuated: "The continuing emergence of intellectual innovations is

thus balanced against a continuing process of critical selection." [53]

3. *Diffusion*—the spread of expectations and values to other nations. As international negotiations agendas are created on the basis of new expectations and values and as negotiation and diplomatic processes begin, diplomats, acting on behalf of a set of ideas as well as a set of policies, "communicate to the leaders of other states their 'theoretical' understanding . . . in addition to signalling their intent on the particular issue at hand. . . ." [54]

Innovation. New or radically different theories, expectations, and values may occasionally arise that "represent the acquisition of a new understanding." [55] Innovation occurs when new meanings and interpretations are generated by individuals within institutional structures. The realization of conceivable expectations depends largely on their practical application, on their timing, and on the ability of those individuals who urge a particular interpretation of the national interest to anticipate the exigencies and needs of the political structures involved in the selection process. From this point of view, innovation is not "blind" but is in a sense preselected, bearing in mind the requirements for selection. [56]

Personal originality, of course, plays an important role in the innovation process as collective understanding is realized through the intellectual performances of individuals; but what matters is that meanings and interpretations are shared. Epistemic communities, defined loosely as a group of intellectuals sharing a common causal understanding on a particular subject and who organize to turn this understanding into action strategies [57] can play an important role in the innovation process, especially when issues depend on some kind of technical knowledge, as most issues now do.

Selection. The actors, structures and processes of the political system determine which expectations and values are turned into policies. The policymaker, in principle at least, serves as judge, jury, and if necessary executioner over the professional output of expectations developed at the institutional level. [58] Expectations and values can thus be satisfied only through policy decision. Those selected are the ones that pass the test of domestic politics. Given that no political idea, whatever its origin or content, is valid a priori but is validated only by the political process, domestic institutions must persuade other actors, especially those at the top of the political hierarchy, of the validity of the ideas advanced by the institutions. What we must ask now is: "On what occasions and by what processes and procedures are institutional expectations and values discredited and abandoned in favor of new or new/old sets of expectations and values?"

My view of the selection process requires a fresh look at the concept of state and the role of institutions, one that transcends the idea of state used by realists and neorealists of the systemic and game-theoretical strands. In my view, states are still the essential actors of international relations; they are made up of many institutions and entities competing for authority, each with its own "embedded orientations or dispositions to act"[59] and each of which can learn different "lessons." The state is not, however, merely an aggregation of bureaus acting according to their "standard operating procedures," as the various bureaucratic and bureaucratic-organizational models often suggest,[60] but a historical entity represented by institutions, each with a particular collective understanding or set of expectations and values. Some institutions will undoubtedly carry more power than others in the selection process and make the critical choices in the international arena, but those choices will be affected by conceptions and understandings developed, in and through politics, by institutions that "work together, neither 'for good' entirely nor 'for ill' entirely, but simply as their joint histories dictate."[61] When a set of alternatives on nuclear arms control reaches the president, for instance, it reflects either a consensus, a compromise, or a choice of ideas that survived political obstacles and may have been selected through the power exerted by political alliances.

The state should not be presumed to be "rational." Rationality must be asserted and proved in every instance, according to the ability of the state to change expectations and values and select political solutions that deal effectively with problems. Thus, the rational state is a historical entity that—pregnant with new and old expectations arising from various groups and institutions that respond in different ways to real problems—is able to learn by selecting political solutions that can deal better with problems.

Two important implications follow from my conceptualization of the state. First, progress in international relations will depend on the extent to which the state can solve problems in such a way as to enhance security, welfare, and human rights across national borders. Second, the national interest is the intersubjective consensus that survives the political process, given the distribution of power in the society. The "objective" national interest is therefore a World 3 product that once produced can have various real intended and unintended consequences. The key question from a becoming perspective, then, is how to effect changes in ideational and ideological assumptions. The preliminary answer is through the creation of new formal or informal institutions that incorporate a new set of expectations and values.[62]

Diffusion: International Cognitive Structures. International collective understandings are constituted and international organization may even take place when institutions of different countries share and coordinate their expectations and values. "The world indeed becomes more organized when participants of the processes build consensus on what factors have caused what events, what has gone wrong, and what has to be done to resume the correct order."[63] The study of international relations then deals with processes by which governments seek to establish their understanding of the world and of phenomena and coordinate their behavior according to a set of causal understandings. Thus, when states negotiate and renegotiate their respective interests, they also implicitly negotiate and renegotiate meanings and understandings. Nations that get together in direct negotiations or that are brought together by strategic interaction and are linked by security, economic, and technological interdependence will affect each other's intentions, plans, expectations, and policies. One way this can happen is by what Robert Legvold has called "interactive" learning, which occurs when one society learns from another.[64] This has been the case with the gradual acceptance by the Soviets of the importance of having secure second-strike, or retaliatory, nuclear forces, which may have been influenced, if not directly affected, by theories of deterrence developed in the United States and by American strategic behavior.[65] Processes of interactive learning and socialization imply, then, that as individuals and institutions transmit to each other their expectations and values, they also transmit *descriptive and normative conceptions of the national interest.*

We can describe the World 3 theoretical understanding of social phenomena that conditions the convergence of expectations of those states that share it as a "cognitive structure."[66] A related though not similar concept is that of "thought collective," developed by Ludwik Fleck.[67] Cognitive structures generate the "evidence" that confirms their validity, and treat those actions that can be considered anomalous to the collective understanding as "errors." Collective understandings can be based either on scientific knowledge or on interpretation of historical events. Cognitive structures, like scientific paradigms, have conditioning and constraining effects on what people consider "right" or "wrong," where they place their attention, and what expectations they develop. Several cognitive structures may coexist at any given time, and power may play a major role in determining which ones will survive.

Because World 3 products produce observable effects, we can justify their importance as ontological constructs. In this sense, I adhere to the observation made by Alexander Wendt in his justification of the ontological status of nonobservable structures, to the effect that even if unobservable, social structures (or in my case international cognitive structures) can produce observable effects and their manipulation can affect the observable world.[68]

Cognitive structures organize rather than constrain behavior; in other words, they apply plastic control to a situation. These structures are "generative,"[69] but only in the sense that they generate foreign policy as if international relations were structured as thought.[70] The world is hence made sensible by interpreting agents who create collective understandings that acquire a life of their own as "objective" products, thus generating policy responses, institutional building, and agendas across national borders.

My theory could be portrayed as structurationist,[71] to the extent that institutional agents play a role in effecting broader collective understandings, at both the domestic and the international level, and subsequently these collective understandings help to organize relations and to condition, in part, the behavior of institutions. I am reformulating somewhat the structuration concept, however. First, my theory deals with two sets of agent–structure relations. In my "national game," institutions are the agents and the structure is transinstitutional. In my "international game," states are the agents and the structure is transnational. Second, the structures I refer to *do not generate* the agents and their behavior[72]; they acquire their causal efficacy as World 3 products once they become part of international political agendas and negotiation processes. Third, agents and structures are not codetermined[73]; rather, the agent through political processes succeeds (or not) in introducing its innovation and turning it into a World 3 product. Later this innovation may have organizational effects on the motivation and behavior of national actors. In other words, the structures I am describing are part of the historical process, explain the actual, and do not fully determine behavior. My theory, then, does not have to deal with structural and historical research simultaneously,[74] because structures and history are complementary.

COGNITIVE EVOLUTION, VALUES, AND PROGRESS IN INTERNATIONAL RELATIONS

A national interest will emerge, or be transformed, because of a combination of descriptive–explanatory understandings with normative judgments.[75] For progress in international relations to take place, the normative content of such national interest as is spread internationally must place a high value—relative to other values—on human beings, regardless of their nationality. Progress in international relations will depend less on the advancement of science per se, or on the cunning of reason, than on the political selection, retention, and diffusion of values that tend to enhance security, welfare, and human rights across borders.

Values

Realism takes value as unproblematic and constant; for example, values are given in game-theoretical studies. Yet how "values are developed, maintained, and changed may be crucial to international politics, and may strongly influence the extent of cooperation"[76] and the prospects for progressive change in international relations.[77] It is meaningful to speak about terminal or end values and instrumental values, as it is to speak about institutional values, which Milton Rokeach defined as socially shared cognitive representations of institutional goals and demands.[78]

Values are mixed with varying amounts of knowledge, beliefs, and expectations because our judgments of what should be are related to our judgments of what is.[79] Thus, although values are back-ward-looking in their frequent justification of past conduct, they also guide anticipatory and goal-directed behavior (i.e., they are linked to expectations).[80] Indeed, the relation between values and expectations did not escape Haas and Karl Deutsch,[81] who saw the evolution toward an international community as resulting from a joint transformation of values and expectations.

Emergence and Evolution of Values and Interests

Human values affect action by influencing our definition of a particular situation and by directing our choice of relevant "facts"[82] or "interests" ("a disciplined understanding of what it takes to advance one's power, influence and wealth").[83] The interdependence of facts and values implies a constant shifting between empirical and normative elements in decision making. Values therefore affect international political behavior, and the transformation of interests, by defining the gratification that establishes and reinforces those interests, and the sources of this gratification.[84]

Values emerge in the political system with problems.[85] In the last forty years the superpowers may have come to value peace more than war, not as a result of a new ethical or moral stand, but because they had to face the problem of nuclear surprise attacks and inadvertent and unintended nuclear war.[86] Certain problems, which can become more perceptually acute through crises, may help to turn previously fringe or "eccentric" values—such as environmental concerns—into more durable and central values.[87] Thus, cognitive evolution may help turn valueless objects or interests into politically valuable and durable objects and interests.[88]

Domestic institutions may help inject into the political process objectives and interests that reflect new values or new combinations of values. Values become politically relevant when they are backed by institutional power, legitimacy, and authority and are most effective when they are not held merely in abstract terms, but are incorporated in political institutions and in habits of political behavior that permit them to be acted on in such a way as to strengthen people's attachment to them.[89]

For example, expectations of peaceful change, coupled with a strong valuation of peace (or a strong negative valuation of war), may help to create an interest in measures such as arms control that may be perceived to enhance the prospects of peaceful change. An interest in arms control then becomes a way to organize values and expectations of international security. Arms control becomes a "searchlight" or "map" that affects attention, diplomacy, and political actions and reactions. Once the habit of arms control becomes established (i.e., when expectations and values become routinized and are taken for granted), we can say that it has become a national interest for x, y, z countries to pursue arms control agreements. Interests are therefore not antithetical to ideational or normative phenomena; they *are*, in part, ideational and normative phenomena and they can be molded, albeit with many constraints.

Progress in International Relations

There are two necessary conditions for progress in international relations: (1) Emergence of new values, redefinition of old values, and a change in the context of valuing that advances human interests across national borders without creating an unbearable harm to other values or human interests. (2) A change in expectations regarding the quality of the outcomes for the agent, including a redefinition of what exists, what can exist, what causes what, what the concomitants of desired actions are, and the like.[90]

The key question is what causes expectations and values that enhance human interests across national borders to be politically selected, maintained, and spread at domestic and international levels. There is probably no single answer, and generalizations would require the study of many cases and comparison of political processes that have led to a reevaluation of a situation and to new expectations. My "Seasons of Peace" in this volume offers one illustration and one set of answers: after World War II, values and expectations of peace and war changed through a combination of learning, modernization, technological changes, and growing security interdependence that challenged some governments to alter the way they advance their power and influence.[91]

Learning does not take place without some active persuasion of decision makers and governmental institutions; deals may need to be cut, alliances may need to be formed before a certain set of values and expectations can win the day. Growing interdependence may persuade policymakers of the need to reevaluate national interests.

But mediating between interdependence and progress are institutions that introduce to the political system theoretical and normative views regarding the implications of interdependence for the national interest. Thus, they create possibilities for progressive change, which must be actualized by political decisions.

Several studies in this volume have found a significant relationship between interdependence, learning, and progress in international relations.[92] On the basis of those studies and my own, we can raise the hypothesis that progress in international relations may take place when interdependence, rising to the level of political collective understanding, helps to break previously held expectations and values about political autonomy in the international arena and triggers a reevaluation process that causes old interests to veer away from war, poverty, and human rights violations because they have suddenly become dysfunctional.

The meaning of learning used in the preceding studies, however, focuses on increasing consensual *scientific* knowledge, which in a context of growing interdependence is believed to lead to the creation of new interests or to the reevaluation of old interests in ways that collective solutions to problems are preferred over unilateral solutions.[93] Yet as I have argued earlier, scientific knowledge (e.g., physics, economics, strategy) can be manipulated to produce several ways to explain the same physical and social phenomena. In the most demanding case, the issue of war and peace, "we have reason for pessimism, for it is not clear what kinds of information or knowledge we could gather or what kinds of scientific research we could undertake that would make it easier than it now is to penetrate the confusions and complexities of policies for maintaining peace. It is particularly difficult if we have several goals, as most of us have."[94] The picture is not very different in the economic realm. Because the operation of the economy depends critically on human expectations about the future and human reactions to those expectations,[95] it is very difficult for economists to provide the kind of consensual knowledge that can bridge different ideologies.

Scientists (in contrast to "science" itself), however, can play an instrumental role in producing shared understandings that can lead to progressive changes. Armed with the authority and legitimacy conferred to them by society, and equipped with a unique understanding in their area of expertise, scientists and other experts, when organized into epistemic communities, can play an important role in the process of intellectual innovation and political selection of ideas and understandings. On the one hand, epistemic communities can provide decision makers with new answers to old questions and help them to redefine and reconceptualize problems. Epistemic communities do not necessarily provide decision makers with "the truth," which because of being "true" helps turn political wheels. They can nevertheless be very influential because they may provide a solution or a key—in the sense that any key mutually recognized as the key becomes the key.[96] On the other hand, together with their innovations, epistemic communities also introduce values and visions that can catch the imagination of decision makers who then, on the basis of their new understanding, may redefine strategic and economic interests so as to enhance human interests across national borders.

Epistemic communities can do much to affect the political selection process. They can help create new institutions or use old ones to push ideas within the government; they may help gain media and public opinion support for their ideas, which can then help persuade decision makers and legislators; and they may be actively involved in creating and participating in coalitions that will promote their innovations.

The success of epistemic communities is historically contingent. Historical contingency is provided by the state of technology; the distribution of power in the international system; domestic political and administrative structures and procedures; and political, economic, and military events. Historical events such as international crises, wars, new technologies introduced into the economy or the military, and perceived changes in economic, political, and military power may help decision makers to see what they were not able to see before. In other words, as the historical context changes, theories or policy proposals that before did not make any sense to politicians may suddenly acquire a political (maybe even urgent) meaning, thus becoming politically viable.

However, the chances of success of an epistemic community will be enhanced when (1) some of its members are brought into state institutions as officials, technocrats, or consultants, who can then affect the political process from within; (2) structures and procedures of government and administration facilitiate the persuasion task of experts by protecting or insulating them from opposing individuals and institutions holding different interests and points of view; (3) there is an ideological affinity between experts and key policymakers; (4) once inside the government, experts are given enough time to formulate their ideas into policies and to implement them; (5) experts formulate their ideas in ways such that policymakers can see their practical application; (6) the ideas advanced address the policymakers' main concerns and interests and give a new meaning to their past experience; (7) the community members are trusted as bearers of legitimate knowledge; (8) key decision makers are willing and able to use their leadership in the political system on behalf of the ideas; and (9) the ideas strike a balance, or find a common denominator, between competing positions within the government and in society, thus helping to beak domestic political deadlocks and creating a *temporary* consensus that enables the implementation of these ideas. (Once implemented, however, they may acquire a life of their own and transcend and outlast the temporary consensus that cleared the way for their promotion by the epistemic community.)

The next section offers two illustrations of the creation, selection, retention, and spread of conceptual and normative "keys" or understandings, which through socialization and interactive learning processes became part of a collective understanding that transcended national borders and resulted in progressive change.

EMERGENCE OF THE NATIONAL INTEREST: TWO CASES OF AMERICAN INNOVATIONS

Superpower nuclear arms control in the last thirty years and the development of a new economic order after World War II are examples of American intellectual innovations that survived and spread, albeit not without changes, because of political power and the role played by experts and epistemic communities in the political processes. In the economic order case, American hegemonic power played an important role in the diffusion of innovation. In the arms-control case, the diffusion of political innovation was characterized by a relatively long intersubjective process involving a slow but noticeable convergence of expectations and values about nuclear war. Both cases were characterized by innovations originating from seemingly "scientific" understandings whose authority and validation were established as a result of domestic and international political processes.

And both cases are illustrations of cognitive evolutionary processes that resulted in *instrumental progress,* which refers to international regimes[97] or cooperative frameworks and institutional structures that nation-states jointly create to deal with problems that, given their nature and scope, are perceived as not solvable by unilateral actions alone.

Nuclear Arms Control

Nuclear arms control was not entirely determined in a structural reality, nor was it entirely determined that during the last thirty years the superpowers would be involved in political cooperation via arms control. Nuclear arms control, both as a concept and as a blueprint for action, resulted from expectations of Americans who, becoming aware of their nuclear weapons vulnerability and concerned about the reciprocal fear of surprise attack, started to anticipate the future in terms of strategic stability. Yet at the end of the 1950s, when the concept of arms control was introduced, stable nuclear deterrence was only a concept that could not be taken for granted; nor could it be ruled out.[98]

I therefore maintain that the epistemic community of strategists and scientists, not only redefined the concept of nuclear arms control and injected an "owlish" ideology into the political process, which until then had been characterized only by "hawkish" (superiority) and "dovish" (disarmament) ideas, but also created the meanings and interpretations of the nuclear predicament and superpower strategic interaction that in time led to political collaboration among the superpowers.

These expectations, together with an idiosyncratic normative understanding of state behavior and war prevention, created a learning process—a common understanding, or a set of cause–effect relationships, about war and peace, about weapons and negotiations, and about conflict and cooperation. This understanding shifted the conception held by academicians and policymakers about international negotiations from measures designed to remove nuclear weapons from world affairs to measures designed to make their presence more tolerable.[99]

The basic assumption behind the new approach developed in the late 1950s was that nuclear deterrence had become unstable and that a catastrophe could now occur against the wishes of the adversary states. These notions about war followed a string of events, such as RAND's (Albert Wohlstetter's) studies on the vulnerability of U.S. strategic forces; the Soviet tests of an intercontinental ballistic missile (ICBM) in August 1957; the launching of "Sputnik," the first Soviet satellite, into space two months later; and the creation by President Dwight Eisenhower of a committee (Gaither) to review the problems of civil defense, which ended up reviewing the whole national security situation and recommending a military buildup across the board.

Some of the scientists who had helped draft the Gaither report, however, became disenchanted with its recommendations and with the trend in U.S.–Soviet relations. Having become members of the presidential Permanent Science Advisory Committee (PSAC), they made their ideas known to the president, who was receptive and supportive. Their concern was shared by a group of strategists working mainly for RAND, who, impressed by the vulnerability of U.S. strategic forces, thought that an indiscriminate quest for military superiority, and a belief in the possibility of winning a nuclear war, would inexorably lead to such a war. Thus, when a Surprise Attack Conference and a conference to discuss a nuclear test ban were convened in Geneva in 1958 (neither of which produced any agreements between Americans and Soviets), the scientists and strategists —most of whom came from Harvard and MIT and thus were dubbed the "Charles River Gang"—formulated a set of shared ideas about how to avoid nuclear war and at the same time protect U.S. national security.

This set of ideas, articulated primarily by the civilian strategists, was indeed a response to technological changes that gave both superpowers an "overkill" and "mutual-kill" capability and to mounting international tensions over Berlin, Taiwan, and Cuba. Yet they also were an evolution of American strategic thinking on nuclear deterrence, strategic war, limited war, and escalation that had started to develop after World War II. As such, they were rigorous theories deduced from a set of hypotheses about technology and stability[100] and whose reference point was not past experience but expectations of the future. Being the disciplined creation of artificial worlds in the strategists' minds, they could not have been determined only by structure.

There have been very few times in international relations history

when a set of ideas and their carriers played such a critical role. Even
though Colin Gray may have exaggerated when he wrote that "contemporary arms-control theory was an invention of the strategic studies
community in the period 1958–60," and although Charles Osgood
may have overemphasized the role of President John Kennedy when
he argued that "this community was largely successful in selling their
ideas to the government with the encouragement and *collaboration* of
President Kennedy,"[101] the fact remains that the community of scientists and strategists developed a set of innovative ideas about
peace and war that were later politically selected and implemented
when a large number of its members went to work for the Kennedy
administration. Once inside, they pushed their arms-control ideas,
created institutions, and persuaded key political actors such as Robert McNamara and Paul Nitze of the need for arms control. The result
was a series of arms-control treaties: the 1963 test-ban treaty, the 1963
Hotline agreement, the 1967 Outer Space treaty, the 1968 nonproliferation treaty, and the 1972 ABM treaty, the latter being the most
faithful to the original expectations and values.

Reflecting on the entire period, Thomas Schelling, who played a
key role in the development of nuclear arms-control ideas, said:

> That 15-year period from 1957 to 1972 is a remarkable story of intellectual
> achievement transformed into policy. Three books appeared in 1961 that
> epitomized an emerging consensus on what strategic arms control should
> be about. Each was a group effort, and each stimulated discussion even
> while being written. . . . a number of participants in the Harvard–MIT
> seminar took positions in the Kennedy White House, Department of State
> and Department of Defense; others from RAND and elsewhere, who had
> been part of this intellectual movement, moved into the government as
> well. So it is not completely surprising that those ideas became the basis
> for U.S. policy and were ultimately implemented in the ABM treaty.[102]

If ideas generated at RAND, at the Harvard–MIT Seminar,[103] and
among the PSAC scientists succeeded in transforming the practices
of deterrence and cooperation with the adversary, what mattered
was not that in the course of their careers personal ideas of the
participants changed, nor how preferences were first proposed, but
how the ideas were ultimately disposed through the presence or
absence of social validation.[104]

The realization of communicable expectations and theories, however, depended largely on their practical application being readily
perceived by policymakers, as was the case with the interdependence

of strategic decisions. Although according to Schelling his theory of interdependent decision was elementary and its practical application evident,[105] it is important because it seems to lend itself to useful and striking political proposals and actions, which in turn are useful and striking because they seem to be based on his theories.[106] "Reality" therefore resulted from a collective redefinition of problems that carried the clout first of "scientific knowledge" and, later on, of political power.

Although the arms-control ideas developed by the American epistemic community between 1957 and 1972 were almost immediately diffused to the Soviets and eventually had a meaningful impact on the international game, almost thirty years had to pass for some of them to be shared by the Soviets wholeheartedly enough to create a unique convergence of expectations and values. This convergence materialized in the 1987 INF arms-control agreement, which opened the way for additional and more ambitious arms control agreements.

At first the Soviets went along with arms control because it fit their own interpretation of what could advance their power and influence: strengthening détente and managing the political environment while developing a full-blown strategic force. To be fair, we must say that at the SALT I negotiations the Soviets were keenly motivated by the desire to avoid a race in ballistic missile defense. But the technical arguments of U.S. nuclear arms control did not impress them greatly. In time, American and Soviet expectations and basic norms regarding war and peace were renegotiated and the U.S. came to follow a more political approach to arms control while the Soviet Union was increasingly socialized by the American concepts, interpretations, and meanings and thus became more receptive and understanding of the American approach. By the end of the 1970s the Soviet leaders had moved beyond arms control as a mere mechanism for lobbying against new American arms programs,[107] agreeing on an arms control regime (SALT II) that promised predictability in the force composition of both sides.

When Gorbachev came to power, he moved with bold strides to the virtual repudiation of the rigid INF arms control stance of his predecessors[108] and his ideas "began to sound reminiscent of the kind of stability and finite limit to nuclear procurement defined by U.S. Secretary of Defense Robert McNamara 20 years earlier as 'mutual assured destruction.' "[109] And as Ronald Reagan and his advisors moved away (at least temporarily) from arms control classical ideas, "Moscow's tacit aims converged with those of classic Western arms control. . . . All the deterrent verities about stability and assured second strike and the destabilizing, trigger-happy nature of the strategic defense that US arms controllers had preached in the '70s suddenly made a great deal more sense to the Soviets of the '80s."[110]

Gradual Soviet acceptance of (1) fragments of American arms control ideas (such as the need to reduce the threat of MIRVed missiles to fixed land-based missiles, to reduce secrecy in order to enhance verification, and to accept equal numerical limitations)[111] and later (2) the notion of placing limitations on and changing the essence of strategic forces, and the asymmetrical reduction of conventional arms in Europe, resulted in the creation of a collective understanding that took years to develop but that now holds the potential for reducing tensions and controlling expectations in the future. What had started as a seed in an epistemic community's collective interpretation of the strategic situation had evolved to become U.S. security policy, and through socialization and interactive learning had further evolved into a cognitive structure regarding issues of national security and nuclear war prevention.

If only because arms control, with superb timing, (1) provided the superpowers with *a* key to avoid Armageddon, which they then turned into *the* key to manage the arms race; (2) induced the superpowers to talk, exchange views, and make each other's doctrines, fears, and hopes better known; and (3) produced crucial time for the Cold War to wane, we can claim that arms-control ideas and practices, reduced the danger of nuclear war and therefore enhanced the human interest. It is a matter of contention whether the world would today be a better and more peaceful place had the superpowers pursued disarmament avenues rather than arms control. We will never know. What we do know in retrospect is that the political selection and diffusion of the arms control conceptual framework in the two-level games of international politics not only became the basis for unilateral measures that enhanced crisis stability but also instituted cooperation between the superpowers (providing the reasons and methods for cooperation) and helped to control expectations and bring them into some convergence.

It is ironic that arms control, which sought to provide a realist alternative to the rationalist and idealist movement of postwar scientists—which predicated disarmament and a world government as the solution to the nuclear predicament—ended up promoting a technical approach based on reason and on the belief that technical solutions, in conjunction with political measures, can and should be applied to the control of the arms race. It is reassuring, however, that intellectual innovation in an issue area where securing restraint against the use of the most powerful weapons and against defensive weapons was, at best, counterintuitive succeeded in making humanity take a few, if only temporary and partial, steps away from the nuclear abyss.

Postwar International Order

The emergence of the postwar international economic order has been recounted more than adequately by others,[112] and my short account on the subject is not the first to focus on ideas.[113] The point, however, is to show the unfolding and changing of international relations as a result of innovation, selection, and diffusion processes. The economic order that emerged after World War II was born in the minds of a small group of key U.S. economists and officials, working mainly at the Treasury Department and operating under the leadership of Under Secretary Harry Dexter White,[114] whose efforts were being replicated on the other side of the Atlantic, especially in Great Britain. For example, the idea for a financial international order can be traced back to two plans, one developed in the United States under White's leadership and the other engineered by John Maynard Keynes in Great Britain. However, the expectations and values that emerged from this intellectual process, and that provided intellectual guidance to political intentions and policies, were negotiated twice: first, in the domestic game, where processes of coalition building, persuasion, and the elimination of plausible alternatives determined the survivors to a large extent; second, in the international game between the Americans, the British, and other European countries in such a way as to reflect not only the original intentions of the innovations but also the preferences and needs of those who were supposed to buy these ideas. Thus, the ensuing understandings, which amounted to a cognitive structure, and even international institutions, such as the International Monetary Fund (IMF), the World

Bank, and the General Agreement on Tariffs and Trade (GATT), resulted in part from cognitive evolution processes.

The international regimes literature has rightly pointed out that the multilateral order that gained acceptance after World War II owed much to American hegemonic power.[115] John Ruggie has enriched our understanding on the subject, adding that the "authority relations that were instituted in the international regimes for money and trade reflected a new balance of state-society relations that expressed a *collective* reality."[116] This collective or intersubjective understanding, which Ruggie called "embedded liberalism" and which anticipated the content and purposes of the new international order, was a compromise between economic nationalism and liberalism: unlike the economic nationalism of the 1930s, embedded liberalism was multilateral. Unlike the liberalism of the gold standard and free trade, its multilateralism was predicated upon domestic interventionism.[117]

The novel conceptual and normative aspects of the American interest in multilaterialism, as they emerged and evolved in the postwar era, arose from a need and desire to create an alternative to the past era of economic nationalism and were directly affected by the last war and by the unique moment of transition from war to peace that helped direct the attention of experts and politicians (increasingly exposed to Keynesian ideas), to efforts of reconstruction and therefore of innovation. The growing preoccupation with the spread of communism in Europe was crucial in persuading political actors in America and Europe to back ideas of embedded liberalism. Expectations also reflected a certain exuberance that evidenced the self-perception of the United States as a hegemonic power, because few Americans anticipated that the powers bestowed upon international institutions could one day be exercised against the United States. Richard Gardner also points out that the architects or innovators zeroed in on a detailed plan for the construction of an economic order and institutions because they remembered the chaos that followed World War I and the negative implications of U.S. failure to join the League of Nations; they interpreted the breakdown of the last peace settlement as a result of inadequate handling of economic problems.[118]

These architects, expressing much genuine idealism, generated a vision of peace and prosperity and expectations of interdependence not shared by all American elites. Nor was this vision readily embraced in Europe. The vision had to survive the hurdles of domestic and international politics before it could be accepted as in the interest of the states involved. Indeed, given the strong isolationist and nationalist ideas of many Americans and the strong political interests and ideological biases against multilaterialism of both the right and the left in Europe, it would have been impossible for the original ideas that motivated the emerging international order to become the basis of international behavior. This is why

> Bretton Woods' sails had to be trimmed to the point where public and Congressional acceptance might be possible—but only after a life and death fight. . . . the package was wrapped in the glittering generalities of a hard political fight designed to get public acceptance and force Congressional approval.[119]

The crystallization of multilateral policies in the United States owed a great deal to the action of individuals and institutions in three nongovernmental arenas: (1) gaining public support for a view that was being sold to the world, including the idea of containment; (2) intense personal and informal coordination with Congress; and (3) private and international consultation with other countries, with feedback to the domestic political arena.[120] Groups at State and Treasury committed to the idea of multilaterialism toured the country explaining, persuading, and putting forward their expectations until the banking community, which formed the strongest opposition to the Bretton Woods agreement, was isolated. Also critical was the creation of a coalition between very strange bedfellows who shared a notion of peace through open markets and thus were receptive to embedded liberalism ideas. The domestic political structure was also an important factor. With respect to trade, Raymond Vernon and Debra Spar stress the fact that because "Congress periodically has exhibited a willingness to delegate the political burden of dealing with the costs and benefits of trade policy, it has been possible for a leader inside the bureaucracy to take on the task of seeking presidential approval for a new trade program and then shepherding it over the domestic and international hurdles."[121]

The British had their own reasons for going along with the American proposals[122] and were careful to draft clauses in such a way that their own interpretations would come out. Yet at the same time a broad range of ideas was negotiated before the countries could reach a consensus. "A process of socialization, furthered by the modification of these normative principles and the coaptation of a variety of European domestic groups, did result in the legitimation of hegemonic power."[123] Socialization, however, was accompanied by active arm twisting, bargaining, persuasion and promises of economic aid and protection on the part of the United States. The loss of power of European rightist and leftist groups opposing embedded liberalism ideas was also consequential.[124]

Once the principle of cooperation survived these processes of innovation, selection, and diffusion, it became habitual and normal. Although several of the original institutions failed to work at first, such as the IMF, or never materialized, such as the International Trade Organization (ITO), "other institutional innovations appeared,"[125] providing continuity to the original understandings and purposes, which were renegotiated at both the domestic and international levels. This continuity was especially evident in the monetary and trade regimes.[126] Hand in hand, once the collective ideas became embedded in institutions and as the latter adapted to changing situations[127] and arrived at new understandings of the situation,[128] these entities acquired new and different functions.

Postwar international institutions originally conceived to manage interdependent relations between developed countries increasingly developed new goals and means to deal with Third World debt, development, and poverty problems and, more recently, with the global environment,[129] and started to reallocate resources to poorer, or even to the poorest, countries.

Also, in its attempt to reform (rather than replace) the postwar economic order, the Third World added new ideas and institutions onto old ones and thus unintentionally bestowed on the old order a minimal measure of legitimacy. Thus, elites from the "North" and the "South" used existing understandings and institutional arrangements to exchange and renegotiate their positions and visions, as well as the normative and epistemic notions on which their respective sets of interests were based.

While certainly not the "best," or a moral, solution from a global perspective, and always subject to setbacks and failure, the postwar order that followed cognitive evolutionary processes produced a very imperfect order, but one that "may be superior to politically feasible alternatives,"[130] and that may have helped to improve the welfare of *some* human beings, mainly in developed, but increasingly also in Third World, countries.[131]

Minimalist progress in the management of international political–economic relations, then, should be measured neither against an abstract and utopian idea of global welfare nor against the notion that in two generations humanity can solve the problem of justice, but against what could have happened to the welfare and security of individuals across national borders if either more radical laissez-faire policies or economic nationalism had continued to be the only intellectual source of "wisdom" on which international economic policies were based.

HUMANIST REALISM

The approach I develop in this study does not challenge realism; it does challenge the structural determinist notions that realists and neorealists have used to make sense out of realist assumptions. From my critique a more dynamic approach emerges, which for lack of a better term I call humanist realism. Humanist realism offers a pragmatic middle ground between the view that nothing changes (which would be debilitating and lead to despair) and the view that everything is possible (which would be utopian). It blends power, structures, interests, and pessimism with bounded optimism, a dynamic view of international politics, and the conviction that some choices do exist and that change can, at times, lead to the enhancement of human interests across borders.

A research program using a humanist-realist approach should therefore be based on the following assumptions, which qualify and amend those framed by Keohane.[132]

1. States are still seen as the principal actors in world politics, although the origins of policies must be traced to domestic institutions. More emphasis is placed on the relation between state and human beings, who play a crucial double role: they shape interests, policies, international agendas, and therefore international negotiations and outcomes, and themselves become the recipients of the "fruits" of progress or the victims of its absence. Without abandoning the nation-state view of international relations, human interests

can and should be taken into account when describing and explaining international politics.

2. Questions of rationality are rephrased to fit a dynamic evolutionary perspective. Rationality is discovered rather than assumed, and it concerns the condition and manner in which governments are prepared to change their expectations and values as time goes on.[133]

3. Power is complementary to values, and behavior is a combination of both. States, representing different cultures, employ numerous ways to interpret, apply, and enhance power (which can be interpreted from more aspects than simply physical (i.e., military) capabilities). According to the principle of complementarity, which is a central tenet of humanist realism, reality in international relations can be seen as an accommodation of opposites[134]; as constituted by different aspects of reality that exclude one another yet add to our understanding of the phenomena as a whole.[135] In a dialectical fashion, the presence of anarchy and the increase of disorder are both needed to bring about management and order. Tensions are reduced because they are caused. Adaptation takes place because there is change. Innovative ideas that can change the way actors relate to each other grow from failure and disappointment. Improvements are made because of dissatisfaction with the present condition. Power and values therefore express two views of the same international reality: power determines the range of possible outcomes, and the human mind determines what is good, bad, rational, and irrational.

I cannot improve upon Charles Sabel's explanation of how this complementarity works:

> It is true that the initial distribution of power and interests between contestants sets broad limits on the possible outcomes of a struggle. But given those limits, the ultimate result depends on the contestants' tactical skill and programmatic boldness, as well as on the web of human sympathy or mistrust that binds or separates allies on both sides. This necessity to maneuver makes possible the transformation of interest in the midst of conflict. . . . a group . . . may gradually revise its claims by applying them to the new circumstances, amalgamating them with those of an ally, or radically extending them in the enthusiasm or desperation of battle.[136]

4. Cognitive phenomena and history are integrated into scientific analysis, based on an epistemology of science attuned to scientific understanding, mainly in the physical sciences and biology, as it has evolved in the twentieth century. This epistemology, by suggesting

a partly indeterminate and emergent physical and social universe, does not give scientists a license to abandon formal scientific research. It instead guides research, armed with a much more dynamic set of concepts and frameworks.

5. It is understood that preference changes result not only from environmental alterations but from human adaptive creativity as well. Therefore, learning processes and outcomes—whether individual, institutional, or international—must be studied.

6. We must understand the intersubjective meanings that international political actors give to situations and events, and how human values, beliefs, and expectations come into play through the meanings and interpretations of actions and events.[137] Humanist realism thus is open to the interpretative kind of work that Haas has pioneered, and should not be confused with approaches that analyze the role of perceptions and misperceptions in world politics.[138] Instead, it means penetrating to the sources of collective human understandings, to the processes that generate them, and to the reasons they so often fail to take shape.

7. The concept of national interest must be more dynamic and plastic, and concerned with how interests are born, how they evolve, and what their descriptive and normative characteristics and qualities are.

8. Finally, a humanist-realist approach will open the door to the study of progress in international relations. The realist side warns us to be very cautious and to expect at best minimalist progress. The humanist side, however, gives us some hope. For it is ironic that as the Enlightenment idea of progress has all but lost its prestige—gone as it were, down the drain of history—it has taken with it the notion that sometimes, somewhere, changes away from "the worst" can and do occur, and that human beings and their values may contribute to such occurrences. It is this idea that should be salvaged, interpreted, and analyzed within the perspective of international relations. Progress in international relations, therefore, can be likened to climbing a precipice: slow, painfully difficult, fraught with setbacks, yet still humanly possible. In international relations we seldom climb toward the top, but mainly away from the abyss.

78   *Emanuel Adler*

ENDNOTES

I am grateful to Don Babai, Beverly Crawford, Ernst Haas, Peter Haas, Stephen Haggard, Peter Hall, Peter Katzenstein, Robert A. Letcher, and Joseph Nye for their critical comments and suggestions.

1. Franklin L. Baumer, *Modern European Thought: Continuity and Change in Ideas, 1600–1950* (New York: Macmillan, 1977), p. 59.
2. Karl R. Popper, *Quantum Theory and the Schism in Physics*, W. W. Bartley, III, ed. (Totowa, N.J.: Rowman and Littlefield, 1982).
3. See Robert O. Keohane, "Theory of World Politics: Structural Realism and Beyond," in Robert O. Keohane, ed., *Neorealism and Its Critics* (New York: Columbia University Press, 1986), pp. 164–165. *Neorealism and Its Critics* is a comprehensive collection of essays on neorealism. The best critique of neorealism is Richard K. Ashley, "The Poverty of Neorealism," in ibid., pp. 255–300.
4. Kenneth N. Waltz, *Theory of International Politics* (Reading, Mass.: Addison-Wesley, 1979), and Robert Gilpin, *War and Change in World Politics* (New York: Cambridge University Press, 1981).
5. R. B. K. Walker, "Realism, Change, and International Political Theory," *International Studies Quarterly* (1987), 31(1):77.
6. Waltz, *Theory of International Politics*, p. 70.
7. Such a system is neatly described by Butterfield: "All the various bodies, the greater and the lesser powers, were poised against one another, each exercising a kind of gravitational pull on all the rest—and the pull of each would be proportionate to its mass, though its effect would be greatly reduced as it acted at a greater distance. When one of these bodies increased its mass, therefore . . . the rest could recover an equilibrium only by regrouping themselves . . . making a necessary rectification in the distances and producing new combinations." Herbert Butterfield, "The Balance of Power," in Herbert Butterfield and Martin Wight, eds., *Diplomatic Investigations: Essays in the Theory of International Politics* (Cambridge, Mass.: Harvard University Press, 1966), p. 132.
8. John G. Ruggie, "Continuity and Transformation in the World Polity: Toward a Neorealist Synthesis," *World Politics* (1983), 35(2):285. See also Stanley Hoffmann, *Janus and Minerva: Essays in the Theory and Practice of International Politics* (Boulder, Colo.: Westview Press, 1987), p. 123.
9. Gabriel A. Almond and Stephen J. Genco, "Clouds, Clocks, and the Study of Politics," *World Politics* (July 1977), 29(4):492.
10. Gilpin, *War and Change*, pp. 13–14.
11. Ibid., p. 15.
12. Ibid., p. 210.
13. The term *reflectivist* was coined by Robert O. Keohane at the presidential address of the International Studies Association. See Robert O. Keohane, *International Institutions and State Power* (Boulder, Colo.: Westview, 1989), ch. 7.

14. Walker, "Realism, Change, and International Political Theory," p. 81.
15. Karl R. Popper, *Objective Knowledge: An Evolutionary Approach* (Oxford: Clarendon Press, 1972), p. 228.
16. Friedrich Kratochwil and John G. Ruggie, "International Organization: A State of the Art in an Art of the State," *International Organization* (Autumn 1986), 40 (4):764–766.
17. Donald T. Campbell, "Evolutionary Epistemology," in Gerard Radnitsky and W. W. Bartley, III, eds., *Evolutionary Epistemology, Theory of Rationality and the Sociology of Knowledge* (La Salle, Ill.: Open Court, 1987). "The logical and methodological arguments are due chiefly to Popper, as are those that are drawn from physics. The biological and physiological support and interpretation come in part from Popper, but also from Lorenz and from such biologists as Sir John Eccles, Sir Peter Medawar, Ernst Mayr, and Jacques Monod. The psychological work can be traced back to Küple and Bühler, and is continued in the work of F. A. von Hayek . . . as well as by Campbell. Campbell has made a fuller, more consistent, and more adequate statement of the position than any other person." W. W. Bartley, III, "Philosophy of Biology Versus Philosophy of Physics," in *Evolutionary Epistemology*, pp. 21–22.
    See also Werner Callebout and Rik Pinxten, eds., *Evolutionary Epistemology* (Dordrecht, Holland: Reidel, 1987). The latter has a comprehensive bibliography on evolutionary epistemology.
18. The new physics works on the assumption of complementarity between physical and perceptual events; biology has history and emergent conditions built in. See Victor F. Weisskopf, "The Frontiers and Limits of Science," *Daedalus* (Summer 1984), 113 (3):191–195.
19. For as "cousin to the amoeba that we are, how could we know for certain?" Donald T. Campbell, "On the Conflicts Between Biological and Social Evolution and Between Psychology and Moral Tradition," *American Psychologist* (December 1975), 30:1120.
20. Ernst B. Haas, "Words Can Hurt You; or Who Said What to Whom about Regimes," in Stephen D. Krasner, ed., *International Regimes* (Ithaca, N.Y.: Cornell University Press, 1983), p. 24.
21. "Learning in the perspective of an evolutionary epistemology must be open, unspecifiable ahead of events in terms of substance, and as unpredictable as evolutionary adaptation. . . . [Thus there] is no fixed 'national interest' and no 'optimal regime.' Different perceptions of national interest, changeable in response to new information or altered values, will result in different processes and in a variety of regimes that will be considered rational by the actors—at least for a while. Collaboration among states . . . expresses no more than the convergence of such interests." Ibid., pp. 25–26, 57.
22. Bartley, "Philosophy of Biology," p. 21.
23. Campbell, "Evolutionary Epistemology"; Thomas S. Kuhn, *The Structure of Scientific Revolutions* (Chicago: University of Chicago Press, 1962); Stephen Toulmin, *Foresight and Understanding: An Inquiry into the Aims of*

Science (New York: Harper & Row, 1961); and Toulmin, *Human Understanding* (Princeton, N.J.: Princeton University Press, 1972).

24. Karl R. Popper, *Conjectures and Refutations* (London: Routledge and Kegan Paul, 1963).

25. Bartley, "Philosophy of Biology," p. 24.

26. Karl R. Popper, "The Place of Mind in Nature," in Richard O. Elvee, ed., *Mind in Nature* (New York: Harper & Row, 1982), p. 54. One can, for example, investigate the structure and function of a theory, or whether it solves a problem, without having to get inside the mind and beliefs of the individual who conceived the theory.

27. Popper's philosophical basis for accepting the real existence of World 3 comes from Alfred Landé: something is real if it can be kicked and can, in principle, kick back. Karl R. Popper, *The Open Universe: An Argument for Indeterminism*. W. W. Bartley, III, ed. (Totowa, N.J.: Rowman and Littlefield, 1982), p. 116.

28. Almond and Genco, "Clouds, Clocks and the Study of Politics," p. 491. See also Popper, *Objective Knowledge*.

29. Popper, *Objective Knowledge*, p. 229.

30. Robert Jervis, "Consistency in Foreign Policy Views," in Richard L. Merritt, ed., *Communication in International Politics* (Urbana: University of Illinois Press, 1972), p. 287.

31. David J. Depew and Bruce H. Weber, "Innovation and Tradition in Evolutionary Theory: An Interpretative Afterword," in David J. Depew and Bruce H. Weber, eds., *Evolution at a Crossroads: The New Biology and the New Philosophy of Science* (Cambridge, Mass.: MIT Press, 1985), p. 240.

32. Toulmin, *Foresight and Understanding*, p. 81.

33. See also Toulmin, *Human Understanding*.

34. Campbell, *Evolutionary Epistemology*. See also Colin Martindale, *Cognition and Consciousness* (Homewood, Ill.: Dorsey Press, 1981), p. 411.

35. James N. Rosenau, "Muddling, Meddling and Modelling: Alternative Approaches to the Study of World Politics in an Era of Rapid Change," *Millennium* (Summer 1979), 8(2):135.

36. Robert D. Putnam, "Diplomacy and Domestic Politics: the Logic of Two-Level Games," *International Organization* (Summer 1988), 42 (3):434. Rosenau has also developed an approach to study change in international relations on the basis of "micro–macro" interaction, wherein "the macro and micro phenomena that make up any large-scale structure, process, institution, or collectivity are linked together in endlessly reinforcing interactions. . . . Macro structures and collectivities may have a life of their own, but they draw their sustenance from their micro components. . . . At the micro level change results from the failure of the memories, beliefs, expectations, and networks to perpetuate themselves, and this failure occurs because circumstances are altered and the memories, beliefs, expectations, and networks no longer serve the needs of the habit-driven behavior for which they evolved." James N. Rosenau, "Be-

fore Cooperation: Hegemons, Regimes, and Habit-Driven Actors in World Politics," *International Organization* (Autumn 1986), 40 (4):868–869. For a sociological study about the micro–macro relationship see Jeffrey C. Alexander et al., eds., *The Micro–Macro Link* (Berkeley: University of California Press, 1987).

37. Stephen Toulmin, "Evolution, Adaptation, and Human Understanding," in Marilynn B. Brewer and Barry E. Collins, eds., *Scientific Inquiry and the Social Sciences* (San Francisco: Jossey-Bass, 1981), p. 31. To "understand political choices, we need to understand where the frame of reference for the actors' thinking comes from. . . . We need to understand not only how people reason about alternatives, but where the alternatives come from in the first place [thus] the task of determining how people actually do behave in situations having game-like characteristics must be turned over to empirical research: research that seeks to determine what values people actually act on, and how they form their expectations and beliefs." Herbert A. Simon, "Human Nature in Politics: The Dialogue of Psychology with Political Science," *American Political Science Review* (June 1985), 79(2):300, 302.

38. Joseph S. Nye, Jr., "Nuclear Learning," *International Organization* (Summer, 1987), 41(3):372.

39. Robert O. Keohane, *After Hegemony: Cooperation and Discord in the World Political Economy* (Princeton, N.J.: Princeton University Press, 1984).

40. Popper, *Objective Knowledge*, pp. 61, 340–361.

41. Ibid.

42. Ibid., p. 66.

43. Ibid., p. 24.

44. Arie E. Kruglanski and Icek Ajzen, "Bias and Error in Human Judgment," *European Journal of Social Psychology* (1983), 13:1–44. Kruglanski and Ajzen's argument is an attempt to build an epistemological background to the problems of judgment, heuristics, and biases in cognitive processes, and provide a corrective to the studies of Daniel Kahneman and Amos Tversky, who argued, basically, that inference models are normative and that judgments that deviate systematically from such models are "erroneous" and indicative of bias in the underlying inference process. See Daniel Kahneman, Paul Slovic, and Amos Tversky, eds., *Judgment Under Uncertainty: Heuristics and Biases* (Cambridge, Mass.: Cambridge University Press, 1982). Kruglanski and Ajzen's "lay epistemology" should not be interpreted, however, to mean that all knowledge is erroneous. They define bias as a "subjectively based preference for a given conclusion over possible alternative conclusions." Error, in turn, is defined as the "type of experience a person might have following an encountered inconsistency between a given hypothesis, conclusion, or inference, and a firmly held belief." Kruglanski and Ajzen, "Bias and Error," pp. 19, 23.

45. The proof is in the "numerous recorded instances of 'laws' . . . that for a time were considered proven beyond the shadow of a doubt, yet were

subsequently falsified and replaced by apparently more believable alternatives." Kruglanski and Ajzen, "Bias and Error," p. 12.

46. "The particular inference reached thus depends heavily on a given individual's epistemic process during which alternative cognitions (comprising premises for the person's conclusions) are generated. Such a sequential process during which cognitions are generated and validated has no unique point of termination. In principle, it could continue endlessly, as alternative competing . . . cognitions are put forth and validated in timeless succession. In actuality, however, the process does come to a halt at some point. At any given time we seem to have in our possession various items of knowledge without which decision-making and action would be virtually inconceivable." Ibid., p. 15.

47. Ibid., pp. 15–16. The decision to stop the cognitive process that generates alternative sets of understandings can be explained by the person's epistemologically relevant motivations and the availability of given conceptions. Ibid., p. 19.

48. Stephen D. Krasner, "Approaches to the State: Alternative Conceptions and Historical Dynamics," *Comparative Politics* (January 1984), 16(2):240.

49. "The mere fact that . . . experiences emerge continuously within our stream of thought, that previous experiences are permanently receiving additional interpretative meanings in the light of these supervenient experiences, which have, more or less, changed our state of mind— all these basic features . . . bar a recurrence of the same. Being recurrent, the recurrent is not the same any more." Alfred Schutz, "The Homecomer," in Arvid Brodersen, ed., Alfred Schutz, *Collected Papers*, II: *Studies in Social Theory* (The Hague: Martinus Nijhoff, 1971), p. 115.

50. G. John Ikenberry, "Conclusion: An Institutional Approach to American Foreign Economic Policy," *International Organization* (Winter 1988), 42(1):234.

51. Edward L. Morse, *Modernization and the Transformation of International Relations* (New York: Free Press, 1976), p. 180. It should be emphasized, however, that not all cognitive change is episodic. Cognitive structures change continuously, but their effect on political action is better described as episodic, because it is only at those critical moments that a cognitive threshold is crossed, and decision makers "discover" that they have to change their behavior. From a cognitive perspective, then, crises represent the culmination of a gradual process that for most of its course may have remained imperceptible.

52. Krasner, "Approaches to the State," and Ikenberry, "Conclusion."

53. Toulmin, *Human Understanding*, p. 140.

54. Michael J. Brenner, "The Theorist as Actor, the Actor as Theorist: Strategy in the Nixon Administration," *Stanford Journal of International Studies* (Spring 1972), 7:109–110.

55. George Katona, "Business Expectations in the Framework of Psychological Economics (Toward a Theory of Expectations)" in Mary Jean Bow-

man, ed., *Expectations, Uncertainty, and Business Behavior* (New York: Social Science Research Council, 1958), p. 66.

56. I owe this insight to Ashton Carter and Joseph Nye. Nelson Polsby is also aware of it in his description of political innovation in America. What "we normally think of as political innovation can be described as a combination of two processes. The first, the process of invention, causes policy options to come into existence. This is the domain of interest groups and their interests, of persons who specialize in acquiring and deploying knowledge about policies and their intellectual convictions, of persons who are aware of contextually applicable experiences of foreign nations, and of policy entrepreneurs, whose careers and ambitions are focused on the employment of their expertise and on the elaboration and adaptation of knowledge of problems. The second process is a process of systematic search, a process that senses and responds to problems, that harvests policy options and turns them to the purposes, both public and career-related, of politicians and public officials." Nelson W. Polsby, *Political Innovation in America: The Politics of Policy Initiation* (New Haven: Yale University Press, 1984), p. 173.

57. The term *epistemic community* was first applied to international relations by John G. Ruggie, "International Responses to Technology: Concepts and Trends," *International Organization* (Summer 1975), 29(3):569–570. See also Peter M. Haas, "Do Regimes Matter? Epistemic Communities and Mediterranean Pollution Control," *International Organization* (Summer 1989), 43(3):377–403, and Emanuel Adler, *The Power of Ideology: The Quest for Technological Autonomy in Argentina and Brazil* (Berkeley: University of California Press, 1987). On a more theoretical basis see Burkart Holzner and John Marx, *Knowledge Application: The Knowledge System in Society* (Boston: Allyn and Bacon, 1979). See also Diana Crane, *Invisible Colleges* (Chicago: University of Chicago Press, 1972). Bureaucracies have also been singled out as a source of political innovation. See, for example, H. Heclo, *Modern Social Politics in Britain and Sweden* (New Haven: Yale University Press, 1974). Peter Hall has emphasized politicians as sources of political innovations. However, he attributes to them the role of choosing among, rather than generating, ideas. See Peter A. Hall, *Governing the Economy; the Politics of State Intervention in Britain and France* (New York: Oxford University Press, 1986), p. 274.

58. Colin A. Gray, *Strategic Studies and Public Policy: The American Experience* (Lexington: University Press of Kentucky, 1982), p. 26.

59. Douglas C. Bennett and Kenneth E. Sharpe, *Transnational Corporations Versus the State: The Political Economy of the Mexican Auto Industry* (Princeton, N.J.: Princeton University Press, 1985), p. 250.

60. See, for example, Graham Allison, *Essence of Decision* (Boston: Little, Brown, 1971).

61. Toulmin, *Human Understanding*, p. 350.

62. Aaron Wildavsky, "Choosing Preferences by Constructing Institutions: A Cultural Theory of Preference Formation," *American Political Science*

Review (March 1987), 81(1):3-21; and Herbert C. Kelman, *International Behavior: A Social-Psychological Analysis* (New York: Holt, Rinehart, and Winston, 1965), p. 578. For a critique of this approach see Michael Brenner in this volume.

63. Chih-yu-Shih, "A Cognitive Approach to International Organization: The Process of Seeking Common Cause—Maps in East-Asia," paper presented at the annual meeting of the American Political Science Association, Washington, D.C., September 3, 1988, p. 6.

64. Robert Legvold, "War, Weapons, and Soviet Foreign Policy," in Seweryn Bialer and Michael Mandelbaum, eds., *Gorbachev's Russia and American Foreign Policy* (Boulder, Colo.: Westview, 1988), pp. 120–125.

65. Ibid., pp. 121–122.

66. I am aware that the notion of cognitive structures has been widely used in social disciplines with various meanings. See, for example, Zenon W. Pylyskyn and William Demopoulos, eds., *Meaning and Cognitive Structure: Issues in the Computational Theory of Mind* (Norwood, N.J.: Ablex, 1986). According to my definition, cognitive structures or collective theoretical understandings, whether or not based on science, when recorded in theories and transmitted can be studied objectively as "products," or World 3 objects, independently of the subjective minds that created them. See Bartley, "Philosophy of Biology," p. 20.

67. The concept of thought collective places the attention on the carriers of collective ideas and was defined by Fleck as a community of persons mutually exchanging ideas or maintaining intellectual interaction that provides the special "carrier" for the historical development of any field of thought, as well as for the given stock of knowledge and level of culture. Ludwik Fleck, *Genesis and Development of a Scientific Fact* (Chicago: University of Chicago Press, 1979), p. 39.

68. Alexander E. Wendt, "The Agent-Structure Problem in International Relations Theory," *International Organization* (Summer 1987), 41(3):352.

69. Ibid. See also Anthony Giddens, *Central Problems in Social Theory* (Berkeley: University of California Press, 1979).

70. Shih, "A Cognitive Approach," p. 14.

71. Wendt, "The Agent-Structure Problem"; Anthony Giddens, *The Constitution of Society: Outline of the Theory of Structuration* (Cambridge, England: Polity Press, 1984).

72. Wendt, "The Agent-Structure Problem," p. 354.

73. Ibid., p. 360.

74. Ibid., pp. 364–365.

75. William E. Connally, *The Terms of Political Discourse*, 2d ed., (Princeton, N.J.: Princeton University Press, 1983), pp. 46–48.

76. Robert Jervis, "Realism, Game Theory, and Cooperation," *World Politics* (April 1988), 40(3):344.

77. Milton Rokeach defines human values as "a relatively small number of core ideas or cognitions present in every society about desirable end-states of existence and desirable modes of behavior instrumental to their

attainment that are capable of being organized to form different priorities." Milton Rokeach, "From Individual to Institutional Values: With Special Reference to the Values of Science," in Milton Rokeach, ed., *Understanding Human Values* (New York: Free Press, 1979), p. 49.

78. Ibid., p. 50.
79. Robin M. Williams Jr., "Change and Stability in Values and Value Systems: A Sociological Perspective," in Rokeach, *Understanding Human Values*, p. 16.
80. Ibid., pp. 20–22.
81. Ernst B. Haas and A. S. Whiting, *Dynamics of International Relations* (New York: McGraw-Hill, 1956); and Karl W. Deutsch et al., *Political Community and the North Atlantic Area* (New York: Greenwood Press, 1957).
82. Norman T. Feather, "Human Values and the Prediction of Action: An Expectancy-Valence Analysis," in Norman T. Feather, *Expectations and Actions* (Hillsdale, N.J.: Lawrence Erlbaum, 1982), p. 277; and Amitai Etzioni, *The Moral Dimension: Toward a New Economics* (New York: Free Press, 1988), p. 127.
83. Albert O. Hirschman, *The Passions and the Interests: Political Arguments for Capitalism Before its Triumph* (Princeton, N.J.: Princeton University Press, 1977), p. 38.
84. Williams, "Change and Stability," p. 24. "Japan is now a much more suitable partner for cooperation than it was in the 1930s, and not only because territorial expansion is neither possible nor economically necessary. Something has occurred that is more basic than changes in instrumental beliefs. Rabid nationalism and the drive to dominate have been transmuted. A Japanese nationalist of the 1930s who saw his country today would be horrified. . . . Because it took a cataclysm to produce such a change, this pattern does not provide an attractive route to a more cooperative world. But it does show both the importance and the mutability of values." Jervis, "Realism, Game Theory, and Cooperation," pp. 343–344.
85. Karl R. Popper, *Unended Quest: An Intellectual Autobiography* (La Salle, Ill.: Open-Court, 1976), p. 193.
86. See my "Seasons of Peace" in this volume.
87. See Peter Haas, "Making Progress in International Environmental Protection," in this volume.
88. Michael Thompson, *The Creation and Destruction of Value* (Oxford: Oxford University Press, 1979), p. 2.
89. Deutsch et al., *Political Community*, p. 47.
90. Williams, "Change and Stability," p. 43.
91. See my "Seasons of Peace" in this volume.
92. See Beverly Crawford, Peter Haas, Robert Kudrle, and Stefanie Lenway.
93. Ernst B. Haas, "Why Collaborate: Issue-Linkage and International Regimes," *World Politics* (April 1980), 32(3):351–405.
94. Herbert A. Simon, *Reason in Human Affairs* (Stanford, Calif.: Stanford University Press, 1983), p. 103.

96. Thomas C. Schelling, *The Strategy of Conflict* (London: Oxford University Press, 1960), p. 57.

97. Krasner defined international regimes as "sets of implicit or explicit principles, norms, rules, and decision-making procedures around which actors' expectations converge in a given area of international relations." Stephen D. Krasner, "Structural Causes and Regime Consequences: Regimes as Intervening Variables," in Krasner, *International Regimes*, p. 2.

98. Lawrence Freedman, *The Evolution of Nuclear Strategy* (New York: St. Martin's Press, 1983), p. 191.

99. Ibid., p. 199.

100. Robin Ranger, *Arms and Politics 1958–1978: Arms Control in a Changing Political Context* (New York: Macmillan, 1979), p. 20.

101. Gray, *Strategic Studies and Public Policy: The American Experience*, p. 72; and Charles E. Osgood, *The Nuclear Dilemma in American Strategic Thought* (Boulder, Colo.: Westview, 1988), p. 36 (emphasis mine).

102. Thomas C. Schelling, "What Went Wrong With Arms Control?" *Foreign Affairs* (Winter 1985–1986) 65(2):223.

103. The RAND Corporation is a think tank created by the Air Force after World War II. It became the source of many of the postwar studies on nuclear strategy and arms control. See Paul Dickson, *Think Tanks* (New York: Atheneum, 1971), ch. 5. The Harvard–MIT Seminar on Arms Control evolved out of a summer study group, which was convened by the American Academy of Arts and Sciences in the Summer of 1960 and became a landmark in the evolution of nuclear arms control ideas. For a list of the participants see Thomas C. Schelling and Morton H. Halperin, *Strategy and Arms Control*, 2d ed. (Washington, D.C.: Pergamon–Brassey's Classic, 1985), pp. 147–148.

104. Wildavsky, "Choosing Preferences," p. 9.

105. Personal communication.

106. Probably the most succint and best exposition of Schelling's arms-control theory is "Reciprocal Measures for Arms Stabilization," in Donald G. Brennan, *Arms Control, Disarmament, and National Security* (New York: Braziller, 1961), pp. 167–186.

107. Legvold, "War, Weapons and Soviet Foreign Policy," p. 116.

108. Ibid., p. 117.

109. Elizabeth Pond, "Ronald and Mikhail: the Summer of Their Content— And a New Detente," *The Christian Science Monitor*, June 16, 1988, p. 17.

110. Ibid., p. 16.

111. Legvold, "War, Weapons and Soviet Foreign Policy," p. 123.

112. See Richard N. Gardner, *Sterling–Dollar Diplomacy in Current Perspective: The Origins and the Prospects of Our International Economic Order* (New York: Columbia University Press, 1980).

113. See, for example, Judith Goldstein, "Ideas, Institutions, and American Trade Policy," *International Organization* (Winter 1988), 42(1):179–217; Peter A. Hall, *The Political Power of Economic Ideas: Keynesianism across*

Nations (Princeton, N.J.: Princeton University Press, 1989); Henry R. Nau, *The Myth of America's Decline: Leading the World Economy into the 1990s* (N.Y.: Oxford University Press, 1990); John S. Odell, *U.S. International Monetary Policy: Markets, Power, and Ideas as Sources of Change* (Princeton, N.J.: Princeton University Press, 1982); John G. Ruggie, "International Regimes, Transactions, and Change: Embedded Liberalism in the Postwar Economic Order," in Krasner, *International Regimes,* pp. 195–231. Also in this volume.

114. Raymond Vernon and Debra L. Spar, *Beyond Globalism: Remaking American Foreign Economic Policy* (New York: Free Press, 1989), p. 78.
115. Robert O. Keohane, "The Theory of Hegemonic Stability and Changes in International Economic Regimes, 1967–1977," in Ole Holsti et al., eds., *Change in the International System* (Boulder, Colo.: Westview, 1980), pp. 131–162.
116. Ruggie, "International Regimes," p. 202.
117. Ibid., p. 209.
118. Gardner, *Sterling–Dollar Diplomacy,* p. 4.
119. Ansel Luxford as quoted in ibid., p. xv.
120. Nau, *The Myth of America's Decline,* chs. 3 and 4.
121. Vernon and Spar, *Beyond Globalism,* p. 54.
122. Gardner, *Sterling–Dollar Diplomacy,* ch. 2.
123. G. John Ikenberry and Charles A. Kupchan, "The Legitimation of Hegemonic Power," paper presented at the Center for International Affairs, Harvard University, March 24, 1988, p. 35. A revised version of this paper entitled "Socialization and Hegemonic Power" was published in *International Organization* (Summer 1990), 44(3). On this point, see p. 300.
124. Ikenberry and Kupchan, "Socialization and Hegemonic Power," pp. 302–303.
125. Keohane, *After Hegemony,* p. 144.
126. Ibid., pp. 184–190.
127. See Ernst B. Haas, *When Knowledge is Power* (Berkeley: University of California Press, 1990).
128. Don Babai, "International Development Policy in the 1980s—Progress, Statis or Regress," unpublished manuscript, Harvard University, 1988.
129. Ibid.
130. Keohane, *After Hegemony,* p. 256.
131. Jock A. Finlayson and Mark W. Zacher, "The GATT and the Regulation of Trade Barriers: Regime Dynamics and Functions," in Krasner, *International Regimes,* pp. 313–314; Keohane, *After Hegemony;* Ruggie, "International Regimes."
132. Keohane has already revised three basic realist assumptions dealing with the state, rationality, and power in his "Theory of World Politics," My proposed assumptions build on Keohane's amended realist position and are inspired by his essay "World Politics and Peaceful Change" (ibid.).

133. Toulmin, *Human Understanding*, p. 84.
134. See John G. Ruggie, "Changing Frameworks of International Collaborative Behavior: On the Complementarity of Contradictory Tendencies," in Nazli Choucri and Thomas W. Robinson, eds., *Forecasting in International Relations* (San Francisco: Freeman, 1978), pp. 399, 402.
135. "Such complementarity situations appear . . . within physics; for example, in respect to the description of an atom in terms of the quantum state or in terms of the location of its constituents. . . . There are different ways of perceiving a situation, ways that may be unconnected or even contradictory, but they are necessary for understanding the situation in its totality." Weisskopf, "The Frontiers and Limits of Science," pp. 191–192.
136. Charles F. Sabel, *Work and Politics: The Division of Labor in Industry* (Cambridge, Mass.: Cambridge University Press, 1982), p. 131.
137. Kratochwil and Ruggie, "International Organization," p. 764.
138. See for example Robert Jervis, *Perception and Misperception in World Politics* (Princeton, N.J.: Princeton University Press, 1976).

3

CHANGE IN REGIME TYPE
AND PROGRESS IN
INTERNATIONAL RELATIONS

Philippe C. Schmitter

Some notion of "progress" seems indispensable for the cumulative development of an academic discipline. Without a clear and shared conception of where things are going, what constitutes an improvement in their status and how knowledgeable intervention may contribute to enhancing that outcome, the collective efforts of scholars are likely to flounder, to disperse across a multitude of weakly related subjects, and to lose all sense of priority.

The study of international relations illustrates the point well. It has gone through periods when it was informed, if not driven, by notions of progress—and prospered as a result of having this sense of direction. It was subsequently inflicted by severe doubts about where its subject matter was moving and whether its efforts could contribute to improving the outcome—and these have threatened to sweep away the previous accumulation of concepts, hypotheses, findings, generalizations, approaches, and theories. More recently, international relations seems to be on the verge of recapturing some of that lost sense of optimism and direction.

REALISM AND IDEALISM AS COMPETING PARADIGMS

When Immanuel Kant wrote a small pamphlet predicting that the spread of republican forms of government would lead eventually to "perpetual peace,"[1] he was engaging in a precocious exercise in political science fiction. At the time (1795), there were perhaps four or five independent states that met the necessary specifications,[2] and their interaction alone could hardly have been expected to change the perpetually conflictual and frequently violent nature of international relations. Moreover, within short order, one of these polities became an empire (France) and deprived three of the others (the Netherlands, Switzerland, and Venice) of their national independence and distinctive governing form. Not a very auspicious beginning for such an audacious hypothesis!

Perhaps for this reason, Kant's ideas were scornfully labeled "idealist" and subsequently dismissed by scholars of international relations. They went on to elaborate a "realist" paradigm of their discipline that not only denies any special relevance to republican/democratic forms of government, but studiously ignores all conditions of domestic politics. Its core postulate that the "distribution of power *among* states constitutes the principal form of control in every international system"[3] permits no deflection because of the distribution of power *within* states. As Ernst Haas has put it, "countries are expected to respond in identical ways irrespective of their domestic peculiarities."[4]

Contrary to the realist paradigm, with its exclusive emphasis on the external structure of power—both at the global and at the regional levels—a few scholars in the post–World War II period began to focus on a new independent variable at the same time that they respecified what international relations theory should be attempting to explain. Led by students of regional integration, they asserted that the most important emergent property was increase in the volume and variety of exchanges between formally sovereign states that they interpreted as producing a condition of rising *interdependence*. This, in turn, was expected to produce not so much a decline in the extent

FIGURE 3.1
The Realist Paradigm of Interstate Relations

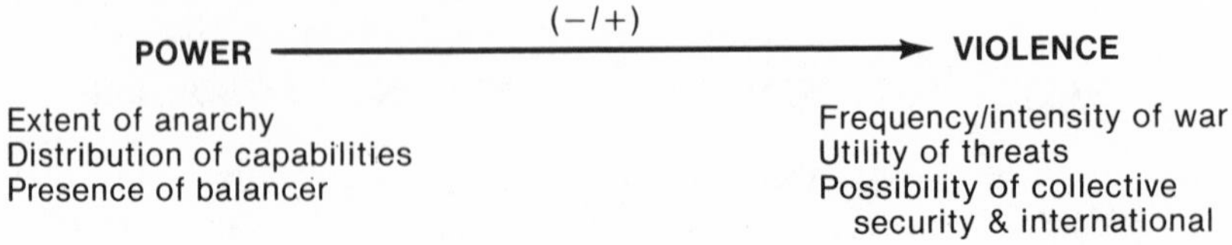

$$(-/+)$$

POWER ⟶ VIOLENCE

Extent of anarchy
Distribution of capabilities
Presence of balancer

Frequency/intensity of war
Utility of threats
Possibility of collective
   security & international

and frequency of international violence as an increase in the extent and frequency of international *cooperation*. These transactionalists, functionalists, and neofunctionalists (as various of them came to be labeled) did not so much ignore the existence of anarchy, the relevance of uneven power distributions, and the potentiality for war in the interstate system as they tended to presume that the prevailing balance of terror and great power stalemate at the military level would permit new forms of cooperation to emerge and eventually to transform the system—most generally, through the functional agencies of the United Nations and, more specifically, through regional organizations in selected parts of the world.[5] Under especially favorable conditions of interdependence and institution building, they even predicted that this cooperation would gradually and consensually give way to international *integration* (i.e., to the development of supranational forms of authoritative allocation and conflict resolution that would supersede the existing separation into allegedly sovereign states).[6] Western Europe was obviously the "privileged site" upon which this sort of inquiry focused. As the European Coal and Steel Community gave way to the more comprehensive European Economic Community and as the latter seemed initially to expand its tasks and resources, the paradigm seemed to be working—until the political obstruction of Charles de Gaulle momentarily stopped it in its tracks, and the economic self-interest of its members subsequently converted it into a forum for intergovernmental haggling.[7] Whether the recent surge toward completing the internal market by 1992 will succeed in reviving interest in the functionalist–neofunctionalist paradigm remains to be seen.

Meanwhile, Kant's idealist scenario, with its emphasis on the internal distribution of power and its external effects, was largely ignored.[8] Central to his argument were two key propositions: (1) that governments accountable to their citizenry would be unlikely to initiate armed violence against other states, since those most likely to pay the highest personal price—death in combat—would effectively resist the temptation of noncombatant elites to exploit momentary power advantages over adversaries; (2) that citizens under a republican–democratic government would be more likely to be free to engage in extensive economic exchanges with potential military adversaries and, therefore, to resist any recourse to violence that would disrupt the profitability of such exchanges.[9] In short, Kant suggested that civilian, constitutional, accountable government would *both* make the disparity in power capabilities between countries irrelevant *and* increase the interdependence and, hence, the cooperative, law-abiding behavior between countries.[10] He was no "integrationist," however. The best he could foresee was some sort of loose confederation among persistently sovereign political units, *à la (pre-1848) Suisse.*

With democracies having recently replaced authoritarian regimes in so many countries, one could now question whether Kant's approach should any longer be labeled "idealist," at least in the sense that it seemed to depend on an unrealizable precondition. Never before in human history have so many ostensibly democratic and republican regimes been spread over such an extensive surface of the globe.[11]

Moreover, it is important to note that never before has the very concept of authoritarian or totalitarian rule seemed so discredited. Even where competitive elections, free associability, and popular accountability have not yet materialized, the pressure for "opening"

FIGURE 3.2
The Neo-Functionalist Paradigm of Interstate Relations

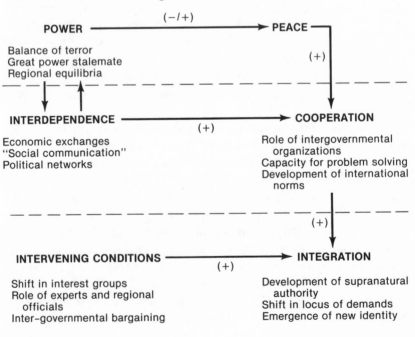

and "restructuring" seems to be pushing in that direction. One could even extend the logic of Kant's basic proposition to suggest that when the demand for democratization is sufficiently intense and widespread, states will be compelled to behave differently with regard to each other. They will be less likely to utilize—or even threaten— armed violence, and more likely to engage in law-abiding, cooperative endeavors.

The approach taken in this study might be considered both critical of and complementary to that advocated in the Adler-Crawford-Donnelly contributions to this volume. It tests the assumption that the nature of the domestic regime—the institutions and rules of national political authority—makes a difference and, therefore, that progressive changes in the realm of international relations may depend upon prior *and* independent changes at the national level. "Learning," and the consequently benevolent redefinitions of the "national interest" that the editors have encouraged us to look for, may not emanate directly from systemic interaction at the international level, but may be contingent upon how "less than national" interests are articulated and constrain the policy options of "less than

FIGURE 3.3
The 'Revised' Neoidealist Paradigm of Interstate Relations

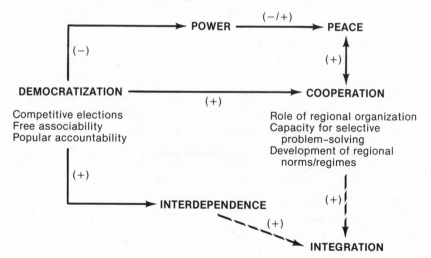

unitary" states. Moreover, this approach takes the view that the impact of "domestic" democratization upon progress is indirect and circular. Only if it can produce or provoke significant changes in the interdependence, threat of violence, cooperation, and/or integration among states is learning likely to take place and to have any lasting impact. In other words, the "idealism" investigated here begins at the national level with changes in practices and rules, not in the international system, with new cognitions and norms.

LATIN AMERICA AS A TEST CASE

Nowhere is it more appropriate in the contemporary world to test our "neoidealism" than in Latin America. This region has experienced short bursts of democratization in the past—first, in the aftermath of World War II and then again in the early 1960s. Subsequently, from the mid-1960s through the 1970s, the entire continent descended into despotism, to use the concept that Kant chose to juxtapose to republicanism. At one point, only three polities maintained some form of democratic rule: Colombia, Costa Rica, and Venezuela. All of the Southern Cone (which shall concern us particularly in this study) went despotic—including two countries that had long respected civil rights, constitutional governance, and competitive politics: Chile and Uruguay—and remained under protracted bureaucratic–authoritarian rule for more than a decade. Only recently have Argentina (1983), Brazil (1985), and Uruguay (1984) emerged from this long night of fear, repression, and arbitrary rule. The fact that these three neighboring countries did so within such a compressed period of time makes our hypothesis all the more pertinent. All things being equal, one would expect that the impact of regime change would be greater if it is clustered in space and time—producing an interactive effect that would differentiate the new subset of democracies from the tyrannies that surround it.[12]

Chile successfully resisted the regional trend until September 1988, when General Pinochet lost a national plebiscite on his perpetuation in power and belatedly triggered a process of transition. This provides our study with an especially valuable "control case." Whatever we discover in the pattern of relations between Argentina, Brazil, and Uruguay, we would expect it not to be replicated with regard to Chile—at least not before December 1989 when (and if) that country holds free, competitive elections. Paraguay remained "beyond the pale" (at least until February 1989, when General Stroessner was removed from power by *coup d'état* and elections were subsequently held). It still lies beyond the scope of this study.

The Southern Cone of Latin America is also an appropriate site for two other reasons. First, it has not been an area of frequent international violence. Threats have been exchanged, especially between Argentina and Chile over border disputes. The Falkland–Malvinas conflict lies at the heart of the Argentine regime transformation, and the militaries of Argentina and Brazil have habitually justified their resources and strategies by playing "war games" on each other. Nevertheless, the central international issue in the subregion involves not avoiding the likelihood of war but exploiting the possibility of cooperative ventures to solve its many economic and social problems.

Second, its countries have not yet attained a high level of interdependence in their exchanges. Despite efforts as early as 1960 through the creation of the Latin American Free Trade Area (LAFTA), trade within the area has always been of marginal importance. For each of its economies, flows of merchandise, services, investments, and technology from the advanced industrial countries are much more significant and constant than the relatively small-scale and erratic exchanges they have with each other. This suggests that, in this part of the world, the regime effect can be isolated and relatively easily observed. There has been no underlying and persistent trend in the volume and variety of economic and social exchanges—independent of who governs. In other words, one can test the idealist hypothesis whether democratization leads to greater interdependence, but the inverse, functionalist or transactionalist, hypothesis is manifestly implausible. There is no way that prior increases in regional interdependence could have brought about democratization—as has frequently been argued in the case of Spain and Greece. Nor is it likely that the low level and high variation in exchanges prior to regime change could have contributed much to reducing interstate violence or inducing cooperative problem solving within the Southern Cone.

Furthermore, neorealist arguments can also be ruled out for this case.[13] The processes of democratization in Argentina, Brazil, and Uruguay had only a marginal impact on the prevailing distribution of interstate power capability within the region. No secessions or massive population shifts occurred. Civil strife did not break out. No productive capacity was destroyed or alienated as a result of the transition. In all three, the political status and public image of the armed forces was affected, most of all in Argentina, where the regime change was driven by defeat in war and gave rise to subsequent indictments and convictions of high officials for crimes against humanity and the people. The Brazilian military extricated themselves from direct responsibility for power with their prestige and internal coherence more or less intact, and by all accounts Brazilian officers continued to play a very prominent role in the subsequent government of José Sarney. The experience of Uruguay lies somewhere in between these extremes. It should be stressed that these circumstances point to an exacerbation, not an attenuation of power differentials. After democratization, Brazil is even more the regional *hegemon*, with Argentina falling farther behind in demographic size, industrial strength, military equipment, and capacity for armed intervention. From a neorealistic perspective, as well as from a neofunctional one, nothing bodes favorably for an increase in cooperative behavior within the subregion.

Nor have definitions of national interest changed significantly as a result of regime transformation. Presumably, Argentines still regard the Falklands–Malvinas as "theirs"; Brazilians still aspire to Great Power status; Uruguayans still wish not to be trampled between their elephantine neighbors. If anything, the *security* dilemma has increased. Argentina's unequivocal defeat in the Falklands–Malvinas opened up an even greater gap in its military power vis-à-vis Brazil. Brazilian successes in armaments production and exports worry its neighbors, as does its continuous demographic expansion into Paraguay and Bolivia. Concerning the other items in the trilogy of progressive goals discussed by Adler, Crawford, and Donnelly—*welfare* and *human rights*—there is little expectation that guaranteeing or improving them necessitates significant foreign policy action at the regional level. As democracies, they would all prefer to have as neighbors other democracies that respect human (and civic) rights, but as we shall see they have not done much to ensure that outcome. Nonintervention in internal affairs remains a relatively strong regional impediment. Also, the transition to democracy was certainly accompanied by popular expectations for enhanced welfare. These were quickly dampened by a deteriorating economic situation, and there is no evidence that they occasioned any major change in inter-state relations.

All this confirms our suspicion that, at least for this region of the world, democratization has relatively little direct effect on the "progressive" redefinition of national interests. It is only after they have increased their interdependence, reduced their threats to use violence, engaged in more cooperative ventures, and moved toward regional integration that the countries involved can be expected to learn new norms and to pursue different interests.

DEMOCRATIZATION AND INTERDEPENDENCE

For Kant and the many other proponents of the *doux commerce* thesis, freedom is contagious. In Kant's version people protected in their civic rights and accustomed to expressing themselves freely on political issues will be more likely to search for and exploit economic and social exchanges with foreigners living under similar conditions. In the more common version, people who enjoy secure property rights and are deeply involved in foreign trade and investment will demand and eventually acquire responsible representative government.[14] As noted earlier, for the *Cono Sur* of Latin America, only the first causal hypothesis is plausible.

In general terms, the timing of regime change for the three cases was not fortunate from the point of view of regional exchanges.[15] For Argentina, Brazil, and Uruguay, mutual trade tended to peak in 1979–1980 and has slipped into a serious decline from which it had only begun to recover when democracy arrived in 1984–1985. For example, in absolute terms, Brazil's exports to Argentina hit an all-time record in 1980 of $1,092 million and diminished by almost one half, until they reached $548 million during the first year of democratic rule (1985). Argentina's exports to Brazil peaked a bit earlier, at $886 million in 1979, and also fell precipitously until they bottomed out at $358.4 million in 1983. They picked up the following year, when Alfonsin came to power, and continued to rise until 1987, when they again receded. Uruguay also slumped from the 1979–1980 peak, although trade with Brazil picked up significantly following the regime transition and has continued to rise since—hitting an all-time high for exports in 1986 and returning almost to peak level for imports in 1987. Chile's dyadic pattern is especially revealing, since it is virtually identical. Its export trade with Argentina, Brazil, and Uruguay also hit all-time highs in 1980 and fell by 50 percent or more until 1985–1986, when it turned up again. There is no sign here that the mode of political domination made much difference.

What lay behind the common pattern of decline in *regional* bilateral exchanges is quite clear: a serious *general* collapse in *total* foreign trade for all four countries. This occurred from 1979 to 1981, prior to, and in my view largely independent of, the advent of democracy. For those who are inclined to read causality into such "world-systemic" movements, it should be observed that the Brazilian and Uruguayan transitions were launched (in 1974 and 1980, respectively) while still in a period of protracted growth in foreign trade. In Argentina, it began after a major decline. Chile suffered a similar bust (especially in imports) one year later—without being thrown into a regime change. In Uruguay total exports grew significantly after democratization; in Brazil they declined slightly; and in Argentina they continued on a trendline established two years earlier.

It may still be possible to "rescue" the idealist perspective on democratization and trade by shifting to a regional level. In a global context of dependency, where national economies are subject to market forces beyond their control emanating from dominant powers, the counter efforts of peripheral actors could be especially important, if they are able to carve out protected and privileged regional markets for nontraditional exports that are relatively immune from the constriction in demand, the limits on credit, and the enhanced competitiveness that can impede trade with central economies. If one first looks at Latin America as a whole and relativizes the importance of regional trade interdependence by analyzing it as a proportion of total foreign trade, the results are not encouraging. For all members of the Latin American Integration Association (which includes the Southern Cone countries), the importance of mutual commerce declined from a high plateau in 1975–1980 of about 16–17 percent to a low of 11 percent in 1983. If anything, regional imports fell even more than extraregional ones![16] Moderately encouraging is the subsequent proportional increase during the "democratic period" from 1984 to 1986, although the results are neither monotonic nor impressive. Intra–Latin American exports as a percentage of total exports have yet to recover their previous level of the late 1970s—when most of these polities were ruled by dictators!

As valuable (and sobering) as these data may be, they are still overaggregated for our purposes. We want to know specifically whether trade between pairs of democracies, even fledgling democracies, has shown any significant increase, especially relative to their total trade pattern. Figures 3.4 through 3.6 show the bilateral export trade between the three pairs of democracies as a percentage of their respective total exports, indexed so that 100 represents the first full year after authoritarian rule. In all cases, we see a relative decline from the heydays of 1979–1980 and some recovery around the moment of democratization. However, closer inspection demonstrates that, although the resurgence of Argentine exports to both Brazil and Uruguay corresponds in time with the regime change and remains monotonic thereafter, Brazilian exports to Argentina plummet in the very year of its transition, and the recovery is erratic. Its exports to Uruguay had already begun to turn up the year before the change and remained relatively unaffected until one year afterward (1986). Uruguay illustrates an even more schizophrenic pattern. The relative

FIGURE 3.4

Bilateral Shares of Argentina's Exports (Indexed to Year of Transition)

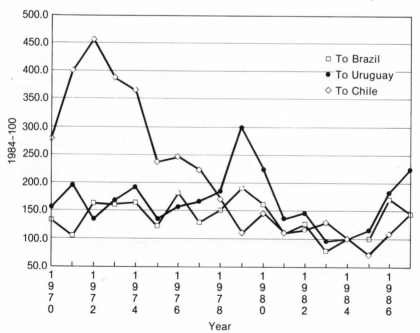

importance of its exports to Argentina took a short plunge when
Sanguinetti came to power in 1985, and its exports to Brazil made a
sharp recovery and went on to record heights the next year!

It this is not confusing enough, consider the bilateral trade patterns of Chile in figure 3.7. Its exports to Argentina hardly changed
when democracy arrived to the latter, but its imports from there
went into a secular decline. One year later, when Brazil changed
regime, imports from there remained unaffected and Chile's exports
to the new democracy went up. Chilean trade with Uruguay is too
insignificant to merit interpretation.

Frustrating as these results must seem from an idealistic perspective, one can be comforted by the thought that trade does not constitute the unique medium of international interdependence. Citizens
of adjacent countries can invest in each other's economies, migrate
to work in each other's territories, organize joint ventures for research and development, visit each other's tourist sites, send each

FIGURE 3.5
Bilateral Shares of Brazil's Exports (Indexed to Year of Transition)

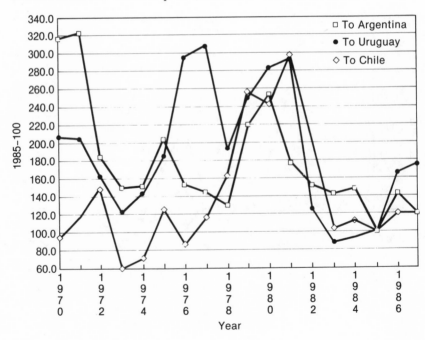

other letters, read each other's press, listen to each other's radio and television programs, and otherwise engage in a multitude of "social communications." This is precisely the sort of diversity in actors and multiplicity in exchanges that Robert Keohane and Joseph Nye have referred to as "complex interdependence" and that they argue is especially likely to contribute to international cooperation.[17]

Although hard evidence on these dimensions is difficult to come by, there seems little reason to suspect that this sort of complexity has been on the increase in the Southern Cone, and even less to suspect that it has greatly increased in the aftermath of democratization. Direct investment of Brazilian firms in Argentina has been estimated at $52.6 million in 1982 and that of Argentines in Brazil at $33.0 million. Chile has received a fair amount of Brazilian capital ($44.1 million), but everywhere the sums involved, compared to total foreign investment, have been minuscule.[18] Moreover, much of what is counted as "regional capital" consists of American or European

FIGURE 3.6

Bilateral Shares of Uruguay's Exports (Indexed to Year of Transition)

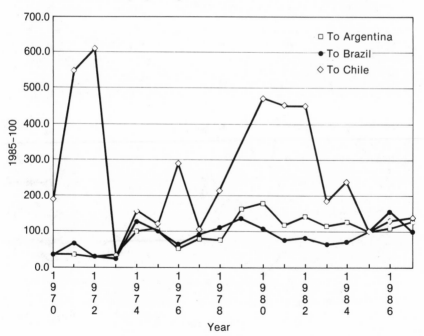

multinational subsidiaries in Brazil or Argentina extending their local reach.

About the other dimensions of "complex interdependence," we know even less. Data on intraregional migration are even more approximative than those on capital investment. In any case, it has never followed formal intergovernmental channels or reached the magnitudes that made the south-to-north flow of "guest workers" such a major component of the postwar European economy.

Tourism among the Southern Cone countries has developed significantly, especially in the case of Uruguay, where receipts from visiting Argentines are an important component of the national economy. Unfortunately, the data from the World Tourism Organization are too incomplete for quasi-experimental purposes, and in any case it would be hard to discern the flows that had been triggered by the new sense of freedom on both sides of a border from those that were motivated by such mundane events as changes in currency restrictions, relative exchange rates, disposable income, and even weather

FIGURE 3.7
Bilateral Shares of Chile's Trade (Unindexed)

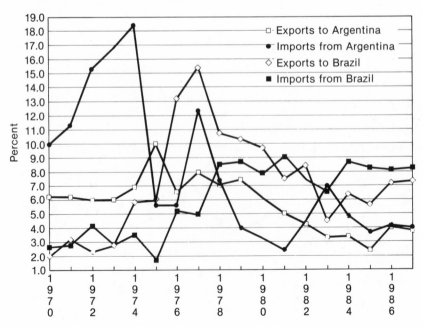

and fashion! For what it is worth, Argentine tourists went in great numbers to Brazil in their first year of liberation (1984) and the number increased even more the following year, when Brazil became democratic. Correspondingly, tourism from Chile to Brazil has diminished monotonically since 1981. So far, so good for our idealistic expectations. The only problem is that Uruguayans going to Brazil also declined during their years of liberation in 1984–1985. To make matters worse, Argentine tourists found undemocratic Chile an increasingly attractive place to visit after 1984. About all one can conclude from this fragmentary evidence is that one should not place much faith in the political consciousness of tourists!

On the other items such as mail flows, media attention, and "social communications" at the mass level, there is little to say. This is not just due to the unavailability of data. One senses that, if something of really significant magnitude were occurring between the mass publics in the newly democratic countries of the *Cono Sur*, it would have attracted someone's attention—at least, anecdotally. What is conspicuous is the inverse: the sense that subregional exchanges remain episodic and feeble—easily subject to the vagaries of macroeconomic forces—while the ones that count, the ones that persist even in times of adversity and indifference on the part of interlocutors, are those that involve asymmetric transactions with extraregional powers. Democracy in this part of Latin America may have increased mutual visibility and, as we shall see, elite political interactions, but it has done little (so far) for "complex interdependence" among the masses. Whether this should be taken as a generally valid refutation of Kantian optimism or as a more specific subproduct of this subregion's dependent and peripheral location in the world system is something that only further comparison can prove.[19]

DEMOCRATIZATION AND THE THREAT OF INTERSTATE VIOLENCE

The last armed conflagration within the *Cono Sur*, the Paraguayan War, ended in 1870. During the period immediately following independence, these "nations" engaged in a good deal of violent confrontation to define their mutual boundaries. Uruguay owes its existence to precisely such a struggle, but once the boundary struggles settled down, war became infrequent. Low population density, especially in frontier regions, plus weak military capacity and a preoccupation with maintaining internal order no doubt contributed to this outcome, although the War of the Pacific in 1890 and the Chaco War in 1930 on the margins of the *Cono Sur* demonstrated that deliberate recourse to violence could not be excluded. The most recent instance of interstate violence was, of course, the Malvinas–Falkland War, in which the defeat of Argentina provided the catalyst that ended authoritarian rule in that country. The failure to reach a mutually satisfactory resolution to that conflict with Great Britain continues to overshadow security calculations within the region, including those between Argentina and its neighbors.

But the real and persistent security issue concerns not the actual use of armed violence and the resolution of its consequences, but the plausibility of threatening to use it in order to gain some advantage in regional conflicts. Latin Americans have an enviable record of rarely going to war with each other, but this does not mean that they have not frequently contemplated doing so—and used the threat to justify increases in military expenditures and/or to attempt to extract concessions from weaker opponents. What democratization is supposed to accomplish, according to the idealist scenario, is to make it decreasingly plausible to exploit such capabilities by making it increasingly implausible that citizens would tolerate their actual use, especially against other democracies.

The newly elected rulers of Argentina and Brazil inherited a number of interstate conflicts that the armed forces of their respective countries had both preserved and periodically reactivated on grounds of "national security." To the traditional rivalry originating in territorial controversies from the independence period and subsequently affected by differences in settlement patterns, racial composition and economic prosperity, recent development had added a few new items: the exploitation of the hydroelectric resources of the Rio de la Plata basin; the prospect that one or the other might produce atomic weapons from their respective nuclear energy programs; the growing penetration of the buffer states of Uruguay, Paraguay, and Bolivia by Brazilian commerce and settlers; the rising industrial and military might of Brazil, especially with regard to weapons production; the relative isolation from international alliance systems of Argentina compared to the close association of Brazil with the United States. Uruguay as a small country with little military capability did not contribute much itself to regional security calculations, but it did retain a strong interest in the balance of power between its much more powerful neighbors.[20]

In the international relations literature, the customary way of assessing the general level of threat perception in an area is to examine military expenditures by its potential belligerents. Despite the region's recently acquired reputation for "militarism," these levels expressed as a proportion of Gross Domestic Product have been relatively modest, although they have increased significantly under military rule. They range from an average high of 7.9 percent for Chile to an average low of 0.8 percent for Brazil.[21] In absolute terms, Argentina and Brazil tended to have about the same level of expenditures during the 1960s, but diverged increasingly after 1970. What is "hidden" in these data is a nonevent that occurred when both countries were authoritarian: the fact that, when Argentina entered into a military buildup prior to the Malvinas–Falkland War, Brazil did not seem to feel threatened and did not increase its expenditures accordingly. Whether this was due to good intelligence about Argentine intentions, explicit (if secret) agreement between the two militaries, or just inattention by the Brazilians is not known.

Despite some problems of comparability (especially with regard to the total Brazilian military budget), the data show conclusively that expenditures on the armed forces have gone down significantly in Uruguay since its regime change.[22] In Argentina, they went down initially but seem to have recovered in 1986. A more qualitative assessment, however, stresses the enormity of changes produced by the civilian government:

> Alfonsin has kept the armed forces' budget extremely tight, forcing personnel lay-offs and necessitating drastic cut-backs in training and operations time. Defense acquisitions from abroad have been practically nil, while the defense industries, primarily owned and operated by the armed forces, have been kept starved of capital and orders. . . . Alfonsin has continually acted to remove critical Army leaders from positions of leadership and to cut back on the service's installations, pay, and privileges.[23]

In stark contrast, military expenditures seem to have remained the same in democratic Brazil[24] and to have increased in authoritarian Chile. Before jumping to the comforting conclusion that this demonstrates that democratization, decrease in international threat perception and decrease in military expenditures are all coupled in a benevolent circle—at least for two of the three cases—one should consider the less idealistic possibility that the dependent variable is a more direct product of the way in which the military were "extricated" from power. Where they completely lost control over who would succeed them (Argentina), they were subsequently "punished" the most in the allocation process; where they managed to set the pace and string out the process (Brazil), they could protect their usual share of governmental resources under the ensuing democratic regime. Uruguay lies somewhere between these extremes; Chile is on another continuum. According to this more realistic view, levels of military expenditure in the *Cono Sur* are determined more by actual competition with domestic political forces than by potential conflict with foreign military adversaries.

The first threatening issue upon which democratization can be said to have a direct effect did not emerge between Argentina and Brazil, but involved the unilateral resolution of a long-standing dispute between Argentina and Chile over their boundary in the Beagle Channel. This had been submitted first to British and then to Papal arbitration. Armed hostilities were only narrowly avoided in 1978. When John Paul II decided substantially in favor of Chile, the Argentine military refused to accept the judgment. Alfonsin moved—shortly after taking office and in the absence of any apparent threat or quid pro quo from the Chileans—to resolve the dispute by accepting the Papal solution and eventually agreeing to territorial concessions. Especially significant from an idealist perspective is the fact that he then submitted the matter to a popular referendum—for the first time in Argentine history. Although the consultation was voluntary and nonbinding on the executive or congress, it set a very important precedent. Some 77 percent of those who voted supported the settlement, despite the opposition of rightist military circles and some Peronists. They demonstrated unambiguously that Kant was right in supposing that citizens would normally oppose using the threat of violence to resolve international disputes—if rulers bothered to ask their opinion. In this case, they even did so with regard to an authoritarian regime for which they clearly had no sympathy. Subsequent to this, the two countries went on to sign several agreements clearing up other border problems and established several *Comités de Frontera* to resolve future ones.

The key to a long-term reduction in threat perception in the subregion, however, lies in the bilateral relations between Argentina and Brazil. Some renewed controversy over the border with Chile or a flaring up of the Malvinas–Falkland conflict could trigger a radical shift in Argentine military posture (and perhaps even lead to a return to authoritarian rule), but this presently seems unlikely. What is crucial is for Argentina to adjust to the fact that the continued greater economic and demographic growth of Brazil—not to mention its higher level of defense expenditures and weapons production—does not necessarily pose a security threat. "Realism" dictates that Argentina should be preoccupied and that it should respond by increasing its power capability. "Idealism" suggests that it may be possible, if democracy prevails, for the two countries to compete and cooperate without regard for their differing capability for inflicting violence.

Ironically, from the Kantian perspective, moves in this direction began in 1979–1980, when both regimes were dictatorial. A tripartite agreement (which included Paraguay) resolving some conflicts concerning the Itaipú dam; the first visit to Argentina by a Brazilian President in 45 years, followed by several other high-level exchanges; an accord on cooperation in nuclear research; some joint naval exercises—all combined to promote a significant change in the geopolitical calculations of both governments. The subsequent deposition of General Videla who had participated in these agreements and Argentina's continued sponsorship of extreme militaristic initiatives involving such things as a coup in Bolivia, assistance to Central American military and intelligence forces, a flaring up of the Beagle Channel dispute with Chile, a proposed South Atlantic naval pact with South Africa, and eventually, the Malvinas Invasion destroyed most of what had been started. As mentioned previously, it is significant that Brazil did not respond to the invasion buildup by triggering an arms buildup of its own. Instead, at least verbally, it gave support to the Argentines and denied Great Britain landing rights during the conflict.[25]

Alfonsin and Sarney were the inheritors of this relative *distensão* in bilateral military relations. The former also inherited a thoroughly discredited and divided military establishment, whereas the latter was dependent upon a relatively successful and unified one. The Malvinas defeat had removed the Argentine armed forces as a security threat to Brazil for some time and compelled them to reexamine their previous obsession with what one author termed their "penchant for casting international relations into a zero-sum geopolitical framework."[26] Both sides seem to have moved skillfully through a series of political agreements (to be discussed later) to defuse further any remaining sources of tension. Brazil has publicly supported Argentina's claim to the Malvinas and handles its diplomatic affairs in Great Britain; both countries have agreed to further cooperation in nuclear research (although no accord on mutual inspection has been reached and neither country has signed the Non-Proliferation Treaty); some Brazilian weapons have been purchased by Argentina and future joint production of combat aircraft has been discussed; joint naval exercises in the South Atlantic have become a regular event. Nevertheless, what is conspicuously missing in all the flood of treaties and declarations that have been issued since 1985 is any formal agreement between the two military establishments themselves. Proposals have been made, but rumors have it that the respective armed forces are opposed to a mutual defense treaty.[27]

It may be premature to conclude that democratization has definitively lowered the threat to use armed violence to resolve interstate conflicts in this part of the world. The evidence since 1984–1985 is certainly encouraging for an idealist outcome (although it should be noted that the process began when both regimes were despotic). Nevertheless, both militaries seem to have kept their options open. If the disparity in capabilities continues to widen in Brazil's favor, Argentina may be tempted to respond by "going nuclear,"[28] and all the recent efforts at mutual reassurance will have been for naught. So far, there are no signs of such an escalation and Alfonsin's assertion of civilian control over nuclear affairs suggests that it is highly unlikely to happen—at least, until he is replaced.

DEMOCRATIZATION AND COOPERATION

If there is one area in which the change in regime type has had an unambiguously positive impact, it is that of international cooperation[29]—at least if this can be measured by the sheer quantity of discussions, declarations, statements of principle, accords and agreements entered into by high-level executives of the region's three new democracies. At no time in history have public officials from Argentina, Brazil, and Uruguay met more frequently and more publicly—sometimes bilaterally, sometimes trilaterally, sometimes pluri-laterally—with varying groups of their Latin American brethren.

In all fairness, it should be pointed out that frequent encounters between *técnicos* of the region began as early as the 1950s with the creation of the Economic Commission for Latin America (ECLA) and increased during the 1960s with the negotiations that led to the foundation of the Latin American Free Trade Area (LAFTA).[30] Meet-ings among Southern Cone *politícos*, however, remained quite rare. When, in 1980, General–President Figuereido of Brazil initiated a series of visits with his neighboring authoritarian rulers, it was re-portedly the first time in forty-five years that the presidents of Argen-tina and Brazil had met one on one! This exercise in regional sum-mitry petered out quickly without leaving much of a trace—only to pick up again with a vengeance once the three countries had gone democratic. From 1985 to 1988, the presidents of Argentina, Brazil, and Uruguay met together—bilaterally or trilaterally—on at least fourteen occasions, and that leaves out a substantial number of mul-tilateral occasions. Moreover, they left behind a veritable "blizzard" of agreements on a wide range of policy issues, and as they enter their fifth year, there is no sign of a slackening of the pace. Moreover, this pattern of interaction conspicuously excluded the remaining nondemocratic polities of Latin America: Chile and Paraguay. Even Panama was shut out of some multilateral meetings when Noriega's dominant political role became too obvious and embarrassing.

The point is well illustrated by the data in Table 3.1, which cover only intraregional visits among presidents. In 1980 and 1981 one can detect the brief flurry of initiatives by authoritarian Brazil (three visits with Argentina and one with Chile), but that failed to become a regular feature of the subregion's diplomacy. Uruguay, which had had a fairly constant set of contacts with its neighbors in the late 1970s, saw these lapse from 1979 to 1982. Suddenly, when all three are democratic in 1985, a very regular pattern sets in. These began as bilateral exchanges between Alfonsin and Sarney and subsequently turned trilateral with the incorporation of Sanguinetti. In 1988 they met three times among themselves, which must be some kind of record for neighborliness among presidents. Inversely, Chile was completely shut out of these high-level encounters. Not a single chief executive from the subregion went there since 1982, when the then authoritarian ruler of Uruguay, General Alvarez, paid General Pinochet a visit.[31]

If one looks at a slightly lower level of public contact, that of ministers and heads of major state agencies, the same pattern of intensified exchanges after 1985 emerges. This is especially apparent in the relations between Argentina and Brazil, but there has also been a less visible set of "technical" visits between democratic Argentina and dictatorial Chile. Presumably, much of this was concerned with working out the details of resolving their previously outstanding border disputes, but it seems to be continuing and expanding into new areas.[32]

In the wake of all this "political tourism," Argentina, Brazil, and Uruguay have been issuing impressive declarations of common intent and signing various sonorous treaties. Behind these professions

TABLE 3.1

Frequency of Presidential Visits: Argentina, Brazil, Chile, and Uruguay, 1976–1988

	1976	*77*	*78*	*79*	*80*	*81*	*82*	*83*	*84*	*85*	*86*	*87*	*88*
Ar. with													
Br.	0	0	0	0	2	1	0	1	0	1	2ª	2ª	3ª
Ur.	1	2	0	0	0	0	1	1	0	2	2ª	2ª	3ª
Ch.	1	0	1	0	0	0	0	0	0	0	0	0	0
Br. with													
Ar.	0	0	0	0	2	1	0	1	0	1	2ª	2ª	3ª
Ur.	0	1	1	0	0	0	0	0	1	1	2ª	1ª	3ª
Ch.	0	0	0	0	1	0	0	0	0	0	0	0	0
Ur. with													
Br.	0	1	1	0	0	0	0	0	1	1	2ª	1ª	3ª
Ar.	1	2	0	0	0	0	1	1	0	2	2ª	2ª	3ª
Ch.	0	0	0	0	0	0	1	0	0	0	0	0	0
Ch. with													
Ar.	1	0	1	0	0	0	0	0	0	0	0	0	0
Br.	0	0	0	0	1	0	0	0	0	0	0	0	0
Ur.	0	0	0	0	0	0	1	0	0	0	0	0	0

Sources: Integración Latinoamericana (Buenos Aires), 1976–1988; *Latin American Regional Reports, Southern Cone* (London), 1981–1989; *Latin American Regional Reports Brazil* (London) 1984–1989; *La Nación* (Buenos Aires).
ª Included are trilateral meetings between the presidents of Brazil, Argentina, and Uruguay, there were one each in 1986 and 1987 and three in 1988.

of mutual faith in "peace, democracy, development and integration,"
however, have come a growing number of more specific (and potentially more binding) protocols. By one count, in the two years after
they were all democratic (1985–1986), they had signed thirty-one
agreements, compared to only four during the previous four years.[33]
The pace continued furiously during 1987 and 1988, with Chile largely
cut out of this orgy of bilateralism. The content of the agreements
ranged widely, beyond the usual goals of promotion of trade and
financial compensation, to cover such things as physical infrastructure, transportation systems, frontier zones, energy networks and
pipelines, complementarity arrangements for specific industries,
technical and scientific cooperation (especially in the sensitive area of
nuclear research). One of them even went so far as to create a
common currency (or, better, unit of account) for Argentina and
Brazil, the *gaucho* or *gaúcho*. Some of these accords have subsequently
run into practical difficulties and political resistance at the implementation stage. Relative prices, entrenched commercial practices, pro-

TABLE 3.2

Frequency of (Nonpresidential) High-Level Visits: Argentina, Brazil, Chile,
and Uruguay, 1976–1988

	1976	77	78	79	80	81	82	83	84	85	86	87	88
Ar. with													
Br.	0	1	1	1	2	0	0	1	1	3	2	2	4
Ur.	1	0	3	0	2	1	1	1	0	2	1	1	3
Ch.	1	2	0	0	0	0	0	1	2	1	2	1	3
Br. with													
Ar.	0	1	1	1	2	0	0	1	1	3	2	2	4
Ur.	0	0	0	1	1	0	0	1	0	0	1	2	2
Ch.	0	0	1	1	0	0	0	0	0	0	0	0	0
Ur. with													
Br.	0	0	0	1	1	0	0	1	0	0	1	2	2
Ar.	1	0	3	0	2	1	1	1	0	2	1	1	3
Ch.	0	0	0	1	0	1	0	0	0	0	0	0	0
Ch. with													
Ar.	1	2	0	0	0	0	0	1	2	1	2	1	3
Br.	0	0	1	1	0	0	0	0	0	0	0	0	0
Ur.	0	0	0	1	0	1	0	0	0	0	0	0	0

Sources: Same as table 3.1

tectionistic pressures—not to mention the debt crisis and raging inflation—have impeded actual trade, investments, and credits from responding so favorably to these negotiated incentives, as we saw earlier in our discussion of interdependence. Very little has been subsequently heard about the *gaucho–gaúcho*. Nevertheless, one can hardly fault the democratic leaders of the three countries for trying to place a whole range of their bilateral exchanges on a more formal, cooperative, and law-abiding basis—as Kant would have predicted.[34]

Moving beyond the immediate subregional context to the issue of foreign policy coordination in general, it becomes more difficult to detect the impact of democratization. Both Brazil and Uruguay have made the right (i.e., "supportive") noises about Argentine claims to the Malvinas–Falklands, but they had taken this position *before* their respective regime changes. On the several occasions in which Argentine democracy was threatened by military coup or insurrection, its democratic neighbors have pledged their unequivocal support for Alfonsin and appeared publicly at his side. Whether Brazil or Uruguay would be prepared to go beyond moral pressure to lend a beleaguered Argentine government military assistance has (fortunately) not been tested. Neither Argentina nor Brazil has joined the international consensus with regard to the Non-Proliferation Treaty (which makes each other and their neighbors nervous). Argentine and Chilean claims to various parts of Antarctica remain *en vigueur*, despite their rejection by other countries of the subregion. Each has negotiated its own arrangement with individual European countries, and there is no joint approach to the European Community in sight.

On the one issue where they might have been expected to profit most from hammering out a common position—reimbursement of international debt—there has been a lot of bilateral and multilateral discussion, without any noticeable results. All three are members of the Group of Eight (actually, Seven, since Panama was "disinvited" because of its questionable status as a democracy). However, the group's last meeting at the level of heads of state in Montevideo in November 1988 could do no better than to come up with platitudes.[35] The United States has often expressed the fear that a "Cartel of Debtors" was being formed in Latin America, but so far the fact that most of those involved are democracies has not been sufficient to overcome differences in their perception of national interest, not to mention differences in their susceptibility to extraregional pressure.[36]

DEMOCRATIZATION AND REGIONAL INTEGRATION

Much of what was classified earlier under the rubrique *international cooperation* has been described and justified by the leaders of the three neodemocracies as contributions to *regional integration*. For example, at their first meeting in 1986, Presidents Alfonsin and Sarney solemnly signed the *Ata para Integração Brasileiro–Argentina*, determined, they said, "to transform (their) permanent links of friendship and cooperation into an integration that consolidates (their) will to grow together."[37] Granted that agreement immediately went on to specify that the course of action would be "gradual," "flexible," "symmetric," and "balanced"—all hints that the initial commitment was modest and that a great deal remained to be worked out, nevertheless, a start had been made. Virtually all the subsequent accords and protocols reiterate the goal of integration and express the conviction that it is somehow essential for the "consolidation of peace, democracy, security and development in the region."[38]

Some have gone even further to suggest that Argentina and Brazil in the mid-1980s are in a situation analogous to that of France and Germany in the mid-1950s: two former arch-rivals who have voluntarily agreed to bury the hatchet and to set a cooperative pace that their neighbors of lesser importance will be compelled (eventually) to follow. Moreover, it has even been argued that they have discovered the functional equivalent for coal and steel in the early stages of European integration, namely, capital goods.[39] If, through complementarity of production and trade in these items, the two can create a basis of interdependence at the core of the process of import-substituting industrialization, then other sectors cannot be far behind.

Before evaluating this scenario and analyzing recent trends in the Southern Cone, perhaps we should make clear the distinction between *cooperation* and *integration*. Unlike the former, where policy coordination between independent actors can be reached through episodic encounters, convergent actions, iterative games, or personal trust, the latter depends on the existence of specific institutions with their own rules, their own arrangements of office, their own purposes, and their own resources. At the extreme, these integrative institutions become large bureaucratic organizations with autonomous capacities to extract resources and initiate policies, and supranational authority to implement these choices. Even if one grants that the European Community has yet to meet all these conditions and may never get completely "beyond the nation-state," it still seems desirable to distinguish between *patterns* of cooperation—however enduring and valuable—and *organizations* of integration—however improvised and subordinate. If there is one constant assumption among the many variants of regional integration theory, it is that only when the relations among states become embedded in a specific, formal, multilateral institution that new systemic properties can appear, whether in the form of an enhanced role for international civil servants and technical elites, a shift in the locus of interest politics, a process of regional party formation, a development of supranational authority, or the emergence of an overarching, common identity.

The relation between domestic democratization and international integration has rarely been explicitly explored.[40] In the case of the European Economic Community, it could be taken for granted. At the time of its initiation, the six members were already democratic, and subsequent decision precluded the entry of those regimes that were not. The neofunctionalist approach presumed not only democracy but pluralism, since its core expansive mechanism, the autonomous action of specialized interest groups at overlapping levels of aggregation, could only operate freely under such conditions. Its failure to pay any attention, however, to the dynamics of domestic party systems and national executive institutions was particularly damaging—as was demonstrated in the 1960s by the subsequent "unanticipated" policies of General De Gaulle and as may be demonstrated in the 1990s by the future "noncompliant" actions of Mrs. Thatcher. The process looks quite different if it is viewed exclusively from the perspective of functionally based, rationally conceived *interests* seeking the site and level that seem to guarantee the highest satisfaction at the lowest possible cost, from the way it would appear if it is approached from that of territorially based, symbolically conceived *passions* that are seeking the greatest security at the highest possible level of national sovereignty. Democracy, in other words, can cut both ways with regard to integration. It can protect a diversity of actors and provide an arena of negotiation in which they can pursue their self-defined interests—and that can involve transferring their attention and effort to new, overarching institutions. Or it can provide them with a legitimate framework within which they can express their collectively elaborated passions—and that may mean defending tenaciously the boundaries and functions of existing political units. If democracies are at least ambiguous with regard to integration, autocracies would seem less so. They stifle or skew the arena of interested negotiation, and they usually assert their passionate defense of national sovereignty.

The (admitted limited) experience of Latin America with schemes for regional integration only partially confirms the preceding generalizations. For a while, the Central American Common Market made some progress despite the heterogeneity of the political regimes that composed it and the limited pluralism of their interest systems.[41] It never fully recovered from the "Football War" in 1969 between two of its members and is currently in disarray because of a variety of catastrophes: revolution, civil war, American intervention, debt crises, and so on. The Latin American Free Trade Area (LAFTA) got off to a less auspicious start with a much lower level of initial commitment and institutional capacity,[42] but it struggled along until the wave of authoritarian take-overs affected most of its members. The abandonment by these governments, especially in Argentina, Chile, and Uruguay, of import substitution policies and the adoption of development strategies based on generalized free trade undermined the contractual obligations of LAFTA. In addition, changes in their exchange rate systems produced wide and sudden fluctuations in the real value of currency that dramatically and negatively affected intraregional trade.[43] Chile formally withdrew from the more ambitious Andean Bloc in 1976, when its neoliberal economic policies conflicted with the group's arrangements for planned industrial complementarity. Faced with a decline in countries' willingness to offer new multilateral tariff concessions and a stagnation in intraregional trade, LAFTA was dissolved in 1980 and replaced with a new organization, the Latin American Integration Association (LAIA—or ALADI in Spanish), described by one commentator as a "pragmatic scheme at a low level of commitment."[44] Its main novelty was to give up on the goal of establishing a uniform system of multilateral regional preferences and to shift to bilateral agreements of more limited scope. Presumptively, these can eventually be made to converge as other members negotiate their inclusion, but nothing guarantees such an outcome. Moreover, it would appear that even those concessions that are made between pairs of countries can be subjected to renegotiation based on the subsequent balance of trade in the items covered. It goes without saying that this retraction in actual commitment came accompanied by a rhetorical promise to contribute to the "establishment, in a gradual and progressive manner, of a Latin American common market"—without any specification of a deadline![45]

This is the integration legacy that the three neodemocracies faced in 1984–1985: a previous free trade arrangement that had met with a "high level of non-compliance, for one reason or another, with quantitative goals and the specific time limits for reaching them";[46] a set of national economic policy instruments that stressed export promotion and insertion into an extraregional trading and production system; a pattern of increasing disparity in rates of economic growth and trade creation; a profile of declining intraregional trade with severe reciprocal imbalances; and a new "Association" with very weak powers and vague attributions. As we have seen, their response was to jump on the LAIA provisions for partial or bilateral agreements with the argument that, by intensifying their interactions, they would be setting the pace for the continent as a whole. At their December 1988 meeting in Colonia, the presidents of Argentina and Brazil even agreed to submit a formal treaty of integration to their respective parliaments for ratification by the end of the coming year. According to one account, it would contain commitments to an Argentine–Brazilian Common Market based on the removal of all tariff and nontariff barriers within ten years and to the establishment of a joint committee to oversee harmonization of economic policies across the two countries![47] Uruguay, which has been brought into the emerging network of bilateral agreements, balked at subscribing to such an ambitious goal and only announced its intention of joining "in the moment considered opportune and convenient."[48]

So far, however, all this impressive cooperative behavior has not been accompanied by any institution building, much less agreement on the establishment of a single organizational site that might eventually serve as a center for the promotion of further initiatives, the accumulation of additional resources, the monitoring of subsequent compliance, or the forging of distinct identities. Except for a few groups of experts and standing committees on specific topics, Argentina and Brazil have studiously avoided such an outcome.[49] The new initiatives have emerged from direct, personal contacts between chiefs of state and their staffs, not from the secretariats of regional organizations such as ECLA, SELA, INTAL, and ALADI.[50]

Another weakness involves the bilateral strategy that the two democracies have been employing. This usually means that the exchanges must be balanced between each pair of participants.[51] While both Argentina and Brazil sell to Uruguay about as much as they buy on the average, this is not the case with the much larger volume of trade between the two subregional "superpowers." In every year since 1980, Argentina imports from Brazil have been greater than its exports to that country—except for 1986 when they were balanced. According to the latest Argentine figures, Argentina bought $U.S. 819 million from Brazil in 1987 and only sold it $US 539 million.[52] Such imbalances in exchanges can lead to a concern with persistent asymmetries and, eventually, to power differentiation within an integrative process.[53]

As one might expect of a part of the world that gave us dependency theory, Latin Americans tend to pay strict attention to the commodity composition of trade. Not all goods are created (and treated) equal. Manufactures are regarded as intrinsically superior to primary goods, either because of the historical evolution of the terms of trade in their favor or because of immediate linkage effects. Only 30.3 percent of Argentine exports to Brazil in 1985 consisted of manufactured goods, whereas 56.7% of its imports from Brazil came from the same category. Argentina did not do so badly in its manufacturing exports to Uruguay and Chile, but everywhere and across the board Brazil did better. As one critic put it, it is not reasonable to suppose that "Argentina will specialize in food stuffs while Brazil will consolidate its industrial advantage."[54]

All this is not to suggest that Brazil is about to convert its superior trading position into some form of domination over the Southern Cone. Quite the contrary, much of the subregional cooperation we have observed since 1985 is dedicated to assuaging such fears and eventually to compensating for such a possibility. Nevertheless, from a strictly realistic perspective, this asymmetry in trade, when combined with the growing disparity in military and industrial capacity, between the two largest powers in the subregion suggest that serious problems lie ahead—if and when these countries get around to establishing the sort of specific organizations that might be expected to promote and direct the integration process.

CONCLUSION

The lessons from the *Cono Sur* are encouraging from a neoidealist perspective, but they are not conclusive. The transition from authoritarian to democratic rule has made a significant difference in interstate relations within the subregion, but it would certainly be premature to draw the conclusion that *"permanent cooperation"* or even *"permanent peace"* has been attained. We have found no conclusive proof of the existence of a "virtuous circle" wherein *democratization* decreases the *threat of war* and increases *interdependence* between newly liberated private citizens of adjacent countries, which in turn leads to *cooperation* and *integration* among these previously sovereign political units, which eventually results in the *strengthening of democracy* at the national level and the *pursuit of human interests* at the international level. All we can say with certainty is that the demise of despotic government has produced a significant decline in the likelihood of recourse to interstate violence and an unprecedented increase in the volume of interstate agreement. However, the citizens of these countries have yet to generate a volume and variety of mutual trade, investment, production, tourism, labor flows, and social communications sufficient to modify their much more important and persistent dependence upon extraregional partners. Also, our cases do confirm Kant's pessimism about the possibility of going "beyond the nation-state" to create overarching transnational organizations with the capacity and legitimacy to impose peace and administer cooperation.

However, it should also be observed that our findings do not foreclose the possibility that the "virtuous circle" will form around these countries in the future. The experiences with democratization discussed in this chapter are quite recent, and it may be simply too soon to test for their impact on such complex and mediated outcomes as a shift in the pattern of interdependence or the development of integrative institutions. In the short run, the democratic leaders of Argentina, Brazil, and Uruguay have accomplished that which comes easiest. They have drafted and agreed upon a normative and legal framework for the peaceful resolution of conflicts and the cooperative management of problems. The rest can be expected to come later as the result either of induced behavior in other actors or of unanticipated spill-over into other domains. Fortifying this optimistic view is the observation that the Southern Cone started from a markedly low level of mutual exchanges and a previous history of failure in meeting commitments to regional institutions. If, for example, one were to compare its experience with that of the Iberian Peninsula, where democratization occurred in the context of a much higher level of multilateralized interdependence and more varied set of prior integrative efforts, one might well conclude that Argentina, Brazil, and Uruguay have not gotten off to such a bad start. The fact that Spain and Portugal seem to have entered the virtuous circle more easily and to have come out with more consolidated forms of democracy should come as no surprise.

Until 1990, dictatorial Chile had been almost completely frozen out of these developments. Now that it too seems to be launched on a transition to democracy, we shall soon be able to test whether existing bi- and trilateral cooperative arrangements will be easily and enthusiastically extended to cover it—as the neoidealist scenario would predict. We might even discover whether Chile's inclusion will provide a new (and much needed) impetus to further progress in interdependence and integration within the subregion.

Another reason we should be cautious in generalizing on the basis of this case also concerns differences in the point of departure. This part of the world could be regarded as atypical because its persistently low level of armed international conflict renders the usual "realist" assumptions about international relations inapplicable. In other words, whatever trends we observe toward cooperation, interdependence, and integration in the relations between Argentina, Brazil, Uruguay (and, eventually, Chile), they could not be expected to hold in other world areas where interstate violence is a more omnipresent prospect. We have seen that threats to resort to arms to resolve interstate conflicts in the *Cono Sur* have not been so rare as is often presumed; however, it may well be that a similar clustering of democratizations in some region where the issues at stake are more intense or where the capacity for superpower intervention is more likely could produce less significant changes than we have observed among these three "pacified" and "peripheral" countries. In a recent essay, Terry Karl has argued persuasively that in at least one region with these unfavorable characteristics—Central America—democracies have still managed to develop new cooperative ventures, even if they too have not accomplished much in terms of interdependence and have lost much of what they had previously accomplished in the area of regional integration.[55]

Finally, there is the delicate issue of temporal consistency in the findings. As we have noted, an optimist would point out that these experiences of democratization in the *Cono Sur* are so recent that it is simply too early to test for their impact upon the other parts of the alleged virtuous circle. The pessimist, however, would no doubt stress that democracy itself is far from consolidated in Argentina, Brazil, and Uruguay and that the modest accomplishments to date would be completely insufficient to protect any one of the three from retrograding to authoritarian rule. Whatever the leaders of these countries may say in their joint statements about solidarity and co-operation, "if push came to shove" and a military coup were under way, it is difficult to imagine that they could or would intervene effectively—without jeopardizing themselves in the process.

A more sobering thought is that, even if democracy as a generic mode of domination were to become consolidated in the subregion, the sort of conflicts and uncooperative actions that have so often been exacerbated in the past by differences in *types of regime* might become embedded in emergent differences between *types of democracy*. Each would have its distinctive social bases, decision rules, symbolic allusions, international allies, and so on, and these, when brought to bear on a specific issue of contention, could become a basis for additional suspicion and misunderstanding and a source for mobilizing distinctive domestic interests and passions. So far, we have reason to believe that democracies do not go to war with each other, regardless of their "internal" differences in institutional, ideational, and policy structures. But if we define "perpetual peace" in maximalist terms, not just as the absence of recourse to violence to settle interstate conflicts, but as a pattern of interdependence in exchanges, cooperation in problem solving, and eventually, integration in governance (*pace* Kant), then such differences between democracies may become quite relevant. As the core calculus of international relations shifts from "who declares war and why" to "who benefits from policies and how," the internal composition of constituencies and the rules determining collective choice become much more salient components determining the outcome—and this is precisely where democracies differ the most. As we have noted, the international experience of Latin American polities is often dismissed on the grounds that the *cui bellum indico?* calculus is insufficiently salient. However, no one could claim that *cui bono?* is not of central political relevance in this part of the world or that both the persistent and the emergent forms that democracy has taken there do not offer a great variety of responses to this eternal question. My neoidealist inference is that the future of international interdependence, cooperation, and integration in Latin America, and even more specifically, in its Southern Cone may depend *less* on heterogeneity between its regime types and *more* on diversity among its democracies.[56]

ENDNOTES

This article was written before democratic elections were held in Chile in December 1989. It is a revised version of a paper entitled: "Idealism, Regime Change and Regional Cooperation: Lessons from the Southern Cone of Latin America," originally presented in the Seminar on "The New Interdependence in the Americas", The Americas Program, Stanford University, February 28, 1989. I would like to acknowledge the financial support of the John T. and Catherine D. MacArthur Foundation and the Americas Program of Stanford University, as well as the research assistance of Kevin Hartigan and Libby Wood. I would also like to thank my colleagues in the seminar and, especially, Terry Karl for comments and criticisms.
   At the request of the editors, this text has been severely abridged.

1. "To Perpetual Peace: A Philosophical Sketch" in T. Humphrey, trans., *Perpetual Peace and other essays on Politics, History and Morals* (Indianapolis/ Cambridge: Hackett, 1983).
2. Kant used the term *republican* in a rather idiosyncratic sense. It was juxtaposed to *despotic*, not *monarchic* rule. Its defining properties were constitutional restraints on the exercise of power, representative mechanisms linking authorities to publics, and an accountable government based on a separation of powers. Kant explicitly mentioned that such a regime could be headed by a king and expressed strong antipathy to mass participation in governance. Our exploitation of his argument to cover modern democracies is, therefore, hazardous—unless those democracies have the sort of liberal properties that Kant admired.
3. Robert Gilpin, *War and Change in World Politics* (Cambridge: Cambridge University Press, 1981), p. 29 (my emphasis).

4. "War, Interdependence and Functionalism," in Raimo Vayrynen, ed., *The Quest for Peace,* (London: Sage, 1987), p. 2.

5. David Mitrany, *A Working Peace System* (London: Royal Institute of International Affairs, 1943); Karl W. Deutsch et al., *Political Community and the North Atlantic Area* (Princeton, N.J.: Princeton University Press, 1957); Ernst B. Haas, *Beyond the Nation State* (Stanford, Calif.: Stanford University Press, 1964).

6. Cf. Ernst B. Haas, *The Uniting of Europe* (Stanford, Calif.: Stanford University Press, 1958); Ernst B. Haas, "The Uniting of Europe and the Uniting of Latin America," *Journal of Common Market Studies* (1967), 5:315–343; Ernst B. Haas and P. C. Schmitter, "Economics and Differential Patterns of Political Integration," *International Organization* (August 1964), 705–737. For the most comprehensive overview of theories of regional integration, see Leon Lindberg and Stuart Scheingold, eds., *Regional Integration: Theory and Research* (Cambridge, Mass.: Harvard University Press, 1971).

7. For an early appreciation of the difficulties, see Stanley Hoffmann, "Obstinate or Obsolete? The Fate of the Nation State and the Case of Western Europe," *Daedalus* (1966), 95:862–915. Also Ernst B. Haas, *The Obsolescence of Regional Integration Theory* (Berkeley: Institute of International Studies, 1975).

8. But not completely. There have been sporadic revivals of interest in Kant's proposition. Cf. Quincy Wright, *A Study of War* (Chicago: University of Chicago Press, 1942), pp. 839–848; Kenneth Waltz, "Kant, Liberalism, and War," *American Political Science Review* (June 1962), 56(2):331–340; Rudolph Rummel, "National Attributes and Foreign Conflict Behavior," in J. D. Singer ed., *Quantitative International Politics* (New York: Free Press, 1968), pp. 187–214; Melvin Small and J. David Singer, "The War-Proneness of Democratic Regimes, 1816–1965," *Jerusalem Journal of International Relations* (Summer 1976), 1(4):50–69; Michael W. Doyle, "Kant, Liberal Legacies, and Foreign Affairs," *Philosophy and Public Affairs,* (1983), 12:205–235, 323–353; Jack S. Levy, "Domestic Politics and War," *Journal of Interdisciplinary History* (1988), 18(4):653–673. Levy concludes that "democratic states have been involved, proportionately, in as many wars as non-democratic states" (p. 661) but that "liberal or democratic states do not fight each other" (ibid.). The latter he calls "as close as anything we have to an empirical law in international relations" (p. 662). Our concern here will be principally with the organization of international cooperation, rather than the avoidance of international war.

9. Here Kant is echoing a frequent theme of the eighteenth century, namely, that the growth of commerce would tend to induce more moderate, more law-abiding, and less violent behavior. This *doux commerce* thesis was developed by Montesquieu and has recently been revived by Albert Hirschmann, *The Passions and the Interests* (Princeton, N.J.: Princeton University Press, 1977).

10. "All men who can mutually influence each other must accept some civil constitution," *Perpetual Peace*, p. 112.
11. According to its annual survey, Freedom House has estimated that in 1988, 39 percent of the world's population now lives "in freedom." That is a record high for the survey's seventeen-year history. *San Francisco Chronicle*, January 4, 1989.
12. I am indebted to Kurt Taylor Gaubatz for this observation.
13. See, for example, Stephen Krasner, "Power, Asymmetries and Mexican–American Relations," paper presented at the Seminar on "The New Interdependence in the Americas," The Americas Program, Stanford University, November 10, 1988.
14. For an interesting, geographically deterministic version of this thesis, see Edward W. Fox, *History in Geographic Perspective: The Other France* (New York: Norton, 1971).
15. In each case the regime "treatment" will be considered to begin from the moment that a chief executive was elected in an open, competitive election of uncertain outcome to succeed an authoritarian ruler. Alfonsin was elected on October 30, 1983; so, in terms of annualized data, 1984 will be considered the first year attributable to Argentine democracy. Sanguinetti was elected on November 24, 1984, so 1985 will be Uruguay's initial democratic year. The election of Tancredo/Sarney was on January 14, 1985; therefore, given the early date, that entire year will be "attributed" to Brazilian democracy. The situation becomes more complicated if one takes seriously the anticipatory hypothesis—namely, that the effect of democracy begins from the moment that it seems likely that a regime change will occur and actors begin modifying their behavior accordingly. This would move Brazil from last to first place. Its transition probably began with the announcement of *distensão* by General–President Geisel in October 1973 and was certainly enhanced by the defeat of the government's candidates in the congressional election of 1974. Uruguay's transition started on November 30, 1980, when the incumbent dictatorship lost a plebescite on its continuing in power. Argentina's began with the defeat in the Malvinas–Falklands War on June 14, 1982.
16. For a detailed analysis of this collapse in trade within Latin America after 1981 that emphasizes that it was particularly severe for the trade in manufactured goods that LAFTA–LAIA had worked so hard since 1960 to build up, see Guillermo Ondarts, "La crisis del comercio intra-ALADI y las perspectivas de la integración," *Integración Latinoamericana*, (June 1986), 113:42–46.
17. Robert O. Keohane and Joseph S. Nye, *Power and Interdependence: World Politics in Transition* (Boston: Little, Brown, 1977), ch. 2.
18. The source for these data on "direct intraregional foreign investment" notes that these are very approximate estimates and are not consistent in the determination of the national origin of capital. It concluded that, "intra-regional investments account for only a very small proportion

(1.5%) of total direct foreign investment" in Latin America as a whole. The only reason for suspecting that the *Cono Sur* may be different lies in the substantial real estate holdings of individual Argentines in Uruguay —which are not included in the preceding estimates. Inter-American Development Bank, *Economic and Social Progress in Latin America*, 1982 Report, pp. 137–140.

19. A third alternative is that it is simply too early to draw any conclusions about such a complex relationship, especially given the low level of departure. The newly democratized countries of southern Europe may have responded with greater alacrity and magnitude, but they had attained significantly greater interdependence beforehand and they entered into multiple networks of intraregional exchange already in existence.

20. Cf. Joseph Tulchin, "Uruguay como estado tapón: Implicancias para la estabilidad del Cono Sur," *Cono Sur* (August–September 1987), 6(4):7–10.

21. Data are from the SIPRI Yearbook and refer to the period 1970–1986.

22. "The Uruguayan military arsenal, particularly its fleet of aircraft, is showing signs of age and many categories of equipment are in need of replacement or refurbishment. Nevertheless, the country is faced with economic crisis, and the new civilian administration has introduced widespread cuts in the defense budget, including a reduction of the army forces by 20 percent. The Government has indicated that no arms purchases will be made during 1987." *Defense & Foreign Affairs Handbook, 1987–88 Edition* (Washington, D.C.: The Perth Corporation, 1987), p. 1091.

23. Ibid., pp. 44–45.

24. According to the *Defense & Foreign Affairs Handbook*, the Brazilian military has expanded its functions and modernized its equipment since the transition to democracy. Ibid., p. 115.

25. Wayne A. Selcher, "Brazilian-Argentine Relations in the 1980s: From Wary Rivalry to Friendly Competition," *Journal of Interamerican Studies* (1984), 27(2):25–53.

26. Ibid., p. 28.

27. The Brazilian military was reported to be reluctant to include defense cooperation on a formal treaty basis along with the other agreements signed between the two countries. Leonides Pires Gonçalves was quoted as saying: "that is not necessary because both militaries already cooperate closely." *Latin America: Southern Cone Report*, December 25, 1986, p. 1.

28. In 1983 the Argentine military made a surprise announcement that through a secret program they had mastered the technology for uranium enrichment and were building a plant. This puts nuclear weapons within easy reach (although the intention has been strongly denied). Presumably, the recent agreements are designed to dampen Brazilian suspicions and deter them from following a similar course.

29. Robert Keohane defines this as bringing the "actions of separate individ-

uals or organizations—which are not in pre-existent harmony—. . . into the conformity with one another through a process of policy coordination." "International Institutions: Two Approaches," *International Studies Quarterly* (1988), 32:380.

30. On the role of *técnicos* in Latin America, see P. C. Schmitter and E. B. Haas, *Mexico and Latin American Economic Integration,* Research Series No. 5 (Berkeley: Institute of International Studies, 1964).
31. For a detailed examination of Chile's diplomatic isolation, see Heraldo Muñoz, *Las relaciones exteriores del gobierno chileno* (Santiago: Ediciones del Ornitorrinca, 1986). For an interesting discussion of Paraguay's marginalization since 1985, see Virginia M. Bouvier, "Paraguay: Aislamiento internacional del regimen de Stroessner," *Cono Sur* (January–February 1989), 8(1):1–5.
32. One should perhaps not insist too much on the novelty of policy cooperation at lower levels since Argentina, Brazil, and Uruguay have gone democratic. On several occasions when the three were all authoritarian, evidence surfaced of exchanges of information and mutual favors among their respective intelligence and police agencies. All one can say with assurance is that since democratization, the substance of policy coordination has shifted to less violent matters and that its procedures have become more public.
33. Mario Reyes Chaves, "La cooperación económica bilateral en América Latina y su relación e influencia en la consecución del proceso de integracion regional," *Integración Latinoamericana* (July–August 1988), Tables 1–10. The president of Brazil put it even more dramatically: "In the last three years, we (Brazil and Argentina) have signed more agreements than in the 100 years of relations between the two countries," *La Nación,* November 11, 1988.
34. Which is not to say that the bilateral agreements have not had any effect. For example, when the Brazilians closed some gates on the Itaipú dam without proper warning, they promptly agreed to indemnify those Argentines downstream who were affected. *La Nación,* November 28, 1988. In previous years, an incident like that might have developed into a full-scale crisis, because the Argentine military was known to fear that Brazil might attempt to blackmail it by withholding water from the Rio de la Plata, which could make the port of Buenos Aires impracticable.
35. *Latin American Monitor* (November 1988), Vol. 5, No. 9.
36. This is especially telling in the cases of Argentina and Brazil. Despite the fact that both followed rather similar policy lines ("Plan Cruzado" and "Plan Austral") and despite *técnicos* in the two countries who knew each other well, it has proved impossible for the two countries to come up with a common position. According to Luiz Carlos Bresser Perreira, a secret plan for a coordinated suspension of interest payments had been worked out with Argentina when he was Brazilian Minister of Finance in 1987, but it fell through when he left the government. His Argentine

counterparts, Mario Brodersohn and Juan Sourrouille, have denied that any such agreement existed. *Veja,* November 16, 1988.

37. For the text of the *Ata,* as well as an early (and critical) analysis of the Argentine–Brazilian integration effort, see Renato Baumann and Juan Carlos Lerda, eds., *Brasil-Argentina-Uruguai: A Integração em Debate* (Brasilia: Editora Marco Zero, 1987). The citation is from p. 154.
38. Ibid., p. 153.
39. Eduardo Gana B., "Tendencias en la integración latinoamericana: el caso de Argentina y Brasil," *Cono Sur* (January–February 1988), 7(1):5–9.
40. Despite its title, Marcos Kaplan, *Democratización, Desarrollo Nacional e Integración Regional de América Latina* (San José: Centro Interamericano de Asesoria y Promoción Electoral, 1987) contains very little on this subject.
41. For an analysis of its peculiar pattern of institutional growth, see my "Central American Integration: Spill-Over, Spill-Around or Encapsulation?" *Journal of Common Market Studies* (September 1970), 9(1):1–48.
42. For a treatment of LAFTA in its early phase, see E. B Haas and P. C. Schmitter, *The Politics of Economics in Latin American Regionalism* (Denver: University of Denver, Monograph Series in World Affairs, Vol. 3, No. 2, 1965–1966).
43. Michael Anderson, "Tipos de cambio bilaterales y comercio intrarregional," *Integración Latinoamericana* (March 1985), 99:3–17.
44. Augusto Aninat del Solar, "Las modalidades de complementación industrial en la integración económica regional: experiencias y proposiciones," *Integración Lationoamericana* (July 1986), 36:15. This author concludes that, after six years, LAIA/ALADI has produced "neither great benefits nor great costs"! p. 17.
45. Articles 1 and 24, Treaty of Montevideo (1980).
46. *The Latin American Integration Process in 1980* (Buenos Aires: INTAL, 1981), p. 41.
47. *La Nación,* December 5, 1988. Also as reported in *The Financial Times,* December 1, 1988.
48. Ibid.
49. One commentator put it even more strongly: "One observation which imposes itself when examining the documents of Brazilian–Argentine integration is the attention paid *not* to create an institutional infrastructure for integration. . . . The refusal to create a bureaucratic complex is clear and understandable; nevertheless, the poverty of the institutional infrastructure could come to prejudice the dynamics of the integration process." Neantro Saavedra-Rivano, "A integraçao económica brasileiro-argentina no contexto do cooperaçao económica sul-sul," in Baumann and Lerda, eds., Brasil-*Argentina-Uruguai,* p. 75.
50. See Felix Peña, "Deuda, ajuste y democracia: un nuevo impulso para la integración de América Latina?" *Integración Latinoamericana* (January–February 1986), 108:3–7 for the most perceptive analysis of this new situation.
51. On the limits imposed by the logic of bilateral equilibria, see Carlos

Palacios Maldonaldo, "Integración economica latinoamericana: los resultados de la balanza comercial intrarregional y la distribución de benefícios," *Integración Latinoamericana* (June 1986), 113:27–39.

52. This has already created some preoccupation. In a joint communique, an Argentine–Brazilian Working Group declared the "great worry of both governments concerning the . . . bilateral commercial deficit that afflicts Argentina, given that the two countries base their accords on the equitable division of costs and benefits." *Integración Latinoamericana*, (September 1988), 138:67.

53. Philippe C. Schmitter, "Intercambio, poder y lealtad en la integración internacional: nuevas perspectivas de teoria y medición", *Integración Latinoamericana* (January–February 1977), 10:5–28.

54. Eduardo Basualdo and Caludio Lozano, "Integración argentino-brasileña: una crítica básica", *Cono Sur* (October–December 1986), 5(5):6.

55. Terry Karl, "Hegemons and Political Entrepreneurs: Dependence, Democratization, and Cooperation in the Americas," paper presented at the Seminar on "The New Interdependence in the Americas," The Americas Program, Stanford University, September 21, 1989.

56. The principal line of divergence among contemporary Latin American democracies is likely to be between what for lack of a better term I would call "class democracies" and "populist democracies." The former will be rooted in competition between coalitions of social groups that are regularly occupied and self-organized; the latter will be constituted around a single party movement that aspires to dominance on the basis of its appeal to an undifferentiated mass of voters, many of whom are marginally employed—if employed at all.

   The recent Argentine elections were structured along these lines, as will be the Brazilian ones. Listen, for example, to what the populist candidate in Argentina, Carlos Saul Menem, had to say about regional integration: "We want to create a united Latin America, as you have with the European Community. We've already made strides with Brazil and Uruguay, *and we want to do the same with Chile, Paraguay or with Russia,* with which we have very good relations. There are two important principles in international affairs: self-determination and non-interference in the internal affairs of another country. Our interest is to do business with everyone" (my emphasis). Interview in *The Financial Times,* November 28, 1988. Imagine, for a moment, the triumph of that (contradictory) attitude in the Argentine elections and in neighboring Brazil, and the precariousness of what has so far been accomplished in the *Cono Sur* becomes readily apparent.

4

SEASONS OF PEACE: PROGRESS IN POSTWAR INTERNATIONAL SECURITY

Emanuel Adler

"A SEASON OF PEACE. WARMING THE WORLD"

Suddenly, a season of peace seems to be warming the world.[1]

Such a lengthy period of peace among the most powerful states is unprecedented.[2]

As a form of activity, war in the developed world may be following once-fashionable dueling into obsolescence: the perceived wisdom, value, and efficacy of war may have moved gradually toward terminal disrepute.[3]

The preceding contemporary statements suggest and reflect this essay's main argument that since the end of World War II an increasingly large number of nation-states, including the superpowers, have fallen into a "peace trap," wherein the expected utility from peace has outweighed the expected utility from war, including a victorious war.[4] This peace trap, which has led to an unprecedented "season of peace" *in the developed world*, has resulted from a gradual devaluation of war in increasingly larger parts of the globe as well as from changes in expectations of the outcome and efficacy of war and of cooperation with the adversary, following the introduction of nuclear weapons to the world scene.

Certainly the community of nations has not reached a "perpetual peace,"[5] and probably never will, and the problems of war, justice, and freedom clearly have yet to be solved. The United States (U.S.) and the Soviet Union (U.S.S.R), have still to settle political and ideological differences; inadvertent and unpremeditated nuclear war is not impossible, and new conflicts and military violence can still occur in Eastern Europe. Many Third World nations, still involved in the painful processes of nation building, modernization, and border adjustments, have not given up war and are using dreadful weapons, such as chemical weapons. Therefore, war continues to take a very large toll on human life and well-being; only minimalist progress in international security is possible under these conditions.[6]

Even without major structural changes in the nature of the actors that make up the international system—primarily nation-states—without changes in the distribution of power, and with political and ideological conflicts remaining unresolved, nation-states can still make minimalist progress in international security by arriving at a shared preference for peace over war, which does not change with increased opportunities to win a war.

Since the end of World War II such progress has occurred because the great powers have reevaluated their national interests and—taking all factors into consideration, such as the chances of winning a war, or risks to core values other than security—have eschewed the initiation of limited or all-out nuclear war, avoided the use of conventional forces in quantities and configurations that might have led to nuclear war, and increasingly eluded international crises that might have raised markedly the danger of unpremeditated or accidental war.

Progress in international security, therefore, should be measured neither against an abstract and utopian idea of global peace brought about by one disarmament stroke nor against the notion that nuclear weapons can do away with the problem of war and injustice in only a couple of generations,[7] but against what could (or even should) have happened between two superpowers, armed to the teeth with nuclear and conventional weapons and divided by irreconcilable differences, but did not. Why, given all the opportunities for war since World War II, has it not happened so far?[8]

International Security

To understand what progress in international security means, we must first define international security, an essentially contested concept.[9] We have traditionally not paid sufficient attention to the complexity of this concept; we have understood its causes and effects poorly, and we have measured it inadequately by dealing only with tangible variables, such as military hardware and money. Here I will attempt to develop a working definition of international security that will be useful for discussing the notion of progress. Such a definition will include the linkage between international security and other values[10]—such as individual security, freedom from probable death or from the threat of nuclear war, and material welfare—and to the trade-offs between security and these values.

Webster's Collegiate Dictionary defines security as the "quality or state of being secure," in which there is "freedom from danger," "freedom from fear or anxiety," or "freedom from want or depriva-tion."[11] Some of these concepts, such as anxiety and fear, are murky and difficult to measure. Yet this definition suggests that interna-tional security can be seen as a systemic state, condition, or quality, characterized by a relative freedom from major war.

We can say that a systemic freedom from, or a low threat of, major nuclear or conventional war has been achieved when great powers perceive a low reciprocal threat to each other's core values and when avoiding war does not come at the expense of sacrificing those val-ues. As a systemic quality, the enhancement of international security is directly proportional to the relaxation, or at least the reduction, of the great powers' security dilemma.[12]

Several important assumptions follow from this definition. First, the most powerful countries determine the extent of international security or insecurity.[13] A decrease in the reciprocal threat to their core values would tend to lead to a decrease in the threat to core values experienced by other states. Directly, it would tend to dimin-ish the threat to other nations from the superpowers' weapons and actions. Indirectly, it might create favorable conditions for the settle-ment of regional wars and disputes that may have been affected, or even fueled in part, by intense superpower competition. Indeed, the lower the reciprocal threat to core values among the superpowers, the more they themselves can play an active role in settling such disputes.

Second, international security is a collective subjective condition or quality, since the perceivers are mainly political, military, media, and scientific–technological elites. A reciprocal low threat to core values can result only from interpretations of the reasons for the existence of weapons and of the nature of the threat. International security arises therefore from a collective interpretation of what constitutes a threat to national security. The meaning and interpretation of international security and progress in international security can be understood only within the context of historical, technological, political, economic, and social forces of a particular era or generation.

For example, both France and Great Britain have nuclear weapons that could destroy each other. Neither the French nor the English however, perceive threats from each other's weapons, nor do they interpret each other's actions as reflecting hostile intentions. In other words, they both share stable expectations of peace, which have been created by historical circumstances and are being enhanced by similar values. Taking everything into consideration, France and Great Britain, in spite of their nuclear weapons, perceive very low reciprocal threats to each other's core values.

Third, disarmament in itself is not a sufficient condition for international security. Those who argue for disarmament without international security, although well intended, place the cart before the horse. As long as we remain organized into sovereign nation-states, the elimination of weapons without the elimination of the grievances that lead to their production will only tend to increase insecurity because of the long-run uncertainty about relative gains from disarmament[14] and because of incentives to cheat, deceive, and conceal. Only after some measure of international security has been achieved can disarmament begin; that is, only when nations come to perceive that weapons are no longer needed, that they have become obsolete and thus wasteful, are they ready to start to disarm in kind.

Fourth, international security cannot mean merely the aggregation of the national security of each of the great powers, nor is it predicated on the security of this or that major power. International security is a relational and systemic condition, achieved only by a *reciprocal* threat reduction. "Efforts to achieve security can become self-defeating, even if objectively successful, if their effect is to raise awareness of threats to such a pitch that felt insecurity is greater than before the measures were undertaken."[15]

Progress in International Security

Increasing the systemic freedom from nuclear or major conventional war is progressive because it reduces threats to the personal security, life, and well-being of individuals, regardless of their nationality. Although individuals may be killed, injured, and impoverished and their freedom and human rights threatened by regional or local wars, drug traffic, the interruption to the flow of critically needed resources, epidemics, and drastic deteriorations of environmental quality, there is probably no greater threat to the security of individuals than nuclear war or conventional war that could lead to nuclear war.

Actions required to deter or win a nuclear war, or to be prepared to win one, can also exert a heavy toll on the physical welfare of individuals around the globe, whether through harm to the global physical environment or through taxing the economic welfare. Progress in international security will take place only when avoiding nuclear war does not come at the expense of human welfare and human rights.

Substantive progress in international security refers to a durable quality or condition in international life in which security is enhanced over time across national borders without creating an unbearable harm to other values and human interests. Instrumental progress refers to international security regimes or other international cooperative frameworks and institutional structures that nation-states jointly create as a means of dealing with their joint security problems that cannot be solved solely at the national level because of their nature and scope. Achievement of instrumental progress, such as the creation of an international organization or the signing of an arms-control treaty, however, does not guarantee that the problems will be solved or, more important, that human interests across borders will be enhanced in the process.

Substantive progress in international security may be achieved in any of three ways. First, a structural transformation may take place, where the system becomes less anarchic because of what Robert Gilpin has called a "systems" change, involving a major change in its character, or because the system undergoes a "systemic change," involving a change in its governance.[16] In this case, the lowering of a systemic threat of war is driven by structural change. For example, a world government may evolve that could seemingly impose peace, while punishing deviant behavior. On the other hand, a significant redistribution of power in the system may help bring about progress in international security by creating opportunities for nation-states to leave the power politics game.

Second, states at war with each other, or experiencing a very high reciprocal threat of war because of exhaustion and mutual persuasion, because of the outcomes of war, or because of the development of common beliefs and goals, may reduce the reciprocal threat through a political settlement of their mutual problems and grievances. In the absence of structural or lasting cognitive changes, however, a systemic low threat of great war resulting from a political settlement would be only temporary and could be shattered by the development of new problems, interests, and grievances.

Third, without structural changes and with political and ideological conflicts unresolved, progress in international security may take place if changed values and expectations lead to a reduction of the expected utility of war. A higher expected utility from peace than from war may lead nations to reevaluate their national interest in such a way that national goals likely to increase the probabilities of war that have been followed as a matter of course in the past, such as military intervention, territorial expansion, and ideological supremacy, are downgraded in the hierarchy of values and goals. Nations may begin to consider, for the sake of their national interest, alternative ways of competing and of enhancing their power.

Thus, to the extent that nations are jointly discouraged from going to war by memories of the tremendous costs of past wars and the expectation of even higher costs of future wars, and to the extent that they raise the value of present and *future* modernization and economic strength, which would be shattered by total war, they can be expected to value peace above national interests that involve a high risk of war. They can then be expected to change foreign policy goals and means in ways that would tend to lower the reciprocal threat to core values, without increasing immensely the costs to other values.

PROGRESSIVE SEASONS OF INTERNATIONAL SECURITY

The state, condition, or quality of international security can be arranged on a scale of progressive degrees, ranging from minimalist to maximalist. I call the different categories "seasons" in order to dispel the idea that progress, as in the Enlightenment view,[17] is a permanent, inexorable, and irreversible process toward "the better." Seasons of progress mean that increasingly progressive stages build on the conditions of previous stages, but there is no deterministic road toward "the better," and any condition could be scaled down, reversed, lost, even lost forever were a nuclear war to take place. Through the use of the season concept, I want also to convey that although certain regions of the globe may be experiencing a season of progress, others may not.

A scale of progressive states serves as a heuristic device by which to measure, albeit in a very rudimentary and qualitative way, the extent of international security. The primary condition necessary for each of these seasons to take place, of course, is the absence of total war. The seasons are differentiated and arranged according to the condition and the quality of peace (or of the absence of war). Seasons of international security are therefore graded according to the stability of expectations of peace and the degree of mutual predictability of behavior, which I assess in terms of the degree of commonality of values—the minimum being agreement over the value of peace (or the negative value of war); the extent of communication and diplomatic interaction; the degree of information exchange and multiplicity of communication channels; the extent to which the long-range future is taken into account by both sides when making security policy; and the extent of each power's autonomy in making security decisions.

Seasons of international security are rated therefore by the degree of complex interdependence[18] between the major powers, the extent to which they are aware of and understand their tightly coupled security systems and processes, and most important, the degree of security policy cooperation,[19] coordination, and integration that results from this awareness and understanding. The quality of the seasons can also be judged by their extent and duration—the more widespread and permanent international security becomes, the closer we get to maximalist progress.

Degrees and scope of instrumental progress, such as arms-control and disarmament agreements, are also a useful measure of the quality of the seasons, because they indicate the degree of preference for stability and peace over war, and to some extent also express the degree of the powers' confidence of avoiding nuclear war. From this perspective, general disarmament would tend to indicate a very low reciprocal threat to core values.

The first three seasons—"general stability," "common security," and "concert"—can be arrived at without systemic structural change, but behavioral changes alone will not suffice for the seasons of "pluralistic security community" and "peace."

1. The least ambitious and truly minimalist season may arrive when the rewards of peace are so high and the expected utility of war so low that "taking all potential benefits, costs, and risks into account [nation-states] greatly prefer peace to war—in the extreme, even to a victorious war—whether crisis stability exists or not."[20] This condition, which John Mueller has called "general stability," can be arrived at when values and expectations of war and peace change due to learning and the reevaluation of the national interest.

General stability can therefore be characterized by the absence of a great war and by changes in international behavior away from foreign policies that entail a high risk of war and toward those aimed at preventing a major war. Independent nation-states may continue to compete for power, authority, prestige, and influence in the international system, but competition stops short of war or of situations that can make war more likely. Instrumental progress may take place to help control weapon systems and expectations and to help sustain preferences of peace. As a result, tacit and explicit rules of the game may be created, such as mutual respect for spheres of influence, a calculated avoidance of direct military encounters, prudent and self-restrained behavior, toleration for awkward arrangements (such as was the Berlin Wall), and abstention from directly undermining each other's leadership.[21]

We should be careful, however, not to confuse general stability with mere prudential behavior arising from a situation of nuclear deterrence. In a season of general stability, nation-states refrain from going to war because of the threat of the adversary's weapons of massive destruction and because they are equally motivated by the promise of peace. On the other hand, since the powers may not actually have given up their quest for military superiority, this season can turn out to be ephemeral. General stability does not mean that all nations have given up war or that other kinds of violent international behavior, such as terrorism, have ceased. Nor does it require high levels of policy cooperation, integration, and coordination; an extensive amount of information exchange; or the sharing of political, economic, and social values.

2. *Common security* is a season of international progress in which

the conditions and qualities of general stability are met and security interdependence has been mutually perceived to such a degree that states develop interdependent security policies and coordinate them to a greater extent than before. Security interdependence exists when one or several powers become dependent in some way on other powers to assure or improve some aspect of their overall security and when unilateral independent moves may not be adequate to deal with a threat to national security.[22]

A season of common security therefore arrives when major powers abandon their search for decisive military superiority and their illusion that one power can "exercise decisive influence over the whole system."[23] They must then reevaluate their own national security in such a way as to continually take into account the security of their neighbor or opponent. "In short, one can no longer be secure from one another, but only with one another."[24]

We should be careful not to define security interdependence from a narrow technological perspective. Nuclear weapons have made the superpowers increasingly dependent on each other's military strategies and have created such a sense of vulnerability that neither superpower can rely upon its own defenses for security.[25] Yet technological interdependence may not be sufficient to bring about a season of common security because the shared common interest to avoid a nuclear war that results from mutual vulnerability can be competitively exploited, as avoiding nuclear war requires only that one side make concessions.[26]

Only when the superpowers come to realize that they cannot shift the burden of avoiding mutual destruction to the other side does the awareness of security interdependence set in, and with it the opportunity to advance toward a season of common security. This realization can come about because of learning, when the sides discover that technological change has its limits or that technology breeds its own obsolescence through action–reaction processes; when they discover domestic political and economic constraints they were not aware of before; or when they become aware of the existence of common threats to their mutual security (e.g., a sharp deterioration of the global physical environment). Such awareness can be asymmetrical, and an agenda for a common security approach can first be proposed by a single power.

A mutual awareness of security interdependence will most likely be expressed by security policies with a long-run perspective. A perception or expectation of secular time,[27] as John Ruggie has called the long-run social time perspective, may be arrived at by means of increased consensus about the political effects of nuclear weapons and other technological changes and also may be determined in part by domestic needs. Superpowers that look inward and set goals of economic development or of industrial revitalization (which can take dozens of years to be realized) may be forced to look at their security with the very long run in mind.

This awareness and time perspective of security must be accompanied by reassurances arising from the achievement of political agreements over increasingly interdependent regional and global issues. A season of common security is thus incompatible with a cold war and can develop only when a season of general stability has helped to create some shared perception of international security.

Instrumental progress can help expedite and formalize changes toward a season of common security. It may entail broader cooperation regarding (1) the Third World and global problems; (2) economic and technological cooperation; (3) the creation of bilateral institutions for gathering, exchanging, and forecasting information; and (4) the creation of international regimes to control technologies that raise optimism regarding the prospects of winning a nuclear war.

3. A *concert*, even if it does not aim to achieve a definitive settlement of disputes, replaces the balance of power system, which is war-prone, with a system based on the ability and willingness of the great powers to manage change peacefully by means of diplomacy and normative behavior. From 1815 to 1854, European leaders enacted such a system. Creating a great power tutelage over the rest of Europe, the concert brought about a "sense of security, a respect for the public law of Europe, a recognition of a commonly accepted standard of conduct, and a willingness to keep one's own conduct within those limits, that was unknown both to earlier and to later periods."[28]

In the future, a season of concert may come about if the great powers, having agreed on common norms and practices and, perceiving a threat to their status and authority from rising economic and military powers, choose to concertize their efforts to manage change, while allowing the system's structure to change only in an incremental way. The creation of a concert can also be hastened by global problems that the great powers confront and try to manage together in a season of common security. Controlling events in the Third World is another incentive for creating a concert. A concert would therefore imply not only a common reaction to security, economic, and technological interdependence, but also a change of attitudes and behavior toward the Third World and toward global organizations that would be empowered by the great powers to implement policies aimed at solving global problems. A concert would also imply that the great powers, in order to take care of environmental crises jointly, nuclear accidents, nuclear proliferation, drugs, terrorism, Third World underdevelopment, poverty, hunger, and the management of the seas and space, would have to deepen their common information gathering, sharing, and forecasting measures; increase their policy coordination; and set common policy-planning facilities to implement joint policies.

A season of concert would therefore entail a much tighter level of security policy cooperation, coordination, and integration. It would require the institutionalization of summitry and policy consultation, and most important, it would entail a much more developed consciousness about the sharing of a common civilization and the use of a common language of international politics. In other words, although in a concert the great powers are not required to agree on economic, social, and political values across the board, they are nevertheless required to share values, common understandings, and interests about the Third World, about the management of global problems, and about common acceptable behavior in spheres of influence.

4. *A pluralistic security community* is integrated to the point that there exists between the units "dependable expectations of peaceful change."[29] It is a community of nations that have produced something close to an "informal government to ensure peaceful change without subordinating all the differences in values, culture, and the like that make the separate units distinctively free and independent."[30] As such, a pluralistic security community is something truly new under the sun.[31]

According to Deutsch, two conditions are necessary for a security community to take hold: a compatibility of political values derived from common political institutions and communication that reflects a "we-feeling" among the members of a community.[32] Both conditions derive their significance not only from economic interdependencies and from the spillover of functional-technical problems to the political realm,[33] but also from the sharing of political values, first and foremost democracy, which inhibits nations from using force against each other.[34]

Western European nations are now experiencing something close to a season of pluralistic security community. Not only have they gotten themselves out of the cycle of war, but they now experience very low reciprocal threats from each other's capabilities and suspect no bad intentions. Expectations of peace are now very stable in Western Europe, and the human interest has been enhanced across national borders, borders that seem to be becoming more invisible, as Europeans rush toward comprehensive market integration in 1992 and toward at least partial political integration in the long run. Furthermore, the increasing democratization of Eastern European nations creates an opportunity for this economic and security community to be broadened in the forseeable future.

A pluralistic security community creates a model that supposedly other regions may replicate or, even more ambitiously, a model for a global security community. The adoption of the European model of security community by other regions of the world is not devoid of large problems, but it is feasible without major transformations in the international system. A global security community, of which the superpowers would be a part, however, lies on the maximalist side of the progressive spectrum, and may not happen without major structural changes in the balance of power and in the nature of the system's actors. If only because of the need for such a structural transformation to take place, not to mention the need for Third World countries to adopt democratic and other Western values, the concept of a global security community is from the point of view of our generation a utopian dream.

5. In a season of *peace*, an even more utopian concept, stable expectations of peace are rooted in an informal world community, or even in a more formal federation of republics, as Kant envisioned in Perpetual Peace.[35] The changes contemplated by world government enthusiasts, and Kant, are so fundamental that we may well equate the concepts of world government and world federation to the most

maximalist ideas of progress in international security. "Perpetual peace" is a utopian, almost perfect state, at odds with the fact that humans are an imperfect breed.

SUBSTANTIVE PROGRESS IN POSTWAR INTERNATIONAL SECURITY

General Stability

The most profound change in the field of international security in the last four decades has been neither the Cold War nor its apparent conclusion, but learning to compete, adapt, and change without a major war. The post–World War II era thus has increasingly been characterized by a season of general stability; the superpowers have avoided resorting to nuclear or to major conventional war and since the early 1960s (with the possible exception of the 1973 Yom Kippur War) have avoided involvement in international crises and in direct confrontations that might have led to nuclear war. General stability has not been without a price, however, as individuals across national borders still live with the constant threat of nuclear war[36] and are still learning the hard way about the futility of even limited wars, such as those in Vietnam and Afghanistan.

John Mueller and Robert Jervis share the proposition that the likely gains from war are now relatively low and that the situation is "generally stable."[37] Furthermore, Jervis agrees with Mueller's proposition that the "set of transformations that go under the heading of 'modernization' have not only increased the costs of war, but have created alternative paths to established goals, and, more profoundly, have altered values in ways that make peace more likely."[38]

Where Mueller and Jervis disagree, however, is on the role nuclear weapons have played in bringing about general stability. Mueller has tried to show that general stability in the post–World War II era resulted from changes in economic conditions and values about peace and war, which had *nothing* to do with the invention of nuclear weapons. Whether nuclear or conventional, Mueller argues, war has become so intolerably costly, unwise, futile, and debased; the memories of World War II are still so deeply rooted with us; the fear of escalation is so pervasive, and satisfaction with the status quo so evident, that war, even a victorious war, is a course of action the superpowers very much wish to avoid.[39]

Jervis, on the other hand, proposes that general stability resulted because (1) in contrast to a conventional war, the devastation of an all-out nuclear war would be unimaginably enormous; (2) in a nuclear war neither side, or for that matter civilization, may be spared from devastation (he reminds us that the winners of World War II were not devastated); and (3) the devastation could occur quickly, within a matter of days or even hours.[40] If I read Jervis right, he seems to be arguing that nuclear weapons have generated a new set of expectations about war that have made war less likely.

I believe that both Mueller and Jervis are right: that international insecurity has decreased since World War II, first because of a change in values about peace and war whose origins go back many decades before the invention of nuclear weapons, and, second, because the nuclear revolution has helped to alter expectations of peace and war, and expectations of cooperation with the adversary.

International structure, at the same time, created a niche within which values and expectations could evolve. From this perspective, the bipolar structure that took shape at the end of the war was a contextual variable; it created structural opportunities for a change in values and expectations. It did not *cause* the change. As Waltz himself argued: "Structure . . . does not by any means explain everything. . . . States armed with nuclear weapons may have stronger incentives [read: preferences] to avoid war than states armed conventionally. . . . Causes at both the national and the international level make the world more or less peaceful and stable."[41]

Values and the "Debellation" of Nations. If we define interests as a "disciplined understanding of what it takes to advance one's power, influence, and wealth,"[42] then it follows that a change in such understanding can lead to a change in the national interest. Furthermore, the notion of interest depends on an understanding of what is needed and which needs should be promoted to the level of interest. A value change,[43] whether abrupt or incremental, can therefore lead to changes in national interests in regard to war as a means of attaining goals (a change in instrumental or means values) and in regard to the pursuit of goals that are likely to produce war (a change in end values).

One of the reasons for the arrival of a progressive season in international security after World War II was a change in values wherein some nations, using a term coined by Michael Howard, have become "debelled" (from the word *bellicism*) and, taking everything else into consideration, have come to prefer peace more than war. Or in the words of F. H. Hinsley, some nations "had so far altered in themselves and in their relation to the given conditions [mainly modernization] that war had since occurred only when the ability to control these conditions had been abandoned."[44]

Thus, at least since the end of World War I and certainly after World War II, a number of nations, many of them the most powerful (and the formerly most powerful) in the world, have removed themselves from the cycle of major wars and have developed a new national interest, namely, the prevention of war. This national interest, in turn, has generated new foreign policy goals and a set of diplomatic and technical means to prevent war. Because of the reevaluation of their national interest, these nations are devoting a large proportion of their resources and political attention to the prevention of war, and thus are reversing the Clausewitzian maxim that war is a means of diplomacy. Instead, diplomacy has now become the means for preventing war.

To understand the change that has taken place since World War I, one must appreciate the "degree of *bellicism* in European society at that time, especially in Central Europe; a bellicism that accounts not only for the demonstrations of passionate joy that greeted the outbreak of war but sustained the peoples of Europe uncomplainingly through years of hardship and suffering."[45] If before World War I war was "almost universally considered an acceptable, perhaps an inevitable and for many people a desirable way of settling international differences,"[46] after the war a revulsion against war took hold and so did and "overwhelming, and so far permanent, if not wholly successful, desire to prevent similar wars from taking place."[47]

Seen in this light, World War II appears not as one more case of total war in the inevitable struggle for power, but as a terrible failure of the international community to stop the "only person left in Europe who was willing to risk another total war."[48] World War II was exceptional because Hitler actually *wanted* war and was willing "to chance an enormously destructive war in order to dominate the world."[49] But as Jervis points out, this argument about Hitler does not mean that another Hitler may not arise again. It does mean that "we should not let either our theories or our policies be dominated by this possibility."[50] Indeed, much of the pessimistic views in the United States regarding the Soviet Union have sprung from intellectual and policy circles that tend to believe that, given an opportunity, *any* Soviet leader would risk war, even nuclear war, for the sake of world domination.[51]

It would be naive, plainly incorrect, and even dangerous, to argue that the superpowers have now abandoned the struggle for power, as Holland did in 1713 while still a powerful state and as other powers did later on.[52] It is less naive to argue that the beliefs about the necessity of struggle and about the inevitability of war are being questioned on both sides of the East–West divide and that changing values about peace and war are creating economic and technological alternative paths of competition and change. The enthusiasm for going to war[53] and the optimism of "winning," in the broad sense of the word, are receding proportionally to an increase in the valuation —for the sake of national interest—of economic and technological power.

But it is not only the memories of the past and a change in values about war that are forcing great powers away from war. The nuclear revolution has created nightmarish images of future wars that have helped to change expectations of war and have forced the superpowers to begin to "measure their power and interests by new criteria and, as well as wishing to avoid war, they have ceased to doubt their ability to avoid it."[54] Value change then was accompanied by a learning process about war and peace and about international cooperation for preventing war.

Expectations and the Nuclear Revolution. The impact of expectations on international conflict and cooperation has been more than amply demonstrated[55] but insufficiently analyzed, with the exception perhaps, of the work of Thomas Schelling and Robert Jervis.[56] An expectation can be described as an image of the future, bounded by what is physically, humanly, and socially possible. To expect is thus to imagine situations and events that this or that available act could make seem possible. "Through exercise of forethought, people motivate themselves and guide their actions anticipatorily. . . . By representing foreseeable outcomes symbolically,

people can convert future consequences into current motivators. . . .
Cognized futures thus become temporarily antecedent to actions."[57]

Two types of expectations are crucial for human behavior: expectations of outcome and of efficacy. An outcome expectation is defined as a "person's estimate that a given behavior will lead to certain outcomes." An efficacy expectation is the conviction that "one can successfully execute the behavior required to produce the outcomes." A person can believe that a particular action will lead to some defined outcome, but may also doubt that he/she can perform the act successfully.[58]

The nuclear revolution has been the most important factor leading incrementally to the transformation of outcome and efficacy expectations of war. Thus, the nuclear revolution has been a source of progressive change because it has robbed war of its contestlike character, in which powers experiencing differential or uneven power growth would go to war to determine which power would be the hegemon.[59] In other words, before the nuclear revolution neither powerful nations involved in a power context nor for that matter anyone else would "know" which power is the "strongest," without fighting a war. After the nuclear revolution, however, we "know." Says Nye:

> Imagine what would have happened if the statesmen who led the world into this century's first great conflagration in 1914 had possessed a crystal ball showing them the world of 1918. The leaders of 1914 expected a short, sharp war, followed by business as usual. One suspects that if the German Kaiser, the Russian Tsar and Austrian Emperor had seen a picture of 1918—with their thrones vacant, their empires destroyed—they would have drawn back from the brink of war that Summer. Today modern leaders know the horrible destruction that would result from any nuclear war.[60]

"Knowing" the outcome of nuclear war in advance, however, is not enough to prevent it, nor is it a sufficient condition for progress in international security. The reason is that given the lack of experience with nuclear war, and given that scientific knowledge about nuclear war is only partial and subject to all kinds of ideological interpretations,[61] American and Soviet elites may have concluded that the outcome of war may be manipulated, that if conditions x, y, and z are achieved, mutual obliteration may not be so certain. This is why progress in international security requires also a transformation of efficacy expectations of war; elites must expect no effective way (through technological wizardry or otherwise) to fight and win a nuclear war. Thus, the expectation of being in control must be, at least, challenged and, at best, debunked.[62]

Progress in international security has so far been minimalist if only because of the relative slowness with which efficacy expectations of war have changed in relation to the change of outcome expectations of war. For every individual arguing that nuclear weapons mean the loss of efficacy and control, another individual could point to the increasing accuracy of nuclear warheads and to shields in space as "proving" that, under certain conditions, nuclear war can still "deliver the goods." Indeed, one of the main obstacles for changing efficacy expectations of war has been the military system itself, which by definition cannot commit suicide by turning its back to what it has been trained to do—fighting and winning wars. Institutional constraints, therefore, may partly explain why military elites have had such difficulty escaping from a prenuclear revolution mentality.[63]

A third important expectation change arising from the nuclear revolution has been the development and strengthening of efficacy expectations of preventing war through cooperation. The more nuclear war was prevented by cautious behavior and cooperative measures, the more confident the superpowers became about their joint ability to avoid nuclear war. By learning how to cooperate in order to avoid nuclear war,[64] states became reassured about their diplomatic and other instrumental means for preventing war. At work here has been a self-fulfilling prophecy in that "believing that the peace could be maintained would make it more likely that the peace in fact would be kept. . . . War will be unavoidable only if decision makers believe it is unavoidable."[65] It follows that general stability is a season that must be nurtured and maintained by continuous diplomatic interaction, by socialization and information exchange.

While during the late 1970s and the first part of the 1980s efficacy expectations of cooperation were lowered and the reciprocal threat to core values increased, general stability did not come to an end, and neither side changed its basic preferences and expected utilities regarding peace and war. Indeed, in the last years, the trend has been reversed. This has been achieved, first, because of instrumental progress in the form of the 1987 INF arms-control treaty, whose main effect has been to increase efficacy expectations of cooperation. Also, the increasing realization by Americans that the maximalist idea of the Strategic Defense Initiative (SDI) was a pipe dream has helped to decrease efficacy expectations of war, which ran somewhat high in the first years of the Reagan administration. Moreso, the state of the Soviet economy and the high price that the Soviets had to pay both for their military intervention in Afghanistan and to catch up with America's SDI program have increased the new Soviet leadership's expected utility for peace. Finally, the recent revolutionary developments in the Soviet Union and Gorbachev's foreign policies, which have *de facto* ended the Cold War, have in a great measure decreased the expected utility of war.

Nuclear Deterrence and the Peace Trap. Since the 1950s the great powers have relied for their security, and that of their allies, on the threat of nuclear retaliation and on a commitment to launch an attack in defense of allies.[66] But although nuclear deterrence, as far as it tended to rely on threats alone, may have enhanced national security and may even have helped to maintain stability in the sense of dissuading the opponent from a first strike, it has not enhanced international security; if anything, it has helped to decrease it. Thus, there seems to be a nuclear deterrence–progress in international security paradox, wherein national security and stability are achieved at the expense of international security: The very threat of nuclear war that is designed to make deterrence work increases international insecurity.

This paradox is real, however, only to the extent that we assume a "constant level of hostility between adversaries, the expression of which is a function of the opportunity to act,"[67] and that we pay attention only to military values and capabilities. A notion of deterrence based on these assumptions has been found wanting by empirical research showing that (1) both the U.S. and the U.S.S.R., at different points in time, decided against war, "despite their expectation that the military balance, seen at the time as highly favorable to themselves, would worsen dramatically in the near future,"[68] and (2) the "principal incentive for aggressive foreign policy appears to be the state's own perceived vulnerabilities which lead its policy-makers to challenge an adversary even when external opportunity to act in the form of a vulnerable commitment is absent."[69] Thus, a "threat-only" notion of deterrence, with its exclusive reliance on military capabilities, may not only have been politically dangerous[70] but may have led to gratuitous, or unnecessarily high, levels of threats.

To the extent that we change our assumptions of deterrence to include the "peace trap," however, deterrence need not be incompatible with making progress in international security because

> deterrence prevails when the expected utility for peace outweighs the expected utility of war. In this sense a deterrence relationship exists not only between the US and the USSR, but also between the US and Canada, and between Bolivia and Pakistan. The usefulness of this approach is that it is not limited exclusively to military considerations, and that it comfortably incorporates such important deterring phenomena as satisfaction with the status quo, as well as the restraining effects of economics, morality, good will, inertia, international opinion, national self-image, etc. Thus it can deal with that multitude of cases in which a militarily superior power lives peacefully alongside an inferior one. The approach can also deal with those cases where a nation has become so distressed by the status quo that it starts a war even when it has little hope of military success.[71]

International insecurity has decreased and a season of general stability has taken hold, then, because the superpowers have been deterred not only by their threats and military capabilities, but also by their expectations of war. Furthermore, they have been mutually reassured through behavior that has carried the message of the promise of peace. Thus, although nuclear deterrence, as interpreted by elites in both superpowers, has tended to increase the threat to each other's values, the "peace trap" may have helped to dampen these threats to a level where a season of general stability could increasingly take hold.

It follows, then, that deterrence theory (and practice) should be expanded, to give promises and reassurances a larger weight. Indeed, a large amount of scholarship,[72] whose origins can be traced back to Schelling,[73] has made the point that promises and reassurances are at least as important as threats. I cannot improve on Jervis' statement that "whether a state will attack is a function not only of the payoffs of such action, but also of the value of the status quo and the expected value of a peaceful future; therefore, increasing these values can persuade a state not to attack."[74]

From a historical perspective we can argue that deterrence theory "has focused upon threats rather than promises for the understandable reason that the theorists were strongly influenced by the Cold

War image of acute international conflict, enhanced by the rapid growth of the strategic strike potential of the Soviet Union."[75] The détente period of the early 1970s did very little to change this approach to deterrence because threats had been designed so broadly that any challenge to the status quo would tend to bring frustration and a backlash.[76] This is indeed what happened in the late 1970s and early 1980s, when American elites and public opinion, interpreting Soviet armament and intervention policies as a challenge to the status quo, became frustrated, overreacted, and exaggerated the extent of the threat.[77] This behavior, in turn, obscured the fact that the situation was generally stable because neither side raised its expected utility from war.

The current situation, however, is very different. As George and Smoke wrote somewhat prophetically fifteen years ago, "in the post–Cold War era of less acute conflict, it would be appropriate for the theory to be extended."[78] The "post–Cold War era" is now, and the extension of deterrence to include the peace trap and the promise of peace is one of the most important intellectual tasks of our present time.

One way to start expanding the notion of deterrence is to reexamine the assumption about the "state of the world" on which deterrence has historically been based, namely, that the "principal communist powers perceive an interest in attacking or encroaching upon various nations or regions within which the United States has an interest in preserving self-determination."[79] Gorbachev's domestic and foreign policy reforms, the Soviet retreat from Afghanistan, far-reaching changes occurring in Eastern Europe, and increasing superpower cooperation in the Third World seem to require such a reevaluation of premises. Expansion of deterrence, would also require consideration of the role of changing values and expectations, questions of timing and cycles of conflict and cooperation; self-binding commitments;[80] notions of risk, including risks to be incurred for peace; and the pervasive effects of security interdependence on international security.

Toward a Season of Common Security?

A new constellation of forces, personalities, and events is creating a propensity for turning the season of general stability into a season of common security in the developed world. Propensities to be realized, however, must be nurtured, the forces at work must be strengthened, and some tough choices must be made. There is therefore no determined road toward a season of common security; there seem to be several contingent paths, and some are worse than others.

At the center of this new constellation of forces lies the Gorbachev revolution, which consists not only of Gorbachev's already instituted and still to be implemented domestic and foreign policy reforms but also of his "new thinking" about national and international security. Though most of the ideas on which this thinking is based were developed in the West in the late 1960s or the 1970s,[81] its newness arises from the fact that the leader of one of the two most powerful nations on earth has partly adopted them and created an international agenda for their implementation.

Three other major forces appear to be at play, creating an opportunity for a common security. First, it is becoming increasingly clear that the "leadership of each super-power is by now convinced that it cannot achieve strategic superiority over the other."[82] Second, an awareness of economic, technological, and security interdependence —whose sources can be traced back to economies becoming more interconnected than ever, to environemental crises and nuclear disasters, and to Third World problems affecting developed countries— seems to be on the rise and more than ever before to have caught the attention of Soviet leadership.

Third, the rise of new economic superpowers seems to be making the world increasingly multipolar, and the post–World War II era of international relations appears to be coming to an end. As Henry Kissinger recently stated:

> For the first time since World War I, it is possible to envisage a plan to reunite Europe with the consent of all its peoples. This could be coupled with the creation of a new security arrangement that could sharply reduce the armed camps that now confront each other in the center of Europe. In Asia too, a new equilibrium is emerging. And regional disputes could become more a matter of diplomatic and economic competition than military conflict.[83]

The winds of change have been blowing from East to West, however, because Soviet elites, perceiving their major threat to come from within rather than from without, had to persuade the West with words and deeds that it too can feel secure from without. Although it is true that many of Gorbachev's reforms have had a domestic content, purpose, and rationale, they could not have been proposed, let alone implemented, had it not been for the fact that the nuclear-armed Soviet Union was far less vulnerable; indeed, as noted, was not vulnerable at all in the traditional sense of the term, and Gorbachev and his colleagues appeared to be aware of the security that they enjoyed as the Brezhnev generation was not.[84] But Western elites, and most strikingly American elites, seemed to share with the Brezhnev generation a lack of awareness of the security they enjoyed. Gorbachev, however, had no time to lose and needed to persuade the West that it had *reasons* to feel secure.

Gorbachev has tried to convince the West by proposing revolutionary measures such as (1) deep reductions in nuclear weapons arsenals; (2) an Atlantic-to-the-Urals arms-reduction zone (an idea first introduced by the West with the aim of reducing imbalances and asymmetries in conventional forces in Europe by means of a Soviet reduction, rather than a Western buildup, which in turn implies legitimizing NATO's fears about the size, structure, and particularly the mode of deployment of Soviet conventional forces in Europe)[85]; (3) placing the Third World off-limits to superpower military intervention[86] (if only because of the cost incurred by the Soviets in their Third World adventures during the 1970s); and (4) upgrading the role of the United Nations and its peace-keeping operations and functional activities regarding Third World development and global problems.[87] Most of these proposals have yet to be implemented, and the superpowers have still to eliminate first-strike weapons that keep the threat of surprise attack relatively high. On the other hand, Gorbachev gave credence to some of his words by implementing symbolic unilateral disarmament actions and by releasing the Soviet grip on Eastern Europe.

At the intellectual root of Gorbachev's agenda was his "new understanding and redefinition of Soviet national security in the nuclear age, under conditions of Soviet–American strategic parity"[88] and an implicit, and sometimes even explicit, invitation to the West to redefine national security likewise. This redefined concept of national security is based on the premise that any nuclear buildup beyond mutual assured destruction (MAD) is meaningless, "and that a much lower level of nuclear weapons . . . will lessen the existing psychological tensions, diminish the danger of an accidental nuclear strike, and increase the security of both super-powers and the world."[89]

The most important component of the redefined concept of national security and the idea more directly related to progress, however, is that of common security:

> The idea behind the concept of "common security" is as simple as it is revolutionary. It proclaims that US reactions to perceptions of military insecurity endanger Soviet military security and consequently do not serve Soviet interests. Soviet reactions to perceptions of military insecurity have the same negative implications for US interests. Therefore, each side must seriously consider the probable impact of its defence policy on the other side—any build-up of military power will likely initiate an arms-race cycle that in the end will not increase the security of either side. . . . If the conceptual modification is implemented in practical Soviet defense policies its importance will be immense.[90]

The "discovery" by Gorbachev of global interdependence is not unrelated to the concept of a common security, and it is certainly an important building block of his reinterpretation of national security. Even ten years ago interdependence was a bad word in the Soviet Union, as it was associated with a capitalist market-oriented approach. There is growing evidence to suggest, however, that the new Soviet leadership is much more aware of the so-called Third Industrial Revolution and the pattern of globalization of national economies.[91] Furthermore, environmental problems, nuclear accidents, nuclear proliferation, and global epidemics, like AIDS, are creating mutual vulnerabilities that can be taken care of only by cooperative action. The Soviets seem to have recognized this point to such an extent that the notion of interdependence "is being acclaimed so frequently that one would think that Moscow invented the concept."[92]

The impact of interdependence awareness on the concept of a common security is simple: " 'interdependence' is conducive to a new way of thinking about international phenomena that stresses shared interests and ceases to view international relations as a 'zero-sum' game."[93] Alas! it took the Soviets thirty years to discover Thomas Schelling; their "discovery" should be welcomed, however, because from a Soviet perspective Gorbachev's redefinition of national security amounts to a true case of cause–effect reevaluation and learning.[94]

Are Americans ready to move toward a season of common security? If recent opinion polls provide any criterion of the American mood, then the answer is "cautiously ready." Daniel Yankelovich and Richard Smoke, who analyzed the results of two major studies of American public opinion, reported that the "current attitude of Americans toward the Soviet Union is different from anything we have seen in forty years. It is not the troubled mood of recent years, of worry about nuclear war."[95] We should be careful, however, when assessing long-range changes from this data, because American attitudes about nuclear issues have been set pretty much from the beginning of the nuclear age, and seem to have changed in a cyclical pattern.[96]

It is instructive (including as an indication of changing expectations of war) to take a look at some of the fundamental changes the polls are reflecting. In 1987 three times as many Americans as in 1980 thought the U.S. should reduce tensions with the Soviets rather than get tough.[97] Looking into the twenty-first century, Americans now prefer a future of cooperative problem solving to one of concentrating on a North American defense by a margin of 9 to 1.[98] In addition, the public increasingly believes that important security problems are no longer East–West in nature but global and that American strength is being challenged by new competitors from a different part of the world; in March 1988, 48 percent of the American public thought the U.S. should focus on terrorism and economic competition.[99]

The American public seems firmly convinced that Gorbachev means it when he says he too wants to reduce the nuclear threat,[100] and the number of Americans that now expect a nuclear war in the next twenty-five years has fallen from 44 percent in October 1987 to 33 percent in March 1988.[101] In 1987 three times as many Americans thought a nuclear war would lead to the mutual devastation of the U.S. and the Soviet Union as had thought so in 1955.[102] And Americans, although uneasy about the Soviets' nuclear advantages, now see the U.S. and the U.S.S.R. to be about equal in nuclear weapons[103] and do not support nuclear superiority. Only 35 percent of 257 generals and admirals polled by Gallup in 1984 felt the U.S. should aim for military superiority.[104]

INSTRUMENTAL PROGRESS IN POSTWAR
INTERNATIONAL SECURITY

By helping to create or to strengthen efficacy expectations of cooperation (i.e., by instilling confidence in the minds of political elites that both the enhancement of national security and the prevention of war can be achieved through cooperative measures), instrumental progress may have helped to sustain not only nuclear deterrence but the season of general stability as well. It may also have helped to enhance human interests in a more direct way, if international agreements, institutions, and injunctions, intentionally or unintentionally, helped produce across national borders a cleaner environment, better health prospects, and the enhancement of economic welfare.

Since World War II, instrumental progress resulted from arms-control treaties, confidence-building measures, and a set of broad and specific injunctions regarding arms-race stability, nuclear proliferation, and the prevention of accidental nuclear war. Instrumental progress in international security can thus be equated to making progress in setting security regimes.[105] Some scholars have dismissed the application of the regime concept to international security, arguing that the anarchic characteristics of this issue area tend to lower incentives for cooperation and regime building.[106] Nye, on the other hand, has shown that once we take the set of agreements, injunctions, and institutions as forming not just one comprehensive security regime but an incomplete mosaic of partial security regimes,[107] the notion of security regimes makes sense.

Indeed, since the late 1950s more than a dozen bilateral and multilateral agreements have helped to constrain short-range, and even in some cases long-range, security interests, although with mixed results. For example, the "SALT agreements formed a partial security regime based on the acceptance of parity, recognition of mutual vulnerability, and agreement to limit both offense and defense. . . . Both sides redefined their short-run interest by adhering to rules . . . and by dismantling nuclear systems that exceeded treaty restraints."[108]

These partial security regimes have led to the creation of understandings about what it takes to negotiate security agreements and what type of norms and rules can be applied and how. In some cases they have helped to institutionalize rules of reciprocity, limit competition, transfer information needed to comply with the agreements, and enhance crisis stability by generating somewhat more stable expectations, including the expectation that diplomacy and negotiations should not be interrupted in the event of international crises. Taken together, and regardless of their various degrees of success, partial security regimes have amounted to a discreet, yet still significant, effort to limit and control autonomous action in the security area.

The partial security regimes built in the post–World War II era can be described as "prudential," not because they resulted from shared political, social, and economic values and goals but because the great powers shared the recognition that cooperation was in their own and different interests. In other words, converging on the recognition of what had to be prevented, they became united by a mutual interest to survive and to be able to compete by peaceful means.[109] In order for prudential regimes such as SALT (1972), the Non-Proliferation Treaty (NPT) (1968), and the Partial Test Ban Treaty (PTBT) (1963), to take hold, however, a partial agreement was needed on what prudential behavior means, and on a set of understandings about how to manage situations when prudence might not be enough.

To understand what is progressive about these partial regimes we must understand that the idea of nuclear arms control that challenged and later displaced ideas of nuclear disarmament and nuclear superiority in the early 1960s, was not entirely determined in a structural reality, nor was it foreseen that during the next thirty years the superpowers would be involved in political cooperation via arms control. Nuclear arms control, both as a concept and as a blueprint for action, resulted from expectations of Americans who became aware of their nuclear weapons' vulnerability and weary about the reciprocal fear of surprise attack and started to think about the future (indeed, anticipating the future) in terms of strategic stability. Yet at the end of the 1950s, when the concept of nuclear arms control was introduced, stable nuclear deterrence was only a concept that could not be taken for granted, not could it be ruled out.[110] Indeed, nuclear arms control was an intellectual innovation of the American strategic and scientific community that, having been adopted by the administrations of Presidents Kennedy and Johnson, created an agenda for negotiation with the adversary, in much the way that the Soviet leadership under Gorbachev is now starting to introduce new concepts and security ideas and is setting an agenda for negotiating them.

What is crucial to understand here is that throughout the 1960s and 1970s other courses of action might have been pursued with seemingly very different results. Thus, when Schelling wrote in 1960 that "there is a vast new area to be explored once we break out of the traditional confinement of 'disarmament'—the entire area of military collaboration with potential enemies to reduce the likelihood of war or to reduce its scope and violence,"[111] he was not merely making an academic point; in a way he was helping to create a contingent alternative world that, although it may not have been the most benign, was seen as realistic for the times.

Although values about war had been changing since World War I, and the nuclear revolution helped to change outcome and efficacy expectations of war, nuclear arms control may have helped the superpowers, and indeed individuals around the world, to realize that the situation could be stabilized by human choice. Prudential nuclear regimes therefore helped to control expectations and beliefs about the inevitability of war and the efficacy of cooperative means to avoid nuclear war.[112]

The importance of arms-control agreements, then, lies not in the control of arms or military expenditures, nor even in the political effect of arms control in any general sense, but in the need to provide to ourselves and the adversary the "proof" that we are achieving intermediate goals and that we are making progress, however minimal, in avoiding nuclear war. This is because if "success calls for sustained effort over a long time, proximal subgoals are needed to provide incentives and evidence of progress along the way."[113] By creating and strengthening efficacy expectations of cooperation, therefore, partial security regimes may have contributed to the strengthening of the season of general stability. For example, the INF agreement, given the small fraction of nuclear weapons eliminated, is quite insignificant from a military point of view. Yet it enhanced efficacy expectations of cooperation by allowing intrusive verification, never allowed before, and by eliminating an entire class of nuclear weapons.

Some arms-control agreements, such s the PTBT, NPT, Antarctica (1959), and Space (1967), may have enhanced the human interest in a more direct way. Thus, although the PTBT had no meaningful effect on halting the arms race, it nevertheless stopped nuclear tests in the atmosphere that were polluting the air with radioactive material, and thereby may have prevented people around the world from the risk of cancer and other nuclear radiation–related illnesses. Likewise, although the NPT regime and institutions may not have prevented India, Israel, Pakistan, and South Africa from entering, uninvited as it were, the nuclear weapons club, they may have enhanced, if only in a very minimalist way, the welfare of individuals in the Third World, by preventing elites from channeling resources to nuclear weapons production and by providing the Third World with the necessary information for preventing nuclear accidents. At the same time, the Antarctica and Space treaties have helped to preserve natural environments from being used for military purposes.[114] In the assumption that military installations and weapons would harm these physical environments and create a new source of threat for individuals across national borders, the preceding treaties have enhanced the human interest. From the human interest perspective the placing of weapons, or "nuclear shields," in space would be progressive only if a hermetic space defense were to be developed. Otherwise, nuclear weapons and shields would only tend to increase the reciprocal threat to core values, and to harm the environment.

CONSTRAINTS TO PROGRESS IN INTERNATIONAL SECURITY

Minimalist progress in international security can be reversed, or further progress can be delayed or prevented, by forces or constraints that limit the effects of value and expectation change:

1. Uneven growth and technological development tend to sow uncertainty and instability, fears from hegemony, and perceptions of decay that raise the level of reciprocal threats and create expectations of war. War may result less from a calculated action of a leader planning to conquer the world than from desperate attempts by one or more powers determined to prevent a perceived decline in their relative economic and/or military power. Miscalculation, misinterpretation, and crisis psychology are still major enemies of seasons of progress in international security.

2. Domestic politics is another foremost constraint. Domestic po-

litical groups merely reflect different interpretations and sets of beliefs about national security causation. Thus, every society holds in its midst political, military, scientific-technical, and media institutions and forces that can mount their own forceful countermeasures. For every such institution that, for example, holds and acts upon the assumption that international cooperation may help increase international security, there are counterpart institutions that hold and act upon opposite assumptions. In this sense, domestic politics is the arena where national security and world order ideas are raised, legitimized, and selected by policy choices, and where they are tested after they have become national policies and have had international effects. International security progress is therefore constrained as much by the lack of domestic agreement as to what national and international security is about, who is friend and who is foe, what risk is worth taking, and why, as by the lack of international agreement.

3. Cultural differences, a different historical experience, and a difference in cognitive understanding of causes and effects prevent further and more rapid progress toward increasingly less minimalistic seasons of international security. We can better understand this constraint as a difficulty in arriving at common meanings and interpretations across national borders, rather than as a problem of misperceptions.

4. Long delays between actions and noticeable results can discourage many of the advocates of change along the way. Because the processes involved in the reduction of reciprocal threats to core values are by nature intersubjective and thus sometimes require long periods of time before they can have some effect, crises and unexpected events can be interpreted from the very narrow perspective of the decision makers in power as meaning the end of a process of progressive change. Only from a broad historical view and after the effects of the events have been worked out can we judge whether the events have really disrupted a season of progress or whether, dialectically, they may have helped to solidify it. Impatience with the lack of apparent success also raises obstacles for progress. Thus, for example, the attempt to get rid of nuclear weapons by means of one disarmament stroke (Gorbachev's maximalist vision) or by means of an infallible shield in space (Reagan's maximalist vision) may be dangerous, because either may threaten whatever minimalist gains

were painfully achieved in the last decades. Making progress in international security, then, also means making sure that whatever gains have been made are not lost.

5. Revolutionary nationalism and ethnic, modernization, and border problems, mainly in the Third World, are a constant threat, compounded by the increasing ease with which nuclear weapon, chemical, and missile technologies are transferred to and developed by Third World nations. The problem is not one of right (i.e., whether Third World countries have or do not have the right to develop and buy the same kind of weapons and vehicles of mass destruction as those owned by countries in the First and Second Worlds). The problem is that throughout the Third World war and violence are still prominent, and many Third World societies have still to be "debelled" to levels of the First and Second Worlds. Unfortunately, we cannot expect major changes in values and expectations of war until most of these countries have surmounted their nation building, ethnic, and integration problems; until they have corrected border problems inherited from a colonial past; and until they are transformed "to a much greater extent by the material and ideological forces that changed the First and Second Worlds."[115]

The threat to the peoples of the Third World, to peoples that seem to have given up war for good in the developed world, and in a broader sense to a season of post–World War II general stability, comes from a dire combination of two factors: a still uninhibited pattern of bellicose behavior, coupled with technologies and weapons of mass destruction. The most dreadful threat to a season of general stability, of course, arises from nuclear proliferation, for although a war is a war, a war with nuclear weapons is a nuclear war. In a more direct sense, a season of general stability is threatened by the prospect of the use of nuclear weapons by countries that, given their linkages to the superpowers and their geopolitical configuration (India, Pakistan, Middle East), can drag the superpowers into a major war.

6. The past may also be a constraint. First, "lessons" from history,[116] mainly about "the last war," may have a deep and lasting effect. Perceptions of the causes of the last war may affect situations long after a war and its direct effects have ended. Those who tend to look back to 1914 as a point of reference for today's national security policies are more attentive to unpremeditated wars but tend to be

more oblivious to wars by design. Those who look back at 1939 for inspiration, however, see a Hitler hiding behind every leader with revolutionary goals, and by proposing a tough stand may help to create propensities for unintended wars. Second, public opinion images of the adversary formed in the past may change at a slower pace than the adversary's actual behavior.

7. Military and strategic doctrines may force decision makers to frame problems and solutions within the usually narrow bounds of doctrinal premises and assumptions. Thus, for example, a doctrine may limit progress in international security by constraining political and military elites to narrow, and even incorrect, assumptions about human nature and the world. By telling decision makers what weapons should be developed and procured, doctrines can lead to the development of weapons that may later "severely constrain unilateral and joint efforts to stabilize the military balance."[117] General doctrines of national security can also be a threat to human rights because, for the sake of national security, governments may curtail people's right to know, or even to be free of unnecessary suspicion. Human rights violations then can turn, and rightly so, into a substantial constraint on instrumental and substantive progress.

8. Alliances may be able to preserve balances of power and thus generate ephemeral stability, but then can also prevent progress in international security because "weapons may be deployed and arms restraints avoided in deference to the strong views of one's allies. Changes in a military strategy and in weapons deployments may also be constrained by allied opinion."[118]

9. Technology has already been mentioned as erecting obstacles to progress. The problem, of course, is not technology itself but what humans choose to do with it, and the social consequences of technological choices.

Thus, technological "hubris," or the belief that national security problems can be solved only by means of technological wizardry, may raise constraints for progress because it does not tend to take into account technological limits, technological reactions of the other side, and the unintended consequences of technological development. Also, a long lead time from research and development to weapons deployment tends to create institutional and political constraints on the elimination of technologies and weapons that may be unnecessary or destabilizing. Developing technologies as mere bargaining chips may constrain progress because if the bargain fails, one ends up developing "the chips." Finally, technological change is a source of complexity, which in turn tends to increase uncertainty about solutions to national security problems. Here the problem may be not only lack of perfect or the right kind of information, but a problem of what sense to make of too much information, and what to do with it.

CONCLUSIONS

To the determinist, preferences and behavioral changes of nations are fully determined in human nature, the international environment, and more precisely in the anarchic characteristics of the international system and in the distribution of power in the system. Once we allow preferences to enter, however, we must also allow that it is not only a hostile environment that plays an active, organizing, and designing role in the evolution of international relations, but also an active search by national actors for a *preferred* environment that since the end of World War II has meant for many nations, including the superpowers, a more peaceful environment.

A preference for peace over war of an increasing number of nation-states that have not given up their conflicts and grievances in a semianarchic world is minimalistically progressive because it increases the personal security and well-being of individuals across national borders and gives expression to a choice between death and life, as old as Moses' advice to his people: "Choose life, that you may live, you and your seed."[119] I have argued in this paper that since the end of World War II an increasing number of nations, most notably in the developed world, have chosen life. The fact that the superpowers, armed with nuclear weapons, have been part of this lot has been significant for the reduction of international insecurity.

This expression of minimalist progress, however, is not nearly complete. It is partial, certainly not irreversible, and not fully recognized by superpower elites that, responding to a historical context of Cold War, have relied almost exclusively on the power of the "stick" and the threat, disregarding almost entirely the power of the "carrot" and the promise that lies behind their mutual preference for peace. Also, the season of general stability that has taken hold since World

War II in the developed world has almost bypassed the majority of Third World countries that still have to be "debelled" and whose bitter struggles of nation building and integration, boundary disputes, and lack of confidence in and expectation of a better economic future have prevented them from following First and Second World countries in developing a higher expected utility from peace than from war.

With these caveats in mind, however, it is not exaggeration to argue that one of the most important changes in the late twentieth century regarding international security in the developed world has been a collective cognitive change about preferences of peace and war. Indeed, we can argue that rivalries and power conflicts may have not decreased, and may have even become more intense, precisely "because they are predicated on and controlled by the axiom that they will not be settled by resort to force and war."[120] What seems to have changed, then, is the pattern of change in world politics itself. Although in the past, hegemonic winners and losers were selected by war, in the nuclear age winners and losers, by necessity if not by choice, must be selected by peaceful means. International security has therefore depended on a collective process of learning to compete, adapt, and change with the aid of peace.

Certainly the nuclear revolution has played a major role in the achievement of minimalist progress, for it has taken away from war its contestlike nature, and thus created a crystal ball regarding the outcome of war, which elites can now consult before deciding to go to war. Nuclear power elites have diminished efficacy expectations of war, that is, less confidence in winning wars, and increased efficacy expectations of cooperation, based on an increased confidence in their mutual ability to prevent war, confidence that was slowly built through the creation of prudential partial security regimes and through intersubjective processes resulting from the exchange of meanings and interpretations about nuclear weapons and their political effects.

Hand in hand, minimalist progress in international security can also be traced back to a change in values of war and peace that is linked to the costs of the two world wars and to processes of modernization, the advancement of material warfare, and positive economic and welfare expectations about the future. No society, whatever its economic system, may want to pay the economic price of a war that, at best, may resemble the total wars of the twentieth century and, at worst, may burn human civilization in a nuclear fire.

But what about the thousands of nuclear and conventional weapons that the superpowers and other nations have still poised against one another? Are they not a proof that progress has not taken place? Indeed, they prove that progress in international security has been only minimalist and that the pattern of change can still be reversed, maybe even in a matter of days or hours. Before nations and their elites can get rid of the soldier, the tank, and the nuclear weapon, however, they have to remove the soldier, the tank, and the nuclear weapon from their heads. The fact that the latter has begun to happen in some corners of the world is too little to comfort us, if we think about an idyllic world that never was, a world of perpetual peace, but it is a tremendous improvement over the perspective of a world of perpetual war.

Thus, as the post–World War II era of international relations draws to an end, and a new era of both new possibilities and enhanced risks begins, additional progress in international security, such as moving toward a season of common security, will depend on the ability of nation-states to keep as high as possible both the costs of war and the benefits of peace. This means, of course, that for the foreseeable time a mutual assured destruction capability will have to be maintained. But it also means that to increase the benefits of peace great powers have to redefine further their national interest and produce economic reforms that can create positive expectations of the future, for their own peoples and for the future of peoples in the Third World that have not been able, as yet, to see the light at the end of the tunnel. In other words, a more secure world will be one in which the expected utility from peace will continue to outweigh the expected utility from war, and in which the stick does not disappear but gets a little smaller and less threatening, and the carrot is introduced and made a little juicier. In a sense, the future may depend on our expectations of peace (i.e., on a self-fulfilling prophecy of peace).

POSTSCRIPT

I finished this essay's final draft before the earth shook under the postwar international order. The revolutions of 1989 in Eastern Europe and in the Soviet Union, and the fact that most of these revolutions occurred peacefully, have now created a crossroads of major historical proportions—comparable only to the Congress of Vienna in 1815 or the Versailles Conference in 1918—which may have major implications for progress in international security. To begin with, the 1989 events already had a powerful influence in persuading the West that war, arising from the East, is now very unlikely. But, even more fundamentally, at stake is nothing less than the restructuring of superpower relations—and that of their allies, and in the case of the Soviet Union, of former allies—within the context of a new "European Common Home." At the center of a new European order lies the European Community and within it, a united Germany. Whether these events will help developed countries to continue to take the road of peace, and advance any further to a season of common security and beyond will depend, however, on a complex combination of political, economic, and technological constraints and opportunities with human will, imagination, and skill.

Thus, the future of a united European Community is still uncertain and so are the ways in which Eastern European countries may be brought back "home." Furthermore, the major parties concerned still have to agree on how to spike the guns of the warring machines in Europe and elsewhere, and especially, on major conventional and strategic arms control agreements, and on the political basis for a new European political order. They also have to agree on whether and how to use the North Atlantic Treaty Organization and the Warsaw Treaty alliances, now almost obsolete, and the Conference on Security and Cooperation in Europe (CSCE) to achieve their common goals.

Also, dormant nationalist conflicts in Eastern Europe, suddenly awakened, and the fear of German hegemonic aspirations may force the developed world to go down the wrong road, thus jeopardizing the current season of general stability. Moreover, while the superpowers seem to have temporarily put the nuclear and chemical weapons genies back in their bottles, the bottles seem to have fallen into the hands of an increasing number of "undebelled" Third World states that, involved in bitter regional conflicts, may one day, purposefully or inadverently, let the genies escape.

The prospects for a season of common security are better than in any time in the recent past. Even a season of concert (in spite, or because, of the problems I raise), or of a pluralistic security community, ranging from the North American West to the Urals, seems less remote and utopian than it did only a few years ago. Only time will tell, however, whether humanity has debelled itself enough, and expectations of the outcome and efficacy of war have changed so significantly, that the revolutions of 1989, unlike the Congress of Vienna and the Versailles Conference, which were followed by regression, will be remembered in history as catalysts for progressive change in international security.

ENDNOTES

I am grateful to Beverly Crawford, William Jarosz, Sean Lynn-Jones, Peter Katzenstein, John Mueller, Joseph Nye, David Welch and to other members of the Avoiding Nuclear War Project (Center for Science and International Affairs), for their critical comments and suggestions.

1. "Stirrings of Peace," editorial in the *New York Times,* July 31, 1988, p. 24E.
2. Robert Jervis, "The Political Effects of Nuclear Weapons: A Comment," *International Security* (Fall 1988), 13(2):80.
3. John Mueller, "The Essential Irrelevance of Nuclear Weapons: Stability in the Postwar World," *International Security* (Fall 1988), 13(2):78.
4. I am, of course, paraphrasing Bruce Bueno de Mesquita's *The War Trap,* in which he developed an expected-utility theory of war. See mainly ch. 3, "The War Trap—The Expected Utility Theory" (New Haven: Yale University Press, 1981). In this study I am interested neither in looking at public choice nor in studying, let alone predicting, the motivations of specific individuals. Yet I feel compelled to make a statement about expectancy theory and Subjective Expected Utility (SEU) models, because of my own use of the term *expected utility.*

   Cognitive psychologists have used a model that explains motivation as the joint workings of "expectancy" and "valence." This model, best known as "expectancy theory," holds that people consciously make choices based on the valence or attractiveness of outcomes that result from a given action *and* the expectancy that this action will produce the desired outcomes. Neither expectancy nor valence alone is sufficient to predict motivated behavior (Kenyon B. De Greene, *The Adaptive Organization: Anticipation and Management of Crisis* [New York: John Wiley and

Sons, 1982], p. 272). For a historical overview of the development of the expectancy theory in cognitive psychology see John W. Atkinson, "Old and New Conceptions of How Expected Consequences Influence Actions," in Norman T. Feather, ed., *Expectations and Actions* (Hillsdale, N.J.: Lawrence Erlbaum, 1982). The prime example of the expectancy model is the theory of SEU, which proposes that in making decisions people weigh the subjective probabilities and the subjective values (or utilities) associated with the various alternative courses of action that are available, and that they choose the alternative associated with the maximum subjective expected utility, that is, the option for which the multiplicative combination of subjective probabilities and utilities is a maximum (Norman T. Feather, "Introduction and Overview," in Feather, *Expectations and Actions*, p. 11).

I find SEU models extremely flawed and unrealistic. (See Herbert A. Simon, *Reason in Human Affairs* [Stanford, Calif.: Stanford University Press, 1983.) Simon has proved to my satisfaction that rational choice can only mean "satisficing" choice (Herbert A. Simon, *Models of Bounded Rationality* [Cambridge, Mass.: MIT Press, 1982], 2 vols.) because choice is bounded by the lack of perfect information by internal cognitive factors (D. Kahneman, P. Slovic, and A. Tversky, eds., *Judgment Under Uncertainty: Heuristics and Biases* [Cambridge: Cambridge University Press, 1982]) and by institutional structures and processes (James G. March and John P. Olsen, "The New Institutionalism: Organizational Factors in Political Life," *American Political Science Review* [September 1984], 78((3):734–749). I also accept Simon's notion that the "task of determining how people actually do behave in situations having game-like characteristics must be turned over to empirical research: research that seeks to determine . . . how [people] form their expectations and beliefs." Herbert A. Simon, "Human Nature in Politics: The Dialogue of Psychology with Political Science," *American Political Science Review* (June 1985), 79(2):300. Thus, the most rewarding way to study international security and the prospects of peace or war is to look at the origins and evolution of values and expectations that end up affecting the choices made by decision makers on the basis of their bounded rationality. Although an evolutionary epistemology such as Ernst Haas and I have proposed (see my "Cognitive Evolution" in this study) may not help us to predict every specific choice made on international security, it nevertheless allows us to study whether changing expectations and values across national borders have produced a change in the utility that nations expect, at a particular historical point in time, from peace or from war. Thus, it allows us to study change and the direction of change in world politics, without having to fall for the unrealistic assumption of maximizing cost–benefit analyses and for the kind of heuristics that Bueno de Mesquita has proposed.

5. Immanuel Kant, *Perpetual Peace*, L. W. Beck, trans. (Indianapolis: Bobbs-Merrill, 1957).

6. See Emanuel Adler, Beverly Crawford, and Jack Donnelly, "Defining and Conceptualizing Progress in International Relations."

7. Realists such as Robert Gilpin, who has claimed that nuclear weapons have not changed international politics because "they have by no means eliminated the problems of war" (*War and Change in World Politics* [Cambridge: Cambridge University Press, 1981], p. 214) are implicitly adopting *the* most maximalist idea of progress, which of course is utopian. In so doing, however, they set such high standards for progress that it is then easy for them to dismiss the idea that more modest progress can really take place.

8. John Lewis Gaddis, *The Long Peace: Inquiries Into the History of the Cold War* (New York: Oxford University Press, 1987), p. 217.

9. According to William E. Connolly, an essentially contested concept is "appraisive in that the state of affairs it describes is a valued achievement, when the practice described is internally complex in that its characterization involves reference to several dimensions, and when the agreed and contested rules of application are relatively *open*, enabling parties to interpret even those shared rules differently as new and unforeseen situations arise." *The Terms of Political Discourse*, 2d ed. (Princeton, N.J.: Princeton University Press, 1983), p. 10.

10. Joseph S. Nye, Jr., and Sean M. Lynn Jones, "International Security Studies: A Report of a Conference on the State of the Field," *International Security* (Spring 1988), 12(4):5–27, and Richard Ullman, "Redefining Security," *International Security* (Summer 1983), 8(1):129–53.

11. *Webster's Ninth New Collegiate Dictionary* (Springfield, Mass.: Merriam-Webster, 1988), p. 1062.

12. The concept of security dilemma was introduced by John H. Herz (*International Politics in the Atomic Age* [New York: Columbia University Press, 1959], pp. 231–243). Barry Buzan has more recently defined the concept as a "structural notion in which the self-help attempts of states to look after their security needs tend automatically (i.e., regardless of intention) to lead to rising insecurity for others as each interprets its own measures as defensive, and the measures of others as potentially threatening." Barry Buzan, *People, States and Fear* (Chapel Hill: University of North Carolina Press, 1983), p. 3. See also Robert Jervis, "Cooperation Under the Security Dilemma," *World Politics* (January 1978), 30(1):167–214.

13. Kenneth N. Waltz, *Theory of International Politics* (Reading, Mass.: Addison-Wesley, 1979), p. 72.

14. See Joseph M. Grieco, "Anarchy and the Limits of Corporation: A Realist Critique of the Newest Liberal Institutionalism," *International Organization* (Summer 1988), 42(3):485–507.

15. Buzan, *People, States and Fear*, p. 19.

16. According to Gilpin, systems change refers to a transformation of the "nature of the principal actors or diverse entities composing the system." A systemic change, on the other hand, "entails changes in the interna-

tional distribution of power, the hierarchy of prestige, and the rules and rights embodied in the system" (*War and Change*, pp. 41–42). See also Waltz, *Theory of International Politics*, p. 70.

17. For a classic discussion of the Enlightenment idea of progress see J. B. Bury, *The Idea of Progress* (New York: Macmillan, 1932).

18. "Complex interdependence" is characterized by multiple channels of communication, the absence of hierarchy among issues, and a decrease in the use of military force. Robert O. Keohane and Joseph S. Nye, Jr., *Power and Interdependence* (Boston: Little, Brown, 1977), pp. 24–25.

19. With the aid of game theory, realist scholars have recently been studying cooperation in order to identify the conditions under which cooperation between sovereign and "egoist" states can emerge. See, for example, Robert Axelrod, *The Evolution of Cooperation* (New York: Basic Books, 1984); Jervis, "Cooperation Under the Security Dilemma," and Kenneth A. Oye, ed., *Cooperation Under Anarchy* (Princeton, N.J.: Princeton University Press, 1986). These studies have shown that cooperation can take place even without major international structural changes, without an end to international conflict among nations, and without a change in values and expectations of peace and war. Egoist nations, in fact, may cooperate only because it is in their national interest to reciprocate cooperation with cooperation (tit-for-tat) and because nations may mutually gain from cooperation by reducing decision costs as well as uncertainty (Robert O. Keohane, *After Hegemony: Cooperation and Discord in the World Political Economy* [Princeton, N.J.: Princeton University Press, 1984]). Thus, cooperation in itself need not enhance human interests across national borders; for all I know, it can harm them. What makes cooperation progressive, however, is its aim. We can take cooperation as an indicator of instrumental progress, then, when it is aimed at reducing reciprocal threats and the chances of nuclear war.

20. Mueller, "The Essential Irrelevance of Nuclear Weapons," p. 70.

21. Paul Keal, *Unspoken Rules and Superpower Dominance* (New York: St. Martin's Press, 1983), ch. 3.

22. Alexander L. George, "Incentives for U.S.–Soviet Security Cooperation and Mutual Adjustment," in Alexander L. George, Philip J. Farley and Alexander Dallin, eds., *U.S.–Soviet Security Cooperation: Achievements, Failures, Lessons* (New York: Oxford University Press, 1988), p. 644.

23. Joseph S. Nye, Jr., "Understating U.S. Strength," *Foreign Policy* (Fall 1988), 72:108.

24. Dieter S. Lutz, *On the Theory of Structural Inability to Launch an Attack* (Hamburg: Institut fur Friedensforschung und Sicherheitspolitik, January 1988), p. 24.

25. Robert Jervis, *The Illogic of American Nuclear Strategy* (Ithaca, N.Y.: Cornell University Press, 1984), pp. 47–51.

26. Ibid., p. 30.

27. John G. Ruggie, "Social Time and International Policy: Conceptualizing Global Population and Resource Issues," in Margaret P. Karns, ed.,

Persistent Patterns and Emergent Structures in a Waning Century (New York: Praeger, 1986), pp. 213–217.

28. Richard B. Elrod, "The Concert of Europe: A Fresh Look at an International System," *World Politics* (January 1976), 28(2):170. For another insightful analysis on Concerts see Robert Jervis, "From Balance to Concert: A Study of International Security Cooperation," in Oye, *Cooperation Under Anarchy*, pp. 58–79.

29. Karl Deutsch et al., *Political Community and the North Atlantic Area* (New York: Greenwood Press, 1969).

30. Lynn H. Miller, *Global Order: Values and Power in International Politics* (Boulder, Colo.: Westview, 1985), p. 85.

31. Ibid., p. 89.

32. Deutsch, *Political Community*, pp. 36, 129.

33. Ernst B. Haas, *Beyond the Nation-State* (Stanford, Calif.: Stanford University Press, 1964).

34. Michael Doyle, "Kant, Liberal Legacies, and Foreign Affairs," parts 1 and 2 in *Philosophy and Public Affairs* 12 nos. 3 & 4 (Summer, Fall, 1983):205–235 and 325–353. See also Stanley Hoffmann, "The Acceptability of Military Force," *Adelphi* Papers (London: ISSS, 1973), 103:2–13, and Bharat Wariavwalla, "Interdependence and Domestic Political Regimes: The Case of the Newly Industrializing Countries," *Alternatives* (1988), 13(2):264.

35. See note 5.

36. Lawrence Freedman, *The Price of Peace: Living With the Nuclear Dilemma* (New York: Henry Holt, 1986).

37. Mueller, "The Essential Irrelevance of Nuclear Weapons," pp. 68–79, and Jervis, "The Political Effects of Nuclear Weapons," 88–90. See also John Mueller, *Retreat from Doomsday: The Obsolescence of Major War* (New York: Basic Books, 1989).

38. Jervis, "The Political Effects of Nuclear Weapons," p. 89.

39. Mueller, "The Essential Irrelevance of Nuclear Weapons."

40. Jervis, "The Political Effects of Nuclear Weapons," pp. 83–84.

41. Waltz, *Theory of International Politics*, pp. 174–175. One of the best explanations the international relations literature has offered so far about the decrease in the use of force after World War II is by Robert Keohane and Joseph Nye, who argue that "the use of force has become increasingly costly for major states as a result of four conditions: risks of nuclear escalation; resistance by people in poor or weak countries; uncertain and possible negative effects on the achievement of economic goals; and domestic opinion opposed to the human costs of the use of force." Robert O. Keohane and Joseph Nye, "*Power and Interdependence* Revisited," *International Organization* (Autumn 1987), 41(4):727. I accept this point of view and, as will become clear in the following pages, we can subsume these four conditions under a change in values and expectations about peace and war. See, of course, Robert O. Keohane and Joseph S. Nye, *Power and Interdependence* (Boston: Little, Brown, 1977).

42. Albert O. Hirschman, *The Passions and the Interests: Political Arguments for*

Capitalism Before Its Triumph (Princeton, N.J.: Princeton University Press, 1977), p. 38.
43. Milton Rokeach defines human values as a "relatively small number of core ideas or cognitions present in every society about desirable and end-states of existence and desirable models of behavior instrumental to their attainment that are capable of being organized to form different priorities." "From Individual to Institutional Values; With Special Reference to the Values of Science," in Milton Rokeach, ed., *Understanding Human Values* (New York: Free Press, 1979), p. 49.
44. Michael Howard, *The Causes of Wars*, 2d ed. (Cambridge, Mass.: Harvard University Press, 1984), p. 272; F. H. Hinsley, "Peace and War in Modern Times," in Raimo Vayrynen, ed., *The Quest for Peace* (Beverly Hills, Calif.: Sage, 1987), p. 77.
45. Ibid., pp. 271–272.
46. Michael Howard, "The Causes of Wars," *Wilson Quarterly* (Summer 1984), 8(3):92.
47. Mueller, "The Essential Irrelevance of Nuclear Weapons," p. 75.
48. Ibid.
49. Jervis, "The Political Effects of Nuclear Weapons," p. 89.
50. Ibid., p. 90.
51. But, as Howard rightly pointed out, the "destruction caused by two World Wars, the deaths in the course of them of some twenty-five million people, is an experience no Russian is likely to want to live through again; a deterrent to the Soviet Union becoming involved even in a conventional war, let alone one in which they would suffer all the terrible consequences of nuclear destruction. This absence of bellicism, to which the existence on both sides of nuclear weapons so powerfully contributes, is the factor which makes any comparison with 1914 or 1939 so misleading." Howard, *The Causes of Wars*, pp. 272–273.
52. Mueller, "The Essential Irrelevance of Nuclear Weapons," p. 73.
53. Howard, *The Causes of Wars*, p. 273.
54. Hinsley, "Peace and War in Modern Times," p. 78.
55. For example, see Axelrod, *The Evolution of Cooperation*. International regimes are defined in terms of convergent expectations. See Stephen D. Krasner, "Structural Causes and Regime Consequences: Regimes as Intervening Variables," in Stephen D. Krasner, ed., *International Regimes* (Ithaca, N.Y.: Cornell University Press, 1983), p. 2.
56. Thomas C. Schelling, *The Strategy of Conflict* (London: Oxford University Press, 1960); Robert Jervis, *Perception and Misperception in International Politics* (Princeton, N.J.: Princeton University Press, 1976). As Karl Holsti argued, the "long-range expectations of policy makers, their images of future states of affairs—new orders—that some statesmen seek to achieve, and the impact these images have on specific courses of action and diplomatic programs are phenomena that have received relatively less attention. They are concerned less with assessment of an opponent's objectives and intentions in a particular situation, and more with the

general sources of its foreign policy, the links between domestic and international politics, the role of ideologies, and the opponent's own long-range plans." "Détente as a Source of International Conflict," in Nissan Oren, ed., *Images and Reality* (New York: St. Martin's Press, 1984), p. 126.

57. Albert Bandura, *Social Foundation of Thought and Action: A Social Cognitive Theory* (Englewood Cliffs, N.J.: Prentice-Hall, 1986), p. 19.

58. Albert Bandura, "Self-efficacy: Toward a Unifying Theory of Behavioral Change," *Psychological Review* (1977), 85:193. See also Norman T. Feather, "Actions in Relation to Expected Consequences: An Overview of a Research Program," in Feather, *Expectations and Actions*, pp. 64–65.

59. See Gilpin, *War and Change*, Introduction and ch. 1.

60. Joseph S. Nye, Jr., *Nuclear Ethics* (New York: Free Press, 1986), p. 61.

61. See Emanuel Adler, "The Emergence of Cooperation: National Epistemic Communities and the International Evolution of the Idea of Nuclear Arms Control" (*International Organization*, forthcoming).

62. According to psychologist Ellen J. Langer, although "people may pay lip service to the concept of chance, they behave as though chance events are subject to control." Thus, there seems to be an "illusion of control," that is, "an expectancy of a personal success probability inappropriately higher than the objective probability would warrant." "The Illusion of Control," *Journal of Personality and Social Psychology* (1975), 32(2):311. This psychological finding seems to be consistent with Thomas Schelling's arguments about enhancing deterrence through "threats that leave something to chance" (*The Strategy of Conflict*, ch. 8), because the more elites would expect to be able to control events, the more prone they would be to challenge deterrence and the opponent.

63. On the conventionalization phenomenon, or the use of prenuclear concepts for explaining nuclear politics, see Jervis, *The Illogic of American Nuclear Strategy*, pp. 56–63.

64. Joseph S. Nye, Jr., "Nuclear Learning," *International Organization* (Summer 1987), 41(3):371–402.

65. Robert Jervis, "The Nuclear Revolution and the Common Defense," *Political Science Quarterly* (1986), 101(5):700. For a study of how Soviet expectations have changed due to the nuclear revolution, see Robert Legvold, "War, Weapons, and Soviet Foreign Policy," in Seweryn Bialer and Michael Mandelbaum, eds., *Gorbachev's Russia and American Foreign Policy* (Boulder, Colo.: Westview, 1988), pp. 97–132.

66. While a whole generation of strategists have hailed deterrence as the only realistic, albeit temporary, way out of the nuclear predicament, some even argue that a stable deterrence that prevents a first strike may be "progressive" because it has ensured peaceful change. Seen in this light, international security is enhanced by a stable deterrent condition that disuades the adversaries from striking first. Robert H. Gromoll, "Nuclear Weaponry and the Idea of Progress" (unpublished manuscript). The problem with this argument, however, is that nuclear deter-

rence stability is achieved only by the power of the stick or the threat. The result therefore is an increase rather than a decrease of reciprocal threats. At best, under nuclear deterrence *international* insecurity persists. At worst, it may increase.

67. Richard N. Lebow, "Deterrence Reconsidered," *Survival* (January–February 1985), 27(1):26.
68. Richard N. Lebow, "Windows of Opportunity," *International Security* (Summer 1984), 9(1):150.
69. Lebow, "Deterrence Reconsidered," p. 26.
70. Lebow, "Windows of Opportunity," p. 183.
71. Mueller, "The Essential Irrelevance of Nuclear Weapons," pp. 70–71.
72. See Alexander L. George and Richard Smoke, *Deterrence in American Foreign Policy: Theory and Practice* (New York: Columbia University Press, 1974); Robert Jervis, "Deterrence Theory Revisited," *World Politics* (January 1979), 31(2):289–324; Lebow, "Deterrence Reconsidered," and Lebow, "Windows of Opportunity."
73. Schelling, *The Strategy of Conflict.*
74. Jervis, "Deterrence Theory Revisited," p. 296.
75. George and Smoke, *Deterrence in American Foreign Policy*, p. 81.
76. Stanley Hoffmann, "Détente," in Joseph S. Nye, Jr., ed., *The Making of America's Soviet Policy* (New Haven: Yale University Press, 1984), p. 259.
77. Nye, "Understanding U.S. Strength," pp. 106–107.
78. George and Smoke, *Deterrence in American Foreign Policy*, p. 81.
79. Ibid., p. 59.
80. See Zeev Maoz, "Self-Binding Commitments, the Inducement of Trust, Social Choice, and the Theory of International Cooperation," *International Studies Quarterly* (1987), 31:177–200.
81. Seweryn Bialer, "New Thinking and Soviet Foreign Policy," *Survival* (July–August 1988), 30(4):291.
82. Ibid., p. 309.
83. Henry A. Kissinger, "A Memo to the Next President," *Newsweek*, September 19, 1988, p. 34.
84. Michael Mandelbaum, "Western Influence on the Soviet Union," in Bialer and Mandelbaum, *Gorbachev's Russia*, p. 374.
85. Bialer, "New Thinking and Soviet Foreign Policy," pp. 295–296.
86. Edward C. Luck and Tobi Trister Gati, "Gorbachev, the United Nations, and U.S. Policy," *Washington Quarterly* 4 (Autumn 1988):25.
87. Ibid., pp. 20–23.
88. Bialer, "New Thinking and Soviet Foreign Policy," p. 297.
89. Ibid.
90. Ibid., pp. 297–298.
91. Ibid., p. 301.
92. Luck and Gati, "Gorbachev, the United Nations, and U.S. Policy," p. 24.
93. Bialer, "New Thinking and Soviet Foreign Policy," p. 302.

94. Legvold, "War, Weapons, and Soviet Foreign Policy." See especially pp. 120–129.

95. Daniel Yankelovich and Richard Smoke, "America's New Thinking," *Foreign Affairs* (Fall 1988), 67(1):1–2. One project is "Americans Talk Security" (ATS), the other is "The Public, the Soviets, and Nuclear Arms," a joint effort by the Public Agenda Foundation and the Center for Foreign Policy Development at Brown University.

96. Andrew Kohut, "Stability and Change in Opinions about Nuclear Weapons Policy, 1945–1987." Paper presented at the August 1987 Aspen Strategic Group Meeting. A shorter version of this paper was published in *Foreign Policy* (Spring 1988), 70:150–165. See also Thomas W. Graham, "The Pattern and Importance of Public Knowledge in the Nuclear Age," *Journal of Conflict Resolution* (June 1988), 32(2):319–334.

97. Yankelovich and Smoke, "America's New Thinking," p. 5.

98. Ibid., p. 6.

99. Ibid., p. 12.

100. Ibid., p. 13.

101. Ibid., p. 10.

102. Daniel Yankelovich and Sidney Harman, *Starting with the People* (Boston: Houghton Mifflin, 1988), p. 49.

103. Kohut, "Stability and Change," Table 8.

104. Ibid., pp. 25–26.

105. Krasner has defined international regimes as "sets of implicit or explicit principles, norms, rules, and decision-making procedures around which actors' expectations converge in a given area of international relations." "Structural Causes and Regime Consequences," p. 2.

106. Robert Jervis, "Security Regimes" in Krasner, *International Regimes*.

107. Nye, *Nuclear Learning*, pp. 391–398.

108. Ibid., p. 394.

109. This idea is based on Terry Nardin's concept of practical association, a "relationship among those who are engaged in the pursuit of different and possibly incompatible purposes, and who are associated with one another, . . . only in respecting certain restrictions on how each may pursue his own purposes." *Law, Morality, and the Relations of States* (Princeton, N.J.: Princeton University Press, 1984), p. 9.

110. Lawrence Freedman, *The Evolution of Nuclear Strategy* (New York: St. Martin's Press, 1983), p. 191.

111. Thomas C. Schelling, "Reciprocal Measures for Arms Stabilization," in Donald G. Brennan, ed., *Arms Control, Disarmament, and National Security* (New York: George Braziller, 1961), p. 169.

112. As Jervis said, "The main purpose of arms control in the nuclear era is to control our expectations and beliefs, not our arms. It is the former rather than the latter that will determine our fates" ("The Nuclear Revolution," p. 702).

113. Bandura, *Social Foundations of Thought*, p. 453.

114. For the Antarctica treaty see Deborah Shapley, "Antarctica: Why Suc-

cess?" in George et al., *U.S.–Soviet Security Cooperation*, pp. 307–335. For the space treaty see Steven Weber and Sidney Drell, "Attempts to Regulate Military Activities in Space," in ibid, pp. 373–432.

115. Ernest B. Haas, "War, Interdependence and Functionalism," in Vayrynen, *The Quest for Peace*, pp. 122–123.
116. Richard E. Neustadt and Ernest R. May, *Thinking in Time: The Uses of History for Decision Makers* (New York: Free Press, 1986); Ernest R. May, *Lessons of the Past* (New York: Oxford University Press, 1973); Jervis, *Perception and Misperception;* Yaacov Y. I. Vertzberger, "Foreign Policy Decisionmakers as Practical-Intuitive Historians: Applied History and Its Shortcomings," *International Studies Quarterly* (1986), 30:223–247.
117. Alexander L. George, "Factors Influencing Security Cooperation," in George et al., *U.S.–Soviet Security Cooperation*, p. 662. For one of the best studies on the development of military doctrine, see Barry R. Posen, *The Sources of Military Doctrine: France, Britain, and Germany between the World Wars* (Ithaca, NY: Cornell University Press, 1984).
118. George, "Factors Influencing Security," p. 666.
119. Deut. 30:19.
120. Hinsley, "Peace and War in Modern Times," p. 78.

5

THE IDEAS OF PROGRESS AND U.S. NONPROLIFERATION POLICY

Michael Brenner

The contributors to this book have set themselves the task of exploring the idea of progress as it pertains to select areas of postwar international relations. It is a twofold undertaking: to ascertain whether and in what respects the pattern of development noted represents a qualitative change in the characteristic interplay of states; and to determine if the direction and nature of such change as is detected conform to one or another conception of progress.

The several elements that compose the idea of progress are clearly delineated in the editors' chapter. Their formulation provides a set of reference marks by which to measure progress, to distinguish among its forms, and to assess their significance. The primary definition of progress they offer is apt and indisputable. It is built around two notions: *achievement* and *improvement*. Achievement implies successful accomplishment, either in the sense of reaching goals or solving problems. When used in the former sense, achievement signifies *advancement*—a meaning that dovetails neatly with the notion of improvement. But, as the editors explain, success in problem resolution, by contrast, need suggest only the amelioration of some specific condition—perhaps the mediation of an outstanding dispute or the protection of a tangible interest. Such accomplishment, which may be short-lived and/or self-contained, need not be part of any lasting improvement in international relations generally. Achievement is measured by an "instrumental standard of values," in the formulation of the editors. It carries no intrinsic capacity for transforming the ways in which states generally define national interests, much less for attenuating their capacity or inclination to use their sovereign powers to satisfy those interests.

The idea of improvement in philosophies of progress conveys something more profound. It has the clear connotation of a favorable change in the way persons and societies live and interact. What is involved is more than a practical measure of success. Improvement entails change in kind that results in a more desired general state of affairs (e.g. it is more pacific; it is more orderly; it realizes more fully the worthy aspirations toward economic welfare and human rights as well as security). Improvement, in this "maximalist" image of progress, entails change that leads to the betterment of things through at least a partial transcendence of the state-based system of international relations. The "maximalist" perspective presumes an affinity (if not identity) of successful accomplishment, improvement through change, human betterment, *and* the institutionalized pursuit of "human interests" freed from the preoccupation with parochial "national interests."

So depicted by Adler, Crawford, and Donnelly, this conception of progress bears a noticeable similarity to the liberal philosophy that has been the preponderant influence on American thinking about international politics. It shares with liberal positivism the belief that discourse guided by an expanded view of self-interest could lead to the attenuation of interstate conflict, and eventually to its supersedence. Underlying this belief is the premise that there is a latent community of interest among the world's peoples. A companion belief expresses an ingrained skepticism that a state-centered politics, however enlightened, could produce "real" change in the way the world's affairs are handled—or in its outcomes. Hence, one sees an emphasis, like that in the philosophy of progress, on achievement through a restructuring of the international system that goes beyond the willful acts of its component sovereign parts.

The affinities of philosophies of progress in international relations with the traditionally liberal American outlook on world politics offer a reasonable basis for viewing the broad contours of American foreign policy as the expression (albeit incomplete and imperfect) of some major strands in progressive thinking. They might fruitfully be examined in tandem.

In analyzing the U.S. nuclear nonproliferation policy, therefore, we have an opportunity to accomplish two purposes contributory to this collective project: to apply concepts and propositions derived from the theoretical construct of progress to observed developments in this sphere of international relations; and to assess how a government, acting in accordance with a related set of ideas, conceived and implemented an avowedly internationalist strategy aimed at institutionalizing a collective interest.

The case for proceeding in this manner is reinforced by the United States' leading role in shaping the world's nonproliferation regime.[1] It clearly bears the imprint of American thinking. In reviewing how that construction has fared, we are in a position to consider the practical manifestations in foreign policy of some "progressivelike" ideas, as well as the systemic consequences of their application. The nuclear nonproliferation regime constitutes a substantial accomplishment in institutionalizing a collective international interest; it has evident successes to its credit in slowing the pace of weapons spread. The experience of American policy, and of the regime it fostered, however, is not one of unalloyed or complete success. In a sense the embodiment of progressive ideas, the nonproliferation regime reveals their limitations and shortcomings as well as their potential for qualitatively improving international life.

NUCLEAR WEAPONS AND NONPROLIFERATION

Progress presumes change. But not all change is for the better. In their framework, the editors properly caution us that only change that furthers human interests qualifies as progress. Nobody can dispute the proposition that all the vicissitudes of international affairs cannot be composed into an integrated picture of how the world works. But a theory of progress does have an especial problem in coming to terms with those noteworthy developments and landmark events that have obvious system significance yet leave us apparently worse off than before. Technological change has a particularly ambiguous nature, as Emanuel Adler stresses in his analysis of security in the nuclear age.

The advent of nuclear arms is the hallmark technical achievement of our epoch, with profound implications for interstate relations. Atomic weapons' demonstratively awesome power raised a unique question: What happens to conventional notions of state interest and power politics when the military instruments of policy become dangerously inflexible tools that threaten national survival? Many, progressives and liberals prominent among them, envisaged an end to *realpolitik* and the inauguration of peace through the collective decision of sober-minded, rational governments. That hope has been unfulfilled.[2]

Some significant change certainly has occurred. The nuclear powers have conceded their mutuality of interest in restraining the impulse toward conflict and in curbing their hostility. Their common recognition that nuclear weapons are ill suited to perform the classic functions of arms has led to earnest efforts at prudently managing their arsenals and at reaching agreements, tacit and formal, that establish nuclear rules of the road. They strive, if only intermittently, to formalize a set of stable expectations. Yet the nuclear powers, like other states, continue to pursue a range of other interests defined in more or less national terms. Their relations are a unique mix of conflictual and collaborative elements. The paradox, and diplomatic challenge, has been to craft the means to institutionalize the prudential logic of nuclear stalemate in a state-centered international system still dominated by the ubiquity of conflict situations. For although security thinking has become more enlightened (i.e., more aware that security depends on reciprocating, restrained behavior), it has done so on an instrumental basis, impelled by the fear of nuclear war whose avoidance has become the overriding end of state policy. Nuclear stability has remained, therefore, very much an achievement of the statist approach.

The collaborative dimension of the superpower relationship is most evident in the concrete steps to restrict the spread of nuclear arms to other states.[3] The United States and Soviet Union have joined together to promote the Nuclear Non-Proliferation Treaty; to restrict, along with other nuclear proficient states, the sale or transfer of sensitive nuclear materials and technologies; and to develop the International Atomic Energy Agency (IAEA) as a multinational monitoring body. The last is most noteworthy, because it embodies the willingness to give institutional form to perceived common interests. Indeed, in creating the IAEA and in endowing it with substantial powers for overseeing the management of civilian nuclear facilities, a slice of state authority was reconstituted at an international level.

This act of institution building was in keeping with the American predilection for formally constituted structures of cooperation. It expressed a preferred method for affirming common interests and objectives.[4]

INSTITUTING THE NONPROLIFERATION REGIME

The energetic postwar American efforts at founding multilateral institutions was grounded in the firm conviction that they had intrinsic value, and capacity, for transforming national interests into collective purpose. Qualitative improvement in the character of interstate relations was foreseen as the outcome of those relations being mediated in an organizational framework based on principles of enlightened self-interest—an outlook very much in keeping with the type of institutional development identified as a necessary condition for progressive change in the international system.

Nowhere is this faith in technique more evident than in President Eisenhower's Atoms for Peace program. The plan generously offered to open to the world the benefits of the peaceful atom. Nuclear energy's latent power to do good was juxtaposed to images of the atom's destructiveness. International cooperation to tap it for benign ends would be coupled to joint efforts at holding in check the malignant atom. A new multinational body, the IAEA was founded to regulate the flow of nuclear materials and technologies.[5] The network of treaties, codes of conduct, and understandings that grew around the IAEA together constitutes the nonproliferation regime. At its heart is a compact whereby pledges of abstinence from weapons acquisition were exchanged for commitments of assistance in the peaceful applications of nuclear power.

The plan's underlying premise was that legal and organizational means could keep the military and civilian applications of nuclear energy in watertight compartments. The United States banked on the belief that it could make available to the world a significant portion of the civilian skills and technology in the American repertoire on terms that embedded them in a safe wadding of protective limitations and controls. Similar judgments were being made by other nuclear-proficient states.

The principle of self-denial on arms coupled with generous, if controlled, access to civilian nuclear technology was extended and solemnized in the Nuclear Non-Proliferation Treaty of 1968. The NPT was the culminating achievement inspired by this desire to engage weapons states and non–weapons states in mutual efforts to keep at bay the nuclear menace. It bound them in a set of undertakings that set more stringent preconditions for the recipients of nuclear assistance (including the placing of all their nuclear facilities under international safeguards), linked the adhesion of non–weapons states to pledges from the weapons state to work toward reducing their own nuclear arms in the interest of global security, reaffirmed the parties' right to participate in the technology's peaceful uses, and strengthened the IAEA's position as regulator and overseer of the rules and programs of nuclear cooperation. There is little doubt that the NPT served to solidify the nonproliferation regime and to reinforce nonproliferation norms.*

The strategy built around the IAEA and the NPT was successful to a large extent. The twin principles of weapons abstention and maximum feasible exploitation of civilian nuclear power appeared, on the whole, compatible. Most states' peaceful nuclear ambitions could be satisfied while safeguards served to assure against the abuse of transferred materials and knowhow. The IAEA, as an organization, appeared credible and effective. Yet this model strategy for international cooperation in regulated technology transfer would prove to have certain flaws. They were serious enough to raise the question of whether there are systematically defined limits on the effectiveness of institutions created to achieve political ends through performance of technically defined functions of management and control. The regime's institutionalized norms and obligations undoubtedly discouraged narrow formulations of national security; and its enforced rules did restrict access to weapons-relevant materials. But could this innovative method for managing nuclear technology transfers fully contain the self-directed security behavior of states? Did it have the capacity to alter the environment of threat in which they live—fundamentally enough as to hold security anxieties below a critical threshold consistent with nonproliferation objectives?

Evidence that the magic of nuclear power had not been wholly

*The NPT was drafted and promoted under the leadership of the United States, the U.S.S.R., and Great Britain. (France was not a signatory but agreed in principle to observe its main precepts —a position taken more recently by the People's Republic of China.) Most of the world's nations have adhered to the treaty with the notable exceptions of several states with potential interest in nuclear arms, *inter alia* Argentina, Brazil, India, Israel, and South Africa.

domesticated came in 1974, when India detonated its rudimentary atomic bomb. That act forced new awareness of the bond between the pacific promise and the military threat of nuclear energy. It also called into question the confident assumption that underlay the American-inspired nonproliferation regime. For India used civilian facilities and materials obtained from the United States and Canada as the technological base and fuel source for its bomb. In the process, it had sidestepped the IAEA safeguards that were supposed to prevent just such an event.[6]

The implications of the Indian explosion went beyond that country's respect for legal forms and diplomatic niceties. More worrisome was that the key critical technology employed, spent-fuel reprocessing, and the key material, plutonium, were on the point of entering the commercial marketplace. The United States, acting on the belief that an open, if partially regulated, transfer of nuclear technology was a step toward internationalizing norms of collective responsibility, had encouraged a vision of the nuclear future that included the recycling of plutonium as a standard feature. For the ensuing decade, successive American administrations would wrestle with the daunting task of braking and redirecting a global movement it had instigated and that now was threatening to undermine the very purposes the United States had set out to achieve and that had been institutionalized in the IAEA.[7] Their anxious point of reference was a fresh realization that modulated technology transfers, even though coupled with a compact on weapons abstention, could no remove the motivations of security and pride that move states to build nuclear arms. Collective institutions designed to raise consciousness about the relevant cost benefits of a weapons program by placing them in a global security context could not, in themselves, overcome everywhere the classic logic that "arms make the state"—even if they could noticeably qualify it in some circumstances.

INSTITUTIONAL DEVELOPMENT AS A STANDARD OF PROGRESS

The IAEA was envisaged by its founders as embodying an international "general will" affirming itself in opposition to the further spread of atomic weapons and in support of collaboration in exploiting the peaceful atom. Moreover, it seemed to have the potential to reshape this dimension of international politics by shifting preference orderings toward a collective, supranational perspective on an essential human interest—reducing the risk of nuclear war. Yet it can be argued that the institutional logic of the IAEA itself made it susceptible to the corrosive influences of security-driven national behavior.[8] A close examination of the institutional development process within the organization shows how this occurred.

The International Atomic Energy Agency exemplifies the characteristics of successful regime construction. It represents a "set of mutual expectations, rules and regulations, organizational energies and financial commitments which have been accepted by a group of states."[9] It incorporates principles and norms that encourage the anticipation of reciprocity, a self-denying injunction on the use of sensitive nuclear materials as a tool of bilateral diplomacy, and pledges of abstinence on weapons development made in exchange for explicit commitments of assistance in exploiting nuclear energy's peaceful applications.[10] It functions like a regime: providing for political burden sharing, reducing transaction costs, and facilitating information flows. It thereby creates interdependencies of interest, keyed to global reference points, which militate in favor of more enlightened state behavior. The IAEA's expanding technical capabilities for opening controlled access to nuclear materials was a sign of the regime's success in fulfilling its mission of furthering cooperation in civilian applications of nuclear energy. This very success in regime construction, though, also generated changes that worked counter to stipulated nonproliferation purposes.

The plutonium issue highlighted by the Indian test posed two crucial questions: (1) Has a genuine regime been achieved unless there is the built-in capacity to adjust to new problems and conditions in part created by the regime's own workings? (2) What determines whether the institutions can generate an extended consensus on new rules for dealing with those problems (i.e., whether its developmental potential points toward enhancement of the world community's welfare)? For the challenge no longer was one merely of regime maintenance, or even development along established paths; it was renovation and renewal that were required. Would the requisite will for extending the range of regime consensus come from within the institution or from member states? If from the latter source, what would the institution contribute to regime renewal?

The practical dilemma was whether and how to restrict the transfer of institutionally approved but dangerous items without compromising the principle of maximum feasible cooperation. Implicit in the agency's enabling statutes and in its official policies was the presumption that the technology for separating plutonium from civilian nuclear waste was benign if properly safeguarded (and even desirable on grounds of resource efficiency and waste management). In fact, India's 1974 atomic test did little to alter the institutional mindset, despite the unmistakable evidence that the Indians had made a plutonium bomb from materials imported for nominally peaceful purposes.

The organizationally conditioned response was to deny that a defect had been exposed in the system for controlled dissemination of nuclear technology and hardware. The IAEA's secretariat was ready to ensure that the operating procedures followed in the safeguards program *would* undergo critical scrutiny. But the argument (pushed hard by the Carter administration) that plutonium had proved too dangerous a commodity to allow becoming a staple of international nuclear commerce was staunchly opposed by agency officials.

Dr. Sigvard Eklund, director general of IAEA, was vocal in his public criticism of President Carter's campaign to postpone indefinitely the commercialization of plutonium fuels, and to tighten access to them. He joined publicly in an active political alliance with nuclear industry leaders and opposing governments to block the U.S. move. His counterattack concentrated on what he claimed was an American attempt to renege on the solemn undertaking to participate fully in the collective enterprise of developing civilian nuclear power for the good of the world's citizens. Washington, he argued, was abrogating an international treaty by failing to live up to the terms of Article 4 (of the NPT) that commits signatories to support full exchange of nuclear knowhow and technology not expressly prohibited as being weapons-sensitive. For to put a lid on technological development would shatter the compact between weapons and nonweapons states that was the essence of the world's nonproliferation regime. By leading the IAEA into opposition to the Carter initiative, Eklund made Washington's uphill diplomatic battle that much more difficult. Above all, it reinforced the conviction of recipient governments that international law confirmed the correctness of their position and that the institutionalized general will of the international community was being threatened by American action. It also allowed the IAEA to serve as a source of expertise that could be exploited to counter the technically grounded arguments and interpretations of the American administration's position.

The IAEA was acting true to organizational form by defending its central mission. But institutional conservatism, in this instance, was leading to radical change (i.e., the spread of a weapons-grade material).* Thus, the irony of regime development. The institutionalization of a common good was resulting in progress being made, but with newly apparent and worrisome side-effects. Here was an instance of institution building so solidly accomplished as to make pragmatic adaptation to deal with undesirable, second-order consequences arduous and costly.

The IAEA-centered nonproliferation regime had suffered, in a sense, the consequences of its success. Regimes are needed, as Ernst Haas cogently has argued, because self-reliance carries too high a price. Regimes provide a form of political load sharing, lessening the demands on finite diplomatic capital.[11] They establish rules that routinize behavior that otherwise would have to be cultivated, cajoled, or coerced. The IAEA has substantially satisfied the interests of the United States (and other proliferation concerned states) at reduced political cost and with greater predictability than otherwise would have been the case. Regimes also can have the capacity for generating system change. Stephen Krasner aptly makes the point that "[r]egimes may change the interests that led to their creation in the first place by increasing transaction flows, facilitating knowledge and understanding, and creating property rights. . . . If a regime increases transaction flows in a particular issue area it can alter interests by increasing the opportunity costs of change."[12]

This is very nearly an exact description of what happened within the nonproliferation regime, but with less than welcome results. Increased transaction flows did alter, or at least modify, some interests; they did help to strengthen collective norms in ways that increased the costs to a government for transgressing them. But in the case of the IAEA, the regime did something else as well. It created

---

*However safeguarded, plutonium's very existence created a condition of latent proliferation, since its illicit diversion could allow for the building of a bomb before detection was made. Moreover, peaceful reprocessing plants could be the models for dedicated military facilities. The potential for unsettling world security was great.

conditions that could encourage a latent interest in weapons acquisition at the possible expense of a declared interest in regulating the transfer of nuclear materials. Indeed, recipients' support for the institutional status quo was strengthened for the very reason that the effective performance of the organization's knowledge and technology transfer function produced a redistribution of power in ways unforeseen but congenial to nuclear-dependent states, especially ones that harbored a latent interest in nuclear weapons development. It was the nuclear-proficient states—above all, the United States—that incurred increased opportunity costs in their attempts to maintain the balance of commercial and nonproliferation interests that was the original basis for regime construction.

In principle, development of international institutions is a progressive step toward achieving collective international goods—from a maximalist and a minimalist standpoint. Institutions incorporate common goals; they operationalize norms; they codify rules. Their conservative effect, overall, is pronounced. They consolidate collective purposes, thereby restricting individual national choices on ends while determining what are proper and acceptable means. But it is not only the disruptive and possibly trouble-making who are constrained. It is also that state, in this instance the United States, that believes it has a valid vision of how enlightened self-interest can improve the quality of interstate relations along with a special responsibility for exercising leadership in dealing with a problem that threatens international stability. Progress then lay in breaking the logic of regime-sanctioned change through a reinvigorated state-centered and state-initiated diplomacy to reset the parameters for institutionalized rule execution.

POLITICAL WILL AND REGIME RENEWAL

The lead role in initiating the effort at regime renewal was played by the United States. As directed by President Jimmy Carter, the American approach exhibited characteristics of both the utilitarian–instrumentalist and ideal–maximalist facets of a progressive approach to international affairs. The latter disposition predominated in the first year of his presidency. Carter's urgent campaign in 1977 to stop the use of plutonium in civilian reactors and to force the world to rethink nuclear energy was a high-priority item during the early months of his administration.[13]

It was conducted in the belief that government leaders, when made to confront reality from the enlightened perspective offered by the United States, would come round to accepting the American lead —the skepticism of major nuclear exporting states, the implacable antagonism of some dependent recipient states, and the IAEA's resistance notwithstanding. Unilateral measures of abstinence by the United States (halting the program for recycling plutonium fuels and guillotining the plutonium-dependent "breeder" project) were acts of witness-affirming conviction and setting example. They conformed to a tradition whereby the United States offers itself as a model for emulation and as guide for others' enlightened self-interest.

The high-pressure campaign to convince other nuclear-proficient states to follow the American lead by restricting availability and tightening terms of export for plutonium-related items accompanied those exemplary actions. The campaign could be viewed as an exercise in political education—with Washington playing the role of virtuous tutor. The strategy's optimism was founded on two interlocking beliefs: (1) that all reasonable governments, if forced to reflect soberly on the question of plutonium, would reach conclusions similar to those of the Carter administration; and (2) that neither ongoing programs, intergovernmental commitments, nor the pledge of nuclear assistance embodied in the NPT and the articles of the IAEA constituted insurmountable obstacles to the winning of support for a drastic change in the rules of international nuclear conduct. The confident assumption that rational leaders acting in good faith would prove like-minded is, of course, a classic feature of liberal idealism.[14] It conforms as well to a progressive outlook on international affairs that stresses consciousness raising as part of a desirable process of cognitive evolution.

The Carter administration's earnest efforts at education on the plutonium issue was only partially successful. Its most tangible accomplishment was to create a new grouping of nuclear-proficient states, the London Nuclear Suppliers Group, intended as a vehicle for governing nuclear commerce and for devising more effective methods for monitoring commercial sales. Its very creation was an accomplishment. But the organizational evidence of a will to cooperate could not conceal the fact that some participants disagreed with the key judgments being made in Washington that the envisaged commerce in plutonium fuels constituted a clear and present proliferation risk. They devalued the dangers of diversion and/or stressed the greater risks of alienating recipient states. To force national governments to confront the proliferation issue was not to presume how they would answer it. The United States could rightly claim to have changed somewhat the perspective of skeptics thanks to its vigorous campaign directed at the highlighting of new, dangerous proliferation conditions. Certain adjustments were made in thinking and in policy. Still, on some important points (e.g., the requirement of "full-scope" safeguards as a condition for nuclear transfers), certain key states reached conclusions about the trade-offs of proliferation ends and means different from those of the United States. The problem in the end was not over the terms of discourse, but over preference scales established in reference to largely self-defined state interests.

The Carter initiatives can be viewed as an exercise in regime renewal. They sought to direct the process of cognitive evolution so that the regime consensus would encompass the newly recognized problems associated with plutonium. The United States wanted an amendment of rules (and, partially, in procedures) in the light of what were judged serious new circumstances. The American administration's initial difficulties, and only incomplete eventual success, owed something to the righteousness of its approach and a relative insensitivity to the tacit norms governing consensus-building within the regime. These outcomes can be explained as well by reference to the inherent conservatism of the institutions at the heart of the regime: *and* the intractability of conditions characterized by equivocal fellow suppliers and eager recipients acting in accordance with national interests that, by their lights, looked quite reasonable.

THE REAGAN APPROACH

After 1981, the question of what weight should be placed on institutional approaches to nonproliferation was posed for the Regime administration in another form. The new administration sought to follow a pragmatic strategy, emphasizing bilateral diplomacy. On the key issue of controlling the spread of weapons-related materials and technology, it steered clear of the dramatic initiatives that characterized the heroic efforts of Jimmy Carter while it benefited from its predecessor's considerable achievements in fostering a new near consensus especially sensitive to the plutonium issue in particular and the civilian–military nexus in general.

Reagan administration officials spoke not in terms of regime, but in terms of mutual interests. They used multilateral forums (the IAEA annual conference; the NPT Review Conference) not to promote bold new agendas for collective action, but rather to protect those programs and agreements that were seen as having some practical value. Washington largely set aside the goal of establishing rigid codes of conduct; it tried instead to build a common denominator of consensus on an ad hoc basis. In keeping with this attitude, the Nuclear Suppliers Group ceased to meet regularly as a collective body, with its members communicating informally and privately, often on a bilateral basis.

These arrangements did take place within a regime framework and derived much of their credibility and force from it. But the administration's relentless pragmatism led to a blurring of standards and to some weakening of the binding force that holds the regime together. Inevitably, there was a compromise of principle. Thus, the Reagan administration pushed for Senate approval of a bilateral treaty of nuclear cooperation with the People's Republic of China, despite disturbing evidence of the latter's past reckless nuclear export policies, and acquiesced in treaty language that bent, if did not violate, the meaning of U.S. statute. It sought, and won, exemption for Pakistan from the Symington Amendment to the Military Assistance Act in order to conclude a multi-billion-dollar military aid deal deemed essential to Pakistan's backing of the Afghan rebels. The Commerce Department applied generous standards in licensing the export of "dual-use" items to South Africa. The list of measures tailored to individual circumstances was a long one.[15]

This highly pragmatic approach expressed the belief that nonproliferation ends were best served by treating each case in its individual terms, even at times when that meant bending principle in exchange for accommodation on other matters. The net effect on nonproliferation was mixed. The record of the Reagan years does show flexibility has its virtues. Bilateral diplomacy, at times, does pay dividends. A statist approach can produce positive change. However, the Reagan years also provided ample evidence that such an approach cannot

handle the type of challenge presented by a shift in systemic properties *or* by the introduction of a major new factor. The emergence onto
the nuclear marketplace of supplier states who did not subscribe fully
to existing arrangements for regulating exports was a change of that
order. During the 1980s, it came to threaten the integrity and effectiveness of the nonproliferation regime. Unlike the plutonium issue,
this threat arose not from the workings of an institutionalized regime, but from conditions on the margins of that regime ((or even, in
some cases, outside it) that eluded its control or direct influence.

The "second-tier" of nuclear suppliers included states that themselves had resisted the imposition of extranational controls on their
domestic nuclear programs *and* that were believed to harbor some
interest in weapons development. Numbered among them were the
People's Republic of China (P.R.C.), India, Argentina, Brazil, and
South Africa. Together, they could make available an impressive
array of technology, hardware, technical assistance, and nuclear fuels.
The mounting evidence in the mid-1980s that they were exchanging
sensitive items among themselves was cause for anxiety. These clan-
destine, if not illicit, transactions might well advance threshold states
to the brink of a weapon capability. They might also encourage other
states to rethink their attitude toward the nuclear option in the light
of new, less constrained or detectable opportunities.

The implication of the "new supplier" phenomenon for the nonproliferation regime was twofold. First, it undermined the network of
arrangements for restricting access to sensitive nuclear weapons by
opening a way to circumvent mainline suppliers. Moreover, much of
the commerce transacted with emerging suppliers would not be under safeguards, because that condition distinguished the traditional
from the new suppliers. Second, it accentuated the problem associated with existing loopholes, and gray area markets, in the nonproliferation regimes coverage of export activity. It put recipient countries
in a position to capitalize on the diversification of suppliers. They
could shop around for the requisite bits and pieces necessary for a
viable military program (as Pakistan did). Growing technical skills
and deepening industrial capabilities meanwhile heightened confidence in a recipient's own abilities to coordinate the operation and
integrate a weapons program's component parts. Thereby a new
measure of proliferation risk was being created for a regime whose

regulation of the international nuclear marketplace was both imperfect and incomplete.

The dangers of disorder in the nuclear trading system could not be addressed on an *ad hoc* basis alone. Bilateral approaches to individual "new" suppliers were made, and in some instance, they did make an impression. The outstanding instance was the United States' negotiations with the P.R.C. on a nuclear cooperation agreement that was used effectively by Washington to bring the Chinese up a steep learning curve on proliferation matters. Beijing came to accept the principle of requiring safeguards on nuclear exports and itself joined the IAEA.[16]

But the experience with China, as with other less forthcoming new suppliers, underscores the essential importance of having internationally sanctioned rules of conduct. *Here the virtues of collective institutions stand out.* They have a potential for authoritative rule making that exceeds that of individual states or groupings of states. Where they are able to establish clear-cut norms, embodying a wider consensus, an essential baseline of acceptable international conduct becomes available. It both guides behavior and creates a basis for determining compliance. The evolution of the P.R.C.'s attitude toward nuclear commerce and proliferation was due not merely to the persuasion and influence of the United States and of other states with whom it sought to have nuclear commercial relations. It reflected the recognition of an institutionalized common purpose, and common interest, that was larger and more enduring than the convergent policies of its member states. To participate fully in the international nuclear community, to derive its benefits, China had to buy into the nonproliferation regime.

Success in modifying the export behavior of other new nuclear suppliers has been less dramatic. Some progress, though, has been made. India and Argentina have given clear signs of following less liberal policies, especially in placing safeguard requirements on their more sensitive export items. In their cases, though, concessions appear to have been made primarily in response to pressures from mainline suppliers, rather than to an institutionalized international will. A practical calculation of the costs that could be imposed on them by the United States or the Soviet Union dictated that they refrain from otherwise beneficial nuclear transactions. These costs were not limited to the sphere of nuclear energy; they entailed other economic and security items on the diplomatic agenda. By contrast, the direct influence exerted by the collective institutions of the nuclear energy *cum* nonproliferation regime were slight. Unlike China, India and Argentina already enjoyed the advantages of IAEA membership; no standard of good behavior need be met for them to gain entry. Indirect influence is more difficult to estimate. Undeniably, though, the very fact that an international consensus on proliferation is embodied in a regime acts as a constant factor weighing in favor of compliance with its norms.

On balance, how has the nonproliferation regime fared in the face of the plutonium dilemma and the challenge of new suppliers? Overall, its integrity has been preserved. It serves an essential function of legitimizing and enforcing rules of prudent nuclear conduct. The redoubled efforts at restabilizing the nonproliferation regime triggered by the plutonium scare had considerable achievements to its credits. A more restrictive set of export guidelines is now observed by mainline suppliers. A new, if incomplete consensus has developed on the dangers of generous technology transfer policies and on the value of nonproliferation relative to other, largely commercial national interests.[17] The more egregious activities of new nuclear suppliers have been curbed; the P.R.C. has been brought into the fold of the nonproliferation regime, reinforcing its credibility. Progress thus has been made both in strengthening collective norms on the monitoring of nuclear exchanges and in enlarging the institutional means for performing collective functions of regime management.

Although the modified regime now in place represents a considerable instrumental achievement, there is reason to refrain from concluding that this success amounts to a supersedence of statist politics. Indeed, there is grounds for judging that the future depends primarily on security calculations of individual nation-states, even if made more enlightened through their participation in the nonproliferation regime.

PROGRESS AND REALPOLITIK

Our review of the nonproliferation regime's evolution, and the approach of American policy toward it, has considered a slice of international reality where progressive ideas have been implemented. A progressive philosophy's value as an organizing construct for understanding and interpreting international relations depends on refining its concepts and testing them against reality, as we have sought to do here. It entails two questions: "What sort of change has occurred and how should one typify it?" and "What measure of consistency is there between progressive goals and the actual means by which they have been reached and/or approached?"

We have confirmed the editors' proposition that instrumental success need not presume an improvement in the nature of political intercourse in world affairs. Even desirable system changes may derive from the play of power, as in the Soviet–American joint push behind the Non-Proliferation Treaty, inspired by convergent fears of how their national security might be threatened by the spread of nuclear weapons. Progress without successful accomplishment is inconceivable. Yet a foreign policy can be effective despite, or regardless of, its being guided by the precepts of a progressive philosophy, or using some of its means. This may be due simply to the unintended consequence of changes unaccounted for in the framing and execution of the policy. Those successes also may be due to constellations of interest that neither represent a qualitative improvement in international relations, in the maximalist sense, nor are likely to endure beyond the circumstances that permitted them to form.

The plutonium issue is a concrete case in point. The U.S. objective of blocking the widespread commercial transfer and use of plutonium has been largely realized—for the time being. But the subsequent slowdown in the recycling of plutonium (with the consequence that it has yet to become available on a wide scale)) may have reflected less worldwide adherence to the American vision of the nuclear world, or acceptance of its government's injunctions, than it did a concatenation of economic circumstances that militates against expansion of civilian nuclear energy, and the use of plutonium especially. They include reduced rates of increase in electricity demand, the drop in oil prices and its improved reliability as a fuel source, and the softening of prices for uranium fields. Thus, the reason for this favorable occurrence might have had relatively little to do with the fundamentals of how nations define their interests, or in the rules that govern their interaction.

The more basic, indeed overarching question is why nation-states

decide whether or not to acquire nuclear arms. Is it because of re-
gime-induced modifications in the way they view interests? because
of regime-maintained nonproliferation norms that embody a collective good for the world community? because of regime-imposed restraints on access to necessary materials? And/or is it because of
judgments by national governments of what is needed to satisfy state
security?

There is no reason to dispute the assertion that the nonproliferation regime has reduced the "rate and degree of proliferation" to
some immeasurable degree.[18] The question is, "Why and how?"
Institutionalized norms and obligations do militate against proliferation insofar as they add to the political and economic costs that a
potential proliferator must take into account. Furthermore, their cod-
ification in solemn international treaties and their institutionalization
lend to them a symbolic meaning that increases their value even
further. But do they exercise much independent influence on states'
definition of *need*—their *security need* above all?

On balance, there is reason to incline toward the view that (1)
security interests predominate in decisions on weapons questions;
and (2) relatively few states have taken up the nuclear option mainly
because their security interests have been satisfactorily attended to
otherwise. By implication the influence of the regime *per se* has been
marginal, if consequential. It is not an unreasonable conclusion that
the instrumental action of the great powers, aimed at meeting national security needs, has been the strongest—although not the only
—force working against proliferation, however uncongenial that idea
may be. Those policies are the essential underpinning to the nonproliferation regime. The regime, in its institutional expression, has
made a significant contribution. But it has been enabled by the heavy
investment of political capital by the superpowers (as supplemented
by that of other nuclear proficient states). That investment has given
the IAEA–NPT focused regime its critical deistic push. The readiness
to provide further impetus for reasons of enlightened self-interest is
likely to determine its resilience and future effectiveness.

Placed in this perspective, the achievement represented by the
Nuclear Non-Proliferation Treaty deserves some skeptical scrutiny. It
often is portrayed as a radical break from the realpolitik tradition that
arms make the state. Indeed, the treaty *is* unique in that nonweapons
states have taken a pledge of abstinence that is, in effect, a self-

denying injunction on the most potent class of arms that exists. The list of signatories constitutes an impressive diplomatic success. However, is this fact, in itself, conclusive evidence of a distinct improvement in the structure of international relations? Is the perceived change of a general nature and will it endure? Beyond such positive changes as might have occurred, is the evidence that behavior (or *some* behavior) with regard to a particular class of armaments has "improved" itself reason to presume that basic dynamic of interstate politics has been altered?

Nuclear weapons do indeed seem to have modified the way some nations (the superpowers certainly) view questions of war and peace (in respect to using or risking the use of those weapons). There is slimmer grounds, however, for confident assertions about how ' ridely that lesson has been learned. The NPT *alone* is not a sufficient basis for saying that states now abjure nuclear weapons as arms too dangerous, and too lacking in utility, to possess. The evidence does allow an assertion that a global consensus has emerged stigmatizing the acquisition of nuclear weapons and, thereby, inhibiting the behavior of national governments. But that consensus is not universal or unqualified. A review of signatories (weapons and nonweapons states) and nonsignatories is instructive on this point.

Indeed, there is even some grounds for the radical judgment that most states that have had both the *means* and the *need* to build nuclear weapons (by some reasonable, objective standard) have done so. Most nuclear-capable adherents to the NPT either have been constrained to observe self-denial (the U.S.S.R.'s Eastern European dependents) or have had their security interests met by a protective ally (nonnuclear members of NATO; Japan; indirectly, the European neutrals). Other states with a concrete security threat with which to cope have gone the nuclear route (China, India, Israel, South Africa, Pakistan) or have striven to keep open the option (Iraq, Iran, South Korea, Taiwan). Apparently, the last two both made affirmative decisions in the 1970s only to bend to extreme American pressure.[19] It is a classic system of protective alliances in a global security environment, overshadowed and rendered stable by fears of world nuclear war, that is the *primary* cause of self-restraint on the part of potential proliferators. Where this logic has not held, and will not hold in the future, is in areas of regional conflict that generate severe security threats inadequately dealt with by conventional defenses and protective alliances. I believe that assertions are supported by the evidence of decisions taken by threshold nuclear states.[20]

A fair judgment would seem to be that the nonproliferation regime has been sustained as much by the deployment of national power, and the manipulation of national interests, as by common conviction as to the value of a global structure of peace. The United States has given the Federal Republic of Germany and Japan iron-clad security guarantees. It threatened Taiwan and South Korea with punitive action while tempting them with attractive aid packages of conventional armaments. Where the mix of classic carrots and sticks has not been potent enough, security-anxious states have found cause to acquire nuclear arms, even when presented with a clear vision of consequences and an enlightened version of their own interest.

Progress then has been made. It is, though, of a minimalist kind: instrumental in reflecting primarily states' formulations of what their interests are; and states' judgments as to the means for realizing them—however exceptional the forms some of these means take (including creation of a multinational, institutionalized vehicle for affirming convergent national objectives). Where state prerogatives have been attenuated, it is at the margins of their sovereign authority. States have yielded that authority to circumstances, not to a radically different conception of how to serve human interests.

CONCLUSIONS

The evidence from the nonproliferation field indicates that overall there has not been a transcendence of a state-based international system whose members habitually follow the logic of *Staatspolitik*. With regard to security, the most elemental of political concerns, the locus of authoritative decision making remains at the level of states. Their calculations of security obviously *have* become more enlightened insofar as they are made in stark recognition that self-reliant means to security may not suffice. Enlightenment properly can be ascribed to an objective condition, the lethality of weaponry, which is an overriding fact of strategic life. This is a lesson clearly etched in the collective consciousness of the great nuclear powers. Yet we should recognize that although the balance of self-reliance and mutuality may have shifted in the nuclear age, it always has figured to some degree in the thinking of *realpolitik* statesmen. Furthermore, in the contemporary world, that shift may well have been considerably less among those minor nuclear powers with serious, conventional security problems than among the great powers.

There is a paradox for American nonproliferation thinking that matches the intellectual paradox of defining security in a nuclear world. It is the following. Although American foreign policy has generally followed a logic that recognizes "raison d'état" as the mainspring of state behavior, it simultaneously tends to conjure a view of the world that disparages power and conflict as staples of international life. Liberal belief remains that they not only can be controlled and moderated, but transcended. Under the influence of that belief, we run the constant risk of confusing two things: our preferred view of how other states should think and act, and those of our actions that influence their behavior. Success, in a progressive–liberal frame of reference, comes to be measured by our presumed ability to surmount power politics. Hence, the misrepresentation of solid accomplishment itself can become a policy liability by making it hard to distinguish between situations that warrant appeals to collective warfare and those that warrant traditional *staatspolitik* in different mixes.[21]

The gravest danger is that we will lose sight of how critical to our nonproliferation efforts have been our security policies and lose patience for dealing with recurring regional problems (in the Middle East, in South Asia). Nonproliferation policy, as Joseph S. Nye has reminded us, "is part of foreign policy" and therefore entails "adjustment of partly conflicting objectives."[22] The conflict is manifest in the classic "dove's dilemma."[23] Military assistance and security guarantees extended to potential weapon states who live in a threatening environment is a key ingredient in a strategy designed to dampen their appetite for nuclear arms. Yet there is a constant anxiety lest we thereby fuel those regional conflicts that engender security worries. In an American political atmosphere where skepticism abounds about the wisdom and affordability of the U.S. overseas commitments, the latitude for providing security guarantees and for fine-tuning military assistance programs may be narrowing significantly. A politically effective argument for curtailing those commitments advocates placing the full weight of our nonproliferation energies behind multilateral strategies for regime construction, expansion, and development. In this way, the "sanitizing" of American foreign policy through the suppression of state-centered, security-minded policies is envisaged. However, if in fact it is state-centered security policies that have been most instrumental in keeping nuclear aspirations in check, there would be a loss of real effectiveness in goal achievement for the sake of apparent success in enhancing the instruments of collective action directed at another, less salient facet of the proliferation problem.

Embedded in the dove's dilemma is the issue of whether informed publics contribute to making substantive progress in realizing the ends of human welfare. In this instance, it can be argued that popular aversion to America's playing the role of world policeman represents a positive factor, encouraging the U.S. government to relinquish its prerogatives of state in favor of a more "systemic" approach to security. There is a differing interpretation, though, that separates the disposition toward restraint in the exercise of state power to achieve nationally defined interests from a readiness to support the development of institutionalized collective perspectives on those interests and building the attendant capabilities to achieve them.

In the United States, philosophies of progress have tended to be populist.[24] But although most Americans have believed strongly in change as leading to the building of a better society, the range of this belief often has been confined to the United States. After all, the country was founded in self-conscious distinction from other nations. Understandably, the United States' self-proclaimed and undeniable capacity for improvement based on enlightened self-interest has not always inspired a commitment to an outward-looking internationalism. For much of its history, the United States was content to present itself as a model for, rather than an instigator of positive change. The more parochial approach to the world, which concentrates on the singularity of the United States, has been reconciled with the universal internationalism of a broadly progressive-minded foreign policy only for the relatively brief if highly significant period after World War II.[25] Hence, an agnostic position on the issue of the relationship between informed publics and the maximalist vision of progress best conforms to the national experience of the United States, at least.

American foreign policy, as evinced in its approach to nuclear nonproliferation, exhibits features that match both the minimalist conception of progress and more traditional *staatspolitik*. The nonproliferation regime of which it has been primary architect reveals a similar mix of influences. Although the assessment offered here has stressed the latter element, it should not be equated with a stereotypic realism. The record does not validate a vision that views the world as a bleak landscape dominated by power configurations whose endless permutations offer the only change, and their management the only opportunity for initiative. There has been evidence that the conceptions and conduct associated with a progressive outlook work. But they best serve the cause of enlightenment and human betterment when modified to accommodate a less than pliable world environment where multiple perspectives, interests, and behaviors are intermingled.

ENDNOTES

1. My purpose in this essay is not to provide a comprehensive assessment of the nonproliferation regime. Nor is it meant to offer a forecast of proliferation risks. Either endeavor would require substantially more space than the format of this book allows. Rather, I focus on some core elements of the proliferation regime in order to illustrate general points about the ideas of progress in the conduct of American foreign policy and in the evolution of the nonproliferation regime.
2. The modification of strategic thinking in the presence of nuclear weapons is a much discussed subject. Among the most cogent appraisals of the change in doctrine and policy are Lawrence Martin, ed., *Strategic Thought in the Nuclear Age* (Baltimore: Johns Hopkins University Press, 1979)—in particular, contributions by Martin and Henry S. Rowen; Michael Mandelbaum, *The Nuclear Question* (New York: Cambridge University Press, 1979); and Fred Kaplan, *Wizards of Armageddon* (New York: Simon and Schuster, 1983).
3. The subtleties of perception and policy in nuclear weapons are addressed with insight and proportion by Robert Jervis, *The Illogic of American Nuclear Strategy* (Ithaca, NY: Cornell University Press, 1985). See also his *Perceptions and Misperceptions in International Politics* (Princeton, N.J.: Princeton University Press, 1976).
4. I have borrowed the broader formulation from Raymond Aron, *Progress and Disillusion* (New York: Praeger, 1968), introduction.

   Technical innovation exemplifies the idea of progress. Technique— defined as organized means used in a prescribed, orderly manner to achieve ends conceived in advance—encompasses both technology (its mechanical expression) and rationalized organization operating according to strict rules and procedures (its institutional expression).
5. The history of Atoms for Peace and founding of the IAEA is reexamined in J. Pilat, S. Pendley, and C. Ebinger, eds., *Atoms for Peace: An Analysis*

After Thirty Years (Boulder, Colo.: Westview, 1985). See also Berstrand Goldschmidt, *The Atomic Complex* (Washington, D.C.: The American Nuclear Society, 1982). Lawrence Scheinman provides us with a penetrating examination of the Agency's current state in *The International Atomic Energy Agency and World Nuclear Order* (Washington, D.C.: Resources for the Future, 1987).

6. Independently, the Indians had constructed the critical plutonium separation plant using knowhow gathered from the U.S. Atomic Energy Commission's training courses. Participants from countries with whom Washington had nuclear cooperation agreements were welcome. Indeed, the commission had a dedicated program to raise skill levels in nuclear engineering among recipient countries. For a contemporaneous account of the issues raised see the Ford Foundation sponsored study *Nuclear Power Issues and Choices* (Cambridge, Mass.: Ballinger Publishing Co., 1977).

7. See my account in *Nuclear Energy and Non-Proliferation: The Remaking of U.S. Policy* (New York: Cambridge University Press, 1981)

8. Brenner, *Nuclear Energy* (ibid.) ch. 3.

9. John G. Ruggie, "International Responses to Technology: Concepts and Trends." *International Organization* (Summer 1975), 34:570.

10. See Robert Jervis, "Security Regimes," in Stephen Krasner, ed., *International Regimes* (Ithaca, N.Y.: Cornell University Press, 1983) for a succinct statement of the distinction between regime and simple agreement in security relations. Jervis's views are considered with reference to nonproliferation regimes by Roger L. Smith, "Explaining the Non-Proliferation Regime: Anomalies for Contemporary International Relations Theory," *International Organization* (Spring 1987), 41(2).

11. Ernst B. Haas, "Words Can Hurt You; or, Who Said What to Whom About Regimes," *International Organization* (Spring 1982), 36(2):207.

12. Stephen D. Krasner, "Regimes and the Limits of Realism: Regimes as Autonomous Variables," *International Organization* (Spring 1982) 36(2):504.

  To put the paradox of the IAEA's evolution in more explicitly functionalist terms, the incremental steps taken in conformity with established institutional procedures to diffuse nuclear technology extended collective rules to cover a wide range of transfer, but did not extend the scope of regulatory rule-making to encompass new and dangerous applications. These issues are deftly analyzed by Ernest B. Haas in *The Obsolescence of Regional Integration Theory*, Research Series, No. 25, Institute of International Studies, University of California, Berkeley, 1977.

13. Brenner, *Nuclear Energy* ch. 4, 5.

14. The notion of a pliable environment owes something to American domestic circumstance as well as to its optimistic philosophy of progress. The entire American experience is popularly viewed as a pageant of progress. Improvement and steady achievement are made possible because resistance (inert or active) will give way to the force of human volition guided by informed goodwill. Carter, a quintessential American

populist, had an abundance of goodwill and optimistic faith in the eventual success of earnest effort.

15. The Reagan administration's nonproliferation policy was a unique mix of unilateral nationalism (inspired by "realist" views of nationalist interest) and "ad hocism." The former led to a downgrading of multilateral approaches and a readiness to qualify the commitment to nonproliferation by introducing other foreign policy concerns. Each case tended to be treated individually as general principles got diluted. As a result, even in those instances in which official Washington attitudes had stiffened, U.S. policy had little effect in strengthening common rules.

16. I examine these and related issues raised by the China treaty in *The US/PRC Nuclear Bilateral Accord* Case Study in Negotiation, Pew Foundation (Pittsburgh, 1986). See also Leonard Spector, *Nuclear Proliferation Today* (New York: Vintage, 1984).

17. The achievement at renovating the nonproliferation regime in response to the crisis of the 1970s is appraised with insight and judicious balance by Joseph Nye, "Maintaining the Non-Proliferation Regime," in George Quester, ed., *Breaking the Chain: Nuclear Proliferation* (Madison: University of Wisconsin Press, 1981).

18. Nye, ibid., p. 33

19. Stephen M. Meyer has systematically examined the state decisions of whether or not to "go nuclear" in his penetrating book *The Dynamics of Nuclear Proliferation* (Chicago: University of Chicago Press, 1984). The evidence he adduces supports the contention that security considerations have predominated, including governments toward an affirmative decision.

20. Ibid., passim. A set of case studies that offers reinforcing evidence are found in Mitchell Reiss, *Without the Bomb: The Politics of Nuclear Non-Proliferation* (New York: Columbia University Press, 1988). He treats Sweden, South Korea, Japan, Israel, South Africa, and India. On India, see also Shyam Bhatia, *India's Nuclear Bomb* (New Delhi: Vikas, 1979); A. Kapur, *India's Nuclear Option* (New York: Praeger, 1976); and Spector, *Nuclear Proliferation Today*. On Pakistan, S. Weissman and H. Krosney, *The Islamic Bomb* (New York: Times Books, 1981) and Spector, *Nuclear Proliferation Today*. On Israel, Peter Pry, *Israel's Nuclear Arsenal* (Westview, 1984) and Leonard Spector, *The Undeclared Bomb* (Ballinger, 1988). An assessment of the British, French, Chinese, and Israeli nuclear policies is also made by McGeorge Bundy, *Danger and Survival: Choices about the Bomb in the First Fifty Years* (New York: Random House, 1989).

For the older nuclear powers, the classic works are Wilfred Kohl, *French Nuclear Diplomacy* (Princeton, N.J.: Princeton University Press, 1971); Andrew Pierre, *Nuclear Politics* (New York: Oxford University Press, 1972); and John Lewis and Xue Litai, *China Builds the Bomb* (Stanford, Calif.: Stanford University Press, 1988).

21. There is a more fundamental contradiction. Success, from a progressive standard, is measured, among other indicators, by our ability to *transcend*

power politics. The task of reconciling power-based means and idealistic ends is akin to squaring the circle. One at times can combine elements of liberal idealism and *realpolitik* in the practice of diplomacy, but devotion to the belief that power politics could and should be transcended is likely to create unavoidable pitfalls for a foreign policy burdened by this dual personality.

The uneasy fit of *realpolitik* concepts and American thinking about foreign affairs is clearly in evidence in the contributions to *Neorealism and Its Critics*, Robert O. Keohane, ed., (New York: Columbia University Press, 1986). Criticisms offered to Kenneth N. Waltz's modest argument for consideration of the classic realist wisdom are most revealing of how enduring the liberal tradition is that denies a place to power politics in its view of world affairs.

22. Nye, "Maintaining the Non-Proliferation Regime," p. 31.
23. For a penetrating re-examination see George Quester's "Introduction" to *Breaking the Chain*.
24. See James H. Billington, "Realism and Visions in Foreign Policy," *Foreign Affairs: America and the World 1986*. The elitism of Fabian socialism and other brands of English progressive thought have produced only a thin resonance in the United States.
25. An insightful interpretation of the ascendance, and now decline, of universalistic internationalism is provided by Thomas L. Hughes in his scintillating essay "The Twilight of Internationalism," *Foreign Policy*, (Winter 1985–1986), 61.

6

EMBEDDED LIBERALISM REVISITED: INSTITUTIONS AND PROGRESS IN INTERNATIONAL ECONOMIC RELATIONS

John Gerard Ruggie

A recurrent theme in the popular press and some academic accounts holds that the postwar economic regimes have already collapsed, or are in the process of doing so, with dire consequences ahead for international economic relations. Monetary disorder, neonationalist protectionism in trade, and a more generalized lack of leadership and external discipline, it is said, are coming to prevail. There is a measure of truth in these claims: Instances of each of these disturbing features can be found in current international economic relations. At the same time, however, there are good grounds to question the extent to which the conventional wisdom has fully grasped actual patterns of continuity and change. Above all, these scenarios of imminent calamity have been with us for nearly two decades now, from the alleged "collapse" of Bretton Woods and the anticipated "trade wars" of the early 1970s.[1] "Not since the 1930s . . ." has been a staple of economic commentary ever since. But two decades is not an unsubstantial period of time. For example, it is equivalent to the *entire* interwar period, which we routinely treat as an era of the twentieth century. Moreover, even when the conventional wisdom is descriptively accurate, the inferences drawn from the descriptions are often exaggerated or yield anomalous conclusions.

If imminence fails to materialize over such an extended duration and if anomalies abound, then it may be worth exploring whether there is something amiss, not in the world of actual state behavior, but in the model of state behavior that analysts are bringing to bear on it. That, at any rate, is the proposition I explore here.

In the first section, I lay out what I take to have been the basic institutional framework by which the capitalist countries sought to come to grips with the twin desires of domestic and international economic stability at the outset of the postwar period—which I capture by the term *embedded liberalism,* in contradistinction to orthodox liberalism. Next, I sketch in the salient features of the postwar monetary and trade regimes through which the embedded liberalism compromise was enacted. I then examine actual patterns of state behavior in monetary and trade relations up to the present and show that what appears as anomalous behavior when viewed through the lenses of the conventional wisdom is quite consistent with the expectations of the embedded liberalism model. Finally, I conclude by suggesting that the bogus fears of the "new protectionism" mask very real progress in international economic relations during the postwar era—"instrumental progress" in the terminology of this volume—insofar as states appear to have institutionalized certain norms and precepts that make a recurrence of the 1930s a low-probability event.

THE EMBEDDED LIBERALISM COMPROMISE

As U.S. policymakers originally envisioned the postwar international economic order, their chief objective was that it be nondiscriminatory, which is to say that it reflect the principle of the open door. No mutually exclusive economic blocs were to be permitted, no beggar-thy-neighbor policies followed. Moreover, the United States favored the reduction of barriers to the flow of international economic transactions, especially those that lacked transparency and were difficult to apply in a nondiscriminatory manner. The international division of labor that would emerge as a result of these measures would enhance not only American but also global welfare, U.S. policymakers believed, while minimizing economic sources of inter-

national conflict. The mutually destructive consequences of the external economic policies states pursued in the 1930s were invoked as
evidence to justify these beliefs.

At the same time, the postwar designs of U.S. policymakers also
reflected another reality of the interwar years: the growing demand
for and acceptability of state intervention in domestic economies,
attempting to stabilize employment and prices in the face of the
cyclical fluctuations that had always inhered in capitalist development. Indeed, the New Deal became an international showcase of
sorts, an inspiration to both the theory and practice of reformist
economic policy formation abroad. Neither the New York banking
community nor the Republican party was much enamored by what
they regarded as New Deal gimmickry, in domestic and international
economic policy alike, but their views, although significant, did not
prevail.

As a result, steps by the United States toward liberalization were
coupled from the outset with measures to safeguard domestic stability. The Reciprocal Trade Agreements Act of 1934 typically is cited as
heralding the American quest for liberalism to come. Yet, as Stephan
Haggard has pointed out, President Roosevelt put off its submission
to the Congress until domestic legislation was in place shielding
business and agriculture from external threats and extending new
guarantees to labor. And even then it contained escape clause provisions, permitting temporary protection of industries injured by liberalizing concessions.[2] What was politically expedient in the United
States in 1934 had reached the status of historical first principle
abroad by 1944: no liberalization without safeguards.

And so emerged the compromise of embedded liberalism, the
grand domestic and international political bargain on which the postwar economic regimes came to rest: unlike the economic nationalism
of the 1930s, the international economic order would be multilateral
in character; but unlike the liberalism of the gold standard and free
trade, its multilateralism would be predicated upon domestic interventionism.[3] Domestically, this was a compromise between the major social groupings (agriculture, labor, and capital), as well as
between export-oriented and import-competing industries. Internationally, it was a compromise between the United States, where
domestic stabilization measures remained the least comprehensive
and systematic, and the most constrained by opposition, and the

European states, where rejection of liberal orthodoxy was universal but the objects of economic protection varied widely among the left, right, and center of the political spectrum.[4]

In sum, the broad expectation was held in governing circles at the dawn of the postwar era that the international economic order would become multilateral in form. Movement toward greater openness in the international economy, however, would be coupled with safeguards that acknowledged and even facilitated the interventionist character of the modern capitalist state. But the measures adopted to effect such domestic cushioning also were expected to be commensurate with the extent of the external disruptions and compatible with the long-term expansion of international economic transactions.

THE BRETTON WOODS REGIMES[5]

On the monetary side, by the time of the Anglo-American "Joint Statement of Principles," issued not long before the Bretton Woods Conference, a consensus had emerged between these two nations that provided for free and stable exchanges, on the one hand, and, on the other, the erection of a "double screen," in Richard Cooper's suggestive words,[6] to cushion the domestic economy against the strictures of the balance of payments.[7] Free exchanges would be assured by the abolition of all forms of exchange controls and restrictions on current transactions. Stable exchanges would be secured by setting and maintaining official par values, expressed in terms of gold. The "double screen" would consist of short-term assistance to finance payments deficits on current account, provided by an International Monetary Fund, and, so as to correct a "fundamental disequilibrium," the ability to exchange rates with Fund concurrence. Governments would be permitted to maintain control over capital movements.

In devising the instruments of the monetary regime, the most intense negotiations were occasioned by the functioning of the "double screen." On the question of the Fund, the British, in the person of John Maynard Keynes, had argued for an international overdraft facility, a Clearing Union. This would have created some $25 to $30 billion in new liquidity, with the overall balance of credits and debits in the Fund being expressed in an international unit of account that was to be monetized. The arrangement would have been self-clearing unless a country were out of balance with the system as a whole, in which case complementary corrective measures were called for on the part of surplus and deficit countries alike. The ceiling could be raised by simple intergovernmental agreement, as additional liquidity was required to finance international trade. The U.S. plan, proposed by Harry Dexter White, the American counterpart of Keynes in these negotiations, originally called for a mere $5 billion Fund, though the United States ultimately agreed to $8.8 billion. However, these funds had to be paid in by subscription, as opposed to being created by agreement. Both access to the Fund and total liability were strictly limited by quotas, as were voting rights, all of which in turn reflected paid-in subscriptions—the initial U.S. contribution was $3.175 billion. Additional liquidity would come from increased gold production and the more costly process of increasing quotas (subscriptions). Moreover, a country that sought to draw on the Fund had to make "representations" that it needed assistance for making payments on current account, and for no other reason. Thus, with the United States, the only major creditor country in sight, seeking to limit its liabilities, the first part of the "double screen" was both more modest and more rigid than the United Kingdom and other potential debtor countries would have liked. But there was no question about its being provided.

On the second part, exchange rate changes, the United Kingdom was more successful in assuring automaticity and limiting intrusions into the domain of domestic policy. The Fund was required to concur in any change necessary to correct a "fundamental disequilibrium," and if the change was less than 10 percent, the Fund was given no power even to raise objections. Most important, the Fund could not oppose *any* exchange rate change on the grounds that the domestic social policies of the country requesting the change had led to the disequilibrium that made the change necessary.

Interestingly, the central issue of international liquidity generated relatively little discussion. In all probability, this was for two reasons. First, under the British overdraft scheme international liquidity would have been a nonissue, or at least only a minor issue, since accounts had to balance out while the ceiling could be raised as needed, and the British were too preoccupied with salvaging their scheme to pay close attention to alternative solutions to the liquidity problem. Second, the United States was not keen to have the issue discussed, counting all along on the U.S. dollar emerging as the chief international medium of national currency reserves. And of course it did. All currencies were valued against the dollar and the dollar against gold; all countries in practice would use dollars to clear their international accounts and the dollar would be convertible into gold on demand. As a result, however, with gold production subsequently being inadequate and quota increases constrained by U.S. voting power, U.S. payments deficits became the major source of international liquidity.

Once negotiations on postwar commercial arrangements got under way seriously, in the context of an International Conference on Trade and Employment, the principles of multilateralism and tariff reduction were affirmed, but so were safeguards, exemptions, exceptions, and restrictions—all designed to protect the balance of payments and a variety of domestic social policies.[8] The proposed Charter for an all-encompassing International Trade Organization became internally so inconsistent that it is difficult to say just what sort of regime it would have given rise to. In any case, the U.S. Senate refused to ratify the Charter, it being too intrusive for some and not activist enough for others, as a result of which a far smaller domain of commercial relations became subject to the international regime than would have been the case otherwise. Among the most important areas excluded thereby were the regulation of commodity markets, restrictive business practices, and international investments. The more traditional concerns of commercial policy—tariffs, quotas, and the like—were addressed by the General Agreement on Tariffs and Trade (GATT), which the United States quickly helped to form and joined by executive order.

The GATT made obligatory the most-favored-nation rule, but a blanket exception had to be allowed for all existing preferential agreements (a U.S. concession to Britain), and countries were permitted to form customs unions and free trade areas (U.S. encouragement to Western Europe). Moreover, quantitative import restrictions were prohibited, but were deemed suitable measures for safeguarding the balance of payments—*explicitly* including payments difficulties that resulted from domestic full-employment policies. They could also be invoked in agricultural trade if they were used in conjunction with a domestic price support program. The substantial reduction of tariffs and other barriers to trade was called for, but it was *not* made obligatory, and it was coupled with appropriate emergency actions, which were allowed if a domestic producer was threatened with injury from import competition that was due to past tariff concessions. The Agreement also offered a blanket escape from any of its obligations, provided that two thirds of the contracting parties approved—the United States promptly availed itself of the opportunity to exclude its entire agricultural trade from international scrutiny. Lastly, procedures were provided to settle disputes arising under the Agreement and for the multilateral surveillance of the invocation of most (though not all) of its escape clauses. The principle of reciprocity was enshrined as a code of conduct, to guide both tariff reductions and the determination of compensation for injuries suffered.

In the minds of White and Keynes, the institutional edifice necessary for a viable international economic order to emerge would require yet a third pillar: the intergovernmental provision of investment capital. Neither thought that private sources of investment funds alone could do the job, and they pointed to the erratic patterns of capital flows in the interwar period as proof positive. Hence, both turned to intergovernmental schemes. Indeed, White's first draft plan for an "Inter-Allied Bank" was more ambitious than his corresponding proposal for a monetary fund. The Bank would have a capital stock of $10 billion and was designed to engage in counter-cyclical investment as well as the stabilization of commodity prices. Keynes's proposal was more tentative, because for him much hinged on whether or not his Clearing Union was adopted, but he leaned toward an international mechanism to coordinate national investment plans. Needless to say, neither the United States nor the United Kingdom was interested in so constraining their national discretion or the future of their national capital markets, a sentiment that was echoed if not amplified by their respective financial centers. The International Bank for Reconstruction and Development (World Bank) that ultimately emerged from the Bretton Woods negotiations was barely a pale shadow of these initial plans.

These efforts to construct multilateral economic regimes did not succeed until the 1950s. Only then had European leaders acquired the confidence to undertake the process of liberalization. The European Economic Community had been formed, the IMF agreements became fully operational, and successive rounds of GATT negotiations got under way that would virtually eliminate tariff barriers to trade and unleash the most sustained period of economic growth

ever. Getting from "here to there" required massive doses of direct
U.S. assistance: economic assistance in the form of the Marshall Plan,
and security assistance in the form of NATO.[9] With the Marshall
Plan bearing the brunt of European reconstruction financing, the
World Bank's initial mission, the Bank slowly turned its attention to
becoming a development finance institutions. These changes went
hand in hand with an overall reorientation of U.S. foreign policy,
whereby the United States moved from being "arsenal" of to an
"agent" for reconstruction abroad.[10] In the process, the monetary
and trade regimes lost the universalism that would have been provided by socialist membership, whereas European and Japanese par-
ticularisms were encouraged.

PATTERNS OF CHANGE AND CONTINUITY

In a major survey of international monetary reform published
in 1985, *The Economist* wrote: "How easy to say that, in the early
1970s, the Bretton Woods system 'collapsed' or was 'swept away.'
Easy but unfortunate." It went on to exclaim: "Of course, fixed rates
were replaced by floating ones—but was that the change that mattered . . . ? Certainly, governments were freed of the external discipline of maintaining parity; but didn't they still face other disciplines
. . . ?"[11] In point of fact, neither the monetary nor the trade regime
has ever functioned as designed. What is more, over the course of
time, specific instruments of the two regimes have been abandoned;
deviations from rules have not been unusual and may be becoming
more frequent; and even core norms are sometimes disregarded with
impunity as governments pursue their national objectives. All of this
is well known and beyond dispute. What remains in contention is its
significance, and what it signifies.

How can perfectly reasonable and intelligent observers differ on
so basic an issue as whether or not a regime has collapsed? Because
they bring very different mind-sets to bear on the question. At least
three such sources of distortion have been identified in the monetary
realm. Peter Kenen cites one: "Without always knowing, most of us
have judged events, decisions, and proposals by an idealistic, cos-
mopolitan criterion. We have asked how far each step has taken us
toward the creation of a world money to which national monies
would be subordinated and by which they might some day be sup-

planted."[12] Seen in this light, most efforts at monetary reform may well look like "slapstick comedy," which is how Robert Triffin dismissed the 1976 Jamaica Accords that enshrined floating exchange rates.[13] Yet the governments involved appeared to take it reasonably seriously. *The Economist* describes another prevalent mind-set. "Some people like to have things written down and agreed: to them, the international monetary system should indeed be a system, complete with charters and pacts. Others feel that messy evolution is inevitable, and better for it." As it happens, governments appear to prefer changes of the messy sort. Finally, Robert Aliber sardonically characterizes yet a third widespread mind-set as the willingness on the part of some analysts to "risk sacrificing the state to save the constitution"—that is, to expect governments to adhere rigidly to rules, no matter what the conditions, and no matter what the consequences.[14] Governments have not been prone to oblige. Similar mind-sets are at work in commentaries on the trade regime, except there the emotive appeal of orderliness and texts if anything is heightened by virtue of the greater involvement of international legal scholars.

Assessing the efficacy of international economic regimes, then, is not an easy or straightforward task, like checking off a list of performance criteria for a home furnace or an automobile engine. The underlying core problem is that, ultimately, there exists no Archimedean point from which regimes can be viewed as they "truly" are. In the final analysis the "reality" of regimes resides in the principled and shared understandings of desirable and acceptable forms of behavior among the relevant actors. Adaptations to new and unforeseen developments, attenuating circumstances, the rationales and justifications for deviations that are proffered, as well as the responsiveness to such reasoning on the part of other states, all are critical in assessing the efficacy of regimes. As *The Economist* put it, "even the breaching gives the government a chance to explain why some departure from plan was necessary or inevitable."[15] Such communicative dynamics may tell us more about how robust a regime is than actual behavior alone.[16]

From the vantage of this perspective, international regimes are not expected to produce saints from sinners, but only to keep their sins within more or less mutually permissible bounds. Nor are international regimes defined by an unwavering commitment to specific instrumentalities, which *should* change so as to accommodate the many situational differences that inevitably emerge over time, but by how compatible these instrumentalities remain with the underlying normative understandings that animate the regimes, given currently prevailing circumstances. Governments in the trenches, not analysts perched on Archimedean points, are the ultimate judges of what constitutes compatibility.[17]

Next, I briefly examine the most commonly discussed changes in the monetary and trade regimes; and I suggest that there is less to fear from the conventional problems than is typically assumed.

The Monetary Regime

Seen against the background of the abusive currency practices of the interwar period, a singular achievement of the postwar monetary regime has been the creation of a nondiscriminatory system of currency exchanges. All major currencies are fully convertible into one another; none is governed by multiple exchange rates or other rationing schemes; and the remaining deviations either are insignificant, which is the case for controlled Third World currencies, or, as in the case of the socialist country currencies, are undergoing the slow and wrenching process of moving toward greater convertibility. This core dimension of multilateralism in monetary relations, the desire for which so animated the Bretton Woods negotiators, is so deeply instituted and taken for granted today that it is rarely even mentioned in assessments of the monetary regime.

When analysts today speak of the collapse of Bretton Woods they have in mind two other—and in my judgment, two lesser—features: fixed rates of exchange, and the gold convertibility of the U.S. dollar. And what they fear most is that excessive variability of exchange rates and increased disaffection with the management of the dollar, in addition to generating economic inefficiencies, will lead to greater monetary and trade protectionism, thereby indirectly evoking discriminatory practices.

Fixed Exchange Rates. Let us begin with fixed rates of exchange. We would do well to remind ourselves that under a system of *truly* fixed exchange rates, governments are expected to subordinate their domestic policies to the maintenance of parity: "monetary policy, as usually conceived, ceases to be a discretionary instrument of policy. The money supply on any meaningful definition must be altered if necessary to preserve the exchange rate."[18] It is safe to say that no government present at the Bretton Woods conference would have accepted this stricture had it been proposed. But of course it wasn't. Under the Bretton Woods arrangement, exchange rates were *expected* to change if necessary to correct "fundamental" disequilibria —a concept that remained undefined because governments would only know one when they saw one.

Thus, exchange rates were not fixed but were on an adjustable peg. This system in turn proved flawed because of several well-known factors. Surplus countries, particularly Germany and Japan, basking in the presumed virtue of surpluses and enjoying the competitive advantage of undervalued currencies, refused to revalue upward as much or as frequently as required. Deficit countries for their part were afraid of losing face and waited until the last minute to devalue. And the United States was prevented from making any change in the value of the dollar against other currencies because its price was fixed in terms of gold. For all practical purposes, then, there never was an effective means of routinely adjusting currency values to fundamental disequilibria. The adjustable peg system therefore was inherently unsustainable; only the timing of its demise was in doubt.

What is more, although controls on capital movements were not formally mandated by the Bretton Woods scheme, Richard Cooper points out that its internal logic required them, and they were expected to remain in place.[19] This too would have proved unsustainable in the long run, as it presupposed the ability to differentiate sharply between current and capital account transactions, a distinction that would have become murky as the volume of direct foreign investment and long-term trade credits continued to expand. But governments in addition deliberately chose to liberalize capital markets as a matter of policy preference. This combination of capital mobility and discrete exchange rate changes in turn "produced the celebrated one-way option for currency speculation" that was responsible for the recurrent exchange rate crises of the 1960s—when decisions to change rates were delayed so long that their inevitability provided a sure bet to speculators.[20] The inherent incompatibility of these two features of the monetary regime, capital mobility and pegged rates of exchange, both of which were deemed desirable in their own right, sooner or later would have forced the abandonment of one or the other. The surging U.S. inflation of the Johnson era, produced by expenditures for Vietnam and Great Society programs that were funded by monetary expansion rather than taxes, provided the proximate cause.

Accordingly, by the time governments adopted floating exchange rates in 1973, the choice *as they understood it* was "not between floating and fixed rates, but between rates changing by small amounts on a day-to-day basis and those changing at longer intervals by substantial percentages and usually only after macroeconomic policy debacles, welfare-reducing direct controls, and repeated foreign exchange crisis."[21] And they adopted a system of floating rates in the hope of securing greater domestic stability while preserving the relatively open trading and financial systems—objectives that surely were in keeping with the political framework of Bretton Woods. Besides, most of the world's currencies do not float even today but are pegged to a small handfull of key currencies that do.[22]

The Gold-Convertible Dollar. We saw earlier that the liquidity provisions of Bretton Woods were ambiguous from the start and proved inadequate in the event. As a result, the dollar exchange standard was already in trouble when the monetary regime first began to function as designed. In 1958, just as the Europeans were resuming full convertibility of their currencies, U.S. gold reserves fell permanently below U.S. overseas liabilities. And before the next year was out, Professor Triffin articulated the famous "dilemma" that bears his name.[23] Throughout the 1960s, a seemingly endless series of stop-gap measures was tried in an effort to devise what Robert Roosa, former Under Secretary of the Treasury, called "outer perimeter defense" for the dollar. Roughly speaking, these measures were designed to make gold conversion of dollars financially unattractive, to increase the capacity of the IMF to supply liquidity, and to increase the capacity of central banks to neutralize the flow of speculative capital. The United States also "taxed" its allies for military services provided by obtaining offset payments from them and through the exercise of seigniorage. And the United States undertook limited domestic measures to reduce its payments deficits while pressuring surplus countries to revalue their currencies. By 1968, however, the dollar had become in effect inconvertible into gold; it was declared formally so in 1971.

It is absolutely crucial to note, however, that although the link of the dollar to gold may have been "psychologically important," it was "technically tenuous."[24] That is so because it had not provided a principled basis for determining the overall world monetary condition in the first place. As Cooper explains, pegging the value of currencies in the manner of the Bretton Woods scheme "determines the price level of each country in relation to the others, but it does not determine the world price level."[25] So long as the United States pursued domestic economic policies that were conducive to international monetary stability, the problem remained masked. As the United States became unable and unwilling to perform that international public service, the problem became unmasked. But it had been no more resolved before 1971 than it is today; the problem has existed throughout.

It should also be noted that none of the major monetary powers has rushed forward with structural solutions to this congenital defect in the Bretton Woods regime. Like the United States, they have been content to patch things up around the edges. When the dollar has gone on one of its periodic wild gyrations—the sharp depreciation of 1978 and the staggering appreciation of 1981–1985 being prime instances—they of course have shown irritation; they have jaw-boned the United States; and the Europeans specifically have sought to limit the dislocating effects among themselves through further monetary integration. These governments have also from time to time coordinated extensive exchange market interventions, as in the Plaza Agreement of 1985 that sought to assure a "soft landing" for the dollar once its ascent had reversed. And they have provided substantial unilateral assistance: the financial analyst David Hale recently quipped that the Bank of Japan should have had to register as a GOP political-action committee in the 1988 U.S. presidential election, so helpful was it to supporting the dollar and thus to the Bush campaign.[26]

But to date none of these governments has been prepared to have their currencies play a truly significant international reserve currency role. There is no desire among them to return to a full-fledged gold standard, nor a consensus to construct a different commodity-based reserve asset, nor even to expand significantly the use of the IMF collectively created Special Drawing Rights. Indeed, so modest a modification as the Substitution Account proposed in 1979, whereby some portion of "unwanted" dollars could have been traded in for an IMF asset, was rejected in part over squabbles about the allocation of exchange rate risks and interest payments—just before the dollar glut was overtaken by a renewed scramble for dollars as a result of the second oil shock.

One final point deserves mention here. The specter of "currency blocs" is often adduced as a possible outcome of current international monetary practices, with the shadow of the 1930s projected ominously over today's exchange markets. The major candidates today are blocs organized around the U.S. dollar, the yen, and the European monetary system. The predicted emergence of these blocs may turn out to be correct; but the implied deleterious consequences simply do not follow. Peter Kenen has put this very well: "A currency bloc does not imply discrimination against outsiders, nor does it necessarily imply the internal exploitation that arose in some blocs during the 1930s."[27] Pegging one's currency to that of a neighbor, or closely aligning currencies within a group, in and of themselves are entirely neutral with respect to the norm of nondiscrimination. Only in the service of discriminatory norms do they become discriminatory practices. In contrast, under present circumstances such blocs actually may be helpful, by muting protectionist pressures on the trade front, reducing the vulnerability of the monetary regime to the fate of the dollar, and lowering the transaction costs of policy coordination among the three leading monetary authorities.

Volatility. Even most critics of the current international monetary arrangements agree that they helped absorb the extreme duress of the 1970s: the two oil shocks, double-digit inflation in the major OECD countries, and a complete and sudden reversal of prevailing current account balances that was unprecedented in peacetime. Floating exchange rates and liberalized capital markets were the central mechanisms of adjustment; the formal apparatus of the IMF played a relatively minor role. At the same time, there exists a growing unease that these mechanisms, far from providing the long-term international stability and relative domestic autonomy their advocates promised, are also responsible for increased volatility of exchange rates that have real and adverse consequences, both domestically and internationally. Once again, the facts are clear but the implications more ambiguous: "Market-determined exchange rates have exhibited wild instability beyond the fondest nightmares of fixed-rate fanatics, yet trade and investment flows seem relatively unaffected by these changes."[28] The answer to what appears to be going on here has two elements.

A clue to the first can be found in the relationship between the U.S. current account balance and the dollar exchange rate between 1981 and 1985: it defied all conventional understanding. While the U.S. trade deficit exploded from some $9 billion to over $100 billion, and as the United States was shifting toward net debtor status, the exchange rate of the dollar *appreciated* some 60 percent in real terms! Trade may well have "the last laugh," as *The Economist* claims,[29] but clearly the capital account gets some chuckles along the way. For what happened in the case of the United States was a vast inflow of foreign funds, attracted by interest rates, investment opportunities, a favorable fiscal environment, and political stability.

This case illustrates a deeper and more profound institutional development in the world economy: international capital markets have been cut loose from their role as servants to international trade. Their relative magnitude now dwarfs world trade flows. In 1984, world trade amounted to some $2 trillion; Eurocurrency deposits alone were about $2.4 trillion; and international capital movements as a whole ranged somewhere between a low estimate of $20 trillion to a high of $50 trillion.[30] Moreover, whereas capital movements historically reflected business decisions to finance trade or to establish production facilities abroad, "it seems apparent that the dominant proportion of the investment funds actually in movement internationally today reflects instead decisions concerning portfolio holdings . . . , shifts among holdings of various kinds of intangible assets."[31] Finally, as far as the international capital markets are concerned, the major currencies in the process have become simply one of those intangible assets. "The central message of the post-1973 experience is that the foreign exchange market is an asset market and that the economic laws governing exchange rates are fundamentally similar to those governing other asset prices, with stock and bond markets providing obvious domestic analogies. In fact, while exchange rates have indeed been volatile, their volatility has been less than that of stock prices."[32]

A clue to the second element of the answer to what is going on follows from the conclusion of the first. If exchange markets indeed have become like other asset markets, then it is entirely possible that economic actors have learned to treat them accordingly. Volatility, therefore, does not *ipso facto* constitute a fatal flaw of the international monetary regime, for volatility in and of itself tells us nothing about actor expectations and anticipation. Students of international regimes should appreciate this point: after all, they define regimes in terms of *convergent expectations*, not actual outcomes. An attempt by Allan Meltzer to differentiate expectations and outcomes across international monetary regimes from the 1890s to the 1980s yields some interesting (though preliminary) results. To begin with, Meltzer finds that not all measures of variability in actual outcomes have in fact increased over time: variability in nominal and real GNP was higher under the classical gold standard than in the post–World War II era, though variance in price level is higher now; money growth shows no consistent pattern. What is most interesting, however, is Meltzer's finding that variation in forecast errors has declined both in absolute value and relative to the variance in actual outcomes. As a result, though some measures of volatility may be higher today, risk and uncertainty are uniformly lower. "By prewar standards, the period of fluctuating exchange rates has been remarkably stable, if stability is measured by short-term predictability (the variance of errors in quarterly forecasts)."[33] In sum, not only actual volatility, but also expectations about it and thus presumably adaptations to it, need to be considered when predicting its effects.

The increasingly complex and indirect relationship between exchange rates, current account balances, and capital flows, together with Meltzer's conclusions about declining macroeconomic risks and uncertainties under managed monetary regimes, take us a long way toward explaining why the obvious volatility in exchange rates of recent years has had only limited effects on trade and investment flows and on the attitudes of governments. They also suggest why exchange market intervention by governments as a means to stabilize exchange rates is bound to be of limited utility. And they indicate why fundamental reform would necessarily entail a measure of new capital controls, and/or a more closely coordinated set of domestic policies, at a minimum monetary policy, among the leading currency countries.[34]

This discussion has not tried to make the case that we live in the best of all possible monetary worlds. We do not. I have suggested only that the regime is not in danger of imminent collapse, at least not from any endogenous source; and I have suggested some of the reasons why. Above all, the monetary regime remains thoroughly multilateral in character. The basic political compromise of Bretton Woods continues to hold among the major monetary powers, and of course it does so most effectively when their governments share a roughly similar political orientation, as they did throughout the conservative 1980s. Moreover, this political compromise continues to hold despite the fact that the Keynesian instruments through which it was enacted in the past have weakened in efficacy. Institutional deviations or inventions on the whole have been undertaken on the belief that previous mechanisms were unsustainable or no longer served their purpose, not to gain unacceptable unilateral advantage. And no other fundamental reforms have been forthcoming because no new consensus has formed among economists, let alone governments, about the viability of fundamentally different institutional designs that would not at the same time deprive governments collectively of policy instruments or market mechanisms that they now hold clear.

The Trade Regime

As a result of successive rounds of negotiations conducted under the GATT, tariffs today are so low as no longer to constitute a significant barrier to international trade: barely 5 percent on industrial products, down from an average of over 40 percent in the immediate postwar years. Moreover, as the 1980s drew to a close, growth in world trade was resuming its postwar norm of increasing well in excess of 5 percent per annum and outpacing the growth of world output.[35] Some two thirds of the absolute increase in world trade during 1988 consisted of exports of capital goods, reflecting a widespread investment boom in the developed market economies and suggesting yet further trade expansion ahead. A number of developing countries in Africa and Latin America still were making little headway in their decade-long struggle against debt, inflation, stagnation, and capital flight, but overall exports from developing countries in 1988 increased by 13 percent. The socialist countries almost uniformly were seeking fuller participation in the world economy, turning their backs on over forty years of central planning and relative economic isolation. And the ongoing Uruguay Round of GATT negotiations was venturing into the uncharted domain of trade in services, while holding out some hope for progress on liberalizing international agricultural trade as well.

Few observers question the significance of these accomplishments. But many do question their sustainability in the face of the so-called new protectionism: the battery of nontariff barriers imposed by the leading economic powers on imports from one another and from the newly industrializing countries. Such measures are decried as doubly damaging the international trade regime: not only do they impose quantitative and other administrative restrictions on trade, but they do so in an inherently discriminatory manner by singling out specific countries for differential treatment. One frequently cited observer has characterized the growing incidence of nontariff barriers, particularly bilateral, "voluntary" export controls as well as multilateral "orderly marketing arrangements," as constituting nothing less than the "collapse of free-trade ideology into retaliatory protectionism."[36] Have we thus struggled for over forty years to create and sustain a multilateral trade regime only to embrace the very protectionism that initially animated our efforts? Let use examine the evidence.

The New Protectionism. The facts are straightforward. A recent GATT study reports the bilateral, voluntary export restraint arrangements (VERs) known to have been in effect at the end of 1987. The product categories affected include textiles and clothing (71 arrangements outside the Multifibre Agreement, an OMA or multilateralized form of export restraint); agricultural and food products (58); steel and steel products (52); electronic products (23); automobiles and transport equipment (20); footwear (15); machine tools (13); and miscellaneous (25). "The majority of the arrangements protect the EEC market or the market of one of its members states, followed by the U.S. market; these two account for just over three quarters of the measures listed. The arrangements mainly limit exports from Japan (38 arrangements), the Republic of Korea (35), the EEC (15), and Taiwan (13)."[37] All told some 30 percent of world trade was affected thereby. In addition, many of these same countries were subject to antidumping and countervailing duty actions. Lastly, it is clear that the use of these mechanisms has increased over the years.

As in the case of the monetary regime, however, it isn't the facts themselves but what they signify that is at issue. The view that these developments indicate a resurgence of "retaliatory protectionism" has to accommodate several sizable anomalies.

First of all, the overall magnitude of nontariff barriers typically is expressed in terms of the *number* of product categories affected; however, those figures tell us nothing about the actual *extent* of effective protection the measures provide. And as we noted earlier both the value and volume of international trade once again are expanding at postwar historical rates. At the very least, then, trade-creating forces are outweighing trade-destroying ones, despite the "new protectionism." What is more, if these export restraints are designed to prevent market penetration by imports, certainly in the United States and perhaps elsewhere they have done a very poor job—and much worse of a job than would be done by tariffs. In a comprehensive survey of every statutory instrument of the so-called new protectionism employed by the United States since 1958, Judith Goldstein concludes that although the government provides adversely affected domestic industries many things, "effective protection was excluded."[38] The U.S. government has been least responsive to pressure from uncompetitive producers and most responsive to instances of unfair trade. But even in the latter, an empirical study shows that a 1 percent increase in the "less-than-fair-value" complaint index yields but a 0.2 percent reduction in import growth rates.[39] Finally, yet another study demonstrates that the effect of these nontariff barriers "is not nearly as large as the protection afforded by tariffs . . . or natural barriers to trade."[40] Thus, when all is said and done, the markets of the industrialized countries are more open today than they were only a decade ago, leading the distinguished international economist Jagdish Bhagwati to conclude: "the growth of protectionism appears significant but its consequences do not."[41]

Compounding the anomaly, governments apparently choose instruments to restrain imports that are not only ineffective, but actually transfer the scarcity rents produced by government intervention to the *exporting* country![42] The case of Japanese automobile manufacturers complying with their numerical quota but exporting more expensive cars to the United States is well known.[43] Less well known is the fact that in some industries a secondary market in quotas has actually emerged, complete with "quota brokers"—the markets for textile quotas in Hong Kong, South Korea, and Taiwan being cases in point.[44] This phenomenon would seem to demonstrate that although VERs may limit the quantity of imports, they also make the trade more profitable to the exporting country. That of course would explain why exporting countries don't complain more; but, at the same time, it makes this a very peculiar form of protectionism indeed.

In short, if it were the intention of governments to institute effective protectionism by means of OMAs, VERs, and similar measures, then those governments are either very stupid or utterly perverse. Without wishing to overestimate the wisdom of public officials, is it not possible that their objectives are otherwise to begin with? It is not only possible, but highly likely. Take the case of the United States.

Patterns in U.S. Protectionism. One of the most striking aspects of the so-called new protectionism "imposed" by the United States is the systematic patterns it exhibits. A "low track" and "high track" pattern was discerned by J. M. Finger and his associates in one of the earliest studies of the actual effects of "administered protection"—antidumping and countervailing duty cases as well as the escape clause mechanism invoked by the United States between 1974 and 1979.[45] The LFV, or "less-than-fair value," cases (antidumping and countervailing duties) are administered on the low track; very elaborate and precise technical criteria exist, and judgments can be appealed to the federal courts. Moreover, the average case size tends to be small. The escape clause mechanism (EC), on the other hand, is administered on the high track: the criteria are vague and the process is highly politicized, ultimately involving a presidential decision. There is no right of judicial review. And the case size on average is upwards of ten times as large. An econometric analysis of the determinants of outcomes reflects these differences. In LFV cases, whether or not less-than-fair-value pricing is found depends on such factors as comparative costs and the narrowness of the product definition involved in the complaint; whether or not injury to domestic producers is determined (and both are necessary for relief to be awarded) also reflects the size of the petitioning industry's labor force. Other domestic, and all international, factors tend to be insignificant.[46] On the high track of escape clause cases, the International Trade Commission issues findings, but the final decision rests with the president. EC cases tend to be politically visible, or involve petitioners who have the influence to make them visible. But—and here is the crucial fact often ignored in popular accounts—highly visible petitions will also attract opposition, and the nature of the high track offers no technical means of resolving the differences. As a result, the president's desire to reap political net gain or minimize net loss from such decisions is best satisfied *not* by coming down on one side or the other, but in trying to avoid them! "This has two implications for the presidential decision. First, it will push the president toward saying no. Negative decisions will discourage further petitions and will reduce the number of times the president will have to say anything. . . . Second, it will push a presidential affirmative decision as far toward a non-decision as his legally defined options allow."[47] As a result, although these mechanisms may be biased toward protectionism, the bias is not large: only 2.2 percent of U.S. manufactured imports were granted relief under the LFV statutes, and 3.8 percent under the escape clause, in the period covered by the Finger study.

A very similar set of patterns if found by Goldstein in her comprehensive study of all statutory restraints imposed since the 1950s.[48] The evidence shows that, "[a]s trariffs decreased and imports decreased their market share in the 1960s and 1970s, American producers did react by petitioning the bureaucracy for protection."[49] But the government's response failed to mirror the increased petition activity. In determining actual outcomes, technical merit seems to prevail in cases on the low track, a complex political calculus on the high track of presidential involvement:

> When confronted by a choice between giving aid or not, the executive gave no aid. When protectionism was mandated by the bureaucracy, the president often chose to give a transfer payment, to give less than recommended or, in the case of countervailing duties, to sanction a tariff waiver. In dumping findings, legislation leaves no recourse but to assess a duty. However, every effort was made to convince the exporter to halt the practice.

The preferred instruments used by the president to avoid mandated actions were OMAs and VERs. Thus, Goldstein's central finding is that although access to the institutions of administered protection has been progressively eased, and although these institutions have been increasingly pressed for protectionist measures, they "have not become increasingly protectionist over time."[50]

In sum, two attributes of the so-called new protectionism U.S. style are becoming increasingly clear and compelling. First, unlike classical protectionism, the instruments of the new variant are not unilaterally imposed, but bilaterally negotiated. And in many instances the scarcity rents from protectionism are actually transferred to the exporting country. Second, the government rarely if ever grants effective protection to domestic producers—not even in so central a sector as automobiles, where foreign producers have been allowed steadily to increase their share of the domestic market. Indeed, the evidence suggests that the government does not seek to do so, and that the executive branch, when it has final say, goes a long way to avoid it. Before trying to explain these apparently anomalous findings, two additional attributes of the new protectionism should be briefly noted.[51]

One concerns the duration of restraints. Many observers assume that, once imposed, trade barriers persist in perpetuity. But here too the "new protectionism" seems to differ. Aggarwal et al. suggest that there are at least three patterns of duration.[52] In some cases, restraints are allowed to lapse after an initial period and are not renegotiated. Color television and footwear imports into the United States provide examples. In other cases, the restraints expand and become more complex over time. The Multifibre Agreement for textiles and apparel illustrates this pattern. Finally, some restraints are allowed to lapse but subsequently may be renegotiated. The steel and automobile industries provide instances. What accounts for these differences? Industry structure, according to the authors. Temporary restraints, they argue, tend to be characteristic of small industries with low barriers to entry and exit. Here, in the face of foreign competition, domestic firms use the adjustment period afforded by the restraints to take their money and run. More permanent institutionalized restraints are characteristic of labor-intensive industries with low barriers to entry but high barriers to exit. These firms are politically important and stuck. Finally, sporadic restraints tend to appear in industries with large firms, high entry barriers, but also high adjustment or exist costs. In the case of steel and automobiles, the firms should have used the opportunity afforded by restraints to adjust, but for a variety of reasons they could not or would not. Yet the long-term preference by the government not to continue the restraints has been established.[53] In short, the import restraints of the "new protectionism" by no means are invariably of indefinite duration.

A final consideration is pertinent to this discussion; it relates to changes in industry preferences. It is well known that export-dependent industries have different preferences regarding protection for import-competing industries. Helen Milner has gone a step further to suggest that the more extensive the multinationality of firms becomes, the less likely they are to demand protection and the more likely they are to resist it, *even if* their industry is under pressure from import competition. Obviously, as firms in the advanced industrial countries become increasingly multinational in scope and ownership, previous pressure for protectionism ought to decline. Milner's case studies of selected U.S. firms in the 1920s and 1970s, and a cross-sectional comparison of U.S. and French firms today, largely confirm the hypothesis.[54] At the same time, however, Milner points out that such firms may increase demands for what has come to be known as "strategic trade policy," that is, demands for governmental action to secure access to foreign markets and to vindicate other norms of fairness in international trade—under the threat of home-country retaliation for failure to comply. Some of the most advanced industrial sectors, including semiconductors, commercial aircraft, and telecommunications, exhibit this pattern.[55] But surely these demands for strategic trade policy are market-opening, not market-closing, in intent.[56]

In the end, perhaps the most confounding anomaly that the "resurgent retaliatory protectionism" view has to accommodate is that, by the logic of its own argument, the 1970s should have been far more protectionist than they turned out to be. The world economy in the 1970s experienced dislocations more severe than any others since the 1930s. Yet there is no comparison at all between the alleged protectionism of the 1970s and the real stuff in the 1930s, and the 1980s, as we have seen, have exhibited even more positive market-opening trends. Something is clearly amiss.

Managing the Public Economy. These anomalies disappear, however, and become fairly consistent patterns of behavior when we view the so-called new protectionism from the vantage point of the management by advanced capitalist states of their public economy more broadly. Consider, for example, Cameron's analysis of different rates of growth in public expenditures among the OECD countries from the 1960s on. As possible explanations, he examines overall economic growth, tax structure, the nature of partisan political competition, and the institutional apparatus of the state. But his major—and to him, startling—finding is that the "openness of the economy is the best single predictor of the growth of public revenues relative to the economic product of a nation." [57] Greater international openness, he finds, consistently compels governments to expand their domestic role via adjustment and distributive policies—and overrides domestic differences in doing so. Obviously, then, as barriers to trade have declined, governments have become more active in managing the consequences.

Cameron's results have been confirmed by numerous other studies, and extended by some. For example, Blais has examined specifically the incidence of government industrial subsidies, finding that their best single predictor—more important than a country's overall level of affluence, size, and rate of unemployment or than the presence of left-wing parties in its electoral system—is the extent of tariff reductions the country has undertaken. For our purposes, however, Blais's most significant finding is this: "Subsidies may thus be a substitute for tariffs, but . . . they are only a partial substitute. Our results support the argument that *governments merely attempt to mitigate the negative effects of trade liberalization on specific industries and not to offset them entirely.*" [58]

These data echo the conclusion of every empirical study of the actual effects of the so-called new protectionism that we cited earlier. And in the words of Blais, they also "support Ruggie's depiction of postwar policy as 'embedded liberalism,' based on a commitment to multilateral trade with substantial safeguards to minimize socially disruptive adjustment costs." [59]

Unilateralism and Discrimination. A final set of issues needs to be addressed: the danger posed to the trade regime by the unilateralism and discriminatory treatment that is said to inhere in the new protectionism.

One charge can be dismissed readily. It is the charge that VERs and similar measures are "coercive," and thus reduce orderly trade relations to the law of the international jungle. If enriching exporting countries at the expense of consumers in the importing countries constitutes a form of international coercion, then perhaps a case can be made. But that definition of coercion is bizarre, and I suspect that, all other things being equal, exporting countries would gladly have more of it. The *ceteris paribus* condition must be stressed because not only the threatened unilateral but *even the available multilateral* alternatives to VERs would leave exporting countries *worse off* than VERs do! As Brian Hindley has pointed out, "for most countries confronted with a request for a VER, the alternative, should they refuse, is not unrestricted trade but an Article XIX emergency action [under the GATT]. In that event, the exporting country will find itself faced with a tariff on its exports or by formal quota restrictions on them with the quota rights going to importers . . . rather than to exporters. In either case, the profits of the exporting industry will be reduced. . . ."[60] And by affecting imports from all countries such a tariff or quota restriction eliminates the transshipment option for the exporting country. What is more, unlike the case of VERs, there is no effective time limit on how long Article XIX safeguards may remain in force; VERs typically do have such a limit at the end of which they either expire or must be renegotiated. Lastly, no country claiming injury under Article XIX has ever had its claim challenged! In any practical as opposed to rhetorical sense, therefore, the charge of coercion is specious.

The second charge is somewhat more complex. It is that VERs are discriminatory, and thus undermine one of the central norms of the trade regime. That they are discriminatory cannot be at issue; it is the very reason they are invoked. The real issue is whether VERs or the legally permissible alternative, again Article XIX under the GATT, do more collateral damage to the trade regime. And it is not obvious that Article XIX should be preferred on those grounds. Article XIX permits alteration or suspension of past tariff concessions in a nondiscriminatory manner, provided that interested parties are consulted. But it is clumsy. Precisely because of the necessity to apply it in a nondiscriminatory manner, the invocation of Article XIX is likely to affect innocent bystanders adversely, bystanders who are not causing injury to domestic producers in the initiating country. Thus, it may require widespread and lengthy renegotiation, or even trigger retaliatory suspension, of past concessions. Those who favor Article XIX have yet to demonstrate that these adverse consequences for the entire trading system are of a lesser magnitude than a VER aimed at a specific party. And simply to retort that Article XIX is to be preferred *because* it is multilateral in character won't do: It is a perfect example of what Aliber describes as "sacrificing the state to save the constitution." No rational government can be expected to follow that precept when well-established and apparently acceptable alternatives are available.[61]

The final charge is too difficult to come to grips with fully here. It concerns unilateralism and its precedential consequences. The culprits here are the so-called Super 301 section of the recent U.S. trade legislation (Omnibus Trade and Competitiveness Act of 1988) and Japan, the main target at which it is aimed—the two are intimately related.[62] On the one side, this dispute has the United States claiming the right to act as accuser, judge, and jury and to impose punishment with no chance of redress. On the other side, the dispute has Japan depicted as being, and sometimes claiming the right to be, a different sort of capitalist economic formation than the more typical competitive market economies but wanting to benefit from the same rules as the others. The potential for deleterious and even destructive consequences for international trading relations certainly is present here, particularly because the measure imposes more severe constraints on U.S. executive branch discretion than its legislative predecessors. Nevertheless, that future potential of deleterious consequences can hardly be cited as evidence in support of the "new protectionism" scenarios that have been propagated for some twenty years now. Moreover, it is important to remember that the goal of the trade regime has been "to maintain a balance of concessions and obligations, not to restructure nations"[63]—which ultimately may well be what is at stake in the U.S.–Japan trade disputes. Finally, if we take the argument and evidence of the present paper seriously, then we are obliged to place at least offsetting bets on the ability of the regime and of the key actors to adapt.[64]

CONCLUSION

There is an inherent danger in writing about progress, whether in international economic relations or in any other domain of human activity, of being dismissed for being Whiggish if not Panglossian. In conclusion, let me briefly anticipate both of those possible reactions.

First of all, I do not consider the developments described herein to have been inevitable. The Nazis could have built the atom bomb and won World War II; and Hjalmar Schacht had given no sign of being poised to propose a Bretton Woods arrangement for organizing the conduct of international economic relations. Nor are all current international economic arrangements necessarily better than those that went before. Multilateralism is clearly superior to Schachtian bilateralism raised to the level of systemic organizing principle, in my judgment and given my values, but there are no *a priori* grounds for concluding that more benign forms of bilateralism are impossible or undesirable—witness the U.S.–Canada free trade pact. Moreover, certain features of the classical gold standard and free trade may well have been superior to those we have today, as some have claimed. My general view on such matters has always been influenced heavily by the writings of Stephen Jay Gould, not by Darwin or Victorian historiographers: play the tape of life again and very different outcomes are likely to prevail; but once a certain path is taken, it conditions what follows.[65] Thus, let me state my point clearly: statesmen learned from the Great Depression, but different statesmen learned different things. That some of them inherited power rather than others is part of life's lottery, not the product of some evolutionary design. But once their preferences were instituted, the institutional arrangements shaped subsequent developments.

As for Dr. Pangloss, I am not oblivious to very serious imbalances that afflict the international economy today or to the dangers they pose for economic stability and economic justice in the world system. Nor do I believe that the current set of monetary and trade arrangements could not be substantially improved. I would add two thoughts, however. First, on social scientific as well as normative grounds, it is necessary and desirable to learn from accomplishments no less than from failures, as unfashionable as that view may appear. And within the confines of their policy spaces the regimes for money and trade do constitute accomplishments, as I have tried to show. They have provided at least some degree of mutual stability of expectations amidst deep conjunctural crisis and profound structural transformation. Thus, in the language suggested by the editors of this volume, the postwar regimes for money and trade at the least constitute an example of "instrumental progress" in international relations. Second, of the many things to be worried about in international monetary and trade relations today, the issue of the so-called new protectionism, for the reasons stated, simply is not at the top of my list.

But to close with the *de rigueur* dash of pessimism, I would posit that a development in which several authors of this volume put great stock, the use of knowledge in policymaking, ironically also constitutes one of the greatest potential threats to the monetary and trade regimes in the years ahead! Both monetary and trade policy rely on reams of statistical information processed by advanced technical means. But the figures aren't adding up the way they used to, because the models on which they are based are increasingly anachronistic; policymaking as a result increasingly comes to resemble a high-stakes game of pin-the-tail-on-the-donkey. Exchange rate policy still assumes that currency values follow the trade account, at a time when capital movements outweigh trade flows by a factor of twenty to one. Trade statistics and hence trade policy still conceive of trade as though it were arms-length exchange between two nationally distinct entities, when in fact production is increasingly globalized while trade overwhelmingly takes place within firms—so that IBM is the leading computer exporter of Japan, West Germany, and the United States, and Sony is the leading exporter of U.S. television sets. Even hallowed GNP figures lie by systematically understating the value of services and high-tech productivity increases that constitute the most desirable and most rapidly growing segment of all advanced economies—for example, by *discounting* national wealth when I chose a faster but *cheaper* software package on which to draft this chapter over a slower but more expensive one. In sum, the conceptual and statistical infrastructure of economic policy and economic regimes is frozen in time, with perverse and potentially catastrophic results ahead.[66]

ENDNOTES

Ernst B. Haas critically scrutinized an earlier draft, as he has most everything I have written since I was his graduate student at Berkeley in the late 1960s and early 1970s. I dedicate this paper to him with great affection, deep respect, and enduring gratitude for being an outstanding role model and good friend.

1. Perhaps the most alarmist among serious commentators was C. Fred Bergsten. In a 1972 article ("The New Economics and U.S. Foreign Policy," *Foreign Affairs* [January 1972], Vol. 50) he wrote: "In the summer of 1971, President Nixon and Secretary Connally revolutionized U.S. foreign economic policy. In so doing [they] encouraged a disastrous isolationist trend" (p. 199), "violated the letter and the spirit of the reigning international law" (p. 200), and sought "to export unemployment to other countries" (p. 203). "The policy could easily lead to the first real international trade war since the 1930s" (p. 204). "Trade wars could become full economic wars, precisely as they did under similar international conditions in the 1930s" (p. 206). "These economic effects would have a disastrous impact on U.S. foreign policy, and on our own national security" (p. 207). By 1976, the intervening years had somewhat allayed Bergsten's fears. He felt "reasonably sanguine" about "the longer-run future. . . . The problem is to get there, by avoiding the trade wars which once again loom on the horizon." *Foreign Policy* (Summer 1976), no. 23, p. 31.
2. Stephan Haggard, "The Institutional Foundations of Hegemony: Explaining the Reciprocal Trade Agreements Act of 1934," in G. John Ikenberry, David A. Lake, and Michael Mastanduno, eds., *The State and American Foreign Economic Policy* (Ithaca, N.Y.: Cornell University Press, 1988), p. 102. Or, as Judith Goldstein has put it, "liberalism was accepted only with safeguards." Goldstein, "Ideas, Institutions, and American Trade Policy," in ibid., p. 188.
3. A more detailed historical discussion of the origins and structure of this compromise may be found in my essay "International Regimes, Transactions, and Change: Embedded Liberalism in the Postwar Economic Order," in Stephen D. Krasner, ed., *International Regimes* (Ithaca, N.Y.: Cornell University Press, 1983).
4. This was true even in Great Britain, where Labour sought to institute systematic national economic planning, which would necessarily have entailed discriminatory instruments of foreign economic policy, while Conservatives remained committed to imperial preferences and the imperial alternative to a universal economic order, which was inherently discriminatory in character. See Richard N. Gardner, *Sterling-Dollar Diplomacy in Current Perspective* (New York: Columbia University Press, 1980), ch. 1. In Scandinavia the overriding objective of domestic economic policy was the achievement of full employment, yet it was perceived to be entirely compatible with multilateralism. Tapani Paavonen, "Reformist Programmes in the Planning for Post-War Economic Policy during World War II," *Scandinavian Economic Historical Review* (1983), Vol. 31, No. 3.
5. For the sake of brevity, I am using the appelation "Bretton Woods" generically here, to include money, finance, and trade, even though the trade regime was not negotiated at the Bretton Woods conference.

6. Richard N. Cooper, "Prolegomena to the Choice of an International Monetary System," *International Organization* (Winter 1975), 29:85.
7. Among the other major sources I have drawn on for this discussion of the monetary negotiations are Gardner, *Sterling–Dollar Diplomacy*; Armand Van Dormael, *Bretton Woods: Birth of a Monetary System* (London: Macmillan, 1978); Fred Block, *The Origins of International Economic Disorder* (Berkeley: University of California Press, 1977); Susan Strange, *International Monetary Relations*, Vol. 2 of Andrew Shonfield, ed., *International Economic Relations of the Western World* (London: Oxford University Press for the Royal Institute of International Affairs, 1976); and A. L. K. Acheson, J. F. Chant, and M. F. J. Prachowny, *Bretton Woods Revisited* (Toronto: University of Toronto Press, 1972).
8. Major sources for the trade negotiations include Gardner, *Sterling–Dollar Diplomacy*; William Diebold, "The End of the ITO," *Princeton Essays in International Finance* (October 1952), No. 16; Gerard and Victoria Curzon, "The Management of Trade Relations in the GATT, in Shonfield, ed., *International Economic Relations of the Western World*, Vol. 1; Jacob Viner, "Conflicts of Principle in Drafting a Trade Charter," *Foreign Affairs* (January 1947), Vol. 25.
9. The United States also undertook more direct measures in the domestic politics of other countries, through the Occupation Authorities in Germany, Italy, and Japan, and through transnational adjuncts of American civil society such as the American Federation of Labor, which was particularly active in France and in Latin America, seeking to moderate the structure and political direction of labor movements, encourage the exclusion of Communist parties from participation in governments, and generally to keep collectivist impulses within acceptable Center-Left bounds.
10. A superb discussion of this shift may be found in Robert Pollard, *Economic Security and the Origins of the Cold War* (New York: Columbia University Press, 1985).
11. "Everybody's Business: International Monetary Reform—A Survey," *The Economist*, October 5, 1985; the citations are from p. 11.
12. Kenan, "An Overall View," in Fabio Basagni, ed., *International Monetary Relations After Jamaica* (Paris: The Atlantic Institute for International Affairs, 1976), p. 7.
13. Robert Triffin, "Jamaica: 'Major Revision' or Fiasco," in Edward M. Bernstein et al., "Reflections on Jamaica," *Princeton Essays in International Finance* (April 1976) 115:47.
14. Robert Z. Aliber, "Fixed Exchange Rates and the Rate of Inflation," in Colin D. Campbell and William R. Dougan, eds., *Alternative Monetary Regimes* (Baltimore: Johns Hopkins University Press, 1986), p. 120.
15. "International Monetary Reform," p. 62.
16. This position is elaborated in Friedrich Kratochwil and John Gerard Ruggie, "International Organization: A State of the Art on an Art of the State," *International Organization* (Autumn 1986), Vol. 40.

17. The possible retort that "anything goes" under this criterion would be factually in error. In the 1930s, for example, governments knew well that they were not collaborating with one another, having set out deliberately to pursue autarchic and beggar-thy-neighbor policies. (See Kenneth A. Oye, "The Sterling–Dollar–Franc Triangle: Monetary Diplomacy 1929–1937," *World Politics* [October 1985], Vol. 38, and Oye, "On the Benefits of Bilateralism: Lessons from the 1930s," paper prepared for the Workshop on Change in the International System, University of Southern California, May 5–6, 1989.) And even today, looking approvingly on some aspects of the "new protectionism" does not preclude appreciating the dangers of the real, neomercantilist stuff. (See Brian Hindley, "Protectionism and Autonomy: A Comment on Hager," *International Affairs* [Winter 1982–1983], Vol. 59, critically commenting on Wolfgang Hager's avowedly neomercantilist: "Protectionism and Autonomy: How to Preserve Free Trade in Europe," *International Affairs* [Summer 1982], Vol. 58.)
18. Richard N. Cooper, "A Monetary System Based on Fixed Exchange Rates," in Campbell and Dougan, eds., *Alternative Monetary Regimes*, p. 88.
19. Cooper, ibid.
20. Richard N. Cooper, "A Monetary System for the Future," *Foreign Affairs* (Fall 1984), 63:170.
21. Rachel McCulloch, "Unexpected Real Consequences of Floating Exchange Rates," in Robert Z. Aliber, ed., *The Reconstruction of International Monetary Arrangements* (London: Macmillan, 1987), p. 25.
22. According to a recent GATT report, of a total of eighty-eight convertible currencies, forty-one are pegged to a single currency; eight are linked to a basket of currencies via the European Monetary System; and twenty-three are otherwise actively managed. Only sixteen float independently —of which the most important are the U.S. dollar, Japanese yen, and British pound. *Review of Developments in the Trading System, April–September 1988* (Geneva: General Agreement on Tariffs and Trade, 1988), Appendix I to Section X, pp. 97–98.
23. In essence, Triffin argued that if the United States corrected its balance-of-payments deficit, the result would be world deflation because gold production at $35 an ounce could not adequately supply world monetary reserves. But if the United States continued running a deficit, the result would be collapse of the monetary standard because U.S. foreign liabilities would far exceed its ability to convert dollars into gold on demand. Robert Triffin, *Gold and the Dollar Crisis* (New Haven: Yale University Press, 1960).
24. Cooper, in *Foreign Affairs*, p. 171.
25. Cooper, in Campbell and Dougan, *Alternative Monetary Regimes*, p. 90.
26. Referred to by Kevin Phillips, in "Western World Tilts Left, Leaving Conservative Cycle," *Los Angeles Times*, August 27, 1989.
27. Kenen, "An Overall View," p. 10.

28. McCulloch, "Unexpected Real Consequences," p. 25.

29. "International Monetary Reform," p. 31.

30. Ibid., p. 42.

31. Robert V. Roosa, *Economic Instability and Flexible Exchange Rates* (Singapore: Institute of Southeast Asian Studies, 1982), p. 4.

32. McCulloch, "Unexpected Real Consequences," p. 25.

33. Allan H. Meltzer, "Some Evidence on the Comparative Uncertainty Experienced under Different Monetary Regimes," in Campbell and Dougan, *Alternative Monetary Regimes*, p. 142; see also Stanley Fischer's commentary "Meltzer on Uncertainty under Different Monetary Regimes," ibid.

34. Rudiger Dornbusch, "Flexible Exchange Rates and Excess Capital Mobility," *Brookings Papers on Economic Activity* (1986), Vol. 1, and Stanley Fischer, "Symposium on Exchange Rates, Trade, and Capital Flows: Comments and Discussion," ibid.

35. GATT, *Review of Developments in the Trading System, April–September 1988;* and United Nations Conference on Trade and Development, *Trade and Development Report, 1989* (New York: United Nations, 1989).

36. Robert B. Reich, "Beyond Free Trade," *Foreign Affairs* (Spring 1983), 61:774.

37. *Review of Developments in the Trading System,* ch. 7.

38. Goldstein, "Ideas, Institutions, and American Trade Policy," and Goldstein, "The Political Economy of Trade: Institutions of Protection," *American Political Science Review* (March 1986), 80:17.

39. J. M. Finger, "The Industry-Country Incidence of 'Less than Fair Value' Cases in US Import Trade," *Quarterly Review of Economics and Business* (Summer 1981), 21:274.

40. Peter Morici and Laura Megna, *U.S. Economic Policies Affecting Industrial Trade: A Quantitative Assessment* (Washington, D.C.: National Planning Association, 1983), p. 11.

41. Jagdish Bhagwati, *Protectionism* (Cambridge, Mass.: MIT Press, 1988), p. 56.

42. David Yoffie, *Power and Protectionism* (New York: Columbia University Press, 1983).

43. In point of fact, even though the U.S. has lifted negotiated quotas, Japan continues to maintain them on its own—"but Japan's major manufacturers note that the action is now an annual political gesture that has no effect on the sales of Japanese cars." "Japan Seen Extending Auto Quotas," *New York Times,* January 12, 1990.

44. Brian Hindley, "Voluntary Export Restraints and GATT's Main Escape Clause," *The World Economy* (November 1980), Vol. 3.

45. J. M. Finger, H. Keith Hall, and Douglas R. Nelson, "The Political Economy of Administered Protection," *American Economic Review* (June 1982), Vol. 72.

46. Finger et al. point out that, although antidumping petitions for steel and automobiles were filed, these sectors did not "belong" on the low track

and were not resolved there; petitioners subsequently transferred them to the high track.

47. Ibid., p. 463.
48. Judith Goldstein, "The Political Economy of Trade," and "Ideas, Institutions, and American Trade Policy." Her analysis includes the invocation of five statutory provisions to restrain imports (escape clause, antidumping, countervailing duties, adjustment assistance, and allegedly unfair practices related largely to patent claims) over a longer period of time, from 1958 into the 1980s.
49. "Political Economy of Trade," p. 169.
50. "The Political Economy of Trade," pp. 180, 178. See also Douglas Nelson, "The Domestic Political Preconditions of U.S. Trade Policy: Liberal Structure and Protectionist Dynamics," prepared for the conference on Political Economy: Theory and Policy Implications, The World Bank, Washington, D.C., June 17–19, 1987.
51. A full comparison with the prevailing practices of the European Community and Japan is well beyond the scope of this paper; both are extremely complex cases. To begin with, the "European Community is not only itself a discriminatory trading arrangement, if looked at as a collection of separate countries, but is embedded in concentric circles of discrimination"—consisting of preferences and export restraints—such that its bound MFN tariff "is largely the tariff applicable to the United States." Martin Wolf, "The European Community and the Developing Countries in the International Trading System," *Aussenwirtschaft* (Heft 1, 1987), 42:56–57. The case of Japan is taken up briefly later.
52. Vinod K. Aggarwal, Robert O. Keohane, and David B. Yoffie, "The Dynamics of Negotiated Protectionism," *American Political Science Review* (June 1987), Vol. 81.
53. In the case of automobiles, the Reagan administration phased out the VER regulating Japanese imports, though as already mentioned, the Japanese themselves have kept it in place. In steel, the Bush administration announced in the summer of 1989 that it would phase out quotas over the ensuing thirty months, whereas the steel industry had expected to be protected for another five years. *Wall Street Journal*, July 26, 1989.
54. Helen V. Milner, *Resisting Protectionism: Global Industries and the Politics of International Trade* (Princeton, N.J.: Princeton University Press, 1988).
55. Helen V. Milner and David B. Yoffie, "Between Free Trade and Protectionism: Strategic Trade Policy and a Theory of Corporate Trade Demands," *International Organization* (Spring 1989), Vol. 41; and Yoffie and Milner, "An Alternative to Free Trade and Protectionism: Why Corporations Seek Strategic Trade Policy," *California Management Review* (Summer 1989), Vol. 31.
56. However, if the openness of markets is judged by bilateral trade balances —for example, if Japanese willingness to import beef is judged by the amount of beef it purchases specially from the United States—then

strategic trade policy becomes a form of neomercantilist market-*sharing* rather than market-opening. See Bhagwati, *Protectionism*, ch. 4.

57. David R. Cameron, "The Expansion of the Public Economy: A Comparative Analysis," *American Political Science Review* (December 1978), 72:1254.
58. Andre Blais, "The Political Economy of Public Subsidies," *Comparative Political Studies* (July 1986), 19:210; emphasis added.
59. Ibid., p. 208. Cf. Robert O. Keohane, "The World Political Economy and the Crisis of Embedded Liberalism," in John H. Goldthorpe, ed., *Order and Conflict in Contemporary Capitalism* (Oxford: The Clarendon Press, 1984).
60. "Voluntary Export Restraints," p. 321.
61. Hindley similarly dismisses criticisms of VERs on the grounds that they are illegal. "A much better analogy is the out-of-court settlement of civil legal actions, a procedure whose outcome is constrained by the law, but which both parties to the dispute expect will leave them better-off than undergoing the expenses of the full judicial process. No legal system will collapse as a result of such agreements (on the contrary, if there were no such agreements, collapse would be very much more likely)." "Voluntary Export Restraints," pp. 331–332.
62. See Jagdish Bhagwati, "Super 301's Big Bite Flouts the Rules," and Leslie E. Grayson, "For Its Own Good, Japan Needs a Shove," *New York Times*, June 4, 1989. I discuss this issue more fully in chapter 4 of my book manuscript, "Return to World Order: The United States and the Future of Multilateralism," on which this paper draws.
63. Patricia Kalla, "The GATT Dispute Settlement Procedure in the 1980s: Where Do We Go from Here," *Dickinson Journal of International Law* (Fall 1986), 5:95.
64. Thus, although the original section 301 of the Trade Act of 1974 eased domestic access to the instruments of administered protection, at the same time it "encouraged the United States to make greater use of the GATT dispute settlement process. . . . [O]f the sixteen GATT complaints filed by the United States between 1975 and 1985, eleven complaints arose out of section 301 investigations." Julia Christine Bliss, "GATT Dispute Settlement Reform in the Uruguay Round: Problems and Prospects," *Stanford Journal of International Law* (1987), 23(1):45.
65. See, most recently, Stephen Jay Gould, *Wonderful Life: The Burgess Shale and the Nature of History* (New York: W. W. Norton, 1989).
66. Fred Block has a good preliminary discussion of the significance of this issue in "Postindustrial Development and the Obsolescence of Economic Categories," *Politics & Society* (1985), Vol. 14, No. 1.

7

PROGRESS FOR THE RICH: THE CANADA–U.S. FREE TRADE AGREEMENT

Robert T. Kudrle
Stefanie Ann Lenway

Progress in international relations among the wealthy liberal democracies lacks the drama of advance in many other spheres. Nonetheless, we think the concept can be useful. This chapter attempts to specify the dimensions of such progress in Canadian–U.S. economic relations by focusing on the Free Trade Agreement (FTA) concluded in December 1987.

Prime Minister Mulroney formally committed himself to FTA negotiations in September 1985. The Canadian decision to propose the FTA negotiations seems to have been based principally on two considerations. First, the U.S. "administered protection" mechanism— that body of law and institutions designed to protect U.S. producers from surges of foreign imports and "unfair" foreign practices—was seen by Canadians as increasingly threatening to their economic well-being.[1] Second, Canada's attempt in the 1970s to engage in a protective industrial policy and to limit foreign investment failed to stop the increasing dependence of the Canadian economy on U.S. trade, although it did precede a decline in Canadian productivity growth.

The United States greeted the Canadian initiative with interest. The FTA promises both lower potential costs and lower probable benefits for the United States that it does for Canada. Nonetheless, the U.S. executive remains committed to the development of more liberal trade, and much of U.S. business showed keen interest in lowering Canadian barriers to both trade and investment.

The issue of free trade has arisen many times in the usually rather tranquil history of Canadian–American relations. Several times an agreement has seemed near, only to be dashed by a changed political climate on one side of the border or the other.[2] To help explain why the negotiation of the FTA became possible in the mid-1980s we posit the national goals of security, autonomy, and prosperity.[3] We will argue that a changed understanding of the causal relationships among various policies and national goals along with a reconsideration of the trade-offs among the goals—in essence, a redefinition of the national interest—has made the FTA possible.[4]

Our approach fits entirely with the suggested concerns of security, welfare, and human rights discussed in the Introduction. Security issues between the United States and Canada have evolved over decades and are now generally regarded as satisfactory by both sides.[5] This state of affairs has both permitted and been encouraged by international interdependence of unequaled complexity. The FTA has resulted mainly from one particularly strong element of interdependence, international exchange, coupled with a cognitive evolution. This evolution, mainly in Canada, concluded that the maintenance of traditional Canadian protectionist policies was exacting a high and possibly sharply rising price, both because of intrinsic economic effects and increasingly active U.S. hostility.

We contend that the situation of the United States and Canada stands as a paradigm for the relations between other developed states experiencing *de facto* economic integration in the absence of intended political convergence. This assumption stems from a close consideration of the term *welfare* (and, for some, perhaps *human rights*). Just as the desire for perceived material well-being is nearly universal, so too, we suggest, is a hunger for identification with a partially self-determining group smaller than humanity itself. We submit that this reveals an entirely acceptable aspect of a desire for autonomy.[6]

Our claim rests solidly on an individualistic evaluation of well-being and merely recognizes that one element of a "more pleasant and better developed life"[7] for most people is identification with a distinct community. Increasing interdependence among the rich countries typically poses the welfare trade-off between diminished autonomy for the community with which the individual holds primary identification and increased material well-being. A successful resolution of the trade-off under changing conditions implies progress, not only for the United States and Canada, but systemically, because others can learn from this pioneering effort.

This chapter first explores changes in the understanding of the relationship between autonomy and prosperity in trade that have made liberalization between Canada and the United States possible. Security issues comprise a large part of U.S.–Canadian relations, but they are handled mainly within NATO and in a series of bilateral agreements. The FTA talks explicitly eschewed "linkage" beyond their declared purpose.

Next, we examine a part of Ernst Haas' work that provides theoretical guidance for understanding the interaction of changing power and cognition as well as the pattern of conflict and its resolution in the bilateral negotiations. With this background, we go on to discuss specific aspects of the FTA negotiations, including the agreement to reduce tariffs on goods and nontariff barriers in services and investment; the agreement reached on the management of conflict in dumping, countervailing duty, and escape clause cases; and the lack of agreement on government subsidy restriction and on trade in culture. In conclusion, we draw some lessons from these negotiations for the multilateral liberalization of trade.

GOALS AND POLICY IN THE UNITES STATES AND CANADA: A STUDY IN CONTRASTS

Many observers conclude with Seymour Martin Lipset that the United States and Canada "probably resemble each other more than any two nations on earth."[8] Yet the differences between the two countries are quite marked and are nowhere more important than when the two deal with each other. The differences become immediately apparent when we consider them in the context of the three goals we suggest to be fundamental.

Security

Much of the difference in security perspective stems understandably from Canada's small size relative to the United States. Many key Canadian magnitudes, such as population and Gross National Product, are roughly one tenth of their American counterparts. During most of the nineteenth century physical isolation from the rest of the world led to a general sense of security for both countries, although the Canadians lived with some threat of American ambitions. To deter the Americans and any other potential aggressors, Canada counted on British military—mainly sea—power. The United States, of course, relied entirely on its own forces, which were nonetheless quite modest by international standards.

In the postwar period Canada has relied on another senior partner: only the United States could protect Canada from its only plausible major enemy, the Soviet Union. By contrast, the United States regarded Canada as one of many weaker allies: one distinguished mainly by a vital strategic location yet so small in relative economic size and population and so removed from central theaters of nonnuclear war as to be constantly tempted to spend very little on national defense.[9]

Prosperity

Each country has seen the other as an important contributor to its prosperity. The United States replaced Britain as Canada's largest trading partner after World War II, and its role grew steadily, until it absorbed 79 percent of Canadian export in 1985. Only 28 percent of U.S. exports went to Canada. The high volume of U.S. savings flowing into Canada, much of it in the form of direct investment, provided an even greater asymmetry until the mid-1970s. This resulted in over 60 percent of Canadian manufacturing being owned by Americans in 1970 and triggered public policy changes. In recent years the inflow of Canadian direct investment into the United States has exceeded the previously dominant reverse flow.[10]

Autonomy

Lipset has argued that Canadian nationalism can be distinguished mainly by what it is not. Canada rejected both the rebellion against Britain and the French Revolution.[11] Dependent on the United States for both its security and much of its prosperity, Canada has been particularly restive about autonomy issues. Although it has been inundated by American popular culture throughout this century, Canada retains its distinct "national myth."[12] It rests on distinctions from America in several dimensions: a greater deference to authority, a more organic view of state and society with a concomitantly greater emphasis on public welfare, more respect for tradition, and a greater attraction to order.[13]

If one considers degrees of autonomy extending all the way from effective domestic control (maximum) to the simple maintenance of national identity (minimum), the Canadians (by almost any historical and comparative standard) seem willing to settle for relationships that cluster at the modest end of the spectrum.

From the American side, the autonomy dimension appears totally different. Even the pervasive and increasing phenomena of international interdependence have affected the American consciousness less than is the case virtually anywhere else, mainly because America continues to possess the largest single role in determining the direction of these relationships. The United States finds itself operating, with continual frustration, toward the control end of the spectrum. A problem of national identity seems almost beyond imagination.

We argue specifically that agreement about the economic value of freer trade and investment between the United States and Canada and the willingness of both states to forego some autonomy to achieve this prosperity has made the negotiation of the FTA possible. This congruence, which we argue is the result of cognitive learning, has led to agreement about the benefits of an open international trading system and the need to harmonize the implementation of unfair trade statutes. But agreement to reduce autonomy is sharply constrained by nationalism. The ceding of some degree of sovereignty on the part of both Canada and the United States, modified by a strong commitment to instruments of cultural identity on the part of the Canadians and a reluctance of the United States to yield unilateral prerogatives, suggests that nationalism may not be "just a necessary stage through which political man has to pass."[14] More exactly, the stage may have remarkable longevity.

PROTECTIONISM: A CLOSER LOOK

The literature on trade protection contains a variety of typologies.[15] For our purposes, a simple set of distinctions will suffice. We identify three broad sources of support for protection: (1) national sentiment that protection promotes prosperity, (2) national sentiment that protection promotes autonomy or security, and (3) the opportunity for gain by heavily affected parties. In addition, to encourage openness, countries retaliate against protectionist initiatives abroad. Observed protection is grounded on a combination of these and other motives.[16]

Sympathy for the notion that prosperity is promoted by protection has historically found far more resonance north of the border than in the United States, although many of the seventy-two research studies of the Royal Commission on the Economic Union and Development Prospects for Canada (the Macdonald Report) overwhelmingly weigh in favor of liberalization.[17] Indeed, many closely resemble material routinely produced by the U.S. executive departments and the Congressional Budget Office decrying protectionism and many other forms of government subsidy and regulation. In the past, however, a large body of both public and intellectual opinion in Canada embraced traditional arguments for protection, mainly some version of the classic "infant industry" argument.

Sir John MacDonald's "National Policy" of 1887 sought to cultivate economic ties between eastern and western Canada that would create an industrial core sufficiently large and concentrated to enable Canadian industry to survive international competition. Nearly a century later, Pierre Trudeau's policies of the 1970s sought to develop natural resources, to rationalize manufacturing for international competitiveness, to increase the role of high-tech industries, and to increase Canadian ownership and control over investment, especially in the resource sector.[18] By the early 1980s many regarded such policies as a failure: Protection seemed to be undermining productivity but failing to arrest ever-increasing trade with the United States.

Although a residuum of the previous orthodoxy persists across the political spectrum, contemporary economic arguments in favor of broad-scale protection came mainly from the left.[19] The left's case, however, rests on insubstantial arguments concerning prosperity. It conflates traditional infant industry arguments, fears about foreign investment, and trade union apprehension about the impact of increased product competition on negotiated wages. Overall, the pro-FTA forces were able to marshall most of the best economic scholarship in Canada in support of their position. Broader, deeper, and more sophisticated analyses of the past performance and present choices facing Canada have contributed to a far sharper understanding of present and future economic costs implied by pre-FTA practices. Many analyses showed not only that would changed Canadian policy be worth paying to gain freer access to the U.S. market, but that many policy changes should be made anyway.[20]

In the United States claims that protection can lead to aggregate economic enhancement have generally not been taken seriously by informed elites in the postwar period. The primary exceptions to the general belief that freer trade enhances prosperity are given expression in the dumping and subsidy statutes.[21] The Congress has been quite responsive to arguments about the "fairness" of foreign competition not based on comparative advantage, and U.S. law takes a stern view of foreign subsidies and discriminatorily low prices. In these cases governmental discretion to impose duties to compensate for subsidies or below-fair-market-value pricing is seen as contributing to prosperity.[22]

Canada has employed commercial policy quite self-consciously toward the goals of autonomy and security as well as prosperity. Commercial policy in the nineteenth century was intended partially to disrupt economic ties between the United States and Canada.[23] Sir John MacDonald's supporters feared that increased economic ties between Canada and the United States would threaten Canadian sovereignty, and the fear that economic integration would lead to unwanted political and social constraints emerged again in the early 1970s as part of the "Third Option."[24] This policy aimed to diversify trade away from the United States to Western Europe, Japan, and the Third World and thus reduce Canadian sensitivity and vulnerability dependence on the United States.

National sentiment grounded on noneconomic motives remains strong in Canada, although it can be applied easily only to a limited number of industries. A broad spectrum of Canadian opinion rejects free trade in popular entertainment and some other cultural goods and services. In contrast, the United States views free trade in these areas as part of a "level playing field" between producers on both sides of the border.

Canadians are ambivalent about other industries traditionally deemed sensitive on autonomy or security grounds, such as energy, banking, and other financial services. They also developed deep concern about loss of control resulting from foreign ownership of the economy. The Foreign Investment Review Agency (FIRA) of 1974 screened all new direct investment coming into Canada. Policy stringency governing FDI in Canada was, however, largely reversed in the early 1980s as many feared a causal link between declining Canadian productivity growth and falling foreign investment.[25]

Noneconomic motives have also generated some trade and investment protection in the United States. In trade, foreign-owned firms may not generally contract with the Department of Defense, although Canada is exempted from much of this restriction. More important, the United States maintains some restrictions on incoming investment, which in President Reagan's words are implemented "only as are necessary to protect U.S. security and related interests."[26] These restrictions, which mandate partial or total ownership or control by U.S. citizens, are found mainly in aviation, ocean and coastal transportation, communications, and energy production.[27] The states maintain some additional restrictions, including ownership restrictions in banking and insurance that seem based on some combination of autonomy fears and special-interest protection.

Directly affected interests play a central role in the determination of protection policy on both sides of the border. In both countries— and all over the world—resistance to liberalization looms most formidably where public sentiment is well disposed to an industry that is positioned to put its case forcefully.

Industrial sectors that feared the agreement would leave them uncompetitive mounted opposition to FTA in both countries. In the United States, lumber, textiles and apparel, steel, uranium, lead and zinc, and the color TV industry all opposed the agreement.[28] In Canada, opposition came from furniture, wine (especially in Ontario), agriculture, arts–motion pictures, and the printing industries.[29] In an analysis of these industries, Litvak concludes that the "industries opposed to free trade are generally weak and are experiencing situations of decreasing production volume and excess capacity caused by rising import penetration."[30]

Historically, industries such as textiles–apparel and steel that oppose trade liberalization in general have been much more organized than those industries that would benefit. In these negotiations, however, a convergence of elite beliefs between the United States and Canada about the central problems was paralleled by an organized political coalition in each country to lobby in support of the agreement.[31] The American Coalition for Trade Expansion with Canada was formed by the chairman of the American Express Company. It included H. J. Heinz, IBM, Dow Chemical, Honeywell, AT&T, and other large firms. The Canadian counterpart was the Canadian Alliance for Jobs and Trade Opportunities, including such firms as Dupont, Union Carbide, Bombardier, and Mutual Life.

The pro-trade forces were supported by respected and widely known econometric analyses indicating that the liberalization of Canadian–U.S. trade is likely to result in increased intraindustry, not interindustry, specialization.[32] Although some economic dislocation is expected to occur within the industries opposed to the agreement, firms will generally tend to specialize rather than disappear. Overall, private economic interest groups favoring free trade seem to have had more resources and organization than their opposing counterparts in both countries. This greatly eased the task of FTA negotiators.

IMPLICATIONS FOR THE FREE TRADE TALKS

The issues just outlined can be usefully considered by employing some distinctions inspired by Haas.[33] He argues that changes in the rules of collaborative games cannot typically be explained solely by changes in cognition or by changes in relative power among states but rather by a combination of the two.[34] And so it is in the present case. Declining U.S. hegemony led to U.S. rejection of some special international economic advantages for Canada during the Nixon administration.[35] This, in turn, helped provoke a reconsideration of Canadian policy and the introduction of foreign investment screening and attempts to diversify trade. Continuing U.S. economic difficulties in the 1970s linked to hegemonic decline focused foreign, and especially Canadian, attention on the growing protectionist potential of the "administered protection" apparatus embedded in U.S. law.[36] Declining Canadian productivity gains and economic recession in the early 1980s led the Canadians to rethink the efficacy of Trudeau's economic policies, and some sectoral free trade possibilities were explored. Finally, as the plummeting U.S. trade balance of the mid-1980s brought unprecedented pressure in the Congress for increased protection, Canada launched the free trade initiative.

Expert opinion about the economic advisability of closer union between the United States and Canada has perhaps never been more consensual on both sides of the border. Some estimates put Canadian gains from an FTA at several percent of GNP; estimates for the United States are much smaller but still substantial.[37]

In the United States, elite opinion, spearheaded by economists, has professed liberal policies over the entire postwar period. Mass support for free trade with Canada is also overwhelming, if scarcely considered. A poll for the Toronto *Globe and Mail* taken in early 1988 found 90 percent support for free trade, although only two-fifths of the respondents were aware that the FTA had been negotiated!

Widespread support for FTA in the United States in a generally protectionist climate demands an explanation. Two factors probably resolve the apparent paradox. First, although Canada did have the second highest absolute trade surplus with the United States over the period 1980–1984 (after Japan), the amount was quite modest relative to total trade between the two countries and it increased very little during the spectacular dollar rise,[38] in large part because the Canadian dollar also rose dramatically. Moreover, Canada's exports are not mainly finished goods, so Canadian products could not symbolize U.S. trade problems the way Japanese products did.

More fundamentally, creeping U.S. protectionism during the period came out of an administrative structure and executive calculations in which those paying had minimum voice.[39] In sharp contrast, the prospects of free trade and investment with Canada immediately engaged the potential winners on a footing at least equal to those disadvantaged, thus performing much the same function as the GATT bargaining rounds.[40] As will be seen, however, the United States resisted relinquishing control over "administered protection," largely for autonomy reasons.

The relative contribution of ideas and evidence to changing political debate cannot be traced with precision,[41] but we conclude that the evidence cited earlier has provided an important impetus for what amounts to a rethinking of the national interest in Canada. Although many Canadian economists have long urged liberal policies for both trade and investment,[42] elite opinion has been sharply divided. Both the Liberal Donald Macdonald, who chaired the Royal Commission on the Economic Union (the Commission was begun under the Liberal Trudeau government) and the Progressive Conservative Brian Mulroney, who launched the free trade initiative, had entertained more protectionist views earlier in their careers. The endorsement of free trade by eleven of the twelve Royal Commission members stunned the country.[43]

A recognition of the threat that domestic protection posed to the welfare of Canada constituted only part of the impetus for redefining the policy implications of the national interest. More immediately important was the discovery that U.S.-administered protection could be employed with dangerous effect. Opinion makers had been relentlessly bombarded with both quantitative estimates of the costs of protection and the perils of Canada's position as the only major industrial country except Japan without assured access to a market of at least 200 million persons.[44] With this concern in mind, the anti-FTA Liberals in mid-1988 tried to argue that the high tide of U.S. protectionism had passed, and this should cause supporters of FTA to rethink their position.

Doubt remains about the economic effects of FTA among many Canadian politicians. The Federal Liberal Party, much of the support for which comes from Ontario, the home of much of Canada's highly protected industry, has maintained a position of skepticism about FTA, although many provincial Liberals support it, while the trade union–based New Democratic Party (NDP) is unambiguously opposed. The NDP case rests partly on the grounds of "cheap foreign labor" from areas of the United States where wages and benefits are low. These opposing voices also place great stress on autonomy issues. Provincial political leaders also raise autonomy issues. They foresee that the need to bring Provincial law into conformance with the FTA will reduce their autonomy from the federal government.

Both countries entered the FTA negotiations facing the trade-off between increased prosperity and a diminution of autonomy, although the potential prosperity gains and autonomy losses loomed far larger for Canada than for the United States. In addition, each state faced the complexities of internal politics. In the following section we consider a framework for analyzing the trade-off between autonomy and prosperity.

A BARGAINING SCHEME

In *Beyond the Nation State*,[45] Haas devises a scheme to examine decision making and conflict resolution in international organizations that we use to structure our analysis of specific issues included in the FTA negotiations (see figure 7.1). He notes that agreement and disagreement can pertain either to causality or to preferred outcomes, and he identifies dispute resolution mechanisms to which various kinds of issues will gravitate.[46]

Although Haas seeks an understanding of the dynamic of intramural decision making within international organizations and its potential for increasing international cooperation, we are challenged to explain the circumstances under which sovereign states will bargain and the character of the resulting agreements.

We begin by stressing that some minimum level of internal agreement must exist on both the causal mechanism and the expected

FIGURE 7.1
Haas' Matrix

| | | Preferred outcomes | |
		Actors agree	Actors disagree
Beliefs about causation	Actors agree	COMPUTATION requires BUREAUCRATIC STRUCTURE	COMPROMISE requires BARGAINING IN REPRESENTATIVE STRUCTURE
	Actors disagree	JUDGEMENT requires MAJORITY VOTE IN COLLEGIAL STRUCTURE	INSPIRATION requires ANOMIC STRUCTURE AND CHARISMA

Source: Ernst B. Haas, *Beyond the National State* (Stanford, Calif.: Stanford University Press, 1964), p. 105.

outcome of an agreement for a state to negotiate with confidence and effectiveness. Where important domestic actors disagree on either causation or preferred outcomes or both, countries will be loath to bargain. In particular, the compromising of internal interests must typically take place before an initial national bargaining position can be formulated.

Where there is bilateral casual agreement with a range of attractive possible outcomes for both parties, bargaining may proceed. On the other hand, where a chasm of causal disagreement looms between two or more potential bargainers, even where there is unanimity within each camp, no agreement will be reached.

The Haas scheme suggests certain aspects of an actual agreement as well as the circumstances under which bargaining can take place. Issues not covered by the agreement remain totally subject to national control and may be candidates for future bargaining (row 1, column 2). Other issues admit to little future compromise because disagreement on both beliefs about causation and preferred outcomes is intractable (row 2, column 2). Issues upon which the struck bargain is complete can simply be implemented by a bureaucracy (row 1, column 1), leaving yet other issues to some kind of negotiation or adjudication where specific causal questions below the scope of the overall agreement may remain in doubt (row 2, column 1). In figure 7.2 we suggest how the FTA issues addressed here fit into the Haas matrix.

THE FREE TRADE AGREEMENT

Agreement on Causality: The Reduction of Tariffs and Nontariff Barriers

One of the primary objectives of the FTA was to eliminate barriers to trade in goods and services as well as investment between Canada and the United States. In these negotiations there was a high level of consensus on causality; that is, that a reduction of tariff levels would result in an increase in prosperity, a goal that was also the objective of both countries. Although the lion's share of total bilateral trade was already duty-free, the Canadians had faced U.S. tariffs of more than 15 percent in chemicals, metal alloys, and clothing among other products. U.S. exporters had been frustrated by a Canadian tariff on most dutiable goods about twice as high as that of the United States.[47] To eliminate the economic distortions caused by tariffs, the United States and Canada agreed to phase out tariffs on most manufactured goods over a ten-year period. The timing of the tariff reductions is designed to allow companies to adjust to new competitive circumstances.[48] The United States also gained a large measure of certainty about availability and price of Canadian energy. Canada may only limit energy exports to the United States in extraordinary circumstances and cannot discriminate in price against U.S. purchasers.[49]

Negotiations Over Automobile Trade. The majority of the negotiations over trade in automobiles between the United States and Canada was also based on the joint understanding that the reduction in trade barriers would create efficiencies for both the United States and Canadian auto industries. Canada, however, was also concerned about its ability to pursue an autonomous automobile policy as a result of its fear that without special advantages it would not be able to attract new auto production. These two concerns were present during the negotiations over the creation of the Auto Pact in 1965.

The Auto Pact was negotiated specifically to avoid a trade conflict over the U.S. claim that the Canadian policy providing duty remissions on imported parts and cars to companies that exported cars to

FIGURE 7.2
The Nature of Disagreement in U.S.–Canada Trade

		Preferred outcomes	
		Actors agree	Actors disagree
Beliefs about causation	Actors agree	Reduction in tariff and nontariff barriers in services and investment	Escape clause dispute settlement
	Actors disagree	Bilateral dispute settlement in antidumping and countervailing duty cases	Culture

the United States constituted an export subsidy. The agreement provided for bilateral free trade in all original equipment parts and vehicles, but not in replacement parts, replacement tires, and used cars.[50] As a part of the agreement, the Canadian government also signed letters of intent with the major auto manufacturers in which they agreed to increase their investment in Canada to maintain their Canadian production sales ratio. This agreement resulted primarily in increased exports of U.S. parts to Canada that returned to the United States as auto imports after being assembled to meet Canadian production requirements.[51] The Auto Pact led to a tremendous increase in trade such that by 1984 over one third of Canada's trade with the United States consisted of automotive products.[52]

The letters of intent were a continual irritant to the United States. Conflict over United States–Canadian auto trade intensified in the 1980s as a result of a new Canadian policy that offered foreign firms duty remission on parts or cars imported from third countries if they exported auto parts made in Canada. Canada also offered foreign auto manufacturers production-based duty remissions. If foreign producers met Canadian production requirements, they could import cars and parts duty-free from all over the world. The United States considered both of these duty remissions to be countervailable export subsidies. The United States also objected to non-Canadian firms (primarily Japanese) establishing production facilities in Canada to obtain Auto Pact status that would allow them to export cars to the United States duty-free.

The negotiations over autos in the FTA focused on this conflict. Canada agreed to terminate both export and production-based duty remissions. The FTA also expanded the scope of the Auto Pact by eliminating tariffs on all autos, tires, and replacement parts after ten years.[53] Finally, duty-free entry was limited to current participants to the agreement.[54]

Negotiations Over Services. The United States and Canada also agreed to principles liberalizing trade in services. Agreement to extend national treatment to services was also based on a shared agreement that the competitive pressures resulting from the reduction of trade barriers would lead to increased prosperity for both Canada and the United States. In this agreement, the FTA moved well beyond matters yet generally treated in the GATT. The new principles would ensure that U.S. and Canadian service firms (e.g., engineering, accounting, advertising, financial, and data processing) would be treated essentially no differently from domestic firms.[55]

The FTA's concern with lowering barriers over a broad range of goods and services can be interpreted quite persuasively using Haas' scheme for thinking about decision making and conflict resolution. The general thrust resulted from the amalgam of economic logic with evidence that trade restrictions explained part of declining Canadian economic performance. This tended to narrow the circle of those influentials prepared to make the case for a Canadian economy protected from U.S. competition and guided by the government. The changed balance, in turn, emboldened policy intellectuals and politicians in the government who forged the Canadian internal and international strategy.

The story is simpler in the United States. Only a few special interests ever provided serious deterrent to free trade in the first place, and the U.S. government was predisposed to bargain with Canada long before Canada took the initiative. In negotiating with domestic interests that were threatened by trade liberalization with Canada, the United States was usually willing to compensate them through modifications of domestic regulatory policy or other support that did not affect the substance of the FTA.

In both countries, much of the agreement can be implemented in a straightforward way by national trade bureaucracies employing little discretion.

The Liberalization of Investment. In investment, just as with trade in goods and services, Canada joined the United States in suspecting that Canadian restrictions were potentially damaging to Canada's long-term economic interests. Just as with services, the agreement on the liberalization of investment under the FTA sets international precedents. At the time of the Treaty of Rome, for example, not only was free trade considered largely in terms of goods rather than services, but the essentiality of direct investment for the international marketing of goods was imperfectly understood. Hence, despite the commitment of the Six to open factor markets, freedom of investment did not receive priority attention. Forecasts suggest, however, that some 70 percent of the increase in U.S.–Canadian trade resulting from FTA will take place within the MNCs of the two countries.[56]

The United States has historically taken among the most liberal positions in the world on direct investment. U.S. federal law allows for virtually unlimited activity except in a few security-sensitive sectors.[57] The FTA will apparently not alter U.S. practice in any substantial way.

Canada's view of FDI arises from a radically different historical experience. Although virtually no major U.S. industry has had foreign ownership above 5 percent until quite recently, Canadians in the 1960s found three quarters or more of some of their major industries in foreign hands. Although the contribution of this investment to Canadian postwar prosperity was widely recognized,[58] political pressure to become more selective about investment grew steadily, leading in 1974 to the establishment of the Foreign Investment Review Agency (FIRA). FIRA, which declared that foreign investment would be evaluated on the basis of "substantial benefit" to the Canadian economy, drew fire from foreign business and from analysts[59] who feared that the necessity for a proposal to enumerate benefits (e.g., the numbers of jobs created) might generate negative reactions in the home country and hence lead to restrictions there and to generally higher levels of investment politicization.

"Investment wars" never became a major issue between the United States and Canada, but FIRA's message that investment in Canada was a matter for surveillance and bargaining became the U.S. business community's principal complaint about its northern partner, and the negotiation of liberalization in investment became a principle U.S. objective in the FTA.[60]

Even more offensive to U.S. business than FIRA's oversight of FDI were the ambitions of the National Energy Program (NEP) of 1980 to reduce substantially the foreign-owned share of Canadian energy resources. The energy price bust of the early 1980s found the government having already purchased some energy assets at excessive prices and on the path of purchasing much more. At the same time, doubts were mounting about the wisdom of restricting investment in general.

The Mulroney government virtually turned the earlier policies around, abandoning many elements of the NEP, renaming FIRA "Investment Canada" and declaring a policy of seriously screening only investments in sensitive sectors and takeovers of very large firms. Thus, in most respects, the change in Canadian investment policy antedated FTA. Yet the more liberal approach was a unilateral policy that could presumably be reversed at any time, making North American corporate planning far riskier than that with an FTA. Thus, an agreement to give largely national treatment to U.S. investors loomed very large on the U.S. agenda.

The FTA declares its intention "to ensure that future regulation of Canadian investors in the United States and of American investors in Canada results in treatment no different than that extended to domestic investors within each country."[61] Very significantly, although Canada retains the right to review U.S. acquisition of Canadian firms and continues to restrict investment in energy companies, the threshold levels for direct acquisitions have been raised substantially. By 1992 the review threshold for direct acquisitions will be $150 million (Canadian).[62] The United States and Canada also agreed to eliminate investment-related performance requirements (such as local content and import substitution requirements) that would distort bilateral trade flows. Any disputes that arise may be taken to the Canada–U.S. Trade Commission, established to oversee the agreement.[63]

What factors led to Canadian reconsideration? First, the U.S. (and other foreign) reaction to FIRA's role as the Western world's nominally most restrictive FDI screening agency,[64] gave the country the reputation of having a "bad business climate," which was widely believed to have deterred some investment that Canada might have welcomed.[65] Second, internal uneasiness was caused by the decline in Canadian productivity growth that accompanied the screening period. Third, starting in the mid-1970s, Canada began investing more in the United States than the United States invested in Canada. By 1984, Canadian statistics suggested that the stock of FDI in the United States was half that of U.S. FDI in Canada.[66] With respect to both the United States and other countries, Canada was increasingly seen as a state that should be treating foreign investment as it wished its own investment treated.[67]

Finally, Canada recognized that much of the negotiated free trade in services—a vital and growing part of both economies—would be rendered meaningless without the necessary investment receiving national treatment. A free trade agreement in the 1980s could not bear the name without a high degree of freedom for direct investment.

Foreign investment policy presents a clear case of increased consensual knowledge reinforced by increasing symmetry in the interests of the two countries. As Canada's best thinking about economic development moved away from the arguably misplaced concreteness underlying both the Auto Pact and FIRA and toward a position based more fully on competition and flexibility, Canada was also becoming one of the world's most important home countries for direct investment. Nonetheless, Canada's industry is still 40 percent U.S.-owned, and the abandonment of most control over incoming investment must seem like an autonomy threat to many Canadians, despite the attendant promise of higher living standards. After the content of the FTA was made public, opposition politicians were quick to accuse Prime Minister Mulroney of "putting Canada up for sale."

Interpreting the changed Canadian position using the Haas scheme, one finds a parallel with the issue of general trade. Logic, experience, and other evidence diminished the group of influentials prepared to defend restrictions, while it emboldened their opponents. This is demonstrated by the unilateral abandonment of much investment restriction even prior to FTA. Moreover, doubts about the wisdom of liberalization could be overridden internally by the recognition that greater access to the U.S. market simply would not be granted unless Canada yielded on the investment front. The United States experienced little change in its position but merely seized on Canadian desires for access to press for investment openness.

Disagreement on Preferred Outcomes: The Negotiations on Subsidies [68]

Simon Reisman, the chief Canadian negotiator, stated at the outset of the negotiations that he would not be willing to settle for anything less than a complete exemption from U.S. countervailing duty and dumping laws. This position was based on a growing fear in Canada that the U.S.-administered trade procedures were not grounded in economic analysis but rather were driven by primarily political concerns. [69] From the Canadian perspective it looked as if the legal rationale for the imposition of countervailing duties (i.e., the finding that a subsidy on goods exported to the United States was injuring a U.S. industry) was being replaced by willingness on the part of the U.S. government to impose countervailing duties, whether they were justified or not. Countervailing duty cases in the 1980s affecting softwood lumber, Atlantic groundfish, and potash had damaged key regional industries; this increased Canadian sensitivity to the uncertainty and potential abuse that could result from the U.S. system of administered protection.

The United States and Canada reached partial agreement that subsidies could, under some circumstances, cause trade distortions. Agreement over preferred outcomes, however, was hindered by political realities on both sides of the border. Canada, because of the political sensitivity of regional development subsidies that are used to create economic opportunities in underdeveloped parts of Canada, cannot yet politically afford to give them up. The U.S. Congress, on the other hand, believes the countervailing duty procedures to be an essential element of autonomy, is convinced that the United States subsidizes very little in comparison to its trading partners, and considers all subsidies as pernicious without regard to their size. The negotiations over establishing some discipline in subsidies were further complicated by the unwillingness of the U.S. Congress to put restrictions on state development programs.[70]

At the outset of the negotiations, the Canadian negotiating team proposed a comprehensive set of measures that included increased discipline on Canadian subsidy practices. The Mulroney government was willing to forego the use of some subsidies because they were becoming very expensive. In part, the government hoped to use the FTA to justify the reduction in subsidy programs.

The Canadian proposal included tests that differentiated "green light" subsidies that would continue and not be countervailable from "red light" subsidies, which would be forbidden even if there was no threat of injury. (Regional development subsidies were left intact.) In exchange, Canada expected the United States both to offer a restriction on its use of subsidies and to exempt Canada from the trade remedy process. Disputes would be resolved within a binding binational Trade Commission.

The United States did not directly respond to the Canadian proposal until August of 1987. U.S. negotiators were concerned that loopholes in the Canadian proposal could make "red light" subsidies look as if they fell into the "green light" category. The United States proposed an alternative test in which subsidies provided to firms or industries that exported over a certain percentage of their production would be prohibited. (These would include regional development subsidies.) This approach allowed the United States to avoid determining which subsidies were benign and which trade distorting. Canada objected that it was much more export dependent than the United States and that test was unacceptable because it would have considerably more impact on Canada than on the United States.

The entire FTA negotiations almost came to an abrupt end because of the inability of U.S. and Canadian negotiators to reach an agreement over which subsidies would be unacceptable. Shortly before the negotiating deadline Reisman walked out over a disagreement on whether to use the Canadian or the U.S. proposal as a basis for continuing the negotiations.

When the two sides met again, attention turned from discipline on subsidies to a discussion of what remedies would be possible if the imposition of a countervailing duty was believed to be unwarranted under national law. Thus, in the context of the Haas scheme, the negotiations shifted from a discussion about refining understandings of causation to one focusing on agreement over preferred outcomes within which some systematic bilateral causal disagreements could persist. Preferred outcomes became restricted to the consistency of countervailing duty decisions with the ostensibly nonprotectionist intent of domestic law. This could be determined without addressing detailed questions of causality. Canada and the United States did agree to undertake separate negotiations within the first five years of the FTA that would attempt to reach an agreement over discipline on the use of subsidies.

Agreement on Preferred Outcomes:
The Bilateral Dispute Settlement Mechanism

As a result of the absence of detailed agreement on causation (i.e., which kind of subsidies are trade distorting), the negotiations focused on the creation of a binding dispute settlement mechanism. In these negotiations both the United States and Canada could agree upon the legitimacy of the appropriate use of domestic countervailing duty laws.

Canada made the establishment of a binding, bilateral dispute-settlement mechanism to handle U.S. complaints of unfair trade practices a *sine qua non* for any agreement.[71] In sharp contrast, the United States found little fault with the Canadian unfair trading mechanism.[72] U.S. negotiators feared, however, that Congress would not approve an agreement that yielded control over the disposition of dumping and subsidy cases to a bilateral organization.

Since the overriding goal of the Canadians was security of access to the U.S. market, the uncertainty created by the apparent politicization of the technical work of the U.S. International Trade Commission (ITC) became a prime target for elimination in the agreement. Canadian fears rested in part on a 1986 decision of the International Trade Administration (ITA) of the Commerce Department that the Canadian calculation of stumpage (cutting right) fees for softwood lumber on public lands constituted a subsidy.[73] In a 1982 petition, a coalition of U.S. lumber producers claimed that the Canadian government subsidized lumber production by selling stumpage rights at bargain prices. In response to this petition, the ITA ruled that Canadian stumpage fees were "generally available" like ports, roads, or schools—and therefore did not constitute a countervailable subsidy.[74]

In response to a similar petition brought by the softwood lumber industry in 1986, the ITA issued a preliminary decision in which it reversed itself, basing its action on a new ruling in the U.S. Court of International Trade. The ITA found the softwood lumber industry in Canada had greater access to the benefits of the stumpage fees than other industries that use wood as an input (e.g., pulp and paper). This greater access was judged to be the result of governmental discretion and as such was countervailable.

Canada viewed the new definition of a countervailable subsidy as threatening to an increasing number of government programs and would not sign an FTA without some assurance that the precedent set in the softwood lumber case would not be the basis for future decisions. After the talks on subsidy discipline became deadlocked, the United States relented with a compromise. A bilateral panel would replace judicial review in both the United States and Canada. The panel would be made up of legal and other experts in international trade law. If either party was not satisfied with a final countervailing duty or dumping determination, the panel would review the administrative record to decide whether the investigating authority of either side made a decision not in accordance with its law.[75] In the context of the softwood lumber case, for example, a ruling would be made on the appropriateness of the ITA's interpretation of the "generally available doctrine" as well as the economic determination of "injury."[76] The United States conceded to the Canadian demand that the decisions of this panel be binding. After further stalemate, the U.S. executive branch agreed to fight any legislative efforts to overturn the panel's findings, and, if this were unsuccessful, to support Canada's right to retaliate.[77]

The agreement stipulates that the bilateral tribunal will adjudicate countervailing duty and subsidy disputes for five years, with the possibility of a two-year extension. During this time, the U.S. and Canada will work to create a substitute system of laws in both countries.[78] If a substitute system is not implemented at the end of that time, either party could terminate the Trade Agreement on six months notice.[79]

In terms of Haas' scheme, it should be noted that few U.S. policy influentials have been admirers of the U.S. system of administered protection. Although estimates of its economic cost vary,[80] most professionals concerned with trade matters in the United States undoubtedly welcomed a challenge to the system. Nonetheless, other influentials expressed concern about the diminuation of U.S. soveriegnty implied by Canadian demands for binding decision making outside U.S. control.[81] These doubts coupled with the pressures of affected interests help explain the final outcome: more monitoring of the consistency and impartiality of the application of U.S. law but no actual change in the procedures themselves.

On the Canadian side, absolute unanimity prevailed that the United States must yield on administered protection: assured access to the U.S. market propelled the Canadian initiative in the first place. Unlike the situation in trade and investment, the United States changed its view and moved to bargaining flexibility, while the Canadians reacted. The scheme also predicts the necessity of a dispute settlement mechanism. "Unfairness" disputes typically involve causation disputes. Hence, a collegial structure becomes vital, even if only to review the application of domestic law.

The Escape Clause. The United States and Canada agreed that both countries needed to retain an escape clause that would allow the imposition of temporary import restrictions if surges in imports cause serious injury to domestic producers. Implementation of the escape clause, however, threatens free trade because politicians often feel pressured to grant protection by the political clout of the industries involved, even if the protection clashes with the spirit of the escape clause. Thus, although the parties agreed on preferred outcomes (the need to protect against import surges), disagreement on causality often prevails (whether specific surges cause injury).

In the FTA, the United States and Canada agreed to limit the use of the escape clause in their bilateral trade. Until 1998, if an industry is found to be injured by an import surge as a result of the FTA, tariffs can be raised only to the most favored nation rate (MFN) and then only temporarily.[82] The agreement further guarantees compensation to the other country, for example, through accelerated duty elimination on another product.[83] After the transition period ending in 1998, escape clause actions can only be taken by mutual consent. Conflict over the legitimacy of an escape clause action or the adequacy of compensation will be resolved by a panel, which is likely to be composed of bureaucrats, political or industry representatives, and experts. If the findings of this arbitration panel are not implemented, the agreement sanctions retaliation.

The Haas scheme suggests the dynamics behind the agreement reached on the escape clause. Domestic political pressures necessitate bargaining over causality. In escape clause cases a positive recommendation for trade protection hinges on whether the industry can demonstrate that it has been "injured" by imports. States, although they accept the necessity for their trading partners to offer domestic industries temporary import relief to allow for adjustment, often disagree with the finding that imports caused injury. Thus, it is also appropriate in disputes over the application of the escape clause to have them mediated by a binational panel.[84]

Disagreement on Causation and Preferred Outcomes: The Special Issue of the Cultural Industries

Nowhere does the perceptual difference between Canada and the United States on free trade loom larger than on matters connected with the so-called cultural industries. The term is highly misleading: completely free trade would have little impact on high culture but would significantly affect trade in entertainment products. Free trade in popular "culture" presented a major obstacle to agreement. The FTA exempts such industries from trade liberalization.[85]

The U.S. position on open trade in these industries relates both to its general ideological biases in favor of maximum choice for individuals and to its national experience of never having been consciously subject to a single large foreign cultural influence.[86] Moreover, virtually all the protectionism lies north of the border.

The United States controls only the maximum foreign percentage ownership in broadcasting organizations, a policy dating to the 1930s and justified on national security grounds. In sharp contrast, Canada has increasingly protected a broad range of cultural industries in recent decades. Most of this protection has come from nontariff barriers, including (1) restrictions on repatriation of royalties and payments; (2) local ownership requirements, personnel restrictions, and discriminatory licensing; (3) subsidies, tax breaks, discriminatory procurement, and government ownership; and (4) quantitative restrictions on imports or distribution.[87]

General Canadian concerns about control of popular culture seem to rest on two objectives: content and competence. Many have forcefully argued that Canadian nationalism and culture are fragile, not only because the country has been so strongly influenced by the United States, but because a strong edifice of largely nonindigenous British and French biculturalism exhausts much of the rest of the cultural space.[88] Many Canadians claim subnational identification over Canadian identity, an idea almost unthinkable anywhere in the United States. An obvious—if not necessarily very effective—response to this problem would attempt to focus Canadians' attention on matters that are more or less exclusively Canadian, or to stimulate thinking about larger issues from a Canadian point of view.

A number of analysts, both within Canada and abroad, have stressed that only the content objective can really be defended. This objective requires attention strictly to the content of the output of the communication and entertainment system rather than on the nationality of owners, writers, and performers.[89] This position contends that the competence criterion does little more than define production by nationals as a collective consumption good. The analysis is derived from Breton's classic discussion of the economics of nationalism,[90] written with Canada as the principal example. The argument implies that the conflation in public policy of Canadian input and output content yields unjustified protectionism, providing certain producers with noncompetitive income and prestige.[91]

The positions of both governments can be quite easily understood on the basis of a trade-off between prosperity and autonomy in the context of murky causal mechanisms. Free trade in "cultural industries" appears very one-sided in Canada. Exports seem unlikely to increase in a large and dependable way, largely because the U.S. market is already open, whereas the impact of cultural imports are varyingly interpreted.

Public opinion polls show that Canadians strongly support both Canadian cultural content and access to the maximum range of U.S. popular culture.[92] In fact, this describes what Canadians have today: 77 percent of periodicals sold, 70 percent of television airtime, and three out of four books sold are foreign, mainly from the United States.[93] The remaining fraction of the market, however, is perceived by many Canadians to be critical for national consciousness. Moreover, even skeptics about that claim might be quite risk averse in the face of troubling if unsystematic evidence. Stories are told of Canadian children who confuse their (very different) Senate with the U.S. Senate, whereas the Royal Canadian Mounted Police is mistaken for the FBI.[94] When phenomena such as these are considered alongside rampant subnationalism, many Canadians are alarmed. The strong support for cultural protection across the political spectrum must be seen in this light. Critics argue that meaningful national content might be achieved more economically, but the risks of nontraditional policies appear excessive to most Canadians.

The U.S. position during the negotiations rested on conflicting motives. Free trade in cultural industries holds the immediate and certain prospect of a large increase in exports, and the United States wanted the issue considered. Yet the United States ultimately and rather predictably backed down. The stakes are confined to an industry with geographic concentration, mainly in California and New York, where strong economic interests supported FTA anyway. Moreover, the problem is self-limiting. Canadians are willing to engage in only a modest amount of "mutual coercion, mutually arrived at" in the service of national identity. As technology continues to favor software over hardware and to increase economies of scale,[95] the price of national discrimination will probably continue to rise. In addition, Canada appears to have given the U.S. assurances that substantial new cultural protectionism will not be attempted.

More generally, the cultural influence of the United States in the contemporary world can be seen largely as the result of a massive web of private voluntary bargains. American cultural hegemony over ordinary world citizens would meet far more private and public resistance if it appeared to be the result of official design. U.S. realization of this reality must explain the absence of firmness about Canadian practices that, if they involved ordinary commerce, would be regarded as completely intolerable. Canadian autonomy fears were allowed to dominate U.S. prosperity—not assertiveness—ambitions. We have seen no evidence of official interest in advancing U.S. cultural hegemony in Canada.

Once again the Haas scheme can be employed. Considerable disagreement exists over both causal mechanisms and outcomes on the subject of culture, broadly construed. Haas suggests that only charismatic leadership could lead to agreement on such an issue, and this is difficult even to imagine. Canadian experts disagree among themselves, and few Americans have considered the issue. Hence, because of the potentially high risks for Canada, the negotiations never seriously dealt with cultural matters, although, in the spirit of keeping the talks general, everything was nominally "on the table." [96] Sensing the great concern of the Canadians and the relatively minor gains for themselves, the Americans pressed other issues.

The FTA and Dispute Resolution

We think the Haas approach satisfactorily explains the areas where FTA was successful. But it does more. Continuing disputes and the decision mechanisms for their resolution can also be persuasively interpreted using the same scheme.

The two columns of the Haas matrix recall the two roads to progress described by Murphy[97]: the functionalist and the realist, although correspondence is not complete.[98] Where there is agreement on causality, issues do not become completely "bounded, distanced from the nation-state, and handed over to the rule of experts, whose methods are those of scientific inquiry."[99] Instead, where future discretion must be exercised we find the creation of various dispute settlement mechanisms and oversight committees to resolve conflicts that may arise. These include, among others, the U.S.–Canadian Trade Commission responsible for disputes over services, investment, and escape clause cases; a separate binational review board to oversee changes in subsidy and antidumping regulations; and a committee to oversee problems that develop in the agreement over auto trade.

All these dispute settlement mechanisms are likely to contain some experts, some bureaucrats, and some political appointees. To the extent that the United States and Canada can agree on ends and these commissions are staffed by experts, perhaps trade will become more insulated from politics and lead to increased productivity in both the United States and Canadian economies. If political concerns dominate, the process through which disputes are resolved may be less technical and influenced more by the relative power relationship between Canada and the United States (i.e., be more characteristic of Morgenthau than of Mitrany).

The FTA also serves a purpose consistent with Murphy's second road to progress, where states have conflicting ends and statesmen rely on traditional diplomacy and customary international law to resolve conflict. Here the bilateral trade regime can help to avoid trade disputes that could escalate into trade wars by explicitly maintaining national control over trade in spite of potential prosperity losses. Thus, the FTA enhances the utility of diplomacy by acknowledging its necessity in dealing with conflicts over subsidy discipline and cultural trade.

BROADER LESSONS

The Canada–U.S. FTA experience sheds light on broader issues in international economic relations.

1. The United States declared from the beginning that it hoped FTA would give forward impetus to worldwide liberalization, particularly to the Uruguay Round of the GATT. Despite declining relative power, the United States continues to exercise assertive leadership in multilateral trade negotiations.[100] It should also be stressed that as the world's largest economy and largest trader, the United States had far more rational prosperity incentives to consider spillover effects in the FTA negotiations on subsequent developments than would smaller

powers (including Canada). The United States may advance some of the approaches successful in FTA during the latter years of the Uruguay Round.

2. The apparently successful bargaining between the United States and Canada suggests that the bilateral alternative to general liberalization may be viable. Whatever happens over the next few years in Geneva, this lesson may be important for such countries as Australia, New Zealand, the non-EC countries of Europe, and perhaps some of the Newly Industrializing Countries as they consider their international economic strategies.[101]

3. Many nations still pursuing activist economic development policies will be watching the Canadian experience carefully. As the two partners grope toward mutually acceptable solutions to the subsidies issue, Canada will surely yield many widely used instruments. Any deleterious results will be charted alongside the almost certain gains in overall national income. Any dramatic increase in the role of foreign capital in Canada will also be noted. Although the logic of modern interdependence may necessitate virtually free investment as a complement to free trade, a large increase in inward direct investment—however unlikely—could generate negative repercussions that could diminish the exemplary character of FTA for other countries (and could give Canadians second thoughts as well).

Fourth, the United States has seen more clearly than ever before how its administered protection apparatus is viewed from abroad. Canadian demands will be echoes by any other potential free trade partner. A constructive experience with the dispute resolution mechanism in the next few years may calm U.S. sovereignty fears and pave the way for similar U.S. concessions in multinational fora.

Finally, the United States wisely relented on the issue of "cultural industries," despite evidence that much Canadian practice is difficult to justify solely on the basis of protecting Canadian identity and culture. This is an area in which the United States must tread carefully because its experience with the issues falls so far outside that of other states. For example, the U.S. was the only state to vote against national vetoes of satellite broadcasting in 1972.[102] From the U.S. perspective, the next few years' experience will show whether the cultural exception to FTA is as self-limiting and relatively innocuous as it presently appears.

CONCLUSION

The negotiations over the U.S.–Canadian Free Trade Agreement demonstrate how learning and the development of consensual knowledge about the consequences of freer trade and investment may contribute to the ultimate depoliticization of economic transactions and an increase in perceived well-being. Carefully pursued, the reduction of government intervention in international trade and investment can be viewed as "progress." This characterization of progress has existed since Adam Smith wrote about "absolute advantage" in 1776.

Pressures from domestic interest groups to keep the state involved in international transactions remain in any discussion of trade policy. The U.S.–Canadian Trade Agreement is no exception. Opposition to the reduction in autonomy motivated in part by rent seeking persists on both sides. U.S. opposition comes primarily from industries that will face increasing import competition. In addition, the bilateral dispute settlement mechanism may appear to some congressional representatives as an intolerable constraint on U.S. autonomy—and their own discretion. In Canada opposition comes from fearful industrial sectors concentrated in the most populous provinces and from general fears of decreased federal and provincial control and even U.S. engulfment.

Approval by both governments in 1989 marked only the "end of the beginning" for the FTA; many obstacles remain. If a sufficiently common view cannot be attained, the agreement will collapse. Nonetheless, the FTA, through the exemption of culture, demonstrates that economic liberalization need not directly threaten national identity. The increase of international transactions need not clearly undermine the viability of the nation-state as as political unit. Instead, in this agreement we find elements of Murphy's two roads to progress. The FTA calls upon experts, bureaucrats, and political appointees to implement the provisions to reduce trade and investment barriers as well as to settle disputes and ultimately to harmonize U.S. and Canadian subsidy and dumping statutes. It also facilitates the use of diplomacy when trade is restricted, a possibility that could arise in the future negotiations over limiting the use of subsidies and was retained for trade in culture. Thus, while we find some characteristics of functionalist cooperation, we also find an increase on the type of cooperation that remains rooted in the tradition of the nation-state system.

ENDNOTES

1. For a discussion of U.S. law and practices, see Robert Baldwin, *The Political Economy of U.S. Import Policy* (New York: Academic Press, 1986), ch. 1.
2. Earl H. Fry, "An Historical Overview of Canada–U.S. Trade Relations," unpublished manuscript presented at the Conference on Trade Liberalization and Socioeconomic Integration in North America: U.S. Perspectives, (October 1986).
3. Robert T. Kudrle and Davis B. Bobrow, "U.S. Policy Toward Foreign Direct Investment," *World Politics* (April 1982), 34:353–379. Kudrle and Bobrow in turn follow Susan Strange, "The Study of Transnational Relations," *International Affairs* (July 1976), Vol. 52, No. 3; and Robert O. Keohane and Joseph S. Nye, *Power and Interdependence: World Politics in Transition* (Boston: Little, Brown, 1977). Stephen Krasner, "State Power and the Structure of International Trade," *World Politics* (April 1976), Vol. 28, has suggested social stability as a fundamental objective, while David Lake, "Beneath the Commerce of Nations: A Theory of International Economic Structure," *International Studies Quarterly* (June 1984) has posited relative (as opposed to absolute) gains of international economic exchange. Lake's objective is interesting but apparently difficult to find historically. Much of Krasner's stability objective can be included as part of prosperity if the latter explicitly includes both the level of economic activity and the distribution of employment as desiderata. The goals are inductively derived. For a more complete discussion, see Davis B. Bobrow and Robert T. Kudrle, "The Middle Level Powers: What Objectives; What Options?" presented at the Annual Meeting of the American Political Science Association, 1984.
4. In addition to these fundamental goals, some states also appear to pursue "national assertion"—the attempt to project national values and culture abroad. Haas discusses a Jacobin strand of liberalism that holds "that the historical mission of the nation is not merely continuous self-perfection but also the global diffusion of the creed." He contrasts it with the polity of the Whigs who "prefer to confine matters to continuous self-perfection"(Ernst B. Haas, "What is Nationalism and Why Should We Study it?" *International Organization* (Summer 1986) 40(3):707–744. Haas identifies the United States with the Jacobin tradition. We contend that this clashes with Canada's obviously more Whiggish reflexes and provides a source of tension between the two countries. Canada's international posture results both from its national myth and its relative lack of power—and we suspect the former is powerfully reinforced by the latter. Canada's sometimes celebrated attempts at postwar peacemaking

do not contradict the point: peace was being sought for its own sake and not in the name of anything specifically "Canadian."

5. This scarcely suggests that the nations see eye to eye on all security matters. The United States urges Canada to spend more, whereas Canada generally counsels a more accommodating U.S. posture in international relations. There are also occasional specific disputes such as control of arctic waters.

6. For the sake of simplicity we are considering the nation-state as the focus of these parochial impulses. In the case of Canada, of course, strong forces supporting subnational autonomy also prevail.

7. Introduction to this book, p. xv.

8. Seymour Martin Lipset, "Canada and the United States: The Cultural Dimension," in Charles F. Doran and John H. Sigler eds., *Canada and the United States: Enduring Friendship, Persistent Stress* (Englewood Cliffs, N.J.: Prentice-Hall, 1985).

9. Charles F. Doran, *Forgotten Partnership: U.S.–Canada Relations Today*, (Baltimore: The Johns Hopkins University Press, 1984), p. 166.

10. Alan M. Rugman, *Outward Bound: Canadian Direct Investment in the United States* (Toronto: C. D. Howe Institute, 1986).

11. Lipset, "Canada and the United States," p. 113.

12. Haas, "What Is Nationalism and Why Should We Study It?" p. 728.

13. Lipset, "Canada and the United States," pp. 113–118.

14. Haas, "What Is Nationalism?" p. 744.

15. Robert E. Baldwin, "The Political Economy of Protectionism," in J. N. Bhagwati, ed., *Import Competition and Response* (Chicago: University of Chicago Press, 1982), pp. 263–292.

16. Economists have recently developed some new rationales for protection that are "strategic" for other than bargaining purposes. They did not play a role in thinking about the FTA. See Paul Krugman, *Strategic Trade Policy and the New International Economics* (Cambridge, Mass.: The MIT Press, 1986).

17. Royal Commission on the Economic Union and Developments for Canada, *Report*, 3 vol. (Ottawa; Queen's Printer, 1985).

18. Peter Moorici, "The Politics and Economics of Bilateral Free Trade: Impact on the United States," in Edward R. Fried, Frank Stone, and Philip H. Trezise, eds., *Building a Canadian–American Free Trade Area* (Washington, D.C.: The Brookings Institution, 1987), p. 59.

19. See, for example, Abraham Rotstein, *Rebuilding From Within: Remedies for Canada's Ailing Economy* (Toronto: Canadian Institute for Economic Policy, 1984).

20. See, for example, the research on Canadian industrial policy summarized in Donald G. McFetridge, *Canadian Industrial Policy in Action* (Toronto: University of Toronto Press, 1985) and on free trade with the United States in J. Whalley, *Trade Liberalization Among Major World Trading Areas* (Cambridge, Mass.: MIT Press, 1985). "If one could start from scratch, no sane individual would or could construct the barrage of industrial

policies that presently exist in Canada with their duplication, overlap, unknown interaction and unmeasured effect," Christopher Maule, "Does Canada Have an Industrial Strategy?" Ottawa: Carleton University Department of Economics, mimeographed, 1984, pp. 22–23, cited in McFetridge, ed., *Canadian Industrial Policy in Action*, p. 2.

21. Judith L. Goldstein, "The Political Economy of Trade—Institutions of Protection," *American Political Science Review* (March 1986).
22. Both sides will attempt to seize upon such conditions, although economic theory suggests that subsidies, if consistently used in the absence of other entry barriers, typically enrich the importing country at the expense of the exporting country (Robert E. Baldwin, "Protectionist Pressures in the United States," in Ryan C. Amacher, Gottfried Haberler, and Thomas Willett, eds., *Challenge to a Liberal Economic Order* (Washington, D.C.: American Enterprise Institute, 1979, p. 236). Gary C. Hufbauer and Joanna Shelton Erb, *Subsidies in International Trade* (Washington, D.C.: Institute for International Economics, 1984) address the question, "Why should the international community concern itself with the subsidy practices of its member nations?" They comment that, "After all if one nation wished to subsidize production or exports . . . isn't the resulting economic distortion principally the misfortune of the subsidizing nation?" (p. 5). They also provide an answer: "Unbridled and competing national subsidies can undermine world prosperity" (p. 8) by galvanizing protectionist forces.
23. Doran, *Forgotten Partnership*, p. 115.
24. The "third" option was meant to contrast with either a static Canadian policy or closer ties to the United States.
25. Evidence suggests that FIRA had little, if any, impact on the volume of U.S. direct investment in Canada. See Robert T. Kudrle, "The Foreign Investment Review Agency and U.S. Direct Investment in Canada," Humphrey Institute Working Paper, 1989.
26. Quoted in Alan M. Rugman, *Bilateral Trade and Investment Policy*, unpublished manuscript presented at the Canada–U.S. Relations Conference of the University Consortium for Research on North America, 1986, p. 48.
27. Harvey E. Bale Jr., "The United States Policy Toward Inward Foreign Direct Investment," *Vanderbilt Journal of Transnational Law* (1985), 18:209.
28. Isaiah A. Litvak, "Freer Trade with Canada: The Conflicting Views of U.S. Business," *Business Quarterly* (November 1986), p. 48.
29. Ibid., p. 49.
30. Ibid., p. 50.
31. The role of multinationals in the support of trade liberalization has long been recognized. For a particularly penetrating statement see G. K. Helleiner, "The Political Economy of Canada's Tariff Structure: An Alternative Model," *Canadian Journal of Economics* (May 1977), Vol. 10.
32. Richard G. Lipsey and Murray G. Smith, *Canada's Trade Options in a Turbulent World* (Toronto: C. D. Howe Institute, 1985), p. 110.

33. Ernst B. Haas, "Why Collaborate?" *World Politics* (April 1980), 32:357–405.

34. Ibid., p. 387. Haas' concern is explicitly multilateral.

35. Doran, *Forgotten Partnership*, ch. 1.

36. I. M. Destler, *American Trade Politics: System Under Stress* (Washington, D.C.: Institute for International Economics, 1986).

37. Lipsey and Smith, *Canada's Trade Options*, p. 40.

38. Fred G. Bergsten and William R. Cline, *The United States–Japan Economic Problem* (Washington, D.C.: Institute for International Economics, 1985), pp. 22–23.

39. J. M. Finger, H. Keith Hall, and Douglas R. Nelson, "The Political Economy of Administered Protection," *American Economic Review* (June 1982), Vol. 72.

40. Stefanie Ann Lenway, *The Politics of U.S. International Trade* (Cambridge, Mass.: Ballinger Publishing Company, 1985).

41. Martha Derthick and Paul J. Quirk, *The Politics of Deregulation* (Washington, D.C.: Brookings Institution, 1985).

42. See, for example, Harry G. Johnson, *The Canadian Quandry: Economic Problems and Policies* (Toronto: McClelland and Stewart, 1963); Paul Wonnacott and R. J. Wonnacott, *Free Trade Between Canada and the United States* (Cambridge, Mass.: Harvard University Press, 1967).

43. Richard G. Lipsey, "Will There Be a Canadian–American Free Trade Association?" *The World Economy* (September 1986).

44. Lipsey and Smith, *Canada's Trade Options*.

45. Ernst Haas, *Beyond the Nation State* (Stanford, Calif.: Stanford University Press, 1964).

46. Haas defines the organizational structures within the cells of the matrix as follows: "A bureaucratic structure is made up of individual experts with large delegated powers in an administrative hierarchy; a collegium is a body of wise men, inspired by a common purpose, and judiciously able to weigh—and vote on if they cannot agree—the causative factors in dispute; a representative body is a body of less expert delegates from some constituency—i.e., party, interest group, nation, or region; and the structure for complete disagreement can only be anomic or charismatic" (ibid., p. 105).

47. Morici, "The Politics and Economics of Bilateral Free Trade," p. 53.

48. Government of Canada, *The Canada–U.S. Free Trade Agreement* (October 1987), p. 44.

49. Government of Canada, *The Canada–U.S. Free Trade Agreement: Elements of the Agreement* (July 1987), pp. 6, 7.

50. Asim Erdilek, "Potential Impact of a Bilateral Free(r) Trade Agreement on U.S. Direct Investment in Canadian Manufacturing," Working Paper No. 1986:5, Research Program in Industrial Economics, Case Western Reserve University, 1986, p. 31.

51. Ibid., p. 6.

52. Morici, "The Politics and Economics of Bilateral Free Trade," pp. 51–52.

53. Government of Canada, *The Canada–U.S. Free Trade Agreement: Elements of the Agreement.*

54. To ensure that the changes in the Auto Pact promote the ability of both the U.S. and Canadian auto industries to compete internationally, the agreement stipulates that a panel of experts be created to propose both public policy and private initiatives aimed at improving the competitiveness of the industry.

55. Government of Canada, *The Canada–U.S. Free Trade Agreement*, pp. 8, 13.

56. Alan M. Rugman, "Living with Free Trade: How Multinationals Will Adjust to Trade Liberalization," *Business Quarterly* (Fall 1987), Vol. 52, No. 3.

57. State law controlling land investment is frequently restrictive, but so far the states have managed to avoid a federal confrontation.

58. See, for example, A. E. Safarian, "Perspectives on Foreign Investment from the Viewpoint of a Capital Receiving Country," *Journal of Finance* (1973), Vol. 28, No. 2.

59. C. Fred Bergsten, "Coming Investment Wars?" *Foreign Affairs* (October 1974), Vol. 53.

60. For a cross section of business views, see Erdilek, "Potential Impact of a Bilateral Free(r) Trade," pp. 50–52. The official U.S. view held that Canada had every right to restrict foreign investment but that the commitments wrung from incoming firms sometimes involved considerable distortions of U.S. trade. A 1983 U.S. complaint decided in the GATT against Canada attacked the import substitution practices that were part of firms' initial entry agreements (Paul Wonnacott, *U.S.–Canada Interdependence: The Quest for Free Trade* (Washington, D.C.: Institute for International Economics, 1986), pp. 5–20.

61. Government of Canada, *The Canada–U.S. Free Trade Agreement*, p. 229.

62. Ibid., p. 229.

63. The U.S.–Canada Trade Commission is responsible for the implementation of the Agreement and is to resolve disputes over its interpretation and application. The principal representatives to the Commission will be the chief trade negotiators of each country. If a dispute is not resolved through bilateral consultations, the commission is empowered to establish an arbitration panel.

64. A. E. Safarian, "Policy on Multinational Enterprises in Developed Countries," *Canadian Journal of Economics* (1978), Vol. 11, No. 4.

65. But see endnote 26.

66. Alan M. Rugman, "Canada in the USA: Foreign Direct Investment Flows Reversed," *Multinational Business* (Spring 1987), p. 12. Department of Commerce estimates, based on different definitions and data, were considerably lower.

67. An irony lies in the massive change in the Canadian net investment position. Although the diminishing inflow to Canada relative to GNP was not caused by FIRA, the U.S.-administered protection apparatus apparently caused an important part of Canadian FDI in the United

States, particularly in the early 1980s. Thus, relatively free trade and investment could once again alter the relative investment flows between the two countries. The greatest current fear on the Canadian side is not a U.S. takeover but the opposite: the departure of capital supposedly only in place to serve the protected Canadian market. Company surveys, the logic of intraindustry trade, and the actual operations of U.S. firms in Canada do not suggest this outcome, however. Instead, they point to a rationalization of North American production that might lead to some reduction in U.S. investment in Canada in the short run, but with a long-run effect driven mainly by the strength of the two underlying economies taken together. (For a discussion see Erdilek, "Potential Impact of a Bilateral Free[r] Trade," pp. 53–54.)

68. This section is based on interviews with U.S. and Canadian government officials who participated in the negotiations. The interviews were conducted March–June 1988.

69. Alan M. Rugman and Andrew D. M. Anderson, *Administered Protection in America* (London: Croom Helm, 1987).

70. It is not clear whether the Provinces would have gone along with the Canadian offer to forego some kinds of subsidies entirely. Whether the Provinces would have been willing to accept what the negotiators were willing to give up cannot be confirmed because the specific aspects of the subsidy negotiations were never discussed at the briefing meetings for Provincial representatives.

71. For a detailing of Canadian complaints, see Rugman and Anderson, *Administered Protection in America*.

72. The Special Import Measures Act governs the resolution of antidumping and countervailing duty disputes in Canada. This statute gives authority for final determinations to the Canadian Import Tribunal (*International Economic Review* (August 1987), p. 6). Unlike Canada, the United States has not faced seemingly capricious changes in the interpretation of subsidy or antidumping statutes. In 1986, twenty-one dumping cases were completed by the Tribunal. Three of these cases involved products from the United States. The Tribunal found injury in eighteen cases, including the three U.S. cases. The United States did not question the interpretation of the decision to find injury in any of the cases.

73. The U.S. dumping and countervailing duty law is designed to protect firms from the "unfair" competition of subsidized imports. Tests must be met for the imposition of a countervailing duty against foreign goods by both the ITA and the ITC; either party can appeal the case to the U.S. Court of International Trade.

74. Gary C. Hufbauer, "Trade Policy in the United States: A Primer on Legislation and Administration," unpublished manuscript prepared for the Conference on Trade Liberalization and Socioeconomic Integration in North America: U.S. Perspective, October 30, 1986, pp. 16–18.

75. Government of Canada, *The Canada–U.S. Free Trade Agreement: Elements of the Agreement*, p. 2.

76. Alan M. Rugman and Samuel D. Porteous, "The Softwood Lumber Decision of 1986: Broadening the Nature of U.S. Administered Protection," unpublished manuscript, 1987, p. 29.
77. *The New York Times,* October 6, 1987, p. 48.
78. Government of Canada, *The Canada–U.S. Free Trade Agreement: Elements of the Agreement,* p. 21.
79. Ibid.
80. See, for example, Gary C. Hufbauer, Diane T. Berliner, and Kimberly A. Elliott, *Trade Protection in the United States: 31 Case Studies* (Washington, D.C.: Institute for International Economics, 1986).
81. Edith Terry, Bill Javetski, Steven Dryden, and John Pearson, "A Free-Trade Milestone," *Business Week,* October 19, 1987, p. 52.
82. Unless imports from the U.S. and Canada are significantly involved in other escape clause decisions, they have agreed to exclude each other from escape clause remedies.
83. Government of Canada, *The Canada–U.S. Free Trade Agreement,* p. 167.
84. The panels created to adjudicate dumping and countervailing duty disputes are separate from those that will resolve escape clause conflicts.
85. Government of Canada, *The Canada–U.S. Free Trade Agreement: Elements of the Agreement,* p. 4. On the background of Canadian policies, see Steven Globerman, *Cultural Regulation In Canada* (Montreal: The Institute for Research on Public Policy, 1983).
86. Steven Globerman and Aidan Vining, "Bilateral Cultural Free Trade: The U.S–Canadian Case," in Fred Thompson, ed., *Canadian–U.S. Interdependence in the Cultural Industries,* proceedings of a Conference held at Columbia University, New York, 1984, p. 5.
87. Ibid., pp. 6, 7.
88. Charles F. Doran, "Three U.S. Hypotheses About Culture and Trade in Search of Canadian Validation," mimeographed, 1986.
89. Ibid., p. 6. See also George H. Quester, "Coping with Transborder Penetration: The Politics of Television," *Journal of Policy Analysis and Management* (1984), 3(4):37.
90. Albert Breton, "The Economics of Nationalism," *Journal of Political Economy* (1964), 72(4):376–386.
91. Some analysts who see Canadian cultural protection largely as the result of private pressures stress the theoretical possibility that increased specialization resulting from cultural free trade could actually increase Canadian employment. While this could occur, the usual FTA arguments for Canadian enrichment based on a more assured market do not apply. The U.S. market is as open to Canadian producers as it ever will be. An even less persuasive argument suggests that the lower cost of various forms of entertainment and communication resulting from free trade might lead to an increase in Canadian absorption of material with Canadian content (Globerman and Vining, "Bilateral Cultural Free Trade," p. 35; Doran, "Three U.S. Hypotheses," p. 17). This ignores the consumption time required to experience more information or more

entertainment, a factor that drastically decreases the argument's plausibility.

92. Globerman and Vining, "Bilateral Cultural Free Trade," p. 17.
93. Donald G. Campbell, "Free Trade: Implications for the Canadian Culture/Communications Industries," *Business Quarterly* (Spring 1986), p. 33.
94. Doran, "Three U.S. Hypotheses," p. 3.
95. Globerman and Vining, "Bilateral Cultural Free Trade," pp. 21–24.
96. Doran, "Three U.S. Hypotheses," p. 8.
97. Craig Murphy, "Color It Mitrany: The Activities of Global Intergovernmental Agencies and Progress in International Relations," unpublished manuscript, 1986.
98. Although the FTA as a whole conforms to Murphy's notion of a "bounded problem," these negotiations were not linked to acid rain or to other disagreements on security issues, so we are discussing only the differences among the issues undertaken in the FTA negotiations.
99. Murphy, "Color It Mitrany," p. 5.
100. For a discussion of assertion as a national motive, see note 4.
101. Some interesting precedents have not been treated in this paper for lack of space. For example, in agriculture several conceptual agreements were reached that could provide precedents for pacts elsewhere. (See William Diebold, Jr., *Bilateralism, Multilateralism and Canada in U.S. Trade Policy* [Cambridge: Ballinger Publishing Company, 1988], pp. 132–133.)
102. George H. Quester, "Coping with Transborder Penetration," p. 540.

8

MAKING PROGRESS IN INTERNATIONAL ENVIRONMENTAL PROTECTION

Peter M. Haas

> For those with no experience of the intricacies of international cooperation, this slow movement is thoroughly frustrating. For those aware of the problems, it is always a pleasant surprise when some progress is actually made.
> —Michel Batisse: "Man and the Biosphere," *Nature* (1975), No. 256, p. 156.

Throughout the 1970s we heard dire warnings that the sustainability of our current mode of life, ecological equilibrium, and even global survival were threatened by transboundary environmental pollution. This heightened sense of international concern about international environmental problems was triggered by the publicity accompanying a series of environmental disasters resulting from industrial and tanker accidents and the 1972 United Nations Conference on the Human Environment (UNCHE). Although these views were not new, and generated a massive literature that challenged their contentions, there was a widespread sense that the sequence of threats now appeared in an unprecedentedly global, accelerating, and interrelated manner. Writers asserted that environmental threats constituted a challenge to national and international security. Economic disruptions could result from resource deterioration or depletion. Governmental legitimacy could be challenged by disgruntled domestic groups that were displaced by environmental deterioration.[1]

Although these apocalyptic predictions may have been overdrawn, environmental protection remains a prominent issue on the international agenda. Many leaders and analysts still feel that global survival may be threatened and that maintaining our present quality of life may be problematic.[2]

This paper argues that some progress has been made in controlling transboundary pollution. The paper starts with a definition of progress for international environmental protection, reviews international efforts at pollution control, and then examines in greater detail the process by which progress is made through an analysis of the Mediterranean Action Plan (the Med Plan). Informed observers regard the Med Plan as the most successful case of international environmental protection. It serves as a model for nine other regional arrangements.[3] Furthermore, it is a "hard case" for indicating progress, as it occurs in a region so rife with antagonisms (North–South economic disparities and interstate conflict) that observers commonly presume that any form of collective action among the states in the region is precluded. Thus, an analysis of the successful Med Plan serves as a critical analysis of how progress is made in international environmental protection overall.

WHAT IS PROGRESS IN INTERNATIONAL ENVIRONMENTAL PROTECTION?

Environmental problems are characterized by their complex array of interrelated elements that are linked functionally, geographically, and temporally. A persistent feature of these issues is the uncertainty about the dimensions of problems, and the channels by which effects are transmitted. Decision makers face not only increasing levels of political and economic interdependence, but ecological interdependence.[4]

Threats to ecological stability emerge from the complex interlinkages between rapid population growth and technological innovation and dispersion that may lead policies to yield many unintended consequences. Effects of decisions made within one issue area or economic sector are transmitted via the physical environment to other sectors or issue areas in a number of ways: pollutants may functionally influence associated issue areas or economic sectors; pollutants may be transmitted physically to neighboring states across borders; and pollutants may influence longer-term decisions within the same issue area through numerous feedback loops.[5]

The 1985 Annual Report of the Executive Director of the United

Nations Environment Program nicely sums up the magnitude of the complex interlinkages involved in environmental problems.[6]

> Increase in the world's population, together with higher standards of living and limited arable land, increase in soil erosion, loss of genetic diversity and the disappearance of productive natural ecosystems, and movements of population from rural areas ravaged by drought to burgeoning urban centres cause traumatic stress on productive agricultural land, both to supply space for housing and to feed those to be housed. In turn, malnourished people are compelled to destroy the world's resources for nourishment and shelter. Land is forced, often by unsound agricultural practices and the use of chemicals, to be more productive than ever. Also, chemicals find their way to man through the food chain, disturb the productivity and natural evolution of the ecosystems, and contaminate the seas, lakes and groundwater by rain run-off; and often with a devastating impact on plant, animal (including marine) and microbial resources and on human health.

Environmental disasters are presumed to result from the failure of decision makers to link activities in one field of action, such as industrial development, with effects in another field, such as fisheries or tourism. Planners pursue the goal of industrialization but fail to heed the attendant longer-term ecological effects. Such concepts related to environmental problems as nonlinear growth, systemic discontinuities, open systems, feedback, carrying capacity, symbiosis, synergism, and even dialectical growth are relatively new to international relations and development planning.[7] Effective social planning requires a recognition of greater systemic interlinkages, and the adoption of policies to internalize international externalities, such as pollution. As the effects of many international environmental problems cross national borders, and hence are shared by countries,[8] international cooperation is also necessary for countries to coordinate their policies and to exchange information about the state of the environment and their own actions. Since actions often have to be reciprocal and compatible in order to limit environmental degradation, states must also cooperate to limit free-rider problems.

Progress consists of minimizing the collateral damage resulting from the pursuit of material welfare maximization in the Industrial Age. Unlike progress in other issue areas, and in contrast to the pure Enlightenment sense of progress where progress consists of more of a good (more security, more food, more trade with more partners), progress here entails balancing trade-offs between economic growth and environmental quality in order to maintain individual health and access to amenities.

A "minimalist" definition of progress is the creation of international arrangements to reduce forms of transboundary pollution. Indicators of such progress would include the conclusion of international treaties to control pollution, in particular the development of standards for multiple types and sources of pollution.

A "maximalist" definition would stress the need to adopt comprehensive arrangements for environmental protection that not only control specific contaminants but also integrate such controls within a more coherent framework in order to reconcile the tension between many interactive social, economic, and ecological forces. In addition to the minimalist collective arrangements for pollution control, maximalist views of progress would stipulate the form of those arrangements. If the ecosystem is part of a self-regulating global whole, as many ecologists argue, then the only true environmental protection would consist of harmonized efforts to maintain a precarious balance between multiple dimensions of social activity and the supporting physical environmental capacities.[9] Maximalist progress would entail the adoption of international and national efforts at integrated economic planning, and possibly even the widespread acceptance of an "ecological, holistic and co-operative ethic."[10] Aldo Leopold, an active American conservationist in the 1930s and 1940s, wrote passionately of the need to develop a respect for Nature, rather than merely adopting remedial management techniques. He wrote disparagingly of "progress" that did not reflect deeper ethical sensitivity for the contribution of Nature to the human spirit.[11]

Indicators of maximalist progress would include the adoption of comprehensive forms of economic planning that include feedback loops and externalities that had been neglected in previous economic plans. A simple measure of maximalist progress would be the number of endogenous variables and feedback loops between them that development planners program into computer models used for drawing up National Plans, or that are considered in the design of World Bank projects.

These definitions omit references to actual improvements in the physical quality of the environment for two reasons. First, there are no good synoptic data to assess worldwide environmental quality. The best current estimates suggest that since 1972 air and water quality in high-income areas with environmental regulations have improved, while deteriorating in low-income areas without regulations.[12] Water quality in many major Western rivers improved from 1970 to 1985. Peak levels of sulfur dioxide concentrations fell from 1973 to 1985 in the advanced industrial societies, although they grew in intensity for many large cities in developing countries (notably Rio de Janeiro and Beijing).[13]

International commons remain threatened, although joint efforts are currently being developed to manage many such problems.

Pollution of the open seas by pollution from tankers and dumping of chemicals and other waste substances has been largely regulated through treaty drafting by the International Maritime Organization, which has banned dumping of specific substances, developed design standards for new tankers, and established navigation and cleaning practices for tankers. Marine dumping in the North Sea has been virtually eliminated, and offshore incineration there is due to be eliminated by 1994. Sewage is now the principal threat to coastal ecosystems.[14]

European forest damage from acid rain has recently reached severe levels, although the European countries have developed a regime calling for a 30 percent reduction in sulfur dioxide emissions.[15] The stratospheric ozone layer is being depleted by emissions of chloroflourocarbons (CFCs), although the 1987 Montreal Protocol on Substances that Deplete the Ozone Layer will limit this depletion to 2 percent over the next 80 years, and in May, 1989 the signatory parties expressed their intent to ban CFCs by the end of the century—well in advance of the schedule laid out in 1987.

Second, specifying suitable quality criteria is itself a highly controversial and difficult exercise. It requires establishing "suitable for what." Different states commonly have different preferences for the appropriate uses of various areas. For instance, in the early 1970s many LDCs preferred to use shared bodies of water as industrial pollution sinks, whereas many DCs, already facing higher levels of degradation, preferred an evaluation that would reflect the quality for use for bathing or shellfish growing. Thus, counting an increase in water judged safe for bathing would mean accepting increased limitations on LDC industrialization as well.

Many LDC diplomats and scholars have asserted that such arguments about balanced economic development are merely façades erected by the elites of the West in order to retard economic development in the developing countries and to keep the Periphery dependent on the Core. Recently, however, many have come to accept the notion of environmental planning as a method to ensure the future flow of income from their present management of their limited resource endowment.[16] World Bank officials have noted that "many development planners now recognize that environmental management is necessary for sustained economic development."[17]

INTERNATIONAL ACTION ON THE ENVIRONMENT SINCE 1972

Since 1972 there has been progress in the field of environmental protection. Following a host of highly publicized environmental disasters worldwide, some of which demonstrated the enormous distance pollutants could travel, countries came to adopt a host of different arrangements to seek to control these newly evident externalities and to cope with the cross-cutting nature of environmental problems. The image of a single, vulnerable global ecosystem was further popularized by satellite photographs taken from *Apollo 11* in 1969. Tanker groundings in the Atlantic, mercury and cadmium poisoning in Japan, mercury poisoning in Iraq, and the discovery of DDT in Antarctic penguins as well as Arctic ice all led to the acceptance of a public image of a complex web of interrelated natural cycles that transmit problems across borders and threaten public health. The 1972 U.N. Environment Conference served to prod governments further to create environmental bodies and adopt collective arrangements to manage such problems. Global concern has persisted following the disasters at Chernobyl, Bhopal, the 1985 chemical devastation of the Rhine River, the thinning of the atmospheric ozone layer, and, more recently, fears of global warming and the loss of genetic diversity. Each subsequent crisis reinforced the sense that scientific understanding was very incomplete of the complex ecosystems that shaped the parameters of human survival on the earth. For the first time, the United Nations convened global conferences during the 1970s that dealt with such environmental issues as population(1974), food (1974), water (1977), desertification (1977), and energy (1981). The Mediterranean Action Plan (Med Plan) is part of mounting global concern about environmental protection.

Environmental concern was galvanized by tangible crises: specific incidents that produced undesirable outcomes for the bordering countries and that signaled to policymakers that prior plans and forms of understanding could give rise to serious, unanticipated consequences.[18] These events were anomalous for government officials, spurring them to seek new information and advice to avoid their repetition. Many analyses of specific environmental arrangements stress the catalytic role played by a dramatic disaster. The 1985 discovery of actual seasonal depletion of Antarctic ozone levels sparked international negotiations on a global ozone treaty[19]; the 1971 refusal of a dumping permit to a ship carrying chlorinated hydrocarbons for marine disposal triggered the adoption of three treaties to control pollution of the North Sea and the Northeastern Atlantic[20] and the fear of the impending death of the Mediterranean encouraged governments to adopt the Mediterranean Action Plan, as discussed later.

For such events to trigger action, studies of 'Operational Codes' suggest, they must be clearly seen as a crisis within actors' perceptual frameworks.[21] Otherwise, they will be dismissed as meaningless. Analogously, natural disasters have been accepted as acts of God about which nothing can be done if they are known to recur periodically, whereas if they are unanticipated they lead to political demands for compensation and for action to be taken to avoid their recurrence, or to reduce their devastating effects.[22] It is only since humanity has believed that it has developed the capability to control Nature that aberrations in the quality of the physical environment are seen as issues subject to international management.

Between 1972 and 1980, there was a proliferation of governmental bodies dealing with environmental and natural resource problems. Environmental ministries or departments were created in 118 countries. In 1972 fifteen DCs and eleven LDCs had such bodies. In 1982 thirty-four DCs and 110 LDCs had them.[23] In 1973 a new U.N. agency, the United Nations Environment Programme (UNEP) was established with a "catalytic" mandate to encourage and coordinate environmental protection activities within the U.N. system, as well as to popularize the issue in the world at large.

Similarly, there was a proliferation of multilateral international agreements made for environmental protection. At first, each was in response to a narrow shared problem. Progress has occurred because the substantive focus of conventions has expanded from controlling oil pollution and marine dumping to the conservation of species, framework conventions, controlling land-based sources of pollution, and various forms of air pollution. Table 8.1 illustrates this progression of concern. The movement to treating land-based sources and air pollution, which are more difficult to coordinate internationally,

TABLE 8.1
Growth in Scope of Multilateral Conventions for Environmental Protection, 1950–1985

	-1- *Oil pollution and dumping from ships*	-2- *Conservation of species*
1950–1959		
Number of environmental agreements (n = 2)	2	0
Percentage of environmental agreements	100	0
1960–1969		
Number of environmental agreements (n = 7)	6	0
Percentage of environmental agreements	86	0
1970–1979		
Number of environmental agreements (n = 21)	8	8
Percentage of environmental agreements	38	38
1980–1985		
Number of environmental agreements (n = 15)	5	2
Percentage of environmental agreements	33	13
Total number of environmental agreements (n = 45)	21	10
Percentage of all environmental agreements	47	22

Source: Alexandre Charles Kiss, *Recueil de Traités Multilateraux Ralatifs à la Protection de l'Environnement* UNEP Reference Series No. 3 (Nairobi: UNEP 1982); UNITERRA (May 1984), p. 23; OECD: *OECD Environmental Data Compendium 1985* (Paris: OECD, 1985) pp. 275–277.
Notes: Totals may not sum to 100 due to rounding.
    The 1974 Convention on the Protection of the Marine Environment of the Baltic Sea (Hel-

is a further indication of progress. These problems are more costly to manage, are more closely tied to industrial interests domestically, and are technically more difficult to monitor. The Ozone Protocols of 1985 and 1987 are the first to treat environmental issues that are fully global.

-3- Framework agreements	-4- Land-based sources of pollution	-5- Air pollution	-6- Other
0	0	0	0
0	0	0	0
0	0	0	1
0	0	0	14
2	2	1	0
9	9	5	0
4	2	1	1
27	13	7	7
6	4	2	2
13			
	9	4	4

sinki Convention) is counted as both an oil pollution/dumping agreement and a land-based sources agreement.
Includes Law of the Sea; does not include nuclear power agreements or EC Directives, of which there are hundreds.

The frequency with which all conventions have been signed has risen from 0.5/year during the 1950s to 0.7/year during the 1960s to 2.1/year in the 1970s, and 3/year for 1980–1985. Within this broad movement indicating increased saliency of the issue, the hard issues have also come to account for a growing proportion of collective attention: from 0 percent in the 1960s to 14 percent of treaties signed in the 1970s to 20 percent in the first half of the 1980s. By widening the scope of international environmental law, the international community has moved to deal with "better problems."

Seventeen of these forty-five treaties were developed under the auspices of the United Nations Environment Programme's Regional

TABLE 8.2
Comparative Expenditures for Pollution Control
(expressed as percent of national GNP and GFCF)

	1973	*1975*	*1977*
USA			
Public and private expenditures/GNP	1.6	2.0	2.0
Public and private investment/GNP	0.37	0.45	
Federal Republic of Germany			
Federal expenditures/GNP			0.759
Federal expenditures and private investment/GNP		0.796	0.95
Japan			
Federal expenditures/GNP			0.34
Federal expenditures and private investment/GNP			0.56
Private investment/GFCF	0.11	0.18	0.07
France			
Environmental Expenditures as a percentage of GDP			
Public Sewage Treatment/GFCF			
Private Sewage Treatment/GFCF			
Total Sewage Treatment/GFCF			
Public Sewage Treatment/GDP			
Private Sewage Treatment/GDP			
Total Sewage Treatment/GDP			

Source: France. Ministère de l'Environnement, *Données Economiques de l'Environment*, edition 1985, 1984, 1983, 1982, and International Monetary Fund, *International Financial Statistics*, various years.
Notes: GNP = gross national product
        GDP = gross domestic product

Seas Programme, excluding EEC Directives. Over 120 states, fourteen U.N. agencies, and twelve other international organizations are involved in these arrangements. Since UNCHE, 48 percent of them were guided by UNEP.

At least in the industrialized countries, private and public expenditures for controlling all sources of pollution rose suddenly in the early 1970s and have remained relatively stable since. Table 8.2 compares the growth of national pollution control in the United States, Federal Republic of Germany, Japan, and France. The proportion of pollution control relative to gross national product (GNP) and gross fixed capital formation (GFCF) grew for each country. For OECD

1978	1979	1980	1981	1982	1983
1.9	2.0	2.2	1.9	1.8	
0.819	0.872	0.914	0.871	0.808	
0.98	1.02	1.09	1.06	1.03	
0.43	0.51	0.50	0.468	0.443	
0.59	0.67	0.66			
0.05	0.05	0.05	0.05		
1.54	1.64		1.7	1.7	1.7
1.3	1.51		1.85	1.75	1.78
0.41	0.34		0.34	0.53	0.54
1.71	1.85		2.19	2.28	2.32
0.28	0.32		0.39	0.36	0.35
0.088	0.073		0.073	0.11	0.11
0.368	0.393		0.463	0.470	0.460

GFCF = gross fixed capital formation
Expenditures = investment plus operating expenses
France includes water management for economic uses—e.g., irrigation—in environmental expenditures.

countries, investment for environmental protection accounts for about 5 percent of total investment (equipment and operating costs).[24] No comparable data exist for developing countries. Fifteen of the twenty-four OECD countries adopted major environmental laws in the 1970s and 1980s, and all adopted legislation regulating pollution of water and air, as well as regulating solid waste disposal.[25]

As a further indication of increasing recognition of ecosystemic interlinkages, twelve multilateral development banks, including the World Bank, adopted the 1980 "Declaration of Principles on the Incorporation of Environmental Considerations in Development Policies, Programmes and Projects." These banks commit themselves to consider environmental consequences of their loans, and organize environmental training workshops in developing countries to assist local planners. UNCTAD's 1983 International Tropical Timber Agreement is the first international commodity agreement to include specific provisions to "maintain the ecological basis of the regions concerned."[26] In 1988 the World Bank created a new Environmental Division as well as hiring environmental specialists in the traditional project and geographic divisions of the Bank to integrate environment considerations better into the project cycle.

Recent evidence from the United States suggests that it may be following this pattern as well. Under pressure from domestic environmental groups, the U.S. Congress linked the administration of foreign aid to the consideration of environmental consequences of the projects that were to be funded. The U.S. Executive Director to the World Bank is instructed to oppose projects that may lead to longer-term environmental degradation, and the Overseas Private Investment Corporation OPIC is adjured to conduct environmental impact assessments of the projects it funds. In 1980 the United States and Mexico concluded an arrangement for Cooperation in Case of Emergency Oil Spills, and in 1983 they adopted an Agreement for Cooperation of Protection and Improvement of the Environment in the Border Areas, principally to control cross-border air pollution from smelters in Sonora and Arizona, in 1985 they concluded an agreement to limit pollution between San Diego and Tijuana, and in 1986 they adopted a treaty on the transport of hazardous substances.

International information collection activities were also implemented during the 1970s, following interests expressed at UNCHE. International facilities for the collection and distribution of environmental information have been developed. Through its three-part Earthwatch Program, UNEP seeks to assess global environmental conditions and collect and transmit data about them. The Global Environmental Monitoring System (GEMS) collects and disseminates worldwide background and monitoring data on air and water quality from twelve national stations, with an annual budget of $2 million (U.S.). It started publishing data in 1981. The International Registry of Potentially Toxic Chemicals (IRPTC), created in Geneva in 1976, has created a computer data base on toxic chemicals, which is disbursed through a newsletter and direct requests from governments. It provides information to users on deleterious effects of chemicals on the environment and workplace. A third information referral system (INFOTERRA) serves as a switchboard to direct environmental questions to appropriate international sources.

At the global level, there has been some movement toward more comprehensive treatment of a broader range of interlinked problems. But the discussion so far has not yet addressed the process by which this occurs. An analysis of the development of the Med Plan remedies this oversight.

THE MEDITERRANEAN ACTION PLAN

The Mediterranean Action Plan (Med Plan) is an evolving collaborative agreement to protect the Mediterranean Sea from marine pollution. With Albania's attendance at the 1985 Meeting of the Contracting Parties, all the littoral states now participate. The Med Plan consists of an interdependent framework, approved in February 1975, with four components: regional treaties, coordinated research and monitoring, integrated planning, and administrative and budgetary support. Parties agreed "to take all appropriate measures . . . to prevent, abate, and combat pollution . . . and to protect and enhance the marine environment."[27] The 1976 framework Convention calls upon Mediterranean governments to control pollution caused by dumping from ships and aircraft, from the exploration and exploitation of the continental shelf and the seabed and its subsoil, and from land-based sources. It also calls for cooperation in dealing with pollution emergencies, monitoring, and scientific and technological cooperation. Region-wide compliance is estimated to cost $10–15 billion.

Beginning in 1976 with seven pilot monitoring and research projects, one protocol banning marine dumping of a variety of wastes, another encouraging cooperation to respond to accidental oil spills, and a framework convention, the participating states have now developed a far more comprehensive program. In 1977 a center was established to promote integrated development planning. In 1982 the Med Plan's headquarters were transferred from UNEP's Regional Seas Programme in Geneva to an autonomous coordinating headquarters unit in Athens, with a Mediterranean staff supported by annual contributions from all the Mediterranean countries. A Trust Fund was created in 1979 to finance Med Plan activities with contributions from all states proportional to their U.N. allocations. The budget is now $4.1 million, an increase of 71 percent in current dollars from the first 1978–1980 budgets. The program is now entirely supported by national contributions after international agencies provided $27.8 million during its first six years. National support by domestic institutions for collective monitoring amounts to another $10 million a year. In 1980 the parties signed a protocol banning pollution from land-based sources. In 1982 they signed another protocol to preserve endangered marine species. In 1980 they completed the first phase of monitoring regional pollution and established the monitoring program as a continuing institution directly supported by governments, rather than by international organizations. The Med Plan produced nearly thirty manuals for conducting monitoring exercises and trained 129 LDC technicians to monitor marine pollution.

The Land-Based Sources Protocol, which entered into force in 1983, is the most important part of the Med Plan, as it sets limits on industrial, municipal, and agricultural emissions into the Mediterranean. These sources account for 85 percent of the pollution in the sea. Emissions of the most toxic substances, included in a technical annex called the blacklist, are to be eliminated. Emissions of less hazardous substances listed in a gray list are to be controlled in a coordinated manner by participating states. Politically, the adoption of this protocol is the capstone of the Med Plan, as it was the most contentious issue negotiated between the developing and developed states. Controlling land-based sources directly influences industrialization policies, about which the LDCs were extremely sensitive.

Its adoption without significant alteration and subsequent rapid ratification by Algeria and Egypt, who initially opposed it, demonstrates a dramatic change in their interests with respect to the desire for marine pollution control, and their toleration for additional costs associated with industrialization. Indeed, the support of these two countries is one of the most interesting puzzles about the Med Plan. In addition, the sources of pollution and the pollutants covered by the Med Plan exceed the range of common concerns initially articulated by the littoral states.

Algeria initially expressed its vehement opposition to pollution control. In the early 1970s Algerian president Houari Boumedienne was a leading figure in the Nonaligned Movement and opposed environmental protection because it threatened to retard economic development. He announced, "if improving the environment means less bread for the Algerians, then I am against it."[28] The Algerian representative to the 1972 United Nations Conference on the Human Environment (UNCHE) stated that Algeria "will not sacrifice development at the altar of the environment."[29] Moreover, many LDC delegates questioned the very desirability of cooperating with the North, suspecting that DC concern with environmental protection was a "trick," by which they intended to condition or retard economic growth in the LDCs. Egyptian delegates were disinterested in environmental protection that went beyond the immediate problems of untreated municipal wastes that Egypt faced.

These political disagreements overshadowed narrow agreement about what types of pollution should be controlled. Initially, leaders only recognized oil pollution as a problem that required collective action. Countries at different stages of economic development encountered different forms of pollution, and ranked the goal of pollution control differently in their development plans. They agreed abstractly that pollution threatened Mediterranean water quality but disagreed over which forms of pollution to control, whether cooperation was necessary, and what development objectives LDCs would have to forgo.

North African states were more concerned with pollution from smaller industries and petroleum refining, as well as dealing with localized problems of untreated municipal wastes, whereas developed European states wished to control industrial pollution, agricultural spraying, and emissions from untreated municipal wastes. French and Italian delegates sought to promote regional legislation compatible with international law, particularly EEC directives, and were principally concerned with problems of industrial and agricultural wastes. States in intermediate levels of economic development fell between the developed and developing country extremes.

Despite their antipathy to environmental cooperation on industrial pollutants, Algerian and Egyptian opposition was reversed. Algeria came to take constructive positions at Med Plan talks by 1979, and adopted framework domestic legislation for pollution control in 1983. Egypt adopted such legislation in 1982, and both promptly ratified the Land-Based Sources Protocol.

The Med Plan successes are related to the recognition of additional sources and forms of pollution, and the development of protocols to control them. Oil pollution, marine dumping, and land-based sources have all been successfully tackled. Emissions from agricultural spraying and discharge of over twenty heavy metals used in industrial processes are now banned or limited under the Land-Based Sources Protocol. Other aspects of environmental protection related to less concrete exercises have been much less successful. Governments have not adopted forms of development planning that would better internalize environmental consequences of industrial policy into the planning process, as developed in the integrated planning component, and the Protocol for Specially Protected Areas, although in force, is widely disregarded. In order for existing commitments to become fully operational, countries must add costly deballasting facilities to their port facilities, and common standards for different types of water usage must be developed. Comprehensive standards are to be developed by 1991. States have also failed to adopt measures to control pollution from mining the seabed and Continental Shelf. As we shall see, the factors that contributed to successful resolution of the differences over land-based sources were not present in the areas in which these failures occurred.

The biggest advances in terms of national compliance with this international program have been the construction of sewage treatment facilities and the adoption of more comprehensive environmental legislation. New sewage treatment plants have been built or are under construction in Tel Aviv, Athens, Naples, Genoa, Marseilles, Nice, Toulon, Alexandria, Algiers, and Tripoli. As a consequence, the percentage of Mediterranean beaches deemed unsafe for swimming fell from 33 percent in 1976 to 20 percent in 1986. Since 1972, French, Spanish, Greek, and Israeli pollution control expenditures have increased slightly in real terms. Nine countries have introduced framework environmental legislation. Governmental agencies responsible for environmental protection were created in all countries but Albania.[30]

Explaining the Success of the Med Plan

The evolution of the Med Plan, and the support of Egypt and Algeria, requires explanation. It was accomplished through a two-stage process of technical consensus and political compromise, masterminded by a core group of ecologists from the United Nations Environment Program (UNEP). The UNEP Secretariat coordinated meetings and produced background documents and proposals for the Mediterranean countries. UNEP created a transnational alliance with like-minded regional marine scientists. When these marine scientists came to staff national environmental ministries, as they were established in many LDCs in the mid-1970s, they informed their governments of the need to control more sources of pollution, and advised their governments to support the Med Plan, to ratify its protocols, and to develop national pollution control policies and legislation consistent with it.

UNEP officials shared an overriding ecological orientation. Created with a "catalytic" and cross-cutting mandate, UNEP was primarily a coordinative U.N. agency, without the staff to conduct fully integrated projects. UNEP had a more integrated focus than the international agencies operating in the region, with their narrower issue or sectoral focuses (navigation for IMCO, fisheries and living resources for FAO, public health for WHO, and cultural heritage and education for UNESCO). The UNEP staff was interested in producing a new program to enhance its position within the universe of U.N. agencies, and actually to control a broad range of sources of Mediterranean pollution, as well as incorporating environmental considerations into national economic planning.

UNEP's leadership wished to develop an entire interlinked program for broadly defined environmental protection, including rationalized land use planning. They were interested in promoting holistic analyses of international problems, and considered pollution as an excellent example of the complex interlinkages between development issues that should be considered when formulating economic development policies. Mostafa Tolba, the present Executive Director, talks of "development without destruction." UNEP's leadership saw pollution as a visible "canary in the miner's helmet" that could be used to demonstrate the need for systems-type approaches. By interesting states in controlling some sources of marine pollution, they hoped to steer them further down a "slippery slope" to controlling land-based sources of pollution, and ultimately to inculcate leaders and planners in a new pattern of thought about doing rational and integrated economic development, as well as adopting more "environmental ethics" reflecting the unquestioned acceptance of the need to protect nature. Thus, UNEP self-consciously promoted a program informed with a maximalist conception of progress. UNEP failed to accomplish these more abstract objectives.

UNEP's ideology was not shared by national foreign affairs officials or by most of the scientific community. The foreign policy officials participated because they hoped to achieve their environmental foreign policy goals, and most of the scientists hoped for research support. UNEP managed adroitly to wed these interests in a broad enough program that satisfied everyone's short-term interests, while incrementally promoting a more all-inclusive program and creating an alliance with the domestic scientists. Ultimately, Algerian and Egyptian foreign policy officials came to support the Med Plan not because they shared UNEP's holistic vision, but because they recognized that land-based sources of pollution now required treatment.

The marine scientists involved in Med Plan discussions came from the whole span of marine science: marine biologists, marine geologists, physical oceanographers, marine chemists, public health officials, and ocean engineers. Generally, they operated independently of the foreign affairs community. They were interested in controlling pollution from a variety of sources, but were also interested in expanding their research budgets. Many of these interests coincided with the interests of international organizations, as the organizations' missions committed them to studying the subject matter of the assorted marine science disciplines.

UNEP forged ties with these scientists based on their common interest in controlling specific sources of pollution. In addition, UNEP made available resources that were not otherwise available to most national scientists. UNEP incorporated the interests of the various marine science disciplines within its broad ecological mandate, so that each group was able to conduct its own preferred research within the Med Plan research and monitoring components, with Med Plan financial support. In addition to funding, UNEP provided monitoring equipment and training that were unavailable domestically. By helping to publicize the scientists' findings, UNEP contributed to their prestige, thereby reinforcing their public image as experts capable of providing valuable advice to their governments. UNEP also sought to reach out directly to the general population by publicizing the Med Plan whenever possible. The Geneva UNEP staff included a full-time public relations officer, responsible for promoting the program to the media as well as for developing close contacts with national nongovernmental organizations.

Marine scientists were also able to obtain current data about Mediterranean environmental quality at biannual meetings convened by UNEP, in conjunction with the IOC and ICSEM. Attending such meetings also established a bond of solidarity among the marine scientists, and with UNEP, as they constituted a relatively small professional community that disseminated information. French scientists could already get most of these resources domestically, and thus were less interested in active involvement with the Med Plan.

UNEP fostered an ambiguous nongovernmental role for participating scientists by inviting them to technical meetings in their individual, professional capacities rather than as governmental representatives. This reinforced their allegiance to UNEP over their governmental identity and extended their distance from their own governments.

These transnational contacts with different ministries and other international organizations facilitated UNEP's acquisition of data. For instance, the French Foreign Affairs Ministry, the formal focal point through which pollution data would be provided to UNEP, was reluctant to provide data on emissions of radionuclides, because the French felt that they would be pinpointed as the principal regional culprit for such pollution. UNEP managed to get this information by getting the French Public Health Ministry to provide the data to WHO. Similarly, the Egyptian Fisheries Ministry gave pesticides data that the Agricultural Ministry would not divulge.

UNEP resolved the political opposition to environmental protection by two interrelated and concurrent processes of technical consensus and political compromise. Political compromise kept everybody involved in the negotiations; technical consensus guided the discussions toward treating more sources of pollution by encouraging the recognition of ecosystemic interlinkages. The development of technical consensus for focused attention on the scientists allied with UNEP and reinforced their claims to expertise. In turn, as the scientists became increasingly involved in their governments, they altered national policies toward a greater internalization of environmental externalities. The technical consensus that these scientists helped form set the agenda that was then resolved through political compromise. Neither consensus nor compromise would have been possible without the other. In conjunction, they created the possibilities for marine scientists to gain access to national decision making, to transform their governments' environmental stance, and to guide them toward convergent policies regionwide.

Progress in the Mediterranean only occurred after marine scientists were in a position to convince their governments of the legitimacy of these new ecosystemic linkages, and of the need to control pollutants that could be transmitted. For LDCs, which were highly suspicious of information emanating from the North, information about this had to come from domestic scientists.

In the aggregate, this dual process contributed to governmental learning. LDC leaders continued to aspire to economic development as their ideal but recognized that economic growth could not be pursued without sustaining environmental costs. Land-based sources of marine pollution had to be controlled to pursue development effectively, because of their influence on other uses of the ocean.

The governments most exposed to UNEP and the marine scientist community learned. Upon hearing of the multiple sources of pollution contributing to the contamination of the Mediterranean, they undertook measures to protect the sea from previously unrecognized sources of pollution. The countries that became the strongest supporters of the Med Plan—France, Egypt, Algeria, Israel, and Greece —were also the countries in which the domestic alliance with UNEP was strongest, and the groups were most strongly embedded in the national administrations. In each of these countries environmental ministries had been transformed into regulatory agencies during the late 1970s and early 1980s and were responsible for drafting and enforcing national environmental legislation. When present on national delegations, they advised their foreign ministry counterparts on technical aspects of the negotiations, and encouraged them to control more sources of pollution and more pollutants.

In France, the Environmental Ministry was established in 1974. In Algeria a coordinative interministerial body was created in 1974, which subsequently transmitted Algerian scientific findings to the rest of the government. In 1983 a regulatory environmental agency was established. In Egypt a cabinet-level environmental agency was created in 1982. In Greece an environmental agency was created in 1976, and a full-blown ministry was established in 1980. In Israel a regulatory agency was put in place in 1976. In each country these bodies were staffed with marine scientists who believed in the need to control marine pollution. At Med Plan meetings and within their governments they promoted these views. Each country—with the exception of France, where the Foreign Affairs ministry was loath to part with responsibility for foreign policy in the historically symbolic Mediterranean—became more constructive toward the Med Plan after the involvement of these groups in environmental policymaking. However, this learning occurred in two distinct ways. Internationally, delegations came to accept the need to deal with broader sources and types of pollution as a result of exposure to technical consensus. Exposed to the explanations of scientific findings by UNEP and the marine scientists, some foreign ministry delegates became persuaded of the need for more extensive regional measures for pollution control, and others were unable logically to reject such consensus with UNEP arranging the meetings and drafting documents. Yet national changes came about after national environmental ministries, in which the marine scientists were active, obtained responsibility for environmental protection. At the national level, learning occurred through political channels, as the environmentalists usurped decision-making responsibility. Internationally, learning was much more of a cognitive process, as individuals on delegations came to accept the implications of new evidence and changed their positions accordingly.

Several factors proved important in contributing to learning and progress. Global environmental disasters helped generate concern about the issues, as well as providing compelling popular images. Uncertainty about the extent of Mediterranean pollution led leaders to feel that they must do something, although they were not yet aware of the high costs that action would entail. Marine scientists' authority was heightened because they were the only group that could articulate the issues involved, and reduce the uncertainty. Able leadership by the UNEP secretariat was also valuable.

Technical Consensus

Technical consensus developed by UNEP and the marine science community contributed to agenda setting and to altering the interests of some delegates. By providing a common understanding of the extent of marine pollution, and the range of policies required to manage such pollution, UNEP and its allies convinced the Mediterranean governments to accept the need to control land-based sources of pollution.

Concerns emerged from observations of clots of oil on Mediterranean beaches in the late 1960s, combined with alarms of the "imminent death" of the sea by Jacques Cousteau and Lord Peter Ritchie-Calder. Although there was fear that the ocean was in danger, it was not clear from what. There was a total lack of scientific information regarding the composition of the pollution, who was affected, or the consequences of the pollution. Most developing countries lacked the equipment and trained technicians to evaluate water quality. In 1974 the situation was summarized thus:[31]

> The attention drawn to the impact of pollution on marine communities is too recent and, as a result, data is still too spare for it to be possible to draw an overall picture of the situation. Furthermore, the word "pollution" is used to cover very different attacks, both in kind and in intensity and pollution may rightly be considered to include thermal effluents just as much as the discharge of excavation waste, industrial waste, and urban effluents.

Information was sufficient to spur states to action, but not enough to identify what action. Specific policy awaited more precise technical understanding of the problems. Even so, pollution was likely to be understood through the filters of the goals and values of the foreign ministries; FAO consultants' assertions of the existence of Algerian industrial pollution were denied by Algerians. Only after domestic scientists were present in Algerian decision making were these filters modified.

Given this broad uncertainty, observers saw sources of pollution wherever they liked. But the uncertainty also led to a very broad scope of the Med Plan. Faced with such possible threats, and without sufficient information to evaluate the extent of the problem, in 1972 governments commissioned the FAO General Fisheries Council for the Mediterranean to draft a treaty to protect the region from all forms of marine pollution. Eventually, this became the text for the 1976 Barcelona Convention. Facing the technical uncertainty surrounding the problem of pollution, and influenced by the environmental furor of the times, the FAO legal drafters, who were themselves sympathetic to UNEP's view, included a full range of sources of pollution that exceeded FAO's formal organizational scope of living resources. Soon thereafter FAO's exercise was included within UNEP's broader Med Plan initiative.

Misunderstanding by leaders facilitated cooperation. In the early 1970s it was widely thought that pollutants circulated so freely that region-wide cooperation was necessary, regardless of the specific causes. UNEP officials realized that the currents were not sufficiently strong (if this were true, as it was subsequently demonstrated, the entire sea would certainly have been dead) to make it a public bad, but chose not to disabuse foreign affairs representatives of this misconception because the argument supported the need for joint action under UNEP's auspices.

A related, and important, consequence of this uncertainty was the empowerment of marine scientists. Faced with massive uncertainty about the extent and causes of Mediterranean pollution, foreign policy makers looked to their marine scientists to minimize the uncertainty. Transferring the burden to scientists would also diffuse pressure from domestic environmental groups.

UNEP's broad aim and definition of pollution has enabled it to link all the competing marine scientific interests within the monitoring component of the Med Plan since 1974. In 1974 the full gamut of marine scientists met to devise a monitoring program for the region. All the different disciplines' substantive foci were included in the program, to respond fully to the wide variety of pollutants identified in UNEP's definition. The seven studies that were proposed, and that served as the core for the first stage of the Med Plan's monitoring component from 1975 to 1980, satisfied the interests of all the concerned parties. The projects study oil on beaches; heavy metals; DDT, PCBs, and chlorinated hydrocarbons in marine organisms; effects of pollutants on marine organisms and their populations; effects of pollutants on marine communities and ecosystems; coastal transport of pollution; and studies of the relationship between coastal water quality and public health.

This package satisfied not only the interests of different countries and international organizations, but also the research interests of the different marine science disciplines. Public health studies satisfy public health officials, the WHO, Egypt, and developed countries. Oil studies satisfy everyone. Studies of marine communities satisfy marine biologists, the FAO, and domestic fishery directors. Ironically, for this group organic pollution is a good thing, as it provides food for fisheries in a relatively nutrient-starved sea. Studies of heavy metals cater to the interests of marine chemists and those concerned with industrial pollution.

The marine scientists' common explication of uncertainty set subsequent agendas. A 1977 UNEP report (the "Med X" report) revealed that 85 percent of pollutants in the Mediterranean were found to originate from land; 80–85 percent of land-based pollutants came via rivers, mostly from industrial waste, municipal sewage, and agricultural pesticides; and over 80 percent of all municipal sewage emitted into the Mediterranean was untreated.[32] In the face of these findings, LDC foreign ministry officials could no longer ignore the issue, although they weren't ready to change their positions about accepting environmental controls on industrial development. The scientific study also reinforced LDC demands for the inclusion of rivers and atmospheric transport in the Land-Based Protocol. New information drove the agenda, although governmental interests and policies were calculated subject to the interpretation of this new information by domestic scientists, and hence policy lagged the introduction of the report by several years. New information was sufficient for agenda setting, but not for determining national positions.

Moreover, when the report was adopted, foreign ministry delegates guaranteed that the data would be presented in difficult-to-read pie chart form. As a result, the magnitude of the problem and the identity of the countries responsible for most of the pollution were obscured, because the proportional relationships depicted on pie charts are very difficult to distinguish.

Scientific consensus drove foreign policy makers to deal with land-based sources of pollution. By 1978 Executive Director Tolba admitted that the early fear of the Mediterranean's death was excessive, and that the sea was merely ill. Now foreign policy makers had no further reason to cooperate. But by this time scientists concurred that land-based sources were insidious, and collective action to control them was called for. Such consensual knowledge was sufficient to get countries to discuss the linkages between terrestrial development and marine pollution that they had previously avoided because they had no alternative source of information.

Given this technical consensus, scientists were able to approve the technical annexes a year before the political delegates could complete the body of the Land-Based Sources Protocol. Despite the economic costs of controlling the pollutants, and political opposition, the scientists concurred on the scientific need to control the fullest list of pollutants that have yet been included in an international treaty.

During negotiations on the Land-Based Sources Protocol, Tunisian and Moroccan delegates were convinced of the need to ban organophosphorous and flouride compounds, even though phosphate mining is an important source of foreign exchange for each country. Confronted with homogeneous advice from their own scientists on their delegations, as well as two volumes of summarized scientific understanding about numerous pollutants provided by UNEP, they were convinced of the need to control additional sources of pollution in order to protect the sea.

Political Compromise

Although states disagreed widely over the range of pollutants to be covered, such disagreements were papered over by political compromise. Short of changing positions, compromises were sufficient to keep the delegates involved in the negotiations. UNEP's unspoken quid-pro-quo was that in return for the benefits it administered, the countries would continue to negotiate, giving UNEP an ongoing chance to reinforce its ties with scientists and to generate new information to encourage the foreign ministry delegates to accept more comprehensive pollution control measures. All governments were partially rewarded for their participation. These benefits were not large enough to alter interests, but they were sufficient to ensure the governments' continued presence at the bargaining table. In addition, UNEP pursued compromises during negotiations to resolve differences.

UNEP was able to moderate conflicts through its strong ecological organizational ideology. The integrative nature of ecology also enabled UNEP to amalgamate all the contending interests within its own umbrella notion of "pollution," borrowed from a 1969 U.N. experts group meeting:[33]

> "Pollution" means the introduction by man, directly or indirectly, of substances or energy into the marine environment resulting in such deleterious effects as harm to living resources, hazards to human health, hindrance to marine activities including fishing, impairment of quality for use of sea-water and reduction of amenities.

Such a definition effectively combined the competing interests of the developing countries in health effects and oil pollution, developed countries in amenities and oil pollution, and the FAO initiative on living resources. Political compromise, as well as subsequent alliance building with regional marine scientists was facilitated by this broad perspective that enabled UNEP to integrate all competing positions within the program.

TABLE 8.3
Distribution of Benefits from Participating in the Med Plan

Type of country	Percentage of region's population (1970)	Percentage of region's GNP (1978)	Total assistance received (in thousand US$, % of total)
Low income	28.2	8.0	477.2 (33%)
Middle income	35.2	26.4	879.9 (60%)
High income	43.3	65.5	106.3 (7%)
Total			1,463.4

Source: Population and GNP from World Bank figures, Med Plan benefits from Athens Headquarters Unit
Notes: Low income: Albania, Algeria, Egypt, Lebanon, Libya, Morocco, Syria, Tunisia

Robert Cox warns against an unreflective acceptance of such types of consensus: "The language of consensus is a language of common interest expressed in universalist terms, though the structure of power underlying it is skewed in favor of the dominant groups."[34] Such hegemony did not occur in the Mediterranean because of the integrative nature of the ecological language promoted by the UNEP Secretariat. Rather than pitting interests against one another, this view was particularly well suited to including them all under a common umbrella.

Building on this fragile base, UNEP maintained states' participation by a strategy of geographic distribution of benefits, so that countries were rewarded for their participation in negotiations. This amounted to discriminating against the French and Italians. The distribution of benefits, insofar as they may be quantified, are presented in table 8.3.

Whenever possible the UNEP Secretariat attempted to involve scientists from the developing countries in monitoring exercises in order to develop national capabilities as well as rewarding them for

Pieces of monitoring equipment worth more than $5,000 apiece (% of total)	Trainees sent to other laboratories (% of total)	Number of participating national institutions (% of total)	Number of research contracts signed with national institutions (% of total)
14 (33%)	46 (34%)	11 (13%)	30 (20%)
28 (67%)	83 (61%)	41 (50%)	84 (57%)
0 (0%)	8 (6%)	30 (37%)	35 (23%)
42	137	82	149

Medium income: Cyprus, Greece, Israel, Malta, Spain, Turkey, Yugoslavia
High income: France, Italy, Monaco

participation. The lower proportion of institutions from the lowest-income countries reflects the relative scarcity of research institutions in those countries. For instance, there are only three marine research centers in Algeria, and there are twenty-eight in France. All the monitoring and research could have been done much more cheaply, and probably with more accurate results, by merely using French laboratories, as the French suggested in 1974. But such a strategy would have excluded the scientists who contributed to the changing policies in the LDCs and failed to provide LDC governments with the national scientific capability that led them to lend more credence to technical arguments. By continuing to participate, the LDCs received sophisticated monitoring equipment, and training in its use, which they would not have had access to otherwise. Algeria and Egypt were among the four countries that received the most assistance from the monitoring program.

Regional headquarters to coordinate other Med Plan projects were also distributed on a regional basis. Regional Activity centers went to France, Yugoslavia, Tunisia, Malta, and Greece. The nationalities on the Athens Headquarters staff are also regionally distributed. Even the equipment distributed within the technology transfer component was American, rather than French.

UNEP actions were constrained by the need to retain credibility with the foreign affairs community. The evidence presented had to be untainted by hints of favoring DC preferences. UNEP was able to supervise the quality of the decentralized monitoring activities because many officials in the Regional Seas Office were marine scientists and had access to other scientists working in laboratories administered by FAO, WHO, and IAEA. In this manner UNEP served as an insulator between North–South tensions and mitigated the direct application of French influence. Greek delegations also played the role of an "honest broker" between the contending parties.

The Land-Based Sources Protocol was settled by compromise as well. Developed and developing countries made substantial concessions. French influence was ameliorated by UNEP's mediating role and by the support the LDCs were able to muster by referring to technical consensus.

Important disagreements revolved about the inclusion of airborne transmission of pollutants, riverborne transmission of pollutants, ambient versus emission standards governing pollutants, and cover-

age of new or existing installations. France and Italy were opposed
to the inclusion of atmospheric transmission because of insufficient
data about its transmission and because scientific knowledge was
inadequate to identify sources, which might be thousands of miles
away, in the territory of nonparticipating states. LDCs argued that
the Protocol's coverage would be incomplete without reference to
atmospheric paths of transmission, especially for petrochemical industries and agricultural activities emitting organohalogens and organophosphorous compounds. They felt that such findings would be
generated by research conducted under the research and monitoring
component of the Med Plan. The parties resolved this conflict by
including atmospheric transport, but deferred specific action on it
until an unspecified point in the future "under conditions to be
defined in an additional annex," and France vetoed funding subsequent monitoring and research on airborne transmission of pollutants.

France and Italy unsuccessfully opposed coverage of rivers in the
Protocol. France also failed to exclude radioactive substances from
the blacklist, for which it is the major regional source. It is not clear
if France's inability to exclude rivers and radionuclides from the
Protocol's jurisdiction is due to the overwhelming evidence for their
inclusion or was a concession to get the LDCs to sign the Protocol.
Following their failure to exclude radioactive substances from the
blacklist, the French ceased submitting data for emissions of radionuclides into the Rhone to the Secretariat.

Industrialized and developing countries disagreed as to whether
the Protocol should apply only to new installations or to older existing facilities as well. With more older industries, the DCs argued that
many of these should be excluded from regulation, or should at least
be subject to a more lenient schedule for compliance, since they
would soon be decommissioned because of their inefficient production. The LDCs felt that such a distinction would give unfair advantage to the developed countries' firms with older installations, as the
newer LDC plants would have to face retrofitting costs not shared by
the DC firms. Delegates and the U.N. agencies were further unable
to develop a satisfactory definition of "new installations," because of
the ambiguity between factories that were planned, contracted for,
or already under construction. The problem was resolved by the
elimination of references to new or existing installations in the final

version of the Protocol in 1980. Rather, it included a new qualification: "The programmes and measures . . . shall be adopted by taking into account, for their progressive implementation, the capacity to adapt and reconvert existing installations, the economic capacity of the Parties and their need for development," thus fudging the issue and satisfying all parties.[35]

The biggest point of dissension was how the substances should be controlled: by emission controls, as preferred by the Europeans, or through ambient standards, advocated by the South. The LDCs, sensitive to the possible economic effects of banning the emission of a number of substances by their industries, argued that their shorelines, because of historically less industrial pollution, were better able to assimilate emissions: hence, the Protocol should refer to the capacity of the receiving environment to assimilate wastes. The industrialized countries, with greater coastal pollution, advocated the adoption of universal emission standards, rather than the ambient standards supported by the LDCs. France and Italy were already committed to following emission standards laid down in a 1976 EEC directive. The Secretariat preferred emission standards, because of their ease in administration. This issue wasn't resolved until the actual Meeting of Plenipotentiaries in 1980. Countries agreed to compromise by applying emission standards to the blacklist and ambient standards to the gray list, following advice by the Secretariat. Such an arrangement totally bans the emission of the more toxic blacklist substances and requires coordinated water quality standards for the less hazardous gray list substances. WHO is responsible for developing discharge quantities and ambient standards for the gray list materials. As a compromise, this means that the Europeans got the LDCs to eliminate the emissions of certain industrial pollutants, such as mercury and cadmium, and herbicides from agricultural spraying. The LDCs, on the other hand, were *de facto* allowed to pollute more than the DCs for the gray list substances, a variety of municipal, agricultural, and industrial wastes.

The Land-Based Protocol was adopted by compromise. DCs also accommodated LDC demands for technical assistance in the fields of training and technology transfer, possibly leading to the LDC concessions on other elements. The LDCs got atmospheric transport, river transport, radioactive wastes, and some ambient standards. They also got a commitment in the text to technology transfer on concessionary terms. The DCs got a full list of substances in both annexes that were largely consistent with EEC obligations, even though France had to accept some controls exceeding those laid out in the EEC directive, and some emission standards. These outcomes indicate progress toward a broader range of pollutants.

Some issues eluded compromise. Greece consistently argued against the selection of Turkish lead laboratories and later refused to allow a Turkish vessel to conduct pollution research in Greek waters, for fear that they were carrying out sonic studies over part of the Continental Shelf claimed by Greece. This also illustrates the conflict between the scientific and the foreign policy communities. In 1976 Morocco proposed the creation of an Interstate Guarantee Fund, to compensate states for the costs of cleaning up in case of emergencies. France fiercely opposed this proposal, maintaining that it would be difficult to determine whether countries would deserve to be compensated for deliberate, accidental, or background cases of pollution. Rather than being included in the framework convention, countries adopted the proposal as a resolution, with the reservation of France.[36] Little has been done since.

The political compromises proved compelling to keep countries involved in the negotiations. However, without the ensuing shifts in national objectives that resulted from technical consensus, the compromises would have been inadequate to overcome Algerian and Egyptian opposition. There were no instruments available to prevent them from free riding. Each state could have continued to participate in the Med Plan negotiations, as did other LDCs, without transforming their domestic practices.

Technical uncertainty, or ignorance, helped facilitate political compromise. Because officials were uncertain about the true dimensions of the problems, they were interested in remaining in the early arrangements in order to receive information, as long as compliance did not become expensive. Also, because they were unsure about the specific interlinkages between pollutants, such fudging as occurred in the Land-Based Sources Protocol was possible. In addition, of course, uncertainty pushed governments to solicit advice from the ecologists and marine science community.

Med Plan Failures

The less successful components of the Med Plan eluded political compromise and technical consensus. The integrated planning component of the Med Plan is both the most ambitious and least successful part of the Med Plan. Aimed at leading national planners to a more integrative and holistic pattern of planning, it has been overlooked by most delegates. These failed efforts were aimed at much more abstract goals than were the control of specific pollution sources. Rather than highlighting individual interlinkages between observed effects and policy causes, these projects aimed at proposing entire new planning methods. The slow ratification of the Specially Protected Areas Protocol may be related to the failure to accept the values of conserving nature, particularly with the cost of accepting the increased navigation costs that would follow.

The Integrated Planning element actually consists of two programs, adopted in 1977. The Blue Plan is a conceptual planning exercise, pursued largely at the behest and funding of the French. This is an attempt to produce a number of prospective studies for Mediterranean planners, based on projected demographic and economic trends. Rather than dealing with pollution, the project deals with the underlying socioeconomic forces that produce pollution. Although approved in 1977, this project never got under way until 1980. In 1984 the first phase of data collection was completed; a second phase of data consolidation was conducted for one year, and in 1985 the third phase of actual development of prospective futures was begun.

None of the other states picked up the French enthusiasm for this enterprise, largely because it is the pet project of the Director of the Research Division of the Environmental Ministry. Few other officials shared his enthusiasm or expertise in prospective planning. The budget for this is annually challenged by the developing countries and is only saved by French intervention. At first, UNEP supported the initiative because it coincided with UNEP's interest in more integrated types of development planning, but UNEP's support lagged following its realization that most Mediterranean leaders were mystified by it. They were interested more in the direct causes and effects of pollution than in the more metaphysical web of functional and physical interlinkages of which UNEP presumed pollution to be the expression.

The second integrated planning feature is a more concrete exercise, called the Priority Action Programme (PAP), intended to appeal to the LDCs. The projects were selected by polling the interested parties and seeking compromises. These are projects that are of immediate concern to the developing countries: soil protection, water resource management, fisheries and aquaculture management, human settlements, tourism, and soft energy technologies. Work on the PAP did not begin until 1984. The problem with this project is that it appeals only to the LDCs, so it is not supported by the DCs.

In terms of the factors accounting for other successful Med Plan projects, integrated planning has been a failure because it lacks technical consensus. As largely a French unilateral initiative, it has not generated the same scientific support as the other Med Plan projects. In addition, it is too ambitious too quickly: rather than treating related problems sequentially, it seeks to promote an entirely new pattern of thinking from scratch. It is not surprising that no other regional seas programs have integrated planning components.

The 1982 Specially Protected Areas Protocol remains in a similar purgatory. Although in force, countries have been remiss in contributing data to the headquarters in Tunis regarding measures taken to create and protect marine parks and preserves for endangered species. Its appeal rests on UNEP's desire to preserve endangered species as part of its holistic mission. The relative failure of this protocol suggests that the range of interlinkages that were recognized by the Mediterranean states is more specific than UNEP hoped. States moved to control individual additional pollution sources, but did not adopt a new integrated approach that would have been reflective of new values about the use of the natural environment.

Little effort has been expended to control pollution from the exploration and exploitation of the Continental Shelf, because it lacks technical support. With little offshore mining or oil and gas development, there is little regional concern.

CONCLUSION

There has been progress in international environmental protection. The Med Plan's evolution sheds light on how such progress is made.

Once alerted to the existence of the problem of marine pollution, Mediterranean leaders attempted to reduce the uncertainty associated with such a problem. This process led to dealing with a broad range of interrelated sources of pollution. Although concerns varied widely, conflicting interests were mollified in the short run through political compromise. Technical consensus led to a reduction of uncertainty and to establishment of scientific domestic constituencies for more comprehensive national policies.

Progress occurred through a complex process of transnational alliance building between international organizations and national scientists. Once they acquired sufficient domestic influence, the scientists transformed their governments' domestic and international environmental policies. They advised their colleagues toward convergent policies and advocated a progressive movement toward treating more forms and sources of pollution. This progress came in part through the fostering of common understanding about ecosystemic interlinkages and in part through the political appropriation of decision making by scientists who hoped to control more sources of pollution. By providing delegates with consensual technical advice, they shaped the international agenda and convinced some delegates of the need to control more forms of pollution. By acquiring domestic authority for environmental regulation, they promoted such activities domestically as well.

Seen as governmental learning, the Med Plan's growth in substantive scope from oil pollution to land-based sources of pollution remains single-loop learning, rather than reflective double-loop learning.[37] Governments accepted the need to control additional sources and forms of pollution. They did not adopt new patterns of reasoning about development, as maximalist advocates of progress deem necessary. In the Med Plan, as in most environmental cases, such action was precipitated by a crisis, which signaled the need for acting and for finding an authoritative group able to attenuate uncertainty. Future crises may trigger similar organizational responses; in October 1988 Brazilian President Jose Sarney announced measures to slow the destruction of the Amazonian rain forest. "The 'red light' that awakened him, Mr. Sarney said, was a disclosure by Brazilian scientists that they had found more than 6,000 man-made fires in the Amazon in a single day."[38]

There are limits on how far such a process may go. Although informed by a maximalist vision of progress, UNEP was only able to accomplish minimalist progress. The more ambitious, maximalist elements of the Med Plan were inhibited by a number of factors that may restrain progress in general. Few governments or international agencies are organized to cope with cross-cutting issues. Moreover, few individuals have the necessary vision to appreciate or understand the multiple positive and feedback loops that must be mastered to formulate integrative policies. Maximalist progress was also deterred by the absence of technical support for holistic approaches.

Environmental progress may be reversible, if the forces deployed by UNEP to create the Med Plan are eliminated. Maintaining technical consensus and scientific solidarity depends on maintaining the transnational alliance between marine scientists. The alliance between UNEP and marine scientists is dependent on UNEP having enough money to avert distributional squabbles among the scientific communities for funds.

Without such support, governments may move to disavow the linkages they had previously accepted. There are factors militating against this occurring too easily. Foreign ministry officials have limited resources and once they have entrusted an issue area to marine scientists or to the environmental ministry, they are unlikely to go back and review the decision, unless there is another disaster to recapture their attention. Even if scientists uncover findings that indicate that such issues are less important than previously thought or that harmonized measures are no longer necessary, as did occur in the Mediterranean, convergent foreign policies are still likely to remain, as foreign policy officials become increasingly distanced from the technical experts they initially consulted.

Progress may be made, but it is halting and slow. Environmental progress is likely to be more minimalist than maximalist, as the holistic transboundary bases of maximalist progress ran counter to deeply seated sovereign and nationalistic forces in international politics. Nonetheless, minimalist progress emerged as a compromise between UNEP's maximalist vision and the recalcitrant efforts of national governments to retain as much control as possible over domestic policymaking and to minimize their international obligations. To the extent that UNEP and its transnational allies may gain bureaucratic influence, progress of a more maximalist sort may be possible.

ENDNOTES

I thank Beverly Crawford, Emanuel Adler, and other participants at the Conference on Progress in International Relations, as well as M. J. Peterson, for their comments on various versions of this paper.

1. Richard A. Falk, *This Endangered Planet* (New York: Vintage Books, 1971); Mihajlo Mesarovic and Eduard Pestel, *Mankind at the Turning Point* (New York: Dutton, 1974); Harold Sprout and Margaret Sprout, *Toward a Politics of Planet Earth* (New York: Van Nostrand Reinhold, 1971).
2. The first Brandt Commission Report concluded that "there is a growing awareness that an equal danger (to warfare) might be chaos as a result of mass hunger, economic disaster, (and) environmental catastrophes. . . . The world is now a fragile and interlocking system, whether for its people, its ecology or its resources." Independent Commission on International Development Issues, *North-South: A Program for Survival* (Cambridge, Mass.: MIT Press, 1980), pp. 17, 33. American Secretaries of State Vance and Muskie expressed similar concerns. *Department of State Bulletin* (May 1980), p. 24; (August 1980), p. 56. Similar sentiments were voiced at the 1989 Paris Economic Summit.
3. Peter Hulm, "The Regional Seas Program: What Fate for UNEP's Crown Jewels?" *AMBIO* (1983), Vol. 12, No. 1. Even the Heritage Foundation regards the Regional Seas Programme as "perhaps one of [UNEP's] most significant achievements." George P. Smith II, "The U.N. and the Environment," in The Heritage Foundation, *A World Without a U.N.* (Washington, D.C.: The Heritage Foundation, 1984), pp. 44–45.
4. OECD, *Economic and Ecological Interdependence* (Paris: OECD, 1982).
5. For a terrifying catalogue of environmental catastrophes see M. Taghi Farvar and John P. Milton, eds., *The Careless Technology* (Garden City, N.J.: The Natural History Press, 1972).
6. United Nations Environment Program, *1985 Annual Report of the Executive Director* (Nairobi: UNEP, 1986), p. 39. John Ruggie refers to a similar array of issues as the "Global Problematique." John Gerard Ruggie, "On the Problem of 'The Global Problematique'," *Alternatives* (1979–1980), Vol. 5.
7. For instance, C. S. Holling, ed., *Adaptive Environmental Assessment and Management* (New York: Wiley, 1978); James A. Lee, *The Environment, Public Health, and Human Ecology* (Washington, D.C.: The World Bank, 1985).

8. Clifford S. Russell and Hans H. Landsberg; "International Environmental problems—A Taxonomy," *Science* (June 25, 1971), Vol. 172.

9. This view corresponds to the views held by Ernst B. Haas's Ecoevolutionists in "Words Can Hurt You," in Stephen D. Krasner, ed., *International Regimes* (Ithaca, N.Y.: Cornell University Press, 1983). The most recent expressions of such views are in World Commission on Environment and Development, *Our Common Future* (New York: Oxford University Press, 1987); J. E. Lovelock, *Gaia* (Oxford: Oxford University Press, 1979); as well as the Worldwatch Institute's annual *State of the World* and the World Resources Institute's annual *World Resources*.

10. Frank Barnaby, ed., *The Gaia Peace Atlas* (New York: Doubleday, 1988), p. 18.

11. Aldo Leopold, *A Sand County Almanac* (New York: Oxford University Press, 1966). For recent arguments from the same perspective see Arne Naess translated and revised by David Rothenberg, *Ecology, Community and Lifestyle* (Cambridge: Cambridge University Press, 1989).

12. Martin W. Holdgate, Mohammed Kassas, and Gilbert F. White, eds., *The World Environment 1972–1982* (Dublin: Tycooly International Publishing, Ltd, 1982); UNEP *Environmental Data Report* (London: Basil Blackwell, 1989).

13. World Resources Institute *World Resources 1988–1989* (New York: Basic Books, 1988), pp. 320–321; 334–335. Although water quality improved according to many indicators (such as concentrations of heavy metals and organic wastes), the levels of salts (nitrates) increased.

14. "The State of the Marine Environment," *UNEP News* (April 1988), pp. 10–12; UNEP *The State of the World Environment 1987* (Nairobi: UNEP, April 1987).

15. Global Environment Monitoring System, *Forest Damage and Air Pollution: Report of the 1986 Forest Damage Survey* (Geneva: United Nations, 1987).

16. Margaret R. Biswas and Asit K. Biswas, "Environment and Sustained Development in the Third World: A Review of the Past Decade," *Third World Quarterly* (July 1982), Vol. 4, No. 3.

17. Robert Goodland and George Ledec, "Environmental Management in Sustainable Economic Development," in W. C. Baum and S. Tolbert, eds., *Investing in Development: Lessons of World Bank Experience* (New York: Oxford University Press, 1985), p. 519. For similar statements by heads of state see Mostafa K. Tolba, *Evolving Environmental Perceptions* (London: Butterworths, 1988).

18. Such concerns were not new. They had been voiced in the nineteenth century in the United States: George P. Marsh, *Man and Nature, or Physical Geography as Modified by Human Action* (New York: Scribner, 1864). Clarence J. Glacken, *Traces on the Rhodian Shore* (Berkeley: University of California Press, 1967) records earlier sentiments. However, for the first time environmental contamination was now potentially global, and mankind was dealing with more toxic contaminants than in the past, such as radioactive and inorganic wastes that are hazardous at low

concentrations and have extremely long residency times in the environment.

19. Peter H. Sand, "Protecting the Ozone Layer," *Environment* (June 1985), vol. 27, No. 5; David Doniger, "Politics of the Ozone Layer," *Issues in Science and Technology* (Spring 1988), Vol. 4, No. 3.

20. Stuart W. Lehman, "Controlling Sediment Contamination by Toxics in North Sea Estuaries," A Report to the German Marshall Fund of the United States (January 1986).

21. Alexander L. George, "The Causal Nexus Between Cognitive Beliefs and Decision-Making Behavior: The 'Operational Code' Belief System," in Lawrence S. Falkowski, ed., *Psychological Models in International Politics* (Boulder, Colo.: Westview, 1979).

22. R. Kates, "The Perception of Storm Hazard on the Shores of Megalopolis," in D. Lowenthal, ed., *Environmental Perception and Behavior* (Chicago: Department of Geography, University of Chicago, Research Paper No. 109).

23. Mark Baker, Libby Bassett, and Athleen Ellington, *The World Environment Handbook* (New York: World Environment Center, 1985), pp. vii, ix.

24. OECD, *Environmental Data Compendium 1985* (Paris: OECD, 1985), p. 271; OECD, *Environmental Policy and Technological Change* (Paris: OECD, 1985), p. 56; France, Ministère de l'Environnement, *Données Economiques de l'Environnement 1985* (Paris: Ministère de l'Environnement, 1985), p. 12.

25. OECD, *The State of the Environment 1985* (Paris: OECD, 1985), p. 242.

26. Ursula Wasserman, "UNCTAD: International Tropical Timber Agreement," *Journal of World Trade Law* (1984), 18:89.

27. Convention for the Protection of the Mediterranean Against Pollution article 4, paragraph 1.

28. "Mediterranean Prospect," NOVA (Boston: WGBH Transcripts, 1980).

29. *El-Djeich* (Algiers) (April, 1972), 107:28.

30. For an extended discussion of national pollution control policies see Peter M. Haas, *Saving the Mediterranean: The Politics of International Environmental Cooperation* (New York: Columbia University Press, 1990), ch. 5, and Peter M. Haas, "Do Regimes Matter? Epistemic Communities and Mediterranean Pollution Control," *International Organization* (Summer 1989), Vol. 43, No. 3.

31. FAO FID:PPM/74/Inf 6 p 1.

32. UNEP/IG 11/INF 5.

33. United Nations, E/5003 (May 7, 1971), p. 53.

34. Robert W. Cox; "Labor and Hegemony," *International Organization* (Summer 1977), 31(3):386. Some of the clearest arguments about LDC interests being excluded from international environmental discussions are offered in the following sources: Johan Galtung, " 'The Limits to Growth' and Class Politics," *Journal of Peace Research* (1973), Vol. 8, No. 2; Hans Magnus Enzenzburger; "A Critique of Political Ecology," in Alexander Cockburn and James Ridgeway, eds., *Political Ecology* (New York: Times Books, 1979); and Philip D. Lowe and Michael W. Warboys, "Ecology and

Ideology," in Frederick H. Buttel and Howard Newby, eds., *The Rural Sociology of the Advanced Societies* (Montclair, N.J.: Allanheld, Osmun, 1980).

35. Jean-Pierre Dobbert, "Protocol to Control Pollution in the Mediterranean," *Environmental Policy and Law* (1980), 6:112–113.

36. Jose Antonio de Yturriaga Barberan, "Convenio de Barcelona de 1976 Para la Protección del Mar Mediterraneo Contra la Contaminación," *Revista de Instituciones Europeas* (January–April 1976), 2(1):88.

37. Chris Argyris and Donald A. Schon, *Organizational Learning: A Theory of Action Perspective* (Reading, Mass.: Addison-Wesley, 1978).

38. Marlise Simons, "Brazil Acts to Slow Destruction of Amazon Forest," *The New York Times*, (October 13, 1988), p. A6.

9

PROGRESS IN HUMAN RIGHTS
Jack Donnelly

What progress, if any, has been made in human rights in the postwar era? Have there been changes in the field of international human rights that have resulted in less violent conflict, exploitation, misery, or injustice? Have states exercised their sovereignty and power in ways that have produced progress in international human rights? In this paper I attempt to answer these questions by examining a variety of international and regional efforts by states to create or strengthen international human rights regimes.

Clearly, any procedures that strengthen respect for and observance of human rights will be progressive according to the definition of progress adopted in this volume. Furthermore, many human rights are intimately connected with economic and social welfare, and because many human rights violations rest on the threat or use of violence, security may also be strengthened by greater respect for human rights.

After reviewing the evidence, I conclude that some minimalist progress can be discerned in the postwar evolution of international human rights regimes but that the international procedures available or likely to become available in the foreseeable future assure that progress in human rights, insofar as it rests on *international* action, will remain quite minimal indeed. Human rights violations are in large measure an exercise of sovereignty. They typically involve acts of states against their own nationals on their own territory, and thus substantial progress on human rights, whether defined minimally or maximally, will depend on either national action[1] or the sort of major structural changes in international relations that past experience gives us no reason to expect. Even such limited, minimal progress is, I argue, noteworthy, but its limits also need to be emphasized.

INTERNATIONAL REGIMES

I define an "international regime" as "norms and decision-making procedures accepted by international actors to regulate an issue area."[2] States (and other relevant actors) accept certain normative or procedural constraints as legitimate, thereby partially replacing "original" national sovereignty with international authority. The transfer of authority, however, may be of varying degrees of significance and take a considerable variety of forms. Figure 9.1 provides a rough typology of regime types.

Regime norms, standards, or rules[3] may run from fully international to entirely national; there are roughly four types.

1. *Authoritative international norms:* binding international standards, generally accepted as such by states.
2. *International standards with self-selected national exemptions:* generally binding rules that nonetheless permit individual states to "opt out," in part. (For example, states may choose not to ratify a treaty, or to ratify with reservations.)
3. *International guidelines:* international standards that are not binding but are nonetheless widely commended by states. Guidelines

FIGURE 9.1
Human Rights Regimes

	National decisions	Promotion or assistance	Information exchange	Policy coordination	International monitoring	International decisions
International norms	Strong declaratory		Strong promotional	Strong implementation		Strong enforcement
International standards with national exemptions				Weak implementation		
International guidelines	Weak declaratory	Weak promotional				Weak enforcement
National standards	No regime					
	Declaratory regime	Promotional regime		Implementation regime		Enforcement regime

may range from strong, explicit, detailed rules to vague statements of amorphous collective aspirations.
4. *National standards:* the absence of substantive international norms.

Three principal types of international decision-making activities (in addition to norm creation) can be distinguished—*enforcing* international norms, *implementing* international norms, and *promoting* their acceptance or enforcement—and at least six important types of regime decision-making procedures should be distinguished.

1. *Authoritative international decision making:* institutionalized, binding decision making, including generally effective enforcement powers.
2. *International monitoring:* formal international review of state practice, but no authoritative enforcement procedures. Monitoring activities can be further categorized in terms of the powers allowed to monitors to carry out independent investigations and make judgments of compliance with international norms.
3. *International policy coordination:* regular and expected use of an international forum to achieve greater coordination of national policies, but no significant international review of state practice.
4. *International information exchange:* obligatory or strongly expected use of international channels to inform other states of one's practice with respect to regime norms.[4]
5. *International promotion or assistance:* institutionalized international promotion of or assistance in the national implementation of international norms.
6. *National decision making:* full state sovereignty in decision making for the issue area.

International *enforcement activities* involve international decision making and the stronger forms of international monitoring. International *implementation activities* include weaker monitoring procedures, policy coordination, and some forms of information exchange. *Promotional activities* may involve international information exchange, promotion or assistance, and perhaps even weak monitoring of international guidelines.

These types of activities also provide a convenient scheme for classifying regimes, as *promotional, implementational,* and *enforcement* regimes (each of which can be further classified as relatively strong or weak). To this we can add the class of *declaratory* regimes, which involve international norms but no international decision making (except in the creation of norms).

A regime's "strength" can be said to increase, roughly, with its normative and procedural "scope"; that is, as we move out from the bottom left corner (no regime) in figure 9.1. But paper formalities are far less important to a regime's strength than the practical realities of its "acceptance" by states and its "coherence,"[5] that is, the extent to which states in fact abide by and make use of the norms and procedures to which they have committed themselves, and the extent to which the parts of the regime operate together as a smoothly functioning whole.

THE GLOBAL HUMAN RIGHTS REGIME

Human rights are regularly addressed today in bilateral foreign policy and in a variety of multilateral schemes. In this and the following section I shall consider only the "universal" or U.N.-centered regime, which for convenience I shall refer to as "the" global human rights regime. Regional and single-issue regimes are discussed in a separate section below. Bilateral policy and human rights policy in nonhuman rights fora (e.g., development banks) are subjects beyond my scope here.

Figure 9.2 presents a schematic diagram of the U.N.'s major human rights bodies and their functions, using the typology developed earlier. It may be convenient to refer to this diagram occasionally as the discussion progresses.

Regime Norms

The most important statements of the norms of the global human rights regime are the Universal Declaration of Human Rights, adopted December 10, 1948, by the U.N. General Assembly, and the International Human Rights Covenants, which were opened for signature and ratification in 1966 and came into force in 1976.[6] The rights proclaimed in the Universal Declaration—the best known, most general, and most widely accepted statement of the regime's norms—are usually divided into civil and political rights and economic, social, and cultural rights, but a more useful and precise classification is possible.

1. *Personal rights,* including rights to life; nationality; recognition before the law; protection against cruel, degrading, or inhumane treatment or punishment; and protection against racial, ethnic, sexual, or religious discrimination. (Articles 2–7, 15)
2. *Legal rights,* including access to remedies for violations of basic rights, the presumption of innocence, the guarantee of fair and impartial public trials, prohibition of *ex post facto* laws, and protections against arbitrary arrest, detention, or exile and against arbitrary interference with one's family, home or reputation. (Articles 8–12)
3. *Civil liberties,* especially rights to freedom of thought, conscience and religion, opinion and expression, movement and residence, and peaceful assembly and association. (Articles 13, 18–20)
4. *Subsistence rights,* particularly the rights to food and a standard of living adequate for the health and well-being of oneself and one's family. (Article 25)
5. *Economic rights,* including principally the rights to work, rest and leisure, and social security. (Articles 22–24)

FIGURE 9.2
Major Bodies in the International (U.N.) Human Rights Regime

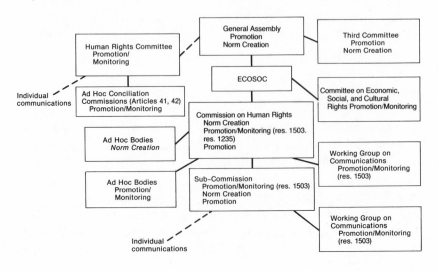

6. *Social and cultural rights,* especially rights to education and to participation in the cultural life of the community. (Articles 26, 27)
7. *Political rights,* principally the rights to take part in government and to periodic and genuine elections with universal and equal suffrage (Article 21), plus the political aspects of many civil liberties.

This list is further elaborated in two International Human Rights Covenants and a variety of single-issue treaties and declarations on such topics as genocide, political rights of women, racial discrimination, and torture. Although these later documents occasionally deviate from the Universal Declaration (e.g., the Covenants prominently add a right to self-determination and delete the right to property), for the most part they elaborate or extend rights proclaimed in the Universal Declaration. Therefore, we can say that the regime's norms are quite coherent. Furthermore, it is generally agreed that these rights form an interdependent and synergistically interactive system of guarantees, rather than a menu from which one may freely pick and choose.[7]

The standard practice of states is to speak of, and thus in a certain sense treat, the norms of the Universal Declaration and the Covenants as international norms (with limited, self-selected national exemptions). Professions of adherence to these norms, and charges of failure to live up to them, are regular features of contemporary international politics. Although domestic practice regularly falls far short of international profession, these rights are widely viewed as more or less binding international standards. Each state, however, retains almost complete autonomy in *implementing* these norms at the national level; regime norms are fully internationalized, but decision making remains largely national.

Decision-Making Procedures

The central *procedural* principle of the contemporary global human rights regime is *national* jurisdiction over human rights questions. The Universal Declaration, although widely accepted as authoritative, is explicitly (only) a "standard of achievement,"[8] and each state retains full sovereign authority to determine the adequacy of its achievements. The Covenants do impose strict legal obligations, but only on those states, currently about one half, that voluntarily accept them by becoming parties to the treaties. Furthermore, as we shall see, national performance is subject to only minimal international supervision.

The regime, however, does verge on authoritative international standard setting or norm creation. States show not merely a willingness but a desire to use the United Nations, especially the Commission on Human Rights, to create and elaborate human rights norms, and the resulting declarations and conventions usually are widely accepted. These norms do allow self-selected national exemptions—declarations are not strictly binding, and treaty obligations not only must be voluntarily accepted but also may be accepted with reservations; and consensual negotiating, which allows any major group of states an effective veto, has limited the output of new instruments. Nonetheless, norm creation has been largely internationalized, and the extent, specificity and acceptance of international human rights norms continue to increase.

There has even been significant acceptance by states of an international role in promoting national implementation of international norms. For example, the General Assembly regularly encourages states to ratify the Covenants and to adhere to other international instruments. A variety of informational, educational, and publicity activities and advisory services such as seminars, fellowships, and consultations are undertaken by the United Nations Center for Human Rights and other bodies. As we shall see, much of the most important work of the Commission on Human Rights is promotional as well. And national foreign policies, both bilateral and multilateral, in the First, Second, and Third Worlds alike, regularly involve efforts to promote the national implementation of international human rights standards. But widespread, vociferous, and usually effective claims of national sovereignty meet all efforts to move from general exhortations even to observations and recommendations addressed to the practice of most particular states, revealing the ultimate weakness of the regime.

Because its norms are strong (i.e., both coherent and widely accepted), the overall strength of the global human rights regime rests on its decision-making procedures. But procedures beyond norm creation, promotion, and information exchange are largely absent.

The Universal Declaration established a relatively strong declaratory regime, but in the forty years since then, although the regime has grown in strength, only rudimentary, principally promotional procedures have been created.

The Human Rights Committee. The parties to the 1966 International Convenant on Civil and Political Rights "undertake to submit reports on the measures they have adopted which give effect to the rights recognized herein and on the progress made in the enjoyment of those rights" (Article 40 [1]). These reports are reviewed by the Human Rights Committee, a body of eighteen independent experts.

The Committee's practice in reviewing reports[9] reflects a narrow reading of its powers. Formal evaluations of, or even comments on, the compliance or noncompliance of individual states have not been made, and the Committee's "study" of reports has been restricted to individual review by each member and, most important, public questioning of state representatives. Nonetheless, this rather haphazard procedure has worked better than might be expected, because many of the experts are genuinely independent, and questioning may be based on information obtained from nongovernmental organizations and other unofficial sources. Questioning, in open sessions, is often penetrating; the Committee is, for a U.N. body, remarkably devoid of ideological partisanship; state representatives often are fairly responsive; and the questioning, by diplomatic standards at least, is neither excessively deferential nor merely *pro forma*. The procedure has even provoked occasional minor changes in national law, and at least a few parties use their dealings with the Committee as an occasion for a genuine review and reexamination of national laws, policies, and practices.

The reporting procedure, therefore, has provided a fairly widely accepted promotional mechanism. But it involves, at most, only information exchange and the weakest of monitoring mechanisms. And even the information exchange procedures are significantly flawed.

The reports of many countries are thorough and revealing. Others however, are farces. For example, many Soviet bloc countries have reported that all the enumerated rights were fully implemented before the Covenants were ratified; many reports consist principally of extracts from national constitutions and statutes; and a significant number are simply evasive.[10] The Committee has tried, sometimes successfully, to obtain better information, but in the final analysis it is powerless to compel more than *pro forma* compliance with even this very weak reporting system—and not even that can always be assured, as illustrated by the extreme case of the report of Zaire, due in 1978 but still not submitted until February 1987 after ten reminders. Finally, this reporting procedure applies only to the parties to the Covenant, which numbered 87 by mid-1989. Thus, about half the countries of the world are exempt from even this minimal international scrutiny.

The one area where guarded optimism may be appropriate is the Committee's consideration of individual petitions under the Optional Protocol of the Covenant, the "best procedure within the U.N. system for the examination of petitions."[11] Particular decisions of compliance or noncompliance can be made in individual cases, giving the Committee moderately strong international monitoring powers. International enforcement, however, still is impossible.

In its first dozen years of operation, through mid-1989, the Committee received 371 communications, with respect to 29 parties to the Optional Protocol. Although more than a third were declared inadmissible, discontinued, suspended, or withdrawn, and a third were still under review, in about a quarter (96) of its cases, the Committee had expressed its views—that is, made a substantive determination on the merits of the case. Although the majority of these decisions involved a single country, Uruguay, the procedure does seem to be relatively open and highly independent, providing genuine, if limited, international monitoring, which in at least a few cases has altered state practice.[12]

But only forty-five countries had accepted the Optional Protocol by mid-1989 that is, about one quarter of the countries of the world are covered by even this modest international monitoring of personal, legal, civil, and political rights. Not surprisingly, almost none of those covered are major human rights violators. As a result, relatively strong procedures apply primarily where they are least needed. Unfortunately, this is only to be expected, given that participation is entirely voluntary.

The International Covenant on Economic, Social, and Cultural Rights also requires periodic reports. Until recently, these reports were reviewed not by a separate body of experts by the Sessional Working Group on the Implementation of the International Covenant on Economic, Social, and Cultural Rights of the Economic and Social Council. A committee of experts (the Committee on Economic, Social and Cultural Rights), roughly analogous to the Human Rights Committee, has, however, been created and has recently begun its work. The fact that the Covenant is explicitly intended to be implemented progressively rather than immediately (Article 2), however, will seriously hamper international monitoring. Furthermore, there is no complaint procedure parallel to that of the Optional Protocol to the Civil and Political Covenant.[13]

The Commission on Human Rights. The Commission on Human Rights, whose central role in norm creation we have already noted, also has important promotional and monitoring functions. Its strongest powers rest on Economic and Social Council (ECOSOC) resolution 1503 (XLVIII) (1970), which authorizes the Commission to investigate communications (complaints) that "appear to reveal a consistent pattern of gross and reliably attested violations of human rights."[14] The Commission, however, is a body of state representatives, not independent experts; although most Commission members are *relatively* nonideological (when compared to, say, their counterparts in the Third Committee of the General Assembly), they are still instructed political delegates. Stringent criteria of admissibility[15] limit the cases considered (although certain second-hand information and communications from non-governmental organizations [NGOs] are admissable). And although individuals communicate grievances, the 1503 procedure deals only with *situations* of gross, systematic violations; there are no procedures for investigating, let alone attempting to remedy, particular violations.

Another major drawback is that the entire procedure is confidential until it has been concluded. Although confidentiality may encourage cooperation by states, it slows the process and largely precludes an activist role for the Commission in helping to uncover and spotlight violations. The Commission has circumvented some of the strictures of confidentiality by publicly announcing a "blacklist" of countries being studied; the practices of some thirty countries have been examined since 1978.[16] Although the resulting international notoriety, however slight, may not be entirely negligible, it is unclear whether we should commend such ingenuity or bemoan the need to resort to it.

Finally, although the Commission may, with the consent and cooperation of the state in question, appoint a committee to investigate a situation, no such investigation has occurred. In the case of Equatorial Guinea, the Commission in 1979 chose instead to pursue a public investigation through a special rapporteur, a process less restricted by procedural constraints. In 1980 the Commission concluded its consideration of the treatment of Jehovah's Witnesses in Malawi, which had been frustrated by official noncooperation, with a resolution that merely expressed the hope that all human rights were being respected in Malawi. Equally modest public actions have been taken with respect to Haiti (1984, 1987), Uruguay (1985), and Albania (1988).[17] Other than these very limited achievements, the public portions of the 1503 procedure have had no apparent impact, although confidential actions almost certainly have had at least a marginal influence on policy in some cases.

The 1503 procedure, therefore, is in practice largely a promotional device involving only sporadic and limited monitoring. Given the sensitivity of human rights questions, even this may be of real practical value. Nevertheless, its weakness is evident.

Much the same is true of the Commission's other activities. For example, the Subcommission on the Prevention of Discrimination and Protection of Minorities' annual discussions, in public meetings, and the Commission's own public discussions, under the authority of ECOSOC resolution 1235 (XLII) and a variety of *ad hoc* procedures, have increased general awareness of human rights issues. Furthermore, the Commission's work has helped to focus international public opinion on deplorable human rights conditions in at least a few particular countries (e.g., Chile) and on a few types of widespread and particularly reprehensible violations, such as torture and disappearances.[18] The Commission, along with the Secretariat, also undertakes a variety of public information activities and coordinates and encourages the use of advisory services in the field of human rights. But virtually nothing has been achieved in the areas of international implementation and enforcement.

The Commission's one real advantage is that it may look into situations—in so far as it is able to look anywhere—in all countries, not only those party to a particular treaty. Therefore, it is in many ways the procedural core of the global human rights regime.

POLITICAL FOUNDATIONS OF THE GLOBAL HUMAN RIGHTS REGIME

The global human rights regime is a relatively strong promotional regime, composed of widely accepted substantive norms, largely internationalized standard-setting procedures, some general promotional activity, but very limited international implementation, which rarely goes beyond information exchange and voluntarily accepted international assistance for the national implementation of international norms. There is no international enforcement. Such normative strength and procedural weakness is not accidental; it is the result of conscious political decisions.

Regimes are political creations to overcome perceived problems arising from inadequately regulated or insufficiently coordinated national action. Robert O. Keohane offers a useful market analogy: regimes arise when sufficient international "demand" is met by a state (or group of states) willing and able to "supply" international norms and decision-making procedures.[19] The shape and strength of an international regime reflects who wants it, who opposes it, and why—and how the conflicting objectives, interests, and capabilities of the parties have been resolved. As Krasner puts it, in each issue area there are makers, breakers, and takers of (potential) international regimes.[20] Understanding the structure of a regime (or its absence) requires that we know who has played which roles, when and why, and what agreements they reached. In this section I examine the interaction of supply and demand that has led to the global human rights regime described earlier.

Prior to World War I, human rights were almost universally viewed as the exclusive preserve of the state; despite occasional references to minimum standards of civilized behavior, there was not even a weak declaratory global human rights regime. In the interwar period, the International Labor Organization (ILO) undertook some minor efforts in the area of workers' rights, but it was functionally restricted to this one class or rights, and its work was of interest primarily to developed, capitalist, liberal-democratic states. The League of Nations' Minorities System,[21] the only other significant international human rights activity in this period, was not only restricted to a single class of rights, but for the most part covered only those states defeated during or created in the aftermath of World War I. With these exceptions, as recently as fifty years ago human rights were not even considered to be a legitimate international concern.

World War II marks a decisive break; the defeat of Germany ushered in the contemporary global human rights regime. Revulsion at the array of human rights abuses that came to be summarized in the term *Nazi* engendered a brief period of enthusiastic international action, culminating in the passage in 1948 of the Universal Declaration.

Although Hitler's actions shocked the conscience of the international community, they did not clearly contravene explicit international norms; for example, at Nuremberg the essential charge of crimes against humanity palpably lacked an authoritative international legal foundation. In such an environment, it was relatively easy to reach general agreement on a set of international principles against gross and persistent systematic violations of basic rights— namely, the Universal Declaration of Human Rights (as well as by the Convention on Genocide, which was even more clearly a direct legacy of Hitler).

It is perhaps surprising that this moral "demand" should have produced even this much in a world in which more material national interests usually prevail. In the years immediately following the war, however, there were willing and able makers, numerous takers, and no significant breakers of a global human rights regime. The moral and emotional demands for a global human rights regime seem to have run relatively deep, even in some important national leaders (strong support came from several countries, including the United States, and none seriously opposed either the Declaration or, later, the Covenants), and no countervailing concerns or interests had yet emerged.

A cynic might suggest, with some basis, that these postwar "achievements" simply reflect the minimal international constraints and very low costs of a declaratory regime; decision making under the Universal Declaration remained entirely national, and it would be more than twenty years until resolution 1503 and nearly thirty years before even the rudimentary promotion and monitoring procedures of the Covenants came into effect. Yet prior to the war even a declaratory regime had rarely been contemplated. In the late 1940s, human rights became, for the first time, a recognized international issue area.

Moving much beyond a declaratory regime, however, has proved most difficult. As we have seen, procedural innovations have been modest. Even the legal elaboration of substantive norms has been slow and laborious: for example, it took nine years to move from a Declaration to a Convention on torture. It is in this relative constancy of the regime (critics and frustrated optimists are likely to say stagnation) that the weakness of the demand is most evident.

To the extent, probably considerable, that the global human rights regime arose from postwar frustration, guilt, or unease, the very proclamation ("supply") of the Declaration, along with the adoption of the Genocide Convention, seems to have satisfied the demand. To the extent, again probably considerable, that it rested on an emotional reaction to the horrors of Hitler and the war, time—sadly but predictably—blunted the emotion. Time also revealed both the superficial, merely verbal commitment of many states and the existence of serious substantive disagreements over particular rights, causing enthusiasm to wane further. And with the Cold War heating up, not only was the desire to move on to other issues strong, but East–West rivalry itself soon came to infect and distort the discussion of human rights.

The most important problem, however, was—and still is—the fact that a strong global human rights regime does not rest on any perceived material interest of a state or coalition willing and able to supply it. In the absence of a power capable of compelling compliance, states participate in, or increase their commitment to, international regimes more or less voluntarily. Barring extraordinary circumstances, states participate in an international regime only to achieve *national* objectives in an environment of perceived international interdependence, and even then usually only when independent national action has proved ineffective or too costly. States are likely to relinquish authority only to obtain a significant benefit beyond the reach of separate national action, or to avoid bearing a major burden. Furthermore, relinquishing sovereign authority must appear "safe," all things considered, to states, who are notoriously jealous of their sovereign prerogatives. A stronger global human rights regime simply does not present a safe prospect of obtaining otherwise unattainable national benefits.

Moral interests such as human rights may be no less "real" than material interests. They are, however, less tangible, and policy, for better or worse, tends to be made in response to relatively tangible national objectives. Moral interests, which are far less likely to be a major political concern of powerful national actors, also are much more easily lost in the shuffle of the policy-making process. They are more subject to political manipulation, because they usually are vaguely expressed and the criteria for determining success in realizing moral interests are particularly elusive. And human rights claims usually are met, justifiably or not, with the politically potent charge of misguided moralism.

The extreme sensitivity of human rights practices makes the very subject intensely threatening to most states. National human rights practices often would be a matter for considerable embarrassment should they be subject to full international scrutiny. In fact, compliance with international human rights standards would in numerous countries mean the removal of those in power.

In addition, and perhaps most important, human rights are ultimately a profoundly *national*—not international—issue. States are the principal violators of human rights and the principal actors governed by the regime's norms; international human rights are concerned primarily with how a government treats the inhabitants of its own country. This situation arises from the basic structure of contemporary international politics: in an international system where government is national rather than global, human rights are by definition principally a national matter, as reflected in the purely national implementation of regime norms, and thus the absence of policy coordination procedures and even rudimentary mechanisms of international enforcement.

Human rights are also a national matter from the perspective of practical political action. Respecting human rights is extremely inconvenient for a government, even in the best of circumstances. And the less pure the motives of those in power, the more irksome human rights appear. Who is to prevent a government from succumbing to the temptations and arrogance of position and power? Who can *force* a government to respect human rights? The only plausible candidate is the people whose rights are at stake.

Foreign actors may overthrow a repressive government. With luck and skill, foreign actors may even be able to place good people in charge of finely crafted institutions based on the best of principles. They may provide tutelage, supervision, and monitoring; moral and material support; and protection against enemies. All this, however, is extremely unlikely, especially if we do not impute unrealistically pure motives and unbelievable skill and dedication to external powers, for whom "humanitarian intervention" usually amounts to little more than a convenient cover for partisan politics. And in any case, a regime's ultimate success—its persistence in respecting, implementing, and enforcing human rights—will depend on *internal* political factors.

A government that respects human rights is almost always the legacy of persistent national political struggles against human rights violations. Most governments that respect human rights have been created not from the top down, but from the bottom up. Domestically, paternalistic solutions, in which human rights are given rather than taken, are likely to be unstable. Internationally, paternalism is no more likely to be successful.

But if international regimes arise primarily because of international interdependence—the inability to achieve perceived national objectives by independent national action—how can we account for the creation, and even modest growth, of the global human rights regime? First and foremost, by the persisting relevance of the "moral" concerns that brought it into being in the first place. Butchers such as Pol Pot and Idi Amin still shock the conscience of mankind and provoke a desire to reject them as not merely reprehensible but prohibited by clear and public, authoritative international norms; even regimes with dismal human rights records seem to feel impelled to join in condemning the abuses of such rulers, and lesser despots as well.

Although cynics might interpret such uses of the language as human rights as merely craven abuse of the rhetoric of human rights, it is just as easily seen as an implicit, submerged or deflected expression of a sense of *moral* interdependence. Although states—not only governments, but often the public as well—often are unwilling to translate this perceived moral interdependence into action, or into an international regime with strong decision-making powers, they also are unwilling (or at least politically unable) to return to treating national human rights practices as properly beyond all international norms and procedures.

A weak global human rights regime also may contribute, in a way acceptable to states, to improved national practice. For example, new governments with a commitment to human rights may find it helpful to be able to draw on, and point to the constraints of, authoritative international standards; we can see this perhaps in the case of the Alfonsin government in Argentina. Likewise, established regimes may find the additional check provided by an international regime a salutary supplement to national efforts; this seems to be the case for many smaller Western powers. And most states, even if only for considerations of image and prestige, are likely to be willing to accept regime norms and procedures—especially norms—that do not appear immediately threatening.

States also may miscalculate or get carried away by the moment, and procedures may evolve beyond what the regime's creators originally intended. For example, ECOSOC resolution 1235, which provides the principal basis for the Commission on Human Rights' public study and discussions of human rights situations in individual countries, was explicitly established in 1967 to focus principally on the pariah regimes in southern Africa, but it has evolved into a procedure with universal application (or at least one that may be applied to any country that a majority of members decides to consider). Such unplanned growth is rare even for relatively weak procedures, but it should not be entirely overlooked.

The current global human rights regime thus represents a politically acceptable international mechanism for the collective resolution of principally, but not entirely, national problems. Because perception of the problem rests on a politically weak sense of *moral* interdependence, however, there is no powerful demand for a stronger regime; even policy coordination seems too demanding, and there is little reason for states to accept international monitoring, let alone authoritative international decision making.

In any international regime, even strong decision-making procedures are largely oversight mechanisms; "enforcement" must be the exception if institutional overload and a corrosive overuse of coercion are to be avoided. Even where a regime includes binding international decision making, the great bulk of the work of implementing and enforcing international norms lies with states.

In conditions of material interdependence, "good faith" compliance can be largely reduced to calculations of long-run national interest. Material interdependence implies that each side has more or less unilateral power to prevent the enjoyment of mutual or reciprocal benefits available only through cooperation. Self-help retaliation, therefore, is likely to be readily available and relatively effective, and good faith compliance with regime norms is roughly equivalent to pursuing long-run self-interest. As a result, policy coordination, or even just information exchange, may be sufficient to maintain a relatively stable and effective regime. Strong international decision-making procedures certainly would strengthen and help to stabilize even a regime based on material interdependence; some benefits of cooperation (e.g., collective goods in conditions with high incentives to free-ride) may be realizable only with strong international procedures. But the "need" for strong procedures is *relatively* low in such conditions.

By contrast, the primarily national character of human rights violations, and the basis of the regime in perceived moral (rather than material) interdependence, drastically increases the need for, while at the same time reducing the likelihood of, international implementation and enforcement. Other states are not directly harmed by a government's failure to respect human rights; the immediate victims are that government's own citizens, making the incentives to retaliate for violations of regime norms low, or at least intangible. Furthermore, "retaliation" is particularly difficult: because the only leverage available, beyond moral suasion, must be imported from other issue areas, such as trade or aid, retaliation is likely to be more costly and involve an escalation in conflict, and because the means of retaliation are no longer clearly and directly tied to the violations, their legitimacy may become questionable.

This is not to belittle the importance of international procedures— the more effective the monitoring and enforcement procedures, the stronger the regime and the more likely it is to achieve its objectives —but rather to stress the fact that regime procedures largely reflect underlying political perceptions of interest and interdependence. Compliance with regime norms rests primarily on authority and acceptance, not force or even enforcement.

An international regime reflects states' collective vision of a problem and its solution, and their willingness to "fund" that solution. In the area of human rights, this vision seems to extend not much beyond a politically weak moral interdependence, and states are willing to "pay" very little in the way of diminished national sovereignty in order to realize the benefits of cooperation. The result is a regime with extensive, coherent, and widely accepted norms but extremely limited international decision-making powers; that is, a strong promotional regime.

REGIONAL AND SINGLE-ISSUE HUMAN RIGHTS REGIMES

Keohane, adopting a metaphor from Vinod Aggarwal, notes that international regimes "are 'nested' within more comprehensive agreements . . . that constitute a complex and interlinked pattern of relations."[22] Although "nesting" implies too neat and hierarchical an arrangement, there are regional and single-issue human rights regimes, which might be considered as largely autonomous, but relatively coherently "nested," international human rights (sub) regimes.

The European Regime

A strong regional regime exists among the (primarily Western European) members of the Council of Europe. Personal, legal, civil, and political rights are guaranteed by the 1950 [European] Convention for the Protection of Human Rights and Fundamental Freedoms (entered into force September 3, 1953) and its Protocols, while economic and social rights are laid down in the 1961 European Social Charter (entered into force February 26, 1965).[23] Both sets are very similar to those of the Universal Declaration and the Covenants. The decision-making procedures of the European regime, however, are of special interest, especially the strong monitoring powers of the European Commission of Human Rights and the authoritative decision-making powers of the European Court of Human Rights.

The principal function of the European Commission of Human Rights, an independent body of experts (one from each member state), is to review "applications" from persons, groups of individuals, NGOs, and states alleging violations of the rights guaranteed by the Convention in the seventeen (of twenty-one) parties that have authorized the Commission to receive applications. If friendly settlement cannot be reached (Article 28–30), the Commission may formally report its opinion on the state's compliance with the Convention (Article 31). Although these reports are not legally binding, they are usually accepted as authoritative by states.

Of the 10,709 applications registered through 1983, only 343 (less than 3 percent) were declared admissible.[24] The criteria of admissibility (Articles 26, 27), however, are reasonable and reasonably applied: domestic remedies must be exhausted and the application filed no more than six months later, and anonymous, redundant, or manifestly ill-founded applications are not allowed. And in about half of the admissible cases the Commission concludes its consideration with a finding that the state is not in compliance with the Convention; another 10 percent typically are resolved through friendly settlement between the petitioner and his or her government.[25] The hurdle of admissibility, therefore, reflects the human rights practices of the parties to the Convention more than anything else.

Within three months of the Commission's report, either the Commission or the state in question—but not the individual victim— may refer the case to the European Court of Human Rights (Articles 47, 48) for binding enforcement action. Through 1983, 72 cases, involving 110 applications, had been brought before the Court. Those cases not referred to the Court are sent to the Committee of Ministers, which, like the Court, is empowered to make legally binding decisions.

These procedures not only are of unprecedented formal strength and completeness, but are almost completely accepted in practice. This acceptance is in considerable measure explained by the impartiality of the procedures, which is ensured by the fact that members of the Commission and judges of the Court are independent experts of the highest standing and integrity, operating almost entirely free of the political influence of the member states.

Any particular set of procedures can be operated in a relatively politicized or a relatively "objective"–technical fashion. And given the political sensitivity of human rights, even the most impartial procedures cannot be substantively neutral; even the "facts" of compliance with or violation of regime norms are morally and politically charged. Therefore, depoliticized, ultimately judicial procedures are of special importance in the area of human rights. Without such impartiality, European states almost certainly would not accept or use the procedures to the extent that they do now, regardless of the depth of their commitment to the regime's norms.

The Convention also allows interstate complaints, but this procedure is used only rarely, and then primarily (although not exclusively) for cases involving foreign conationals (Greeks in British-controlled Cyprus, Austrians in Italy, Irish in Ulster, and Greek Cypriots in Turkish-held territory). The peripheral nature of interstate procedures underscores the point made earlier that human rights are primarily a national matter. Except in extraordinary cases such as the Greek junta, only victims, fellow citizens, or (co)nationals can be counted on to struggle to see that human rights are respected.

Economic and social rights, laid out in the European Social Charter,[26] are supervised through separate, significantly weaker, procedures. Implementation is entirely through biennial reports (Article 21), which are reviewed, along with comments from national organizations of employers and workers, by a Committee of Experts (Article 24). Individual communications are not permitted by the Charter, nor are interstate complaints, and there is no machinery for authoritative enforcement.

Nonetheless, in practice reporting has yielded some policy coordination and rather strong monitoring: the Committee of Experts is not restricted to official sources of information; it may and regularly does make comments on compliance; and in recent years the Committee of Ministers, to whom the experts ultimately report, has begun to exercise its powers of recommendation. Furthermore, and most important, the genuine commitment of the parties to the regime's norms often makes the give-and-take discussion of reports adequate incentive for policy changes, especially given the official participation of workers' and employers' organizations and the national political pressure they and other private groups can exert "from below."

That states accept the European Convention and Social Charter is its real strength. Formal procedures may support and strengthen national resolve, but in the final analysis they largely supplement national commitment and state acceptance; strong procedures are less a cause than a reflection of the regime's strength. In any international regime, strong procedures serve primarily to check backsliding, apply pressure for further progress, remedy occasional deviations, and provide authoritative interpretations in controversial cases.

Although these are hardly negligible functions—they are precisely what is lacking in the global regime—strong international procedures, as noted earlier, rest ultimately on national commitment.

I have argued that a regime's shape and strength could be explained largely by perceptions of interdependence, the benefits states expect to receive (or the burdens they hope to avoid), and the risks they expect to incur in turning over authority to an international agency. The strong national commitment of the European states to human rights greatly increases the perceived value of the "moral" benefits states can expect to achieve, suggesting that moral interdependence can indeed rival material interdependence in political force when national commitment to moral goals is particularly strong. Furthermore, relatively good national human rights records reduce the political risks of strong international procedures.

The European regime is also "safe" because it operates within a relatively homogeneous and close sociocultural community. This greatly reduces the likelihood of radical differences in interpreting regime norms and dramatically decreases the risk of partisan abuse or manipulation of the regime. Perceived community also helps to increase the perception of moral interdependence.

Thus, although it may be literally true, as Ralph Beddard observes, that "few applicants have been made better off, except in peace of mind, by applying to the European Commission" (recall the very small number of cases actually investigated by the Commission), this largely misses the point. Beddard himself implicitly admits this when he goes on to note that often the "individual has benefited either because of the mere presence of the treaty and its machinery or through the application [complaint] of someone else in a similar position,"[27] especially because Commission and Court decisions have significance as possible precedents for all member states.

National compliance is the key. If this is achieved voluntarily, as it is for the most part in Europe, so much the better; if the regime's impact is primarily indirect, it is no less real.[28] As long as states conform their behavior to the regime's norms—and in Europe they clearly do—the relatively infrequent use of authoritative regional decision-making procedures is, if anything, desirable rather than regrettable.

Having said this, though, we should belittle neither the strength nor the significance of the European regime's enforcement measures.

Not only is completely voluntary compliance a utopian ideal, but the European case suggests a process of mutual reinforcement between national commitment and international procedures. A strong regime is a device to increase the chances that states will enjoy the best that they "deserve" in that issue area; that is, the best to which they will commit themselves to aspire, and then struggle to achieve.

The Inter-American Regime[29]

The American Declaration of the Rights and Duties of Man, adopted in 1948, presents a list of human rights very similar to that of the Universal Declaration. The 1969 American Convention on Human Rights, a binding treaty, is, like its European counterpart, limited to personal, legal, civil, and political rights (plus the right to property), in recognition of the inappropriateness of strict, universal legal obligations with respect to economic and social rights, given the low level of economic development of most American countries. The Inter-American regime's norms are rounded out by a variety of single-issue treaties, such as the Inter-American Convention on the Granting of Political Rights to Women (1948). (There is no American equivalent to the European Social Charter or the International Covenant on Economic, Social and Cultural Rights.)

The Inter-American Court of Human Rights, which was established in 1979 and sits in San José, Costa Rica, may take binding enforcement action. As in the European regime, individuals have no direct access to the Court, although the Commission may bring cases involving individuals to the Court. The Court may also issue advisory opinions requested by members of the Organization of American States (OAS); through early 1987 it had issued seven such advisory opinions, largely on technical matters of interpretation. In 1988 it heard its first substantive case, which was decided against Honduras.

The Inter-American Commission of Human Rights, however, is the procedural heart of the regime. The Commission is empowered to develop awareness of human rights, make recommendations to governments, respond to inquiries of states, prepare studies and reports, request information from and make recommendations to governments, and conduct on-site investigations (with the consent of the government). The Commission also may receive communications (complaints) from individuals and groups concerning the practice of *any* member of the OAS, whether a party to the Convention or not. An "autonomous entity" within the OAS, the Commission has vigorously exploited this autonomy.

In the past twenty years the Commission has adopted decisions and resolutions arising from individual communications from more than twenty countries in the region—including the United States! It has issued Country Reports documenting particularly serious human rights situations in more than a dozen countries, most of which have been followed by renewed and intensified Commission monitoring. And it has adopted special resolutions on major regional problems, such as the 1978 resolution on states of siege.

The wide-ranging nonpartisan activism of the Commission can be largely attributed to the fact that its members serve in their personal capacity; it is more a technical, quasi-judicial body than a political body. But how are we to explain the fact that the American states, many of which are not notably solicitous toward human rights, allow the Commission to be so active? Why, given that the dominant political culture is not one in which official respect for human rights is deeply ingrained, have such strong procedures been established?

It is often argued that the power of a single hegemonic state is crucial to the establishment (although not necessarily to the maintenance) of strong, stable regimes.[30] Although hegemonic power had virtually nothing to do with the European regime, the Inter-American human rights regime would seem to owe much to the influence and power of the United States. There is always a U.S. member of the Commission, and there is even a U.S. judge on the Court (nominated by Costa Rica), despite the fact that the United States is not a party to the Convention. Furthermore, the United States has often acted to persuade reluctant, even recalcitrant, governments of the wisdom of cooperation with Commission investigations, despite the peripheral place typically assigned to human rights in U.S. bilateral relations with the region.

Such an account, however, obscures a much more complex reality.[31] The United States did have an effective veto within the OAS, which it did not exercise at the time of the creation of the Commission. For a variety of reasons (including concern over Castro's Cuba and communism in the Americas more broadly) the U.S. has even provided some support for the creation and operation of a relatively weak Inter-American regime. But its creation was more the result of a convergence of interests between the United States and certain democratic governments in the region. "Hegemonic leadership" seriously overstates the U.S. role and significantly misdescribes the political dynamics of the Inter-American regime.

Nonetheless, U.S. support has often been important to the operations of the Inter-American Commission. For example, in 1978 a combination of U.S. political pressure and economic concessions helped to convince the Argentinean military government to permit an on-site investigation by the Commission. More generally as well, the support of the Carter Administration was very important in revitalizing the Commission in the late 1970s. This (at least episodically) supportive role of the regional hegemon has been important to the relative flourishing of the Inter-American regime in the face of a regional human rights record throughout the postwar period far worse than that in Europe, and a record that in the mid and late 1970s had become extremely discouraging. The hegemonic power of the United States, supported and often encouraged by democratic governments in the region, has played an important, although rarely a leading, role in some of the more important activities of the Commission.

Consensual commitment and hegemonic power are to a certain extent functional equivalents for establishing state acceptance. Despite the importance of largely voluntary compliance and the limited ability of even hegemonic power to overcome persistent national resistance, coercion may produce a certain level of limited participation from states that otherwise would not accept a regime. The very immateriality of the moral interdependence underlying human rights regimes may even make hegemonic power unusually effective, should the hegemon choose to exercise it.[32]

Material interdependence in an issue area limits the use of even hegemonic power. Consider the case of trade. A hegemon is likely to prefer an open trading regime—the most productive gain the most in a liberal–free market order. But there are severe constraints on using force to open any but very weak economies (which are not likely to be of much value). Material *inter*dependence implies that even middle powers command valued resources or opportunities outside of the control (at a reasonable cost) of the hegemonic power; material interdependence entails countervailing power (specific to that issue) on the part of the (overall) relatively weak, whose cooperation is essential to realizing the joint benefit that rests on that interdependence.

When the interdependence is moral, however, issue-specific countervailing power is largely absent, especially in the case of human rights, where the benefit (namely, respect for human rights) is largely under national control. If a hegemon chooses to exercise its power through or on behalf of a human rights regime, the weak repressive government does not have much countervailing power available to it; the repressive government's noncooperation cannot forestall mutual enjoyment of some material joint benefit.

Nonetheless, the relative mix of coercion and consensus does influence the nature and functioning of a regime. In particular, coerced participation is sure to be marked by constant, and often effective, national resistance, and regime procedures are likely to be more adversarial. Hegemony may ensure a certain degree of international monitoring, and in extreme cases hegemonic power may be mobilized to ameliorate a situation that otherwise would be beyond the reach of an international regime, but even a hegemon can impose only a limited range of changes. The result is something of a paradox: the Inter-American Commission is relatively active and effective in the worst cases, which by their very extremity mobilize relatively strong pressure or support from the United States; but it is relatively less active in less serious situations, which therefore are in many ways not "easier" but harder to ameliorate through international action.

Africa, Asia, and the Middle East

The African Charter on Human and Peoples' Rights, drafted in Banjul, The Gambia, in June 1980 and January 1981, was adopted by the Organization of African Unity (OAU) in Nairobi in June 1981.[33] There are some interesting normative difference between the African (Banjul) Charter and all other international human rights regimes, most notably the addition of and emphasis on collective or "peoples' " rights (Articles 19–24),[34] such as the rights to peace and development, and the particularly prominent place the Charter gives to individual duties (Articles 27–29).

The Banjul Charter creates an African Commission on Human and

Peoples' Rights (Articles 30–46), allows for interstate complaints (Articles 47–54), and even envisions the receipt of individual communications (Articles 55–60). However, all these provisions are quite vague, there is no reporting system, and the best we can say at this early date is that they leave the Commission, once it is in operation, a limited opening to establish itself as a (weak) monitoring body. There is, however, no judicial organ or any other mechanism for authoritative regional enforcement decisions.

The African Charter only recently entered into force, and the Commission held its first meeting in 1987, so we have little experience on which to base an assessment. Nonetheless, virtually all the factors identified above as important to strong, successful decision-making procedures seem to be absent.

The regional organizational environment is extremely unconducive. The OAU not only is highly politicized but is the most deferential of all regional organizations to sovereignty. Although this is quite understandable, given the weak states and strong subnational loyalties in most of black Africa, there is no reason to expect the OAU to deviate from its standard practice in an area as sensitive as human rights. And previous efforts at regional or subregional cooperation in other issue areas have not been very successful.

The prospects appear no better when we look at national practice. Over the last twenty years, the human rights record of the typical African country has been about average for the Third World, despite lurid and relatively overreported aberrations such as Idi Amin and "Emperor" Bokassa. Nonetheless, in the absence of strong pressure by a regional hegemon, the national human rights record of the typical African government suggests a high degree of aversion to international monitoring. Furthermore, the low level of autonomous economic, social, and political organization in most African states suggests that this situation is unlikely to be changed soon through mass popular action.

Even the currently unclear procedures of the African regime, however, are far more developed than those in Asia and the Middle East. In Asia there are neither regional norms nor decision-making procedures. The Association of South East Asian Nations (ASEAN) is perhaps the most promising subregional organization, but even there the level of cooperation and perceived regional community remains relatively low.

The League of Arab States established a Permanent Arab Commission on Human Rights in 1968, but there are no substantive regional human rights norms: the Arab Charter of Human Rights has languished largely ignored since it was drafted in 1971, and the 1979 Draft Arab Covenant on Human Rights seems destined to a similar fate. Not surprisingly, the Arab Commission has been notably inactive. One commentator has discreetly observed that "rather sparse information is available about the results achieved."[35] The principal reason for this is that the Commission's few concrete activities seem to have involved publicizing the human rights situation in the Israeli-occupied territories.[36] This is hardly a basis for even the weakest of regional regimes.

Single-Issue Regimes

Quite a different type of "nested" human rights (sub) regime is represented by universal membership organizations with a limited functional competence, and by less institution-bound single-issue regimes. Single-issue regimes establish a place for themselves in the network of interdependence by restricting their activities to a limited range of issues (e.g., workers' or women's rights) in order to induce universal participation in a single area of mutual interest.

The first international human rights regime of any sort was the functional regime of the International Labour Organization (ILO),[37] an organization established by the Treaty of Versailles. ILO Conventions and Recommendations in the interwar years, however, were largely concerned with technical issues of working conditions; most of the regime's substantive norms were developed after World War II, including important conventions on freedom of association, the right to organize and bargain collectively, discrimination in employment, equality of remuneration, forced labor, migrant workers, workers' representatives, and basic aims and standards of social policy. Although developed autonomously, these rules can be seen as complementary elaborations of parallel substantive norms of the global regime.

Since regime norms are formulated in individual Conventions and Recommendations, which states adopt or not as they see fit, there is neither universality nor uniformity of coverage. Nonetheless, states are required to submit all Conventions and Recommendations to competent national authorities for consideration for adoption, and they may be periodically required to submit reports on their practice with respect to Conventions they have *not* ratified. Most important, periodic reports are required on compliance with ratified Conventions.[38]

Reports are reviewed by the highly professional Committee of Experts on the Application of Conventions and Recommendations, which has available to it some independent sources of information in addition to the state reports themselves. Although the Committee of Experts may only make "observations," it does so with vigor and considerable impartiality, and Committee observations have often induced changes in national practice.

Much of the explanation for the success of this reporting-monitoring system lies in the ILO's "tripartite" structure, in which workers' and employers' delegates from each member state are voting members of the organization along with government representatives. With the "victims" represented by national trade union representatives, it is relatively difficult for states to cover up their failure to discharge their obligations, especially if some national workers' representatives adopt an internationalist perspective and question practices in countries where labor is less free.

The very issue of workers' rights has also been important to the strength and success of the ILO regime, providing a reasonable degree of ideological homogeneity across a now genuinely universal membership. Certainly Western, Soviet bloc, and "socialist" Third World regimes have quite different interpretations of the meaning of "freedom of association" and other relevant norms, but all face serious internal ideological constraints on overt noncompliance. Along with the relatively high level of autonomy and neutrality of the monitoring system, this has been crucial to maintaining a relatively strong regime.

To the extent that these factors of organizational structure and ideological appeal explain the success of the ILO's functional human rights regime, the prospects for other functional regimes seem dim. Tripartism has not been, and almost certainly will not be, replicated in other organizations. Furthermore, very few other separate human rights issues possess the near universal appeal of workers' rights. One exception, though, is for racial discrimination, the second major single-issue human rights regime.

The 1965 International Convention on the Elimination of All Forms of Racial Discrimination (entered into force January 4, 1969) provides a clear and powerful extension and elaboration of the global regime's norms against racial discrimination. The ratification of the Convention by over 120 countries makes it a major normative instrument. Its implementation provisions, however, are weak.

The Committee on the Elimination of Racial Discrimination, a body of experts established under the Convention, has very narrowly interpreted its powers to "make suggestions and general recommendations based on the examination of the reports and information received from the States Parties" (Article 9[2]). Furthermore, the interstate complaint procedure (Article 11) has never been utilized, and barely a dozen states have authorized the Committee to receive communications from individuals (Article 14). Even the information exchange elements of the reporting procedure are not without flaws: by the summer of 1985, more than 10 percent of the required reports had not been received, with some reports being as much as nine years late despite a dozen or more reminders. Furthermore, the public examination of reports, although sometimes critical, is less thorough or penetrating than that of the Human Rights Committee.

Why did the Committee adopt such a narrow view of its mandate? The simple answer is that this is the most plausible interpretation of the relevant provision of the Convention. Why, though, was the Committee's mandate drawn so narrowly? Much of the explanation lies in the very different institutional environments of the ILO and the political organs of the United Nations.

Most ILO Conventions are truly technical instruments regulating working conditions (e.g., hours of work, minimum age, weekly rest and holidays with pay, seafarers' identity documents, radiation protection, fishermen's medical examinations, and exposure to benzene), so that most of the work of the Committee of Experts deals with relatively uncontroversial technical matters. In the course of this work, expectations of neutrality are established and reconfirmed. Therefore, when reports dealing with human rights issues are considered, they are examined in a relatively depoliticized context as only one part of the work of an essentially technical body of experts. In addition, there are literally hundreds of ILO Conventions and Recommendations, and the organization has existed for over sixty years. States thus are often closely tied into a web of interstate, transgovernmental, and transnational relationships centered on the organization. The Racial Discrimination Committee does not enjoy these advantages.

The one other human rights issue with nearly universal appeal is torture. The Convention against Torture and Other Cruel, Inhuman or Degrading Treatment or Punishment was opened for signature and ratification by General Assembly resolution 39/46 of December 10, 1984, and entered into force, remarkably quickly, in the summer of 1987. Part I is a strong elaboration of norms against torture, building on the 1975 Declaration on the Protection of All Persons from Being Subjected to Torture. . . . And the procedures outlined in Part II are potentially relatively strong.

A Committee Against Torture will be established to receive and review periodic reports from states' parties every four years. Much will depend on how the Committee interprets its powers to "make such general comments on the report as it may consider appropriate" (Article 19), but the potential exists for rather strong monitoring. The Convention also contains optional provisions that allow the Committee to receive communications analogous to those permitted under the 1503 procedure, interstate complaints, and individual communications. The effects of such provisions, of course, will depend on how many and which states exercise the option to authorize such monitoring and the emerging practice of the Committee. For now at least there is a relatively strong declaratory regime on torture that is likely to develop into a perhaps notable promotional regime within the next decade.[39]

Ongoing promotional activities should be noted as well. For example, in 1981 the United Nations established a Voluntary Fund for Torture Victims, which by 1986 had made sixty-nine grants totaling nearly $2 million to forty-six programs in twenty-five countries.[40] And the recent Amnesty International campaign on torture has been an important effort by an NGO to publicize a major problem. Amnesty has a much higher profile than most, but NGO efforts—especially promotional activities such as publicity, information gathering, and local monitoring—can be of considerable significance in the day-to-day operations of all the regimes we have considered.

The final major single-issue human rights regime is that for women's rights, which has traditionally been something of a step-child in the field of human rights. Although racial discrimination is considered in the U.N. Commission on Human Rights, and throughout the U.N.-centered regime, discussion of sexual discrimination as a human rights issues has been largely segregated in the U.N. Commission on the Status of Women.[41] In the last ten years, though, there has been a substantial normative and procedural evolution of the women's rights regime,[42] and women's rights issues are beginning to move closer to the mainstream of international human rights discussions.

The Commission on the Status of Women, a subsidiary body of ECOSOC established in 1947, has played a role in norm creation very similar to that of the Commission on Human Rights, having drafted both a variety of specialized treaties, such as the 1952 Convention on the Political Rights of Women, and the major general treaty in this area, the 1979 Convention of the Elimination of Discrimination Against Women. The Commission has also engaged in a variety of promotion and assistance activities. And in 1984 it began studying individual communications, although so far little if anything seems to have come out of this study. Although it is still too early to say how this procedure will operate, the lack of a mandate to monitor individual country practice is likely to restrict the process to very general promotional activities. The fact that the Commission meets only biennially further reduces its potential impact, although there does seem to be some sentiment to move to annual sessions, at least once the current financial crisis has been weathered.

In some ways more promising is the reporting procedure under the Convention on the Elimination of Discrimination Against Women, which entered into force September 3, 1981, and by early 1987 had 92 states parties. It appears that the Committee on the Elimination of Discrimination Against Women, which has meet annually since 1982, will function much as the Human Rights Committee (although without the optional complaint procedures).[43] Like other treaty-based promotion and monitoring bodies, though, the Committee may only consider conditions in countries that are parties to the Convention. Therefore, the weaker powers of the Commission are of continuing importance to the regime. As in the global regime, there is a political trade-off between the strength of a particular set of procedures and their coverage.

The recent strengthening of the women's rights regime can be traced primarily to the changing awareness of women's issues in the

1970s, a process of perceptual change that at the international level centered around the designation of 1975 as International Women's Year, and the associated World Conference in Mexico City. In conjunction with political and "consciousness raising" activities of national women's movements, a major international constituency for women's rights was created; a growing set of regime makers (including such countries as the United States and United Kingdom) and regime takers emerged, and potential regime breakers were deterred from active opposition by either domestic ideological stands or the emerging international normative consensus.

Table 9.1
Change in International Human Rights Regimes

	1945	*1955*
The International Human Rights Regime	None	Declaratory
norms	none	guidelines
procedures	none	weak promotion
Regional Human Rights Regimes		
The European Regime	None	Implementation
norms	none	guidelines/ regional norms
procedures	none	promotion/ monitoring
The Inter-American Regime	None	Declaratory
norms	none	guidelines
procedures	none	none
The African Regime	None	None
norms	none	none
procedures	none	none
Asia and Middle East	None	None

PROGRESS IN HUMAN RIGHTS

What, if anything, can we say in general about the nature, creation, and evolution of international human rights regimes? In particular, are there any patterns of progressive historical change across the individual regimes discussed earlier?

Table 9.1 presents a summary overview of each of the international human rights regime at ten-year intervals from 1945 to 1985.

The most striking pattern is the near complete absence of international human rights regimes in 1945 in contrast to the presence of

1965	1975	1985
Strong Declaratory strong guidelines promotion	Promotional standards with exemptions strong promotion	Strong Promotional standards with exemptions strong promotion/ weak monitoring
Implementation/ Enforcement regional norms monitoring/ regional decisions	Enforcement regional norms regional decisions	Enforcement regional norms regional decisions
Weak Promotional guidelines promotion	Promotional standards with exemptions monitoring	Strong Promotional/ Enforcement regional norms monitoring/ regional decisions
None none none None	None none none None	Declaratory standards with exemptions none None

several in all the later periods; that is, the postwar creation of human rights as an international issue area. We can also note the gradual strengthening of most international human rights regimes over the last 30 years. But even today promotional regimes are the rule, the only exceptions being the regional regimes in Europe and the Americas and workers' rights, all three of which are "special cases" (cultural homogeneity and good human rights records in Europe, U.S. hegemony in the Americas, and tripartism, institutional history, and the issue of workers' rights in the ILO).

Once states accept norms stronger than guidelines, declaratory regimes readily evolve into promotional regimes; if the regime's norms are important or appealing enough for states to make a commitment to, then it is hard to argue against promoting their further spread and implementation. But the move to implementation or enforcement involves a major qualitative jump that most states strongly resist—usually successfully.

Most of the growth in international human rights regimes, therefore, though important, has been "easy" growth that does not naturally lead to further growth. Regime evolution may be gradual and largely incremental within declaratory and promotional regimes (and perhaps within implementation and enforcement regimes as well). There seems to be, however, a profound discontinuity in the emergence of implementation and enforcement activities. Promotional regimes require a relatively low level of commitment. The move to an implementation or enforcement regime, however, requires a major qualitative increase in the commitment of states. This commitment is rarely forthcoming.

The one partial exception that cannot be explained by special environmental factors is the monitoring procedure of the Optional Protocol to the International Covenant on Civil and Political Rights. But barely three dozen countries are covered by this procedure. The weak monitoring of the 1503 procedure presents perhaps the greatest opportunity for making the jump to implementation or enforcement, given the relatively subtle nature of the required changes. Experience with the procedure to date, however, provides no evidence that such an evolution is on the horizon. The torture regime has some very promising procedures, but it is still too early to say how they will operate in practice, and they will apply only to some states with respect to a single right.

In the course of discussing individual regimes, we have already considered some of the central factors that explain this pattern of (limited) growth. To begin with, we can note the importance of awareness and power in the creation of international human rights regimes, which usually are created or mobilized in the case of human rights by conceptual changes in response to domestic political action or international moral shock. Awareness and power may galvanize widespread support for the creation or growth of a regime, while delegitimizing opposition; supporting power is mobilized, and opposing power is demobilized. Together these changes make moral interdependence increasingly difficult for states to resist.

In the case of racial and sexual discrimination, the conceptual transformations triggered by national movements for decolonization, civil rights, and women's rights created a broad, cross-national demand that helped to mobilize the power of potential regime makers and takers. The rise of national labor movements prior to World War I, and their loyal performance during the war, probably had an analogous impact on the creation of the ILO workers' rights regime. The shock of Hitler provoked a similar empowering conceptual reorientation in the global (U.N.), European, and Inter-American regimes. The barbarities of Amin, Bokassa, and Macias Nguema in the 1970s probably encouraged the formation of the African regime. Most recently, progress on a regime against torture seems to have been triggered by widespread revulsion at the increasing frequency and severity of torture, virtually across the globe. But conceptual changes leading to a wider perception of moral interdependence alone suggest only weak (declaratory or promotional) regimes.

On the basis of the preceding cases, we can also stress the importance of national commitment, cultural community, and hegemony, which largely explain the unusual strength of the European and Inter-American regimes.

National commitment is the single most important contributor to a strong regime; it is the source of the often mentioned "political will" that underlies most strong regimes. If a state has a good human rights record, then not only will a strong regime appear relatively unthreatening, but the additional support it provides for national efforts is likely to be welcomed. The European regime's unprecedented strength provides the most striking example of the power of national commitment.

The importance of cultural community is suggested by the fact that the only enforcement regimes are regional. In the absence of sociocultural and ideological consensus, strong procedures, as noted earlier, are likely to appear too subject to partisan use or abuse to be accepted even by states with good records and strong national commitments. Although the United States presents an exaggerated version of such fears—most strikingly in the U.S. Senate's resistance to, for example, the Genocide Convention and the International Covenant on Civil and Political Rights, with which U.S. law and practice already conform in almost all particulars—they are, in a less extreme form, common and widespread. As we saw earlier, there is a trade-off between regime strength and inclusiveness.

The importance of relatively close cultural community seems to be confirmed by the pattern of opposition to stronger international human rights regimes; opponents of stronger procedures in the global human rights regime and in single-issue regimes include major countries from the First, Second, and Third Worlds with good, mediocre, and poor national human rights records alike. The very scope of all but the regional regimes undercuts the relative homogeneity that seems almost a necessary condition for moving beyond a promotional regime.

Finally, we must stress the importance of dominant power and hegemony that, following Gramsci more than the "hegemonic stability" literature, should be kept analytically distinct.[44] Beyond mere dominant power, hegemonic leadership requires ideological hegemony, a crucial element in the acceptance of, or at least acquiescence in, the authority of the hegemon.

Consider the Americas. U.S. economic, military, and political power has been periodically exercised on behalf of the Inter-American Commission, despite the frequent use of U.S. power on behalf of repressive Latin American governments and against social democratic regimes committed to human rights improvements. But much more important has been the ideological dominance of the idea of human rights, as we can see, for example, by the failure of much more strenuous U.S. efforts to exercise hegemonic "power" over the definition of regional rules for nationalizing foreign-owned property, a topic of much greater concern to the United States. The effective exercise of hegemonic power usually requires not merely dominating material and organizational resources, but an ideological justification sufficiently powerful to win at least acquiescence from nonhegemonic powers.

Leaders require followers; regime makers need takers. The reasons for taking a regime may be largely accidental or external to the issue: for example, Stein argues that the Cobden–Chevalier Treaty, which ushered in the British-led "free trade" regime of the nineteenth century, was concluded principally because of French political concerns entirely unrelated to trade.[45] Sometimes, however, the reasons for taking a regime are connected with the ideological hegemony of the proposed project: Ruggie's account of "embedded liberalism" and the importance of the ideology of the welfare state in the creation of postwar economic regimes might be read in this way.[46]

The seemingly inescapable ideological appeal of human rights in the postwar world is an important element in the rise of international human rights regimes. This is not to deny the importance of power, in the sense that the term traditionally has had in the study of international politics, but rather to stress that true hegemony often is based on ideological "power" as well. The ideological hegemony of human rights concepts has been at least as important as dominant material power, and undeniably more important than the power of a single hegemon. Even weak regimes require the backing of major powers, but a hegemonic idea such as human rights may draw power to itself; power may coalesce around, rather than create, hegemonic ideas such as human rights and the regimes that emerge from them.[47]

For example, the overriding ideological appeal of the idea of workers' rights has been crucial to the success of the ILO. In Europe, the "hegemonic" power behind the very strong European regime came not from any single dominant state but from a coalition built around the ideological dominance of the idea of human rights. In Africa, the ideological hegemony of human rights is essential to explaining the creation of an African human rights regime in the face of the OAU's notorious respect for even the tiniest trappings of sovereignty. And the emergence of the universal, U.N.-centered human rights regime cannot be understood without taking account of this impulse, discussed earlier in terms of perceived moral interdependence.

But hegemonic power does ultimately require material power, and even hegemonic ideas have a limited ability to attract such power. Hegemonic ideas can be expected to draw acquiescence in relatively weak regimes, but beyond promotional activities (i.e., once significant sacrifices of sovereignty are required), something more is needed. In other words, hegemony too points to the pattern of limited growth observed earlier.

Therefore, the evolution toward strong promotional procedures can be expected to continue. But once that stage is reached we can expect states to resist further growth and efforts to cross over to implementation and enforcement activities. There seems to be no reason, in other words, to expect significant qualitative change in the short and medium run. The relatively easy phase of growth has largely passed, and the same factors that explain this growth suggest relative stagnation or only the slowest future growth. The preceding analysis provides little reason to expect that the 1995 column of table 9.1 will show many significant changes from 1985. In the spring of 1990 the only change has been a modest strengthening of the regime against torture.

Not only do the constraints on the further growth of international human rights regimes need to be emphasized, but we must also admit that from a maximalist perspective progress in international human rights has indeed been minimal. Taken as a whole, the procedures discussed earlier have at best led to minor reductions in injustice. The impact of international human rights norms is much more elusive, probably more important, but still minor relative to the magnitude of human rights violations in the world. As was stressed earlier, human rights are ultimately a matter of national practice. Therefore, "real" (maximalist) progress in human rights is only loosely connected to progress in *international* human rights. This has been underscored by the dramatic changes in Central and Eastern Europe, which although undertaken in response to new opportunities presented by a more tolerant Soviet Union, rested largely on internal political processes.

Having admitted all this, however, the reality of the (minimalist) progress traced earlier seems the appropriate place to close. In the case of human rights there has been notable progress in postwar international relations, and as a result our world is at least a bit less unjust than it otherwise would have been. And as this progress has come in an area where the material and security interests of states can rarely be mobilized to provide an incentive for progressive cooperation, even such incremental, minimalist progress is noteworthy.

ENDNOTES

I thank Beverly Crawford, Dave Forsythe, Glen Hayslett, Peter Katzenstein, Tim McKeown, Craig Murphy, and John Vincent for comments on earlier drafts. This paper is a revised and shortened version of "International Human Rights: A Regime Analysis," *International Organization* (Summer 1986), 40:599–642.

1. For an extended argument stressing the limits of both bilateral and multilateral international action on behalf of human rights, see Jack Donnelly, *Universal Human Rights in Theory and Practice* (Ithaca, N.Y.: Cornell University Press, 1989), ch. 13.
2. Compare Ernst B. Haas, "Why Collaborate? Issue-Linkage and International Regimes," *World Politics* (April 1980), 32:357–405, at p. 358 and Robert O. Keohane and Joseph S. Nye, *Power and Interdependence: World Politics in Transition* (Boston: Little, Brown, 1977), p. 19. For alternative interpretations, see Stephen D. Krasner, "Structural Causes and Regime Consequences: Regimes as Intervening Variables," *International Organization* (Spring 1982), 36:185–205. See also Oran R. Young, "International Regimes: Problems of Concept Formation," *World Politics* (April 1980), 32:331–356 and Oran R. Young, "International Regimes: Toward a New Theory of Institutions," *World Politics* (October 1986), Vol. 39. For a good discussion of theoretical weaknesses in the current regimes literature see Stephan Haggard and Beth A. Simmons, "Theories of International Regimes," *International Organization* (Summer 1987), 41:491–517.
3. Although I use these terms more or less interchangeably, Krasner "Structural Causes and Regime Consequences," p. 186, distinguishes *principles* from *norms*—"beliefs of fact, causation, and rectitude" from "standards of behavior defined in terms of rights and obligations"—and treats *rules* as "specific prescriptions or proscriptions for action," which he considers as more akin to procedures than *principles* or *norms*. Although Krasner puts this distinction to good use in his discussion of regime change, it seems rather arbitrary, especially in distinguishing *norms* from *rules* largely by the greater specificity of *rules*. In ordinary usage, *"rules"* has at least as wide a range as norms—consider not only often loose *"rules of the game"* but also *moral rules à la* Kant—but in the interest of clarity I shall, at least in part, defer to the authority of Krasner's precedent and use the relatively neutral term *norm* to refer to the full range of a regime's normative principles (in contrast to its decision-making procedures). For my purposes, however, Krasner's distinction between principles, norms, and rules is of no interest or importance.
4. Clearly, "higher" types of decision-making involve information ex-

change as well. In fact, each "higher" type generally encompasses the powers available in the "lower" types, although the relative strengths of policy coordination, promotion, and information exchange may vary with issue area. For a similar categorization of forms of international decision making see John Gerard Ruggie, "International Responses to Technology: Concepts and Trends," *International Organization* (Summer 1975), 29:557–584, at pp. 570–574.

5. Compare Ernst B. Haas, "Regime Decay: Conflict Management and International Organizations, 1945–1981," *International Organization* (Spring 1983), 37:189–256, at p. 193.

6. U.N. resolutions 217A (III) and 2200 (XXI). They are widely reprinted, for example, in Walter Laquer and Barry N. Rubin, eds., *The Human Rights Reader* (New York: New American Library, 1979); and Ian Brownlie, ed., *Basic Documents on Human Rights*, 2 Ed. (New York: Oxford University Press, 1981).

7. For one rather simple demonstration of the deeper philosophical basis of this coherence, in the form of an argument that international human rights norms arise form the principles of personal autonomy and equality, see Rhoda E. Howard and Jack Donnelly, "Human Rights, Human Dignity and Political Regimes," *American Political Science Review* (September 1986), 80:801–817. The only significant exceptions to the claim that all classes of human rights are interdependent are (1) arguments that are still occasionally made that economic and social rights are not truly human rights (Maurice Cranston has made something of a second career out of rehashing this argument for twenty years now; for his latest version, see "Are There Any Human Rights?" *Daedalus* (Fall 1983), 112:1–17; and (2) a tendency among many Third World commentators to undercut their professions of the interdependence of all human rights by claims of the priority of economic and social rights. I examine and criticize these two (almost mirror image) deviations in *The Concept of Human Rights* (London: Croom Helm, New York: St. Martin's, 1985), ch. 6, and "Recent Trends in UN Human Rights Activity: Description and Polemic," *International Organization* (Autumn 1981), 35:633–655. On the interdependence of all human rights, considered from a more practical point of view, see Rhoda Howard, "The 'Full-Belly' Thesis: Should Economic Rights Take Priority Over Civil and Political Rights?" *Human Rights Quarterly* (November 1983), Vol. 5, and, more briefly, Jack Donnelly, "Human Rights and Development: Complementary or Competing Concerns?" *World Politics* (January 1984), 36:255–283, at pp. 279–282. One reason that I prefer the seven-fold division of rights presented earlier—aside from its greater accuracy and specificity—is that the conventional division into civil and political rights and economic and social rights too easily lends itself to misguided or partisan arguments for priority of one set or the other.

8. The Universal Declaration may plausibly be argued to have attained the status of customary international law. Any legal force it has, however,

would thus rest on state practice (which is discussed later) and is entirely independent of the fact that it is a U.N. resolution. Furthermore, as I shall illustrate in considerable detail, this normative force has not been translated into strong procedures.

9. See Farrokh Jhabvala, "The Practice of the Covenant's Human Rights Committee, 1976–1982: Review of State Party Reports," *Human Rights Quarterly* (February 1984), 6:81–106; and Dana D. Fischer, "Reporting Under the Covenant on Civil and Political Rights: The First Five Years of the Human Rights Committee," *American Journal of International Law* (January 1982), 76:142–153.

10. For example, the report of Guinea claimed that "citizens of Guinea felt no need to invoke the Covenant because national legislation was at a more advanced stage" (A/39/40 para. 139). Bulgaria reported that "all the rights and freedoms stipulated in the Covenant were covered in the appropriate national laws" before ratification (A/34/40 para. 112). And the Mongolian representative, in response to a question by a member of the Committee, proudly claimed that there had never been a complaint about torture or cruel or inhuman treatment made in his country (A/35/40 para. 108).

11. Ton J. Zuijdwijk, *Petitioning the United Nations* (Aldershot, Hampshire: Gower, 1982), p. 361. The Covenant also contains optional provisions (Articles 41–42) for interstate complaints, but these have not been, and are not likely to be, used.

12. See the 1989 Annual Report of the Human Rights Committee, U.N. document A/44/40, para. 612–617. Decisions have also been taken with regard to communications concerning Canada, Colombia, Zaire, Finland, Italy, Madagascar, Mauritius, Sweden, Surinam, and Venezuela.

13. On the activities of the Working Group, see Kamleshwar Das, "United Nations Institutions and Procedures Founded on Conventions on Human Rights and Fundamental Freedoms," in Karel Vasak and Philip Alston, eds., *The International Dimensions of Human Rights* (Westport, CT: Greenwood Press, 1982), pp. 333–334, and Dana D. Fischer, "International Reporting Procedures," in Hurst Hannum, ed., *Guide to International Human Rights Practice* (Philadelphia: University of Pennsylvania Press, 1984) pp. 173–176. On the new committee, see Philip Alston, "Out of the Abyss: The Challenges Confronting the New United Nations Committee on Economic, Social and Cultural Rights," *Human Rights Quarterly* (August 1987), 9:332–381. For an excellent set of recommendations on the implementation of the Covenant, see "The Limburg Principles on the Implementation of the International Covenant on Economic, Social and Cultural Rights," U.N. document E/CN.4/1987/17, reprinted in *Human Rights Quarterly* (May 1987), 9:122–136.

14. For an excellent, thorough discussion of the procedure, see Howard Tolley, "The Concealed Crack in the Citadel: The United Nations Commission on Human Rights' Response to Confidential Communications," *Human Rights Quarterly* (November 1984), 6:420–462. Tolley's book *The*

United Nations Commission on Human Rights (Boulder, Colo.: Westview Press, 1987) is the standard source on that body. See also Dinah L. Shelton, "Individual Complaint Machinery Under the United Nations 1503 Procedure and the Optional Protocol to the International Covenant on Civil and Political Rights," in Hannum, ed., *Guide to International Human Rights Practice.*

15. See Antonio Cassese, "The Admissibility of Communications on Human Rights," *Revue des Droits de l'Homme/Human Rights Journal* (1972) 5:375–393; and Zuijdwijk, *Petitioning the United Nations,* pp. 30–39. The Secretariat initially screens the communications. Those that are deemed worthy of substantive review are examined by a working group of the Subcommission, then the whole Subcommission, and then a working group of the Commission, before they even reach the Commission. (See Tolley, "Concealed Crack," pp. 432–447.) For a petition to reach the Commission, therefore, it must present a very strong *prima facie* case, and referral to the Commission "is often interpreted as at least demonstrating that the allegations in a communication have some merit." Shelton, "Individual Complaint Machinery," p. 65.

16. See Jack Donnelly, "Human Rights at the UN, 1955–1985: The Question of Bias," *International Studies Quarterly* (September 1988), Vol. 31, Table 8, and U.N. documents E/1988/12 para. 386 and E/1989/20 para. 422.

17. For a brief review of the Equatorial Guinea case see Randall Fegley, "The UN Human Rights Commission: The Equatorial Guinea Case," *Human Rights Quarterly* (February 1981), 3:34–47. An on-site visit did take place, but not under the 1503 procedure and only because the offending Macias Nguema regime had been overthrown. (The Rapporteur's report is available as UN document E/CN.4/1371 of 12 February 1980.) On Malawi, Haiti, Albania, and Uruguay see Commission decisions 10(XXXVI), 1984/109 and 1985/107, resolution 1987/13, and documents E/1980/13, E/1984/14, E/1985/22, E/1987/18, and E/1988/12.

18. See David Weissbrodt, "The Three 'Theme' Special Rapporteurs of the UN Commission on Human Rights," *American Journal of International Law* (1986), 80:685–699 and Tolley, *U.N. Commission,* pp. 104–110.

19. Robert O. Keohane, "The Demand for International Regimes," *International Organization* (Spring 1982), 36:325–355.

20. Stephen D. Krasner, "United States Commercial and Monetary Policy: Unravelling the Paradox of External Strength and Internal Weakness," in Peter J. Katzenstein, ed., *Beyond Power and Plenty* (Madison: University of Wisconsin Press, 1978), p. 52.

21. See C. A. Macartney, *National States and National Minorities* (Oxford: Oxford University Press, 1934), Part II; Lucy P. Mair, *The Protection of Minorities* (London: Christophers, 1928); Inis L. Claude, Jr., *National Minorities: An International Problem* (Cambridge, Mass.: Harvard University Press, 1955); and Julius Stone, *International Guarantees of Minority Rights,* (Oxford: Oxford University Press, 1932).

22. Keohane, "The Demand for International Regimes," p. 334.

23. I shall restrict the term *European human rights regime* to the norms and procedures established in these documents. For a good, brief introduction to the European regime, see Rosalyn Higgins, "The European Convention on Human Rights," in Theodor Meron, ed., *Human Rights in International Law: Legal and Policy Issues* (Oxford: Clarendon Press, 1984), and Karel Vasak, "The Council of Europe," in Vasak and Alston, eds., *International Dimensions*.

24. European Commission on Human Rights, *Stocktaking on the European Convention on Human Rights, The First Thirty Years: 1954 until 1984*, Strasbourg, 1984, p. 312. These figures refer only to petitions registered by the Secretariat; a substantial number are routinely refused registration because they patently do not fall under the Convention. Details of cases can be found in European Commission on Human Rights, *Decisions and Reports*.

25. Computed from *Stocktaking on the European Convention on Human Rights*, Strasbourg 1982, Appendix D, Tables III, V and Vasak and Alston, eds., *International Dimensions*, Table 16.2. See also *Stocktaking* (1984), pp. 312, 320–324.

26. Parties to the European Social Charter agree to a comprehensive list of nineteen rights (Part I) and must agree to be legally bound by a set of these rights (specified in more detail in Part II) individually selected by each state according to the rules of the "double minimum floating nucleus," which requires acceptance of five of seven basic rights—the rights to work, to organize, to bargain collectively, to social security, to social and medical assistance, and the rights of the family to social, legal, and economic protection, and of migrant workers and their families to protection and assistance—plus others totaling ten (of nineteen) full articles or forty-five (of sixty-eight) numbered paragraphs. Such complexity "bears witness to the desire of the Member States of the Council of Europe to show their political unity in the social field while taking into account their economic disparities." (Vasak and Alston, eds., *International Dimension*, p. 538).

27. Ralph Beddard, *Human Rights and Europe: A Study of the Machinery of Human Rights Protection of the Council of Europe*, 2d ed. (London: Sweet and Maxwell, 1980), pp. 174, 175.

28. One particularly interesting indirect effect is the impact of regime norms on new and revised European constitutions. See Christian Starck, "Europe's Fundamental Rights in Their Newest Garb," *Human Rights Law Journal* (1982), 3:103–140.

29. For a thorough and up-to-date discussion of the procedures of the Inter-American regime, see Thomas Buergenthal and Robert E. Norris, *Human Rights: The Inter-American System* (Dobbs Ferry, N.Y.: Oceana, 1982–1984) and updates, 3 vols. More briefly, see Thomas Buergenthal, "The Inter-American System for the Protection of Human Rights," in Meron, ed., *Human Rights*.

30. The most subtle verson of the theory is in Robert O. Keohane, *After

Hegemony (Princeton, N.J.: Princeton University Press, 1984). For representative critiques see Duncan Snidal, "The Limits of Hegemonic Stability Theory," *International Organization* (Autumn 1985), 39:519–614; Arthur A. Stein, "The Hegemon's Dilemma: Great Britain, The United States, and the International Economic Order," *International Organization* (Spring 1984), 38:355–386; and Timothy J. McKeown, "Hegemonic Stability and Nineteenth Century Tariff Levels in Europe," *International Organization* (Winter 1983), 37:73–91.

31. This paragraph draws heavily on the chapter on the Organization of American States in David P. Forsythe, *International Human Rights: Patterns and Prospects* (Lexington, Mass.: Lexington Books, forthcoming). Forsythe has convinced me that my original account, which is very similar to that outlined in the preceding paragraph, seriously overstated the nature and importance of the U.S. role.

32. The question of why a hegemon would choose to exercise its power for such purposes is well beyond my scope here; my argument will be simply that should it choose to do so, the absence of issue-specific countervailing power may make that exercise especially efficacious.

33. See Richard Gittleman, "The Banjul Charter on Human and Peoples' Rights: A Legal Analysis," and Edward Kannyo, "The Banjul Charter on Human and Peoples' Rights: Genesis and Political Background," in Claude E. Welch, Jr., and Ronald I. Meltzer, *Human Rights and Development in Africa* (Albany: State University of New York Press, 1984), and Olusola Ojo and Amadu Sessay, "The O.A.U. and Human Rights: Prospects for the 1980s and Beyond," *Human Rights Quarterly* (February 1986), 8:89–103.

34. The Banjul Charter, however, at least does clearly distinguish between human rights (i.e., inalienable rights of individuals) and the rights of peoples, which helps to clarify the potential conflict between these quite different types of rights. In contrast, in U.N. circles peoples' rights usually are treated as merely a new generation of human rights. On such misguided tendencies, with special reference to the so-called right to development, see Jack Donnelly, "In Search of the Unicorn: The Jurisprudence and Politics of the Right to Development," *California Western International Law Journal* (Summer 1985), 15:473–509.

35. A. H. Robertson, *Human Rights in the World*, 2d Ed. *International Dimensions*, (New York: St. Martin's Press, 1982), p. 164.

36. B. Boutros-Gali, "The League of Arab States," in Vasak and Alston, eds., pp. 577–581.

37. For general discussions of human rights in the ILO, see Ernst B. Haas, *Human Rights and International Action* (Stanford, Calif.: Stanford University Press, 1970); Nicolas Valticos, "The International Labour Organization," in Vasak and Alston, eds., *International Dimensions;* Lee Swepson, "Human Rights Complaints Procedures of the International Labor Organization," in Hannum, ed., *Guide to International Human Rights Practice;* Ernst B. Haas, *Beyond the Nation State* (Stanford, Calif.: Stanford Univer-

sity Press, 1964), ch. 9, 11, and 12; and Francis Wolf, "Human Rights and the International Labor Organization," in Meron, ed., *Human Rights*.

38. There is an established procedure for interstate complaints, but it is very rarely used. Of more importance is the special complaint procedure for freedom of association cases arising under Conventions 87 and 98, which works through national and international trade union complaints, reviewed by the Governing Body's Standing Committee on Freedom of Association. See Haas, *Beyond the Nation State*, ch. 12.

39. For a further discussion of the torture regime see Jack Donnelly, "The Emerging International Regime Against Torture," *Netherlands International Law Review* (1986), 32(1):1–23.

40. See U.N. document A/41/706.

41. Even in U.N. human rights organs, subtle denigrations of women's rights still occur regularly; for example, the Secretariat's referral of family separation communications to the Commission on the Status of Women, as if they involved women's issues only (see E/1984/15 para. 69), and the Human Rights Committee's lumping of questions of family life and sexual discrimination in its review of issues considered under the Optional Protocol (see A/39/40).

42. The following discussion draws heavily on Margaret E. Galey, "International Enforcement of Women's Rights," *Human Rights Quarterly* (November 1984), 6:463–490, which is particularly good on procedures, and up to date through the spring of 1984.

43. The reporting record, however, is not very good. By April 1, 1987, twenty-eight of eighty-one reports were more than six months late. See U.N. document A/42/38 Annex II. The questioning, however, seems forceful, informed, and relatively unideological. See, for example, the back-to-back reviews of the reports of Poland and France in U.N. document A/42/38, pp. 44–62.

44. For Gramsci's analysis of hegemony see Quintin Hoare and Geoffrey Nowell Smith, eds., *Selections from the Prison Note books of Antonio Gramsci* (New York: International Publishers, 1971), pp. 52–65, 76–84, 102–106, 169–185, 210, 228–229 and *passim*. On hegemonic stability, see note 30 earlier. Keohane's *After Hegemony* does at least mention Gramsci, but this is clearly the exception in the hegemonic stability literature. And even Keohane gives relatively scant attention to the ideological or superstructural side of hegemony, which seems particularly important to explaining the maintenance of established regimes during the decline of a previously dominant state and the creation of regimes in the absence of dominant material power exercised by a single state. It may be that the very immateriality of the interdependence underlying human rights regimes is important to seeing this side of hegemony in an especially clear light.

45. Stein, "The Hegemon's Dilemma," pp. 364–366.

46. John Gerard Ruggie, "International Regimes, Transactions and Change:

Embedded Liberalism in the Postwar Economic Order," *International Organization* (Spring 1982), 36:379–415.

47. Just what makes an idea hegemonic is an interesting and important issue, but one that obviously lies well beyond our scope here. Gramsci suggests that hegemony arises from the conjunction of the development of material forces of production and largely accidental and local factors of history and human action. In the case of human rights, we can perhaps see an analogous process of technologically induced interdependence and changing standards of national political legitimacy being crystallized by the shock of Hitler.

10

ASSISTING THE PALESTINIAN REFUGEES: PROGRESS IN HUMAN RIGHTS?

Benjamin N. Schiff

The Middle East, perhaps the least stable region of the world today, provides a tough testing ground for measuring international progress. In the Middle East, friendly relations between states and national groups are limited and transient. The stakes of outside powers in the region are large. Technological cooperation in the region is minimal. Under such conditions, the kinds of cooperation and development that Ernst Haas analyzed in the more stable industrialized West are unlikely to take place, and progress is hard to detect.

In his efforts to find progress predicated upon cognitive change, scientific cooperation and technological development, Haas guided us to look at small indicators, rather than cosmic developments to find grounds for optimism. Organized behavior might be significant, even if fragmented; changed patterns of cognition might result in important cross-national alliances of bureaucrats, even if they were not primary political actors. International consensus over values might lead to political accommodations.[1] Pursuing Haas' logic, the Adler, Crawford, and Donnelly framework explains that demands for evidence of international progress should be modest.

In the Middle East, and particularly for the conflict that created the Palestinian refugee problem, maximalist progress can be imagined in the three categories outlined in the introduction: a peace settlement might eliminate violence between Palestinians and their neighbors; economic development might improve their welfare and transform the political conflict; new international agreements might enable exercise of the full panoply of human rights as defined in international covenants.

But the peace settlement, egalitarian economic development, and implementation of agreements on human rights remain in abeyance. These forms of maximalist progress are distant, if even possible. In the Middle East, as elsewhere at the international level, the minimalist criteria of enhancing human values at the individual level give us more reasonable measures of progress. Minimalist progress entails reduction of violence, misery, or injustice; it is progress when states act so that these values are promoted despite or in concert with pursuit of state interests.[2]

Since World War II, nations have increasingly agreed over human rights values. Jack Donnelly argues that the international commitment to rights, demonstrated by the establishment of organizations such as the United Nations High Commission for Refugees (UNHCR) and agreements such as the human rights covenants, indicate progress as compared to the prewar period.[3] One aspect of this new human rights commitment is an international concern for refugees.

Refugees are of particular interest in a system defined by state sovereignty because they are people who lack sovereign protection. Refugees are the responsibility of no state. How the international community deals with these orphans of the system provides some measure of the degree to which human values balance against sovereign interests.[4]

Estimates of the total world refugee population now range up to about 15 million.[5] Refugees are generally defined in international law as people outside of their country of residence who have lost the protection of their government and have reason to fear persecution should they return.[6] The three "durable solutions" to refugee problems enunciated by the U.N. and other international organizations are (1) return to the country of origin, (2) settlement in countries of first asylum, and (3) resettlement in third countries. Of these, the first is statistically the most prevalent, the third is most rare. Pending settlement, international organizations, frequently coordinated by the UNHCR, seek to support the refugees by providing emergency assistance and interceding with governments to protect refugee rights.

Estimates of the number of international refugees vary considerably, and thus calculations of change in the numbers must be sus-pect. In the immediate post–World War II period, estimates are that 35–40 million people were moving around Europe and to North America as a consequence of the war. This included people fleeing from the fighting as Germany collapsed, prisoners of war sent back to their countries of origin, survivors of the Holocaust seeking refuge in Europe and/or seeking to leave for Palestine and North America, and people displaced in Eastern Europe by fighting seeking not to return there or to the Soviet Union. As a percentage of global popu-lation of around 2.3 billion people, then, approximately 1.5 percent of the global population could be termed refugees, in a loose sense of the term.

During the period of 1947–1951, the International Refugee Orga-nization (IRO), using much stricter definitions of refugees and deal-ing with them after a significant number of people had been repa-triated and/or resettled by its predecessor, the United Nations Relief and Rehabilitation Administration (UNRRA), claimed to have reset-tled and repatriated approximately 1.1 million people, or (again using the 2.3 billion figure) 0.05 percent of the globe's population.

The United States Committee for Refugees (USCR) has counted refugees more broadly than U.N. organizations, including in its numbers reports from governments and voluntary organizations, in addition to UNHCR and U.N. Relief and Works Agency (UNRWA) figures. Their counting procedures have changed over the years, most notably in the 1980s, when they began explicitly dividing inter-nal from international subtotals. USCR's numbers have exceeded UNHCR estimates by a factor of up to ten times (partly because of the inclusion of "internal" refugees, but also because of inclusion of large numbers of people not officially recognized by UNHCR) and exceed official U.S. numbers by about one third. They provide a more consistent basis for observation than the other sources, how-ever. Table 10.1 compares the USCR's estimates of refugees world-wide to the global population.

The numbers do not show maximalist global progress in the refu-gee area. They look worse when "internal refugees" are taken into account. Four factors should be borne in mind. First, nonformal defi-nitions under which people are considered refugees, such as those employed by the Committee, have broadened as the postwar world has become increasingly sensitive to the kinds of persecution and privation that cause people to flee their homes. Second, improvement in international communications has probably resulted in better reporting of the numbers of refugees. So although the numbers are not decreasing, there is greater concern about them, which might be regarded as a form of progress. Third, as a percentage of total global population, it is not clear that there is a trend in the numbers of refugees. Things may not be getting better, but they also may not be getting worse. Fourth, since there are many more countries than previously, it should be easier for a refugee to become officially recognized—since one primary criterion is flight across an international boundary—than before. There are more "opportunities" to become a refugee and to be noticed internationally, but the numbers have not jumped accordingly.

USCR, official U.S., and UNHCR refugee tallies include Palestinian refugees. However, the Palestinian refugees are a special case. Their repatriation was called for under U.N. General Assembly Resolution 194 (1948). They were defined explicitly later in the course of relief efforts as people who lived in Mandatory Palestine for at least two years prior to the end of the Mandate, who departed their former residences due to the 1948 conflict and in so doing lost their means

TABLE 10.1
Estimated Numbers of Refugees

Year	1960	1970	1975	1980	1985	1990
Global pop.[a] (billions)	3.0	3.7	4.0	4.5	4.9	5.3 (est.)
Refugees[b] (millions)	15.0	18.2	14.2	16.0	10.1	14.4 (1988)
Additional internal refugees					12.2	20.4
Percent of refugees of global pop.	0.49	0.39	0.35	0.36	0.21	0.27
Percent including internal refs.					0.63	0.65

[a] *Source:* From U.S. Bureau of the Census, *Statistical Abstract of the United States: 1965, 1989.*
[b] *Source:* From U.S. Committee for Refugees, annual reports. "Internally displaced" populations were included in USCR's numbers until the early 1980s. Their estimates are not totaled, as they say they are not "comprehensive." They are included here to show the effect of adding in USCR's upper estimates of the "non-comprehensive" data on the percentages of total population. USCR's lower to upper estimates vary by approximately a factor of 2.

of livelihood. The direct descendants of the original refugees are also considered refugees.[7] There are currently more than 2.3 million registered Palestinian refugees out of a global population estimated to be more than 4.5 million.[8]

Having played a major role in the circumstances leading up to the Palestinians' departure from their homes in 1948, the U.N. General Assembly took responsibility for the refugees, defining the conditions under which their status would be considered resolved. Resolution 194 says that they remain refugees until they are permitted to return to their places of residence and/or are compensated for their material losses, and the choice between these alternatives should not be forced upon them. To end their refugee status, either Israel would have to permit the refugees to return and provide compensation for the losses of 1948 or the United Nations would have to replace Resolution 194 with some other set of conditions under which Palestinians' refugee status would be redefined.

In 1950 the United Nations created an organization to assist the refugees for the period prior to fulfillment of the conditions of Resolution 194. This chapter evaluates the progress in international relations indicated by treatment of the Palestinian refugees, examining the role and record of that organization: the United Nations Relief and Works Agency for Palestine Refugees in the Near East (UNRWA). It argues that UNRWA indicates minimalist progress in international relations at the systemic level and that this progress has helped Palestinians. In that this is a new kind of commitment, it represents a systemic-level "change for the better."[9] The positive effects of the organization, however, have not translated into progress toward peaceful settlement of the underlying conflict, because the organization is irrelevant to the conflict's dominant dynamics. The UNRWA case shows that progress is not uniform in effect: what's good for the individual, group, or nation, and indicative of systemic progress, may not be directly connected to maximalist progress in regional politics.

DISCONTINUITIES IN PROGRESS

UNRWA represents an international commitment to the economic and social rights of the Palestinian refugees. The organization is unique: no other intergovernmental international organization exists to protect the rights of a particular national group. International determination to take care of the Palestinians until the political problems that created their refugee status were resolved represented a new phenomenon in international politics.

Though unique, the commitment to the refugees is limited. UNRWA is funded by voluntary contributions. It is only an interim measure until the conditions of Resolution 194 are fulfilled. It is charged with carrying out operations to ameliorate the hardships of the refugees' existence through emergency assistance and, in its early years, sought to establish small-scale economic assistance programs and large-scale development projects that would enable the refugees to integrate into the countries of first asylum. These projects proved to be politically infeasible and economically unsound. UNRWA turned increasingly into an education, health, and welfare organization. Not party to any political negotiations, UNRWA became the primary agency for tending to refugees' material needs.

Since UNRWA is formally irrelevant to an Israeli–Palestinian political accommodation, it is inappropriate to demand that, in order to be considered progressive, it must play a direct role in a Middle East settlement. Since the lives of the people with whom it deals are primarily constrained and controlled by sovereign governments, these governments, not UNRWA, must bear the responsibility for progress or regress in reaching political solutions to the refugee problem. UNRWA is a service organization, not a political forum. If, in the end, its activities reinforce the status quo, encourage stasis or regression, then responsibility lies at the door of those who established and maintain it: members of the United Nations General Assembly (UNGA). Vital judgments can still be made. Has the Agency contributed positively to individual Palestinians? What are its effects on the Palestinian community? Particularly in the light of continuing violence in the Lebanon and the *intifada* (Palestinian uprising beginning in December, 1987) in the Israeli-occupied territories of the West Bank and Gaza Strip, does UNRWA contribute to or hinder maximalist progress in the region?

UNRWA's critics assert that the existence of the organization has reified, for Palestinians, their refugee status; that the refugee camps UNRWA serves have been breeding grounds for nationalist violence; that its employees have led nationalist uprisings; and that its facilities have been used for military purposes. Although critics see these effects negatively, for Palestinian nationalists, they are desirable. Critics on both sides believe that UNRWA had made the refugees more comfortable, thereby perpetuating their status by (1) reducing their discontent and therefore undermining incentives to assimilate and/or emigrate or (2) reducing their discontent and undermining revolutionary consciousness. UNRWA's defenders argue that refugee consciousness would exist with or without UNRWA; that nationalist agitation is bred by the political and material circumstances, not by an organization that attempts to improve the lives of the refugees; that UNRWA employment has little effect on revolutionary consciousness or activity but that educated and professional people do tend to be more politically active and aware than others; and that UNRWA's efforts to educate the refugees and improve their quality of life is pacific, in that it gives them skills and hope that reduce their frustration and violence. Both sets of assertions are important for deciding whether UNRWA is desirable or not, but the evaluation is always carried out from a particular nationalist group's or country's standpoint: the conclusions depend upon the political preferences of the observer.

UNRWA's role in the Middle East constitutes a progressive commitment at the international level that is also constructive at the individual level but that is ambiguous in its effects on regional peace and security. Measures taken to improve the lives of Palestinian refugees signify a new kind of international commitment, and they work: the refugees benefit from UNRWA. But since maximalist objectives do not command international agreement, it is impossible to separate the evaluation of UNRWA's impact from sovereign (or individual) preferences. There is no objective maximalist measure by which UNRWA can be evaluated.

UNRWA exists by virtue of U.N. resolutions, and it has inescapable operational responsibilities. It cannot terminate itself (unless it runs out of money). Because of its operational role, it can be evaluated for the degree to which it has successfully carried out these responsibilities. Although perhaps not a measure of systemic international progress, organizational learning and successful implementation of its mandate are more positive signs for progress than organizational failures would be. There is strong evidence for these kinds of institutional successes. The population for which UNRWA cares is increasingly healthy, the refugees have become a well-educated group of people within the Arab world, with much credit due to the Agency's schools, and the Agency's bureaucracy has matured. UNRWA has learned what kinds of objectives it can attain and has expanded programs in areas of success, avoiding fruitless activities. It has improved its ability to raise funds, thus increasing organizational stability.

Under the definitions used in this book, international commitments to human welfare represent systemic progress, and thus UNRWA is a piece of positive evidence. This does not imply that the precedent of its commitments or its institutional structure should or will be replicated. Its successes in providing services to the refugees, however, may make its programs useful models for other refugee and development organizations.

This chapter's following sections detail the founding and role of the Agency; how its programs evolved and are evaluated by supporters and critics; how its activities place it squarely in the midst of political conflicts on which it has little effect; how it has shifted slightly toward active protection of refugee rights; and finally, how this case illuminates the complex nature of progress in international relations.

ORIGINS AND MANDATE OF THE ORGANIZATION

UNRWA is an indicator of international responsibility for the Palestinians, a left-over from incomplete decolonization. Great Britain turned over control of its Palestine mandate to the United Nations, effective on May 15, 1948. The UNGA, heavily influenced by the United States, had voted on the previous October 29 to partition Palestine, establishing separate areas of Jewish and Arab control. The partition proceeded against the protests of the Arab population. As the British departed, Arab–Jewish fighting erupted, eventually pitting irregular Jewish forces against the armies of surrounding Arab states. The war resulted in the expansion of the Jewish-controlled area, the Arab areas were reduced to territories under the control of Jordan (on the West Bank of the Jordan River), and Egypt (in the Gaza Strip), leaving approximately 170,000 Arabs within the newly declared state of Israel.[10]

The war produced approximately 750,000 Palestinian refugees, many of whom were threatened by starvation, disease, and exposure to the elements.[11] Church groups operating in Palestine during the waning days of the British Mandate shifted from other tasks to providing aid to the victims of the war. The American Friends Service Committee (AFSC), International Committees of the Red Cross (ICRC), and the League of Red Cross Societies (LRCS) first by themselves, then under the aegis of a U.N. umbrella called United Nations Relief for Palestine Refugees (UNRPR) dealt with the dislocated Palestinians from 1948 through May, 1950.[12]

Unlike the post–World War II European refugees, who were eventually able either to return to their homes or to be admitted into countries of asylum and qualify for citizenship,[13] the Palestinian case remained fluid. The end of the fighting in 1948 did not result in territorial settlement and citizenship rights for the former refugees. Nor did the refugees relinquish their claims on their homeland. In reaction to the perceived injustice that had befallen the Palestinians and seeking to establish means for its resolution, U.N. General Assembly Resolution 194 of 1948 established the Palestine Conciliation Commission (PCC) to act as mediator between the Arabs and Israelis in settling the conflict, and in paragraph 11 resolved that

> the refugees wishing to return to their homes and live in peace with their neighbours should be permitted to do so at the earliest practicable date, and that compensation should be paid for the property of those choosing not to return and for loss of or damage to property which, under principles of international law or in equity, should be made good by the Governments or authorities responsible. . . .[14]

Given the increasing burden of providing services to the refugees and the lack of an apparent resolution to their status, the voluntary organizations sought to end their Palestine refugee operations. In response, the General Assembly declared in Resolution 302 of 1949 that it

> Recognizes that, without prejudice to the provisions of paragraph 11 of General Assembly resolution 194 (III) of 11 December 1948, continued assistance for the relief of the Palestine refugees is necessary to prevent conditions of starvation and distress among them and to further conditions of peace and stability, and that constructive measures should be undertaken at an early date with a view to the termination of international assistance for relief. . . .

and established UNRWA

(a) to carry out in collaboration with local governments the direct relief and works program as recommended by the Economic Survey Mission;
(b) To consult with the interested Near Eastern Government concerning measures to be taken by them preparatory to the time when international assistance for relief and works projects is no longer available. . . .[15]

The repatriation and compensation steps called for in Resolution 194 having not been accomplished, and the need for relief and services remaining, the UNGA has periodically renewed these resolutions and continued the "temporary" existence of UNRWA. In 1990, UNRWA was still temporary, although trailing a forty year history behind it. It was authorized to continue through 1993. UNRWA operates in five "fields": Lebanon, Syria, Jordan, and the Israeli occupied West Bank of the Jordan River and Gaza Strip. Of the approximately 2.3 million currently registered refugees (many of whom have become self-supporting and do not use UNRWA services) approximately 764,000 live in refugee camps. UNRWA runs school programs for about 351,000 Palestinian refugee children, runs health clinics visited approximately 5.2 million times in the reporting year 1988–1989, and provided food and other relief for approximately 142,000 individuals through the "special hardship" program. Additional emergency assistance has been extended to refugees in Lebanon, which at its height served about 177,500 individuals in 1982, and is currently flowing to the West Bank and Gaza Strip.[16]

UNRWA is the largest operational U.N. agency when measured by total number of employees (over 17,000). Only about 135 international civil servants work for the Agency. The rest of its employees are local Palestinians, the majority of whom are school teachers. For its first five years of operations UNRWA spent an annual average of about $30 million. Its current annual budget is approximately $210 million, supplemented during two years of the *intifada* (1988, 1989) on the West Bank and Gaza Strip by approximately $40 million.[17] All of its funds were raised from voluntary donations except for salaries of U.N. international staff that come from the U.N.'s assessed budget. Budgetary uncertainties have played a major role in the history of UNRWA's program development, in relations with donor and host countries, and even with its clients. The majority of U.N. members do not contribute to UNRWA, and it has been chiefly supported by the United States, Western European and Scandinavian countries, and periodic contributions from several of the Arab states.[18]

Since the refugees are not likely to return soon to Palestine or to be compensated for their losses, and given the small probability that the United Nations General Assembly will soon replace UNGA Resolution 194, it appears that UNRWA will continue to operate indefinitely. Although UNRWA has played little direct role in high-level political efforts to solve the Arab–Israeli conflict, it has had a tremendous impact on the Palestinians themselves, eased the burden of the refugees on the host countries, and reduced the Israelis' ability to deal arbitrarily with refugees in the Occupied Territories. At the operational level it confronts continual difficulties especially in locales where its clients and the sovereign authorities are in conflict.

INSTITUTIONAL PROGRESS AND PROBLEMS

Over its forty-year existence, UNRWA has changed its administrative routines and its programs. Fund raising and financial control have been improved. Programs have been modified to improve efficiency and effectiveness, steer away from futile efforts, and improve the living conditions and economic potential of the refugees.

Fund Raising

Fund raising has been a persistent problem for UNRWA. Its operations have no regular funding from any assessed U.N. budget: it subsists on voluntary contributions.[19] East bloc and Arab nations have as a matter of course not contributed, contending that since the problem was created by the West (when it supported the partition of Palestine), dealing with its consequences is the West's responsibility.

Major donor states—primarily the United States, European Economic Community, and Scandinavian countries—support UNRWA as part of their efforts to stabilize the region regardless of progress (or lack thereof) toward peace attained by diplomacy or war. Donor countries contribute to UNRWA less because of commitments to transcendant economic and social values than because of convictions that terminating UNRWA services would create a political explosion. Meanwhile, UNRWA's activities accord with the belief that increasing individuals' economic stakes in the status quo reduce their violent revolutionary tendencies.

Fund-raising duties fell to the Commissioners-General as soon as

U.N. start-up funds were expended. Because the Agency has no Board of Governors or other similarly committed set of states established by statute to depend upon, it cannot assume that any support will be forthcoming if it fails to raise its own funds.

Agency funding has been unstable and limited when compared to the predictable and large demands placed upon the organization. Because of UNRWA's autonomy and voluntary budget structure, its fund-raising techniques and budgetary methods developed idiosyncratically within the U.N. family.[20]

Until the mid-1980s, UNRWA's primary strategy was to exaggerate budgetary needs by including all desirable construction and other expansionary programs, and then to decry the likelihood of severe shortfalls. When donors failed to come up with the requested funds, UNRWA cut expenditures.

From the standpoint of some critics in donor countries, UNRWA's ability to survive despite the cuts showed that the original requests were inflated. But by the mid-1970s, the cuts went beyond program expansion and frills. At the end of the decade, UNRWA was in a real financial crisis. Increased numbers of refugees, a downturn in the regional economy, and deterioration of old buildings and of the water infrastructure resulted in rapidly rising operational costs. Since the Agency is prohibited from taking loans, selling bonds, or running deficits, the only alternatives were to curtail services and seek additional contributions.

Finally facing the possibility that large numbers of employees would have to be fired—and because of its labor intensity, firing people is the only way to save significant amounts—in 1982 the Agency went so far as to print termination notices for teachers in the Jordanian UNRWA schools. But emergency contributions temporarily staved off the collapse. At the same time, UNRWA began to overhaul its control and fund-raising operations.

A new Comptroller began to modernize the Agency's budgeting process in 1984. The Commissioner-General established a Division of External Relations to develop ongoing contacts with donor countries and to reduce the burdens falling directly on him for soliciting contributions.

In May 1986, a first informal donors meeting was held at the Vienna Headquarters, and a new rationalized budget proposal was presented, long-term plans enunciated,[21] and inflated projections abandoned. Agency officials said they received a positive response to their presentation. U.S. officials said that the new financial control and budgeting system would not only improve Agency efficiency but would help them to convince reluctant members of Congress that allocations to UNRWA are being well spent. The exercize was repeated in summer, 1987.[22] These informal meetings coincidently established a basis on which to call another meeting in the spring of 1988 for UNRWA to consult with the donor states about its response to the *intifada* and the U.N. Secretary-General's report on the situation in the Occupied Territories. (These are addressed later in a discussion of UNRWA's response to the *intifada*.)

It is odd that an organization dependent upon voluntary contributions would take so long to get its financial house in order. However, the delay may be explained by UNRWA's unique status within the U.N. system. The combination of a voluntary budget, very small administrative structure, focus on operations, and isolation from the regular accounting and administrative procedures of the rest of the United Nations allowed it to evolve without the benefit of contacts with the modernizing U.N. system. Commissioners-General felt that only by representing the Agency at the highest levels could money be raised from governments: there was little scope seen for professional staff fund raisers, especially given the imperative to devote the most personnel possible to operational duties.[23] In response to the financial crisis of the early 1980s, UNRWA has faced its financial problems, developing budgeting and fund-raising systems that appear better able to provide the contact and arguments necessary to engender government donations.

Programs

When UNRWA was established, it took over ongoing projects initiated by the voluntary organizations. It inherited health, relief, and volunteer educational programs and was called upon by the General Assembly to implement large-scale "works" projects outlined in the report of the United Nations Economic Survey Mission for the Middle East.[24]

Its accomplishments over the next four decades constitute organizational success. The Agency is getting better at what it does, and the refugees are better fed, better housed, healthier, and better educated than they would otherwise have been. UNRWA has also helped insulate parts of refugee life from direct political control by the host and occupation governments.

Works. The UNRWA "works projects" were intended to create temporary employment and eventually to result in continuing demand for agricultural labor, enabling refugees to settle permanently in the areas to which they had fled during the war. The Economic Survey Mission called for small-scale works projects during an interim period prior to larger undertakings for cooperative development of water resources in the Jordan Valley. The subsequent plans of 1953–1956 that emerged from U.N. and U.S. consulting studies echoed the logic of the U.S. Tennessee Valley Authority.[25] These plans, however, never reached fruition.

Implementation of the Economic Survey Mission's proposals was supposed to solve the refugee problem by affecting individual refugees' economic calculi: it would not address the national or civil rights of the Palestinians. The projects were intended to enable the refugees to "reintegrate"[26] into stable communities, superseding desires for a return to Palestine. As an economic solution to the problem, it was attractive to the United States because it would avoid the political problems involved in dealing with Palestinian demands for repatriation and compensation.

Since repatriation and compensation were highly unlikely, the proposals were in one sense more realistic than UNGA Resolution 194. But since they required high-level cooperation between Israel, Syria, and Jordan, needed massive funding by donor states, and ignored the importance of repatriation as a political symbol for the refugees and for Arab governments, they were extremely optimistic.

By June 1955, only about $19 million of a projected $200 million "reintegration fund" had been spent, mostly on small projects. Awaiting agreement on a consolidated Jordan Valley irrigation plan that U.S. negotiators were pursuing with Syria, Jordan, and Israel, UNRWA large-scale programs were dead in the water. By 1957 it was clear that the necessary political agreements would not be forthcoming at all. By June 1957, small-scale projects costing approximately $38 million had resulted in the permanent departure from the relief rolls of about 24,000 people, and the temporary departure of approximately 140,000, but it was a very expensive business.[27]

UNRWA had difficulties in negotiating agreements with the countries in which the refugees were residing even for the small-scale works projects. The host governments feared that UNRWA projects would threaten their sovereignty and that efforts conducive to permanent settlement of the refugees would prejudice their claim to repatriation and compensation. As negotiations bogged down, and the projected departure of refugees from the relief rolls that would follow from the employment-creating projects failed to occur, UNRWA had to keep raising its budgetary allocations for relief. UNRWA scaled down its objectives. The "works" part of the Agency atrophied, and by 1960 the focus had fully shifted to economic empowerment of individual Palestinians through education.

The works projects proposals and small-scale development efforts pursued a logic that was common in the 1950s, that economic improvement would modify political commitments. There was little evidence that supported this optimism in the 1950s and 1960s, when theorists (particularly in the United States) subscribed to these ideas.[28] The Palestinian example, where the political barriers to political agreement were particularly high, has demonstrated that there may be no connection between economic improvement and political quiescence. Many Palestinian refugees' living standards improved in the period from 1948 to the present, but their political discontent and agitation have increased.

Education. Expanding the ongoing education program was much less difficult than trying to gain agreement on grandiose multinational development plans. Educational development was relatively apolitical, could be expanded incrementally, and required no outside international agreements to move forward. UNRWA wound up dealing with Palestinians as individuals—socially and economically—not as a collective. Education was supposed to help Palestinians become employable without influencing their choices about where to pursue individual or collective "reintegration."[29]

Contemporary accounts of life in refugee camps immediately following the 1948 conflict note that classes for children had been set up in tents by volunteer teachers. When the AFSC terminated its services in Gaza in 1950, internal documents show that serious consideration had been given to development of a school system supported by voluntary agencies.[30] When UNRWA took over, it rationalized and institutionalized ongoing activities.

The UNRWA education program was directed both at students and at developing teachers. Many of the volunteer teachers, having begun their activities in the tents of 1948, were not professionally trained or qualified. Rather than replace these dedicated individuals and search for more educated teachers, at UNRWA's request UNESCO developed an extensive in-service training program to bring them up to standard. In addition, UNRWA established teacher training colleges to provide postsecondary skills that could lead to employment within UNRWA and in the Middle East generally.[31]

By the early 1960s, UNRWA began vigorous development of vocational schools to train refugees for practical employment. The school system replaced the works projects as UNRWA's main effort to assist the refugees. Students from the poorest families were given preferential access to the vocational and teacher training schools, under the assumption that they would become breadwinners for their extended families.

By the mid-1960s, and especially as the oil boom led to rapid development in the Gulf states and in Jordan, an UNRWA graduation certificate became practically a guarantee of employment for vocational and teaching jobs. The individually oriented programs were successful. Remissions to refugee families from members employed in the Gulf became a mainstay of the Palestinian economy. At least until the early 1980s, UNRWA schools were considered superior to state-run schools in the host countries. In all of the fields Palestinian students' performance on standardized *(Tawjihi)* exams administered by the governments equaled or (more frequently) exceeded those of their government school peers. In Jordan the UNRWA–UNESCO in-service teacher training and vocational systems became models for the development of government programs.[32]

The educational system currently absorbs approximately 65 percent of UNRWA's budget. It is the largest and least controversial of the Agency's programs. Although there is general agreement by sovereign authorities, UNRWA officials, and the refugees that the schools have performed well, conflicts still emerge over the education operations. Teachers' political role, the quality and censorship of textbooks, political agitation by students, and one instance in which an UNRWA facility was apparently used for PLO military training have created tensions between UNRWA and governmental authorities.

Avi Plascov claimed in his book about the refugees in pre-1967 Jordan that UNRWA teachers were central to the development of the Palestinian nationalist movement.[33] Plascov's work is based largely on direct interview data, and there is no reason to doubt his claim. School teachers in most of the Third World play a central role in community organization and politics, and the Palestinian community is no exception. Plascov does not claim that the teachers used classroom time for political purposes. One of the major roles of the international civil servants in the fields is to maintain the standards of professionalism and U.N. political neutrality of the Agency's employees in execution of their official duties. The latitude of teachers to address political issues in class and to become politically visible is largely dependent upon the strictness of the Field Education Officer and Field Director. Some directors have been lax, and others quite firm in their control of teachers' activities. This issue is currently most serious in the occupied territories, where critics charge that UNRWA education breeds anti-Israeli feelings. They claim that UNRWA teachers use their positions to preach against peace with Israel, that educational materials are anti-Jewish and anti-Israeli, and that the schools are centers for hostile propaganda and political organizing.

The Jordanian curriculum is used in the West Bank, the Egyptian curriculum in the Gaza Strip. Thus, the political slant of the curricula is shaped by these governments. UNRWA education officials (local supervisors and the international officials) try to limit teachers who overstep the accepted boundaries of what is permissable in class. This does not solve the problems of what the teachers do outside of class and of the content of government-approved textbooks.

The actions of teachers outside of class are, like all other security matters, out of UNRWA's hands. UNRWA teachers and all local UNRWA employees are subject to the legal systems of the governmental authorities where they work, and as such are subject to arrest and detention, as are any other residents. When UNRWA employees are arrested or detained, the Agency asks the authorities whether detention or arrest was due to actions carried out in service to the Agency (in which case a protest is lodged) and investigates whether the person was inappropriately apprehended in UNRWA facilities or during working hours. Israeli officials routinely ignore UNRWA's inquiries and simply explain their actions as matters of "security". UNRWA usually does not gain access to arrested or detained employees or other refugees, having no way to force the authorities to comply with its demands.[34]

Class materials are a more complicated matter. Since the program is carried out in pursuit of a U.N. General Assembly mandate, UNRWA and UNESCO (which provides the education experts who established and now supervise the program) consider the program bound by U.N. standards. They consider racist textbooks or ones that endorse violence to be contrary to the spirit of the United Nations. Especially because the Israelis have complained strenuously about some of the texts used in the Jordanian and Egyptian curricula, because of their portrayal of Israel and Jews, a system of textbook clearance has been set up in which UNESCO reviews published teaching materials.

The UNESCO clearance system has worked relatively well, reducing friction between UNRWA and Israeli education officials. However, problems remain, because many texts are withheld but the students are still held responsible for passing their *Tawjihi* exams based on the standard curricula.

The Gaza case is instructive. Textbooks proposed for UNRWA school use come from Cairo. One copy goes to the Israeli Education Ministry in Jerusalem. Another copy goes to UNESCO via UNRWA headquarters. Israeli and UNESCO officials evaluate the texts. They each reject some books (sometimes, but not always, the same ones). Some books that enter the UNESCO process simply do not reemerge; in 1986, ten of forty-six books under consideration at UNESCO appeared not to have been rejected, but had been there for well over a year. Israeli officials also reject some texts. Books must be approved by both parties in order to be used in the territories' UNRWA schools.

Israel has at times produced censored versions of texts and distributed them to non-UNRWA schools. Thus, Palestinian students who attend the government schools have better access to (censored) standard texts than do the UNRWA students. UNESCO prohibits the use of such books because their reproduction (and censoring without permission from the authors) constitutes a violation of international copyright standards. According to the UNRWA Gaza Field Education Officer, in 1986 approximately eighty-five titles were used at the elementary and preparatory (junior high school) level by Cairo, of which only thirty-nine could be used in Gaza.[35]

UNRWA's critics also claim that its facilities, including schools, have been used to support Palestine Liberation Organization (PLO) military activities. They cite the 1982 Israeli army discovery that the Siblin Vocational Training Center in southern Lebanon had been used for PLO military training as the most egregious example of UNRWA's politicization. UNRWA officials found upon investigation that the PLO, in control of the Siblin area, had forced or convinced school officials to require the vocational students to take military training after school hours in order to qualify for their graduation diplomas. UNRWA officials attribute the breakdown of its standards to the remote location of the Center, weak control from field headquarters in Beirut, and the essential sovereignty of the PLO in the area.[36]

To mitigate the seriousness of the charges about Siblin, UNRWA officials point out that the students reportedly fled from the fighting during the Israeli invasion instead of participating and that they had apparently undergone the military training under duress. Although very embarrassing to the Agency, the lapse was not militarily significant. Because of the difficulties of controlling Siblin, it has not consistently been in operation since 1982.

During the *intifada* in the West Bank and Gaza Strip, schools, including UNRWA's, were shut down by the Israelis. UNRWA schools were not singled out for closure, demonstrating that from the Israeli security perspective the problems of UNRWA schools are similar to those of government and private institutions.

The principle of UNRWA education is uncontroversial. Were UNRWA to depart, the local governments would be faced with absorbing the financial and administrative costs of educating the refugees that now attend UNRWA's large school system. From UNRWA's standpoint the main problem it faces, aside from school closures and book censorship in the occupied territories, is that the refugee student population is growing faster than UNRWA's financial ability to construct new classroom space. Old facilities, rented (small) classrooms and a lack of classroom space necessitate double- and triple-shifting and hiring more teachers than would be necessary if classroom sizes were larger. (See Table 10.2.) To alleviate these problems, UNRWA seeks special contributions for capital construction of additional school space, but these funds have been very hard to procure.

Health. Palestinian refugee health has never been as bad as might have been expected, given the stringency of conditions in the early years following 1948. Despite the harsh winter of 1948–1949, poor shelters, polluted water, and nutritional deficiencies, reports from the voluntary agencies noted with surprise the lack of widespread disease among the refugees.[37] They massively used any available health facilities and continued these patterns of usage when UNRWA came into existence. UNRWA's health program, developed

Table 10.2
Population, Rations, School Students

Year	Registered Refugee Population	Number Eligible for Rations	Number Receiving Rations	% Receiving Rations of Population	Students in Schools (elem. & prep.)
1951	904,122	879,667	877,520	97	42,122
1956	996,338	922,279	847,253	85	114,300
1961	1,151,024	1,039,996	870,266	76	140,508
1966	1,317,749	1,145,147	861,122	65	191,446
1971	1,468,161	1,183,169	834,878	57	256,542
1976	1,668,205	1,312,787	654,142	39	309,295
1981	1,884,896	1,466,619	825,726	44	338,386
1986	2,145,794	108,726	102,318	5	348,639
1987	2,201,123	117,697	111,090	6	349,388
1988	2,268,595	135,375	127,439	6	350,000
1989	2,334,637	141,843	133,385	6	351,100

Source: Ration statistics: Annual Reports of the C-G to the General Assembly for the years shown. A/1905, A/3686, A/4861, A/6313, A/8413, A/31/13, A/36/13, A/41/13, A/42/13. School enrollments: "UNRWA Past Present and Future" . . . cited in note 7.
Note: The difference between the number of refugees eligible for rations and the number that received them (1951–1981) is due to a ceiling placed on ration allocations. Because of limited funding, the ceiling meant that for additional refugees to receive rations, others had to be taken off the ration rolls. Since the ceilings were set and held constant while the population increased, the percentage of refugees receiving rations steadily declined. In addition, in years when contributions fell short, the rations themselves became smaller. After 1981, the Agency focused on the "special hardship" cases and eliminated the general ration program.

under World Health Organization (WHO) officials, focused on fundamental measures, such as innoculation, clean water supplies, and basic nutrition.

UNRWA's health programs must be considered a success. Infant mortality has declined rapidly among the refugee population, keeping pace with or exceeding the rate of improvement of analogous populations in the host countries. UNRWA, with WHO, pioneered the oral rehydration method of dealing with infant gastric disorders, which was crucial in reducing mortality rates. While sophisticated and expensive curative health measures are still beyond UNRWA capabilities, the clinic and preventive programs have produced a relatively healthy population. (See Figure 10.1.)

The Palestinian population is not only fairly healthy, but also rapidly expanding, threatening the health and relief programs' successes and putting pressure on limited available infrastructure. UNRWA has had limited success in family planning, despite availability of WHO experts and services. According to officials, the refugees are disinterested in limiting the size of their families. This is partly due to traditional values associated with fertility and large numbers of children, but birth control is also perceived to be politically counterproductive. The refugees believe that the larger the Palestinian population, the harder it will be to ignore.[38]

Relief. UNRWA took over the emergency feeding operations begun by the voluntary organizations, and these operations evolved into a rations program that was terminated only in the early 1980s. UNRWA officials attribute the long delay in conversion of the program to a "needs-based" system to the symbolic importance of the program to the refugees. Responding to fighting in Lebanon and the *intifada*, UNRWA has recently broadened distribution through the relief program, and in the three fields it has termporarily stopped the welfare investigations necessary to update UNRWA special hardship case files.

When UNRWA was established in 1950, approximately eighteen months of relief experience had demonstrated to the voluntary organizations that the refugees required considerable resources for subsistence. It already looked like a long-term problem. The AFSC was particularly adamant in efforts to terminate its effort, citing the im-

FIGURE 10.1

Incidence Trends of Selected Communicable Diseases (Rate Per 10,000 Eligible Population)

POLIOMYELITIS

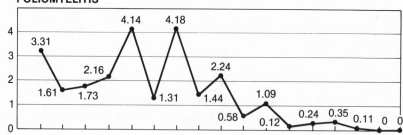

MEASLES

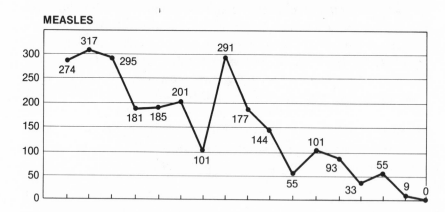

TUBERCULOSIS

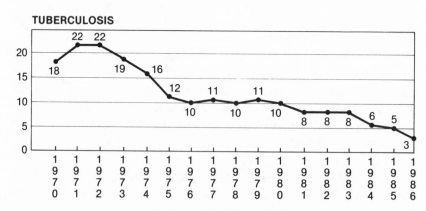

Source: Report of the Commissioner-General of UNRWA to the General Assembly, 1986–1987 (A/42/13), 33.

possibility of remaining apolitical, and the large financial requirements of the task.[39]

UNRWA's relief program took on the burdens of the voluntary
agencies' efforts. Shelter and food assistance were crucial in helping
the refugees to survive in the early years, and until tented refugee
camps were replaced with more permanent structures, UNRWA spent
most of its efforts providing basic necessities of life to the refugees.
By the early 1960s, UNRWA camps no longer contained significant
numbers of tents, and local employment and remissions led to improvements in refugee welfare.[40]

Immediately upon taking over from the PVOs and UNRPR,
UNRWA initiated a program of "refugee roll rectification." Because
of multiple registrations, unrecorded deaths, and departures, the
number of refugees on UNRWA relief rolls was considered to be
substantially in excess of the real number of refugees needing aid.
UNRWA and national officials sought to eliminate deceased persons
and multiple registrations, but this was obstructed by the Palestinians. These problems are typical of refugee relief operations,[41] but,
especially in the charged political context of the Middle East, contribute to a negative view of the Palestinians and of UNRWA.[42] As the
relief program has shrunk, the impact of these problems has declined.

Relief roll rectification was made difficult not only by the refugees,
but also by host country governments that resisted Agency census
taking. Especially in Jordan, the government avoided officially determining how many Palestinians there were, apparently because of a
fear that such information would undermine the legitimacy of the
Hashemite monarchy. In the Lebanon of the 1970s, census taking
operations were politically explosive for the population at large, as
well as for the refugees. In all fields, the problems of roll rectification
were partly solved by establishing ceilings on the number of relief
recipients. To register new family members for assistance, other people had to be dropped from the rolls, creating an incentive to report
deaths and departures. However, the expanding refugee population
meant that these ceilings did not necessarily correspond to the real
number of refugees needing assistance.

Because of the improving welfare of the refugees and climbing
costs of services to them, in the mid-1960s UNRWA officials began to
consider reorienting the relief program away from general rations to

all registered refugees, toward some means-tested program of limited welfare assistance.[43] This was politically very sensitive. UNRWA ration cards were considered by the refugees to be proof of their refugee status, and relief supplies had become a normal, although relatively small, part of their incomes. Until 1982, UNRWA continued general ration distributions, although at ever diminishing levels. (See Table 10.2.)

In 1982 the general ration program was abandoned. The justification for initial suspension of the program was that funds were necessary for emergency relief to the refugees embroiled in the Lebanese war. Instead of restarting general rations when the Lebanese crisis abated, UNRWA replaced it with its "special hardship case" program, under which only the demonstrably neediest refugees would receive rations and shelter renovation assistance. UNRWA officials consider the shift to be a major victory in the rationalization of Agency programs.

The change led to considerable unrest among the refugees, particularly in the occupied territories. From their standpoint, an entitlement was being taken away from them, and the criteria for "special hardship" assistance were much too restrictive. Under the new rules, only families without a male out of school and between the ages of 18 and 60 can be eligible for aid, if the total income for the family is less than one half of the starting salary of the lowest-grade UNRWA employee (regardless of the size of the family). If there is a male family member out of school and of the appropriate age, the family is ineligible for aid, regardless of his actual employment status and the location of his residence, unless he is a welfare case in his own right because of disability, is in prison for more than two months, or is serving in compulsory military service.[44]

From the standpoint of UNRWA administrators, a corrupt and unnecessary program was replaced with a targeted system that, although flawed by the difficulties of implementation and the need for very restrictive criteria, made the best use of severely limited funds. Because of the deteriorating regional employment and economic situation at present, pressures to alter the criteria and expand the program are growing.

UNRWA as a Misguided Welfare Bureaucracy

The Agency's critics charge that it has become a typical welfare bureaucracy: a make-work organization that mostly helps refugees by employing them, hires them through cronyism and other forms of favoritism, and consequently delivers services inefficiently and ineffectively. Even worse, critics charge that the Agency carries out programs counterproductive to political progress in the region.

UNRWA's defenders argue that the Agency's per-pupil and per-patient costs for education and medical attention are extremely low by international standards and that UNRWA is performing its services very cheaply. Good scores on the *Tawjihi* exams and falling disease and mortality rates imply that UNRWA is effective, even if its efficiency can be questioned. Its lack of funding for maintenance and construction and its consequently poor facilities serving a large number of clients indicate that it is in fact stretching its finances quite far. UNRWA is a labor-intensive organization, because health and education are labor-intensive activities. The majority of its employees are teachers, and average class sizes are large. The inefficiency claim is very unlikely.

Bias in hiring may be a more important criticism. UNRWA's formal system for filling jobs officially hires people exclusively on the grounds of merit, with preference given to refugees. International civil servants supervise the local employees and sit on hiring boards. They are supposedly unaffected by nepotism or favors and ascribe to "Western" and "objective" management principles, limiting non-merit ("Eastern," subjectively based, family, clan, friendship, or financially effected) hiring. Still, critics charge that hiring is affected by cronyism, favoritism, bribery, and nepotism. It is very difficult either to substantiate these claims or fully to reject them. Even international UNRWA officials agree that in some cases, job selections seem to have been made on less than totally objective bases. But the distinction between the two cultural tendencies is probably overdrawn, and UNRWA's personnel difficulties are much the same as those that face most large organizations.

Over its forty years, UNRWA effectively delivered the emergency assistance, health, and education services that are its main missions. The assistance activities once so very important to most of the refugees are now important to only the poorest, "special hardship cases" and to people temporarily affected by the dislocations of the *intifada* (and in Lebanon). Low limits on the number of people qualifying for the special hardship program are largely due to limited available funds for UNRWA (although this has at least temporarily changed due to the *intifada*, about which more later). When emergencies have arisen, however, UNRWA's delivery of assistance has been exemplary.

Much more serious than charges of inefficiency and ineffectiveness are charges that the assistance delivered by the Agency makes the refugees more comfortable with their status; paradoxically, both Palestinian and Israeli critics view the refugees' "comfort" as deleterious to their respective causes.

As with most welfare and assistance agencies, the harshest charge against UNRWA is that it creates a dependent population. From some Israeli critics' standpoints, UNRWA perpetuates the Palestinians' refugee consciousness, preventing positive change. Other Israeli critics believe that UNRWA lifts a significant part of the occupation's financial burden from the government's shoulders. The first kind of critic believes that UNRWA's departure would force the Palestinians to face reality, emigrate or be quiet; the second kind of critic believes that UNRWA's departure would force the Israelis to face more of the true costs of the occupation, and thus perhaps to terminate it.

Some of UNRWA's Palestinian critics charge that the Agency has outlived its utility. Lacking the Agency, Palestinian community organization, political mobilization, and autonomy would develop more rapidly. UNRWA breeds complacency, perpetuating refugee consciousness and undermining efforts to create political mobilization. If UNRWA disappeared, there would be short-run privations, but community action would grow and spread as a result. In 1986 UNRWA began to respond to charges that it was contributing to refugee dependence by beginning to develop refugee self-support activities in cooperation with private voluntary organizations, especially in the Gaza Strip. The uprising has created new impetus for further development of these activities and enabled UNRWA to raise funds for other long-standing program needs in the territories.

UNRWA has shaped its programs to meet the needs of the refugees, within the boundaries of its General Assembly mandate. Changes in its programs have been caused by political limitations in the region

—such as the inability of Jordan, Syria, and Israel to work together on a Jordan Valley river plan. Aside from political realities, financing has been the major constraint. The works program disappeared because of its political and economic unworkability. It was replaced by the education program, which succeeded in vastly increasing the employability of the refugees. The health and relief programs contributed to improving the life expectancies of the refugees, reduced infant mortality, and have been rationalized within the confines of restricted funds. From the standpoint of welfare bureaucracy measures, UNRWA has rationalized and expanded its services, and the refugees' welfare has improved as a result. This is progress: the international commitment to Palestinian economic and social rights has led to improvements in their physical and economic conditions.

REGIONAL EFFECTS

Although UNRWA does not directly contribute to political change in the Middle East, it has indirect political effects. UNRWA's political role in the five fields differs according to its relations with the local authorities and the government's relations with the refugees. These relationships have varied over time, and thus UNRWA's status has also changed. At present, UNRWA relations with Jordan and Syria are relatively routine and not politically very salient. In Lebanon, the lack of governmental authority means that UNRWA operates in a power vacuum, needing to consult and bargain with many factions and militias to keep its operations going, and to try to mitigate the effects of the many-sided conflict upon the civilian refugee population. In the occupied territories, it serves as a partial buffer between the Israeli authorities and the refugees, a role of some importance during the recent *intifada*.

Assigning an international organization to improve refugee welfare despite the inherent tensions between organizational authority and governmental sovereignty indicates an international commitment to social and economic rights, even as they intrude on the organizing principle of the international system. Interposition between the occupiers and the refugees, until recently an unintentional role for UNRWA, helps to retrieve a small part of the civil rights that the refugees lack by virtue of being stateless. International institutionalization of the delivery of aid and a small measure of protection for these refugees constitute significant, though minimalist, progress.

Jordan

Jordanian authorities do not consider UNRWA a totally benign influence, because it in some ways rivals governmental authority. However, it is an important contributor to Jordan's economic survival, and Jordanian and UNRWA officials closely coordinate their activities in order to make the relationship as productive and as conflict-free as possible. The Agency's funding of refugee education, health, and welfare programs saves large amounts of money for the government and helps keep the large refugee population relatively content.

Immediately after the "Black September" of 1970, when Palestinian fighters were driven out of Jordan following their effort to establish, in effect, a sovereign Palestinian state within Jordan, UNRWA delivered emergency food rations to civilian refugees. Jordan dealt harshly with the fighters but has pursued a policy of cooptation and economic development, along with careful monitoring and control of political opposition, to prevent a recurrence of the war. All of Jordanian society, including the refugees (especially in the refugee camps), is heavily penetrated by the government's security apparatus.

Relations between the government and the Agency are relatively routine. Local UNRWA employees are screened by the government for security risks. Until 1988, when King Hussein formally relinquished authority over the West Bank to the PLO, UNRWA coordinated with the Ministry of Occupied Territories Affairs (MOTA) on all matters dealing with the refugees, including those on the West Bank. With the dissolution of MOTA, UNRWA no longer formally interacts with Jordan on West Bank matters.

As the refugee camps have "normalized" (i.e., become increasingly like other villages or urban areas) and as UNRWA's financial resources have been strained, Jordan has increased its infrastructure services to the camps. UNRWA welcomes this gradual transfer of sponsorship. Palestinians (except 1967 refugees from Gaza) can obtain full Jordanian citizenship and passports. The situation in Jordan comes closest to the ideas of "reintegration" that were current at UNRWA's founding.

Syria

Syrian–UNRWA relations have been relatively consistent and of much less significance to Syria than relations between UNRWA and the other governments where it operates. The Palestinian and Palestinian refugee population as a percentage of total Syrian population is much lower than that in any of the other areas, and although Palestinians in Syria cannot become Syrian citizens and are drafted into a separate military organization from other Syrians (the Palestine Liberation Army [PLA] which is under the control of the Syrian government), they are governed by the same laws, subject to the same controls, and experience the same kinds of opportunities that regular citizens do.

The Syrians have demanded, and UNRWA has accepted, representation of the government's ministry for Palestinian refugee affairs (GAPAR) on UNRWA hiring boards, and keeps closer watch on UNRWA employment activities than do the other governments. Since the refugee population is relatively small, UNRWA cannot be said to alter significantly the politics of the state or its relations to the refugees. The Syrians tend to be suspicious of all outside influences, and this includes UNRWA; however, since Syria continues to subscribe to the "rejectionist" position with regard to the future of the Palestinians, it accepts UNRWA's role as part of the continuing international commitment to their eventual return to Palestine.

Lebanon

Because of ongoing civil war, UNRWA operations in Lebanon are more hazardous, episodic, and emergency oriented than activities in the other fields. UNRWA installations have been repeatedly destroyed by local forces and by Israeli bombing. Camp residents have been on the verge of starvation because of interruptions of UNRWA supplies caused by attacks from various militias and internecine battles. UNRWA has continued operating despite these difficult conditions, and at times has been the only thing that has stood between the camp residents and starvation.

To the extent possible, UNRWA has also kept schools open, teachers and students in attendance (except when the shooting gets too bad), and health clinics operating. Because UNRWA can have formal relations only with governments, it continues to deal with the Lebanese government as necessary, although dealing informally with the factions that control the territory in which it operates and through which its employees travel. Some local employees have been kidnapped, and UNRWA has worked, mostly successfully, for their release. So far, UNRWA internationals have not become targets for kidnaping, although a British newsman on assignment with UNRWA's public relations division was kidnapped and apparently executed. UNRWA has withdrawn its international civil servants of target nationalities from Lebanon.

Because it is impossible to carry out special hardship case investigations and because of great general need for medical assistance and food, UNRWA relief efforts in Lebanon now appear to be throwbacks to the early years following the 1948 war. UNRWA has had great difficulty in limiting food supplies only to registered refugees, and unofficially extends assistance to all Palestinians who come to distribution centers for help. UNRWA has drawn the line at giving assistance to non-Palestinians, however. At one point during battles between the Shia Amal militia and Palestinian fighters in refugee camps, Amal demanded that in return for allowing UNRWA vehicles into the camps with food supplies, it should also supply local hungry Shias. Viewing this as a contravention of its mandate, the Agency arranged for other voluntary organizations to donate food for the locals, and for UNRWA vehicles to assist in distribution.

For UNRWA, any governmental control of its environment is preferable to the chaos of the intercommunal battles that now rage. During the Israeli occupation, and before that during the PLO control of the "state within the state," UNRWA was able to carry out its mission. In that sense, it is truly a nonpolitical organization. However, since its clients are participants in regional politics and UNRWA increases their visibility and assists them materially, it does have political effects.

Gaza Strip and the West Bank

Unlike in its other fields of operation, or pre-1967 West Bank and Gaza, in the territories since 1967 UNRWA has been caught between the occupiers and the occupied: in order to carry out its mandate, it has to cooperate with a government perceived by the refugees as directly hostile to their interests. The Agency is faced with conflicting imperatives: cooperation with the authorities, necessitated by the government's right to expel the United Nations from the territories, and support for the refugees. UNRWA treads a thin line between collaboration with the occupiers and advocacy of the occupied.

Since 1967, relations between UNRWA and Israeli authorities have generally been correct, if at times less cooperative than either side might have desired. Relations are formally based on a letter exchange of 1967 between then Commissioner-General of UNRWA Lawrence Michelmore and the Israeli Political Adviser to the Foreign Minister and Ambassador-at-Large Michael Comay.[45] Under the agreement UNRWA continued its operations as it had during Jordanian and Egyptian control of the territories, and with the exception of matters pertaining to "military security," UNRWA's installations and activities remained inviolable and governed by the UN's standard Privileges and Immunities document. The definition of "military security," of course, remains up to the governmental authorities, and the occupation authorities have a complete monopoly on the use of force. The most that UNRWA can do in cases where it decides that its privileges and immunities are being transgressed is to complain to Israeli officials and attempt to invoke higher U.N. authority in support of its local operatives.

UNRWA's role is frequently not clear-cut. As might be expected, the Palestinian clients and employees of the Agency try to interpose it between themselves and their community, on the one hand, and the occupation authorities, on the other. At the same time, UNRWA officials, particularly the international civil servants, understand that for the Agency to carry out its duties, it must maintain reasonably good relations with the Israeli authorities and that the refugees' efforts to use the Agency as their advocate must be resisted. The Agency's role is developed through practice, not by declarations of intent.

UNRWA has to "coordinate" its activities with the authorities because it has to use, or connect its installations with, Israeli utilities, and it must transport materiel over Israeli roads and across Israel's borders, and because Israel is in sovereign control of the people living in the territories. "Coordination" can mean anything from advising the authorities of measures to be carried out to seeking acquiescence in plans to construct or modify UNRWA facilities. On the other hand, UNRWA must obtain the cooperation of the refugees if it is going to be able to carry out its programs. Refugee and employee strikes, destruction of UNRWA property, and representations to headquarters have at various times been used as a means of protest against disliked Agency policies or activities.

Israeli views of UNRWA differ between officials and across bureaucratic levels and positions. The Foreign Ministry tends to view it benignly, as part of the exasperating but sometimes useful U.N. family, to be dealt with while maintaining diplomatic decorum. The Foreign Ministry tends to take U.N. international legal immunities seriously and is the authority to whom UNRWA appeals when the Defense Ministry (under which the occupation authorities are organized) appears to have transgressed its privileges or immunities.

The occupation authorities, under the Ministry of Defense, have sometimes seen UNRWA as constructive—in that it carries out activities such as welfare, health, and educational services that in the Agency's absence Israel would have to undertake—but other times have seen it as obstructionist and difficult. UNRWA seeks to discourage the army from, for instance, intruding into its school buildings and classes in search of suspects during school hours, at least without first clearing its actions with UNRWA school officials, and tries to make sure that proper procedures are followed in the event that a local UNRWA employee has been arrested or detained.

Particularly in the Gaza Strip, where the Israeli authorities have tried to encourage refugee camp dwellers to move to government-supported housing projects, there has been continuing tension between UNRWA officials and the Israelis over construction permissions, boundaries of camps, and the Israeli demand that for refugees to take advantage of the housing program, they must demolish their refugee camp dwellings. Israeli officials resent claims of transgressions that appear in the Agency's Annual Reports to the General Assembly. They charge that they are unfairly singled out for criticism while the governments of other fields carry out much worse deeds. UNRWA claims to report on all fields equivalently.

Carrying out operations in the occupied territories, UNRWA depends upon Israel to maintain physical security and to supply infrastructure requirements provided by Jordan prior to 1967. At the same time it tries to maintain its U.N. neutrality in the midst of tense

Palestinian–Israeli relations. Until the accession of Shimon Peres as prime minister of the Unity Government in 1984, Israeli officials generally regarded UNRWA with suspicion, and the military administrators of the occupied territories viewed UNRWA as a hindrance to their ability to carry out their task in Palestinian areas.

UNRWA does not have a mandate to protect refugee civil rights, but its employees and clients do seek to involve it in their efforts to control the degree to which the occupiers exercise authority over their lives. This is especially apparent in efforts of long-time employees to use UNRWA to press Israel into living up to what they regard as the legal role of a military occupier and to resist Israeli actions tantamount to annexation.[46]

Although Israelis charge UNRWA with allowing Palestinians to use the Agency for their purposes, Palestinians charge that sometimes it cooperates too much with the occupation. UNRWA employees and clients seek to involve it in their efforts to control the degree to which the occupiers exercise arbitrary authority over their lives. When UNRWA fails to live up to their expectations, they accuse it of selling out to the authorities.

One example of an alleged Agency "sell-out" occurred in 1984, when UNRWA responded to Israeli demands that it prevent Palestinian students from stoning Israeli vehicles on roads near West Bank UNRWA schools. Israeli security forces closed off refugee camp entrances, pursued alleged stone throwers, and disrupted classrooms while searching for the stone throwers. The authorities informed UNRWA that if the stone throwing did not stop, the schools would be closed. The West Bank UNRWA field office faced two undesirable alternatives. It could attempt to prevent the stone throwing, which put it perilously close to maintaining security for Israel, or it could allow the Israelis to close the schools, which would prevent it from carrying out its educational duties.

UNRWA chose to keep the schools operating by having high fences built around the schools. Detractors charged that in contracting and paying for the fences, UNRWA collaborated with the authorities. Defenders argued that keeping the schools open was the overriding imperative, and the fences made possible the continued education of the refugees.

Another example of the overlap of operational and political imperatives dates from the 1967 departure of large numbers of Palestinians from the refugee camps near Jericho. After the refugees left, Israel did not permit significant numbers of the former residents to return.[47] Some Palestinian UNRWA officials argued that the camps should be physically maintained as if the refugees were about to return, making the point that the Israelis were acting illegally in preventing the return. They charged that failure to maintain the camps constituted UNRWA acceptance of the Israeli action. Agency officials argued that since funds were short, services to the refugees had to have priority over maintaining abandoned camps. Detractors saw UNRWA's position as one in which pragmatism constituted collaboration, whereas defenders saw in the pragmatic course the only option that would permit UNRWA's mandate to be fulfilled.

The largely abandoned Jericho camps reemerged as an issue throughout the 1970s as Israeli military authorities requested that they be demolished. They said that demolition was necessary for health and security reasons: the old huts were places where rats, bugs, and terrorists could hide. In 1986, uninhabited parts of the old Jericho camps were bulldozed (by Israeli military bulldozers guided by UNRWA officers) under an Israeli–UNRWA agreement that preserved the U.N. immunity of the camp areas. Some Palestian observers considered the UNRWA–Israeli arrangement a sell-out, whereas others took some heart in the fact that the few remaining inhabited dwellings were not demolished, and large signs were posted defining the UNRWA camp areas.

UNRWA treads a thin line between collaboration and advocacy because the interests of its clients and of the occupation authorities are in conflict. Operational decisions are frequently made under pressure, and the nature of those decisions depends upon the personalities and orientations of the field officers. Palestinian employees as well as Israeli authorities are very sensitive to the internationals' attitudes; where one field director may be seen as a "reasonable man" by the Israelis and "soft" by the Palestinians, another may have the reputation of being unreasonable and anti-Israel on one side and a "friend" to the other. Because the Agency's position is so sensitive, UNRWA officials explain their actions in pragmatic rather than symbolic or political terms. Given the politicized environment, it is impossible for the Agency to remain truly apolitical.

UNRWA and the *Intifada*. During the current Palestinian uprising in Gaza and the West Bank, news reports frequently featured quotations of and statements by UNRWA officials describing the situation and, by implication, criticizing the occupation authorities. UNRWA officials' unusual public visibility is one aspect of changes taking place in UNRWA's self-conception and its operational emphasis in the occupied territories.

UNRWA's response to the uprising has been to tilt more toward advocacy of refugee interests. The tilt has been legitimated by a report and recommendations from the U.N. Secretary-General that built upon the findings of Under-Secretary-General for Special Political Affairs Marrek Goulding's inspection tour of the occupied territories early in 1988.[48] As a consequence, UNRWA is increasingly interposed between Israeli authorities and the refugees. New economic assistance projects may help build Palestinian organizational capabilities and independence.

Under the Secretary-General's findings, UNRWA's task is now being described as part of "general assistance" protection of the refugees, rather than as merely humanitarian assistance. The Secretary-General defined four varieties of protection:

(a) . . . physical protection, i.e. the provision of armed forces to deter, and if necessary, fight any threats to the safety of the protected persons;

(b) . . . legal protection, i.e. intervention with the security and judicial authorities, as well as the political instances, of an occupying Power, by an outside agency, in order to ensure just treatment of an individual or group of individuals;

(c) . . . also a less well-defined form, called in this report "general assistance," in which an outside agency intervenes with the authorities of the occupying Power to help individuals or groups of individuals to resist violations of their rights (e.g. land confiscations) and to cope with the day-to-day difficulties of life under occupation, such as security restrictions, curfews, harrassment, bureaucratic difficulties and so on;

(d) Finally . . . the somewhat intangible "protection" afforded by outside agencies, including especially the international media, whose mere presence and readiness to publish what they observe may have a beneficial effect for all concerned; . . . "protection by publicity."[49]

The Secretary-General made explicit in his report the desirability of using UNRWA international employees to help reduce the harshness of the occupation. The Secretary-General's report put it somewhat elliptically:

> UNRWA is clearly best placed to provide additional general assistance.
> . . . In paying tribute to the invaluable service that UNRWA Palestinian
> staff have been rendering to the refugees in very difficult circumstances, I
> believe that international staff can at present play an especially valuable
> role. It is usually easier for them to gain access to Israeli authorities in
> emergency situations; and their mere presence at points of confrontation
> has a significant impact on how the civilian population (including UNRWA
> Palestinian staff) is treated by the security forces and helps it psychologi-
> cally by making it feel less exposed.[50]

UNRWA could rapidly respond to the Secretary-General's report because it had already improved relations with donor states. Building on earlier meetings in late February 1988, it convened a third donor group meeting. The report stated that because of the situation in the occupied territories, the United Nations generally, and UNRWA in particular, needed to consider what new measures might help move the conflicting parties toward a political settlement. UNRWA needed to provide assistance to the Palestinians to alleviate their increased hardship and to "provide credible support for the political initiatives of governments."[51]

UNRWA presented proposals for "Emergency Measures for the Occupied Territories" (EMOT) and an "Extended Program of Assistance" (EPA). Donor states were enthusiastic, and their contributions enabled the two proposals to be implemented by UNRWA. The EMOT includes emergency health services (necessitated by the tremendous rise in casualties in connection with violent confrontations between the Israeli security forces and the refugees), emergency food distributions (necessitated by curfews), physical therapy care (for *intifada* casualties), cash grants for emergency housing (necessitated by shelter demolitions), and extra staff to provide these services. The EPA is aimed at rehabilitating shelters; improving environmental sanitation and water supplies; expanding health services, especially through the construction and equipping of additional and improved clinics; expanding employment, training, income-generating, and self-support projects; improving agency installations and funding some education projects.[52]

New positions for international civil servants were created in two categories. Refugee Affairs Officers (RAOs) were to "circulate throughout the refugee camps for the purpose of reporting to the Field Office on any urgent requirements or unusual or abnormal circumstances"; to visit Agency installations to make sure that they are not being misused; to report on problems affecting the welfare of the refugees; to compile reports and information about the refugees; to facilitate delivery of needed supplies during curfews; and as necessary to liaise with the local military governors and civil administrators on matters affecting the Agency's operations or refugees' welfare.[53] By mid-1989, there were ten RAOs on the West Bank and nine in the Gaza Strip hired on six-month, one-time renewable contracts. The assumption and experience is that the job is so demanding that no one should do it for more than one year.

New "Legal Assistance Officers" (one in Gaza and one on the West Bank) have been added to staff to give legal advice to the Field Directors and the other international officials, and to monitor trials of UNRWA personnel and refugees generally. They have been used largely to improve liaison with the authorities, making more time available to the Field Directors to tend to other Agency matters. They are hired on one-year renewable contracts.[54]

In response to the *intifada* UNRWA has also relaxed its restrictions on the distribution of relief supplies. During crises, when identification of registered refugees is difficult anyway, and when many other Palestinians are in as much need as are the registered refugees, the Commissioner-General has instructed field officials to distribute aid without regard to refugee status. Prior to the uprising, only in Lebanon were UNRWA services flowing beyond the registered refugee population.

The success of efforts to fund the EPA enables it to plan infrastructure repairs and improvements, but military controls, strikes, and disruptions thwart implementation. The EPA has further significance, however. It represents the first time that Arab governments have assented to UNRWA allocating its resources unequally between its five fields of operation, and may signify a tacit acceptance of the idea that UNRWA is aiding what will eventually become a Palestinian state in less than all of Palestine.

Since the onset of the uprising UNRWA officials' willingness publicly to criticize the occupation authorities' actions demonstrated how negatively they view the Israeli response to the uprising, but was also consonant with the UN Secretary-General's idea of "general assistance." They told foreign press representatives about security operations inaccessible to the media, and they released information gathered from their health clinics showing the numbers and severity of physical attacks upon refugees. UNRWA health officials brought to the attention of the media, the UN, and international health authorities Israeli troops' use of riot-control gasses in confined areas where they constituted a lethal hazard, and have publicized the lethal effects of plastic coated bullets.

Israeli officials are quite aware of UNRWA's statements to the international press, innovations in the delivery of services, and increases in international staffing. UNRWA officials and Israeli representatives use curiously similar adjectives to describe their relationship. Both say that relations are normal at the high levels, but that at the ground level problems sometimes arise. Israelis speak of errant UNRWA international employees who misrepresent the nature and consequences of Israeli security measures in the territories. For UNRWA representatives, the problem is that Israeli Defense Forces personnel on the ground sometimes obstruct discharge of UNRWA's duties.

Israeli representatives stress that UNRWA's proper role is a humanitarian one. From their standpoint, the mandate calls for UNRWA to carry out its medical, educational and relief program as before, and they say that Israel seeks fully to cooperate with those programs. They take exception, however, to UNRWA statements about the condition of refugees as a result of Israeli security measures during the *intifada*, particularly the claim that they have used riot control gas inappropriately. They object further that although criticizing the way Israel has carried out its security measures, UNRWA personnel haven't urged the Palestinians to desist from the behavior that necessitated those measures.

Avoiding explicit politicization, with the Secretary-General's blessing pushing a vague mandate further in the direction of refugee "protection" than ever before, the Agency is now tilting in a direction opposite of the one it appeared to take during the 1984 stone throwing and 1986 Jericho bulldozing incidents. Consequently, its reputation among refugees has improved. Donations for the agency from Arab states have increased substantially, and UNRWA's traditional donors regard it more highly as a way to be constructively involved in the problems of the Palestinian residents of the occupied territories. Reacting to the *intifada,* UNRWA has become more politically relevant, and its activities reflect an increased humanitarian concern by the international actors for the rights of refugees.

CONCLUSIONS

The fact that the numbers of refugees worldwide are not declining in absolute or relative terms is evidence that oppression and strife continue to propel people out of their home countries, seeking refuge in states of first asylum and frequently needing to be assisted by international humanitarian agencies. The numbers also demonstrate increased international awareness of the refugee phenomenon, as the scope of the definition of who is a refugee expands. The general picture remains gloomy; measuring the number of refugees, it cannot be argued that the world is becoming a more tolerant place. The Palestinian case is special, but a somewhat promising instance of a global commitment to refugee assistance. Despite the failure of high-level political agreement to solve their problem, the international commitment to the Palestinians has had positive consequences.

UNRWA indicates minimalist progress because it demonstrates the new, post–World War II international commitment to economic and social rights of peoples and individuals. It is seen by some observers to produce a suboptimal status quo, where revolution, discouragement, and assimilation of Palestinians, or radical changes in Israeli politics might follow if UNRWA withdrew. But these views are based on powerful political interests in particular outcomes for the Arab–Israeli conflict. Apart from these strongly held views, the Agency demonstrably improves the individual welfare of those it is committed to serve.

The UNRWA case demonstrates that progress in international relations does not necessarily proceed congruently at different levels of aggregation. Minimalist progress constituted by international concern with individual welfare and organizational improvements in delivering services to those people does not automatically lead toward maximalist progress. Maximalist progress is much more difficult than minimalist progress to define apart from sovereign interests. We should probably continue to look for fragmented, low-level indicators as Ernst Haas has shown us, rather than becoming totally frustrated in attempts to derive transcendent measures for maximalist progress.

UNRWA is also instructive as a model for other refugee programs. Its greatest successes have been in emergency assistance and providing educational opportunities to the Palestinians. Its in-service training system, developed under UNESCO leadership, can and has served as a model for national policies. Its excellent record of vocational training and placement demonstrates what education can do to help individuals in regions where demand exists for skilled labor. The health program has addressed basic health problems, shifted to preventive medicine, and extended Palestinian life expectancies. The Agency's fund-raising apparatus was primitive for many years but has finally been modernized. With the development of the external relations division, UNRWA came of age, rationalizing its operations. With new planning measures it has begun to face up to its likely future. Progress, in the sense of organizational evolution, is thus evident in UNRWA's case.

No other refugee or national group has enjoyed the exclusive commitment of an international organization to its welfare. Because of the U.N.s involvement in the creation of the state of Israel and the consequent dispossession of the Palestinians at the close of the colonial epoch, it is unlikely that the United Nations will be faced with an analogous situation in the future. Because of the protracted nature of the commitment and the political sensitivity of U.N. involvement in it, it is unlikely that even given the chance, the United Nations would easily repeat its commitment. Nonetheless, the Agency's operational programs can serve as demonstrations to other development organizations within the U.N. family, and perhaps to other nationalist groups and governments, such as the African National Congress and the developing countries of Africa, about where to place their emphases in development of welfare, health, and educational programs.

UNRWA cannot reconcile the political conflicts of the Middle East. To do so is outside its capability and outside its mandate. But UNRWA does indicate international progress. It shows an international commitment to the rights of a people despite enormous sovereign interests in the conflict that surrounds them, it has made organizational progress in rationalization of its operations, and its programs have helped individuals and can serve as models for other organizations.

ENDNOTES

I thank the editors of this volume and anonymous readers for their very helpful comments. I also thank the many present and former UNRWA officials, governmental officials, and commentators on the situation in the Middle East who have aided me in this project. The AFSC was very helpful to my research into the early period of aid to the Palestinians. Oberlin College has provided vital support for my research, as did the Foundation for Middle East Peace.

1. Ernst Haas, *The Obsolescence of Regional Integration Theory*. Research Series 25, (Berkeley: Institute of International Studies, University of California, 1975), pp. 32–39.
2. Adler, Crawford, and Donnelly, paper 1 of this volume.
3. Jack Donnelly, paper 5 of this volume.
4. The history of refugee and immigration policy is rife with examples where the sovereign interests dominate human values objectives—even when refugee interests wind up being served. Still, even the possibility of contrasting human interests and national interests, and the frequent invocation of the former to justify the latter demonstrate the power of human interests as a norm at the international level.
5. Gil Loescher and John Scanlon, *Calculated Kindness: Refugees and America's Half-Open Door 1945–Present* (New York: Free Press, 1986), p. xiii.
6. G. S. Goodwin-Gill, *The Refugee in International Law* (Oxford: Clarendon Press, 1983), ch. 1.
7. UNRWA's definition had to be specified in order to determine who qualified for its services. In 1954 it reported to the General Assembly that it considered a Palestinian refugee for its purposes to be "a person whose normal residence was Palestine for a minimum of two years preceeding the conflict in 1948, and who, as a result of this conflict, lost both his home and his means of livelihood and took refuge in 1948 in one of the countries where UNRWA provides relief. Refugees within this definition and the direct descendants of such refugees are eligible for Agency assistance if they are: registered with UNRWA, living in the area of UNRWA operations, and in need." A/2717, Add. 1, Part III, Para. 19 (1954), as quoted in UNRWA, *UNRWA, Past, Present, and Future: A Briefing Document.* (Vienna: UNRWA, 1986).
8. Refugee figure from UNRWA, "Report of the Commissioner-General of the United Nations Relief and Works Agency for Palestine Refugees in the Near East 1 July 1988–30 June 1989". UN General Assembly 44 Supplement 13 (A/44/13). Total population estimate from: Alasdair Drysdale and Gerald H. Blake, *The Middle East and North Africa: a political geography* (New York: Oxford University Press, 1985), p. 284.
9. Adler, Crawford, and Donnelly, paper 1 of this volume.
10. Don Peretz, *Israel and the Palestine Arabs* (Washington, D.C.: Middle East Institute, 1958), p. 95.

11. United Nations, *Final Report, UN Economic Survey Mission for the Middle East* (Lake Success, N.Y.: UN, 1949), part 1, pp. 18–19.

12. Edward Buehrig, *The United Nations and the Palestinian Refugees* (Bloomington: Indiana University Press, 1971), pp. 29–31.

13. Loescher and Scanlon, *Calculated Kindness* ch. 1.

14. U.N. General Assembly Resolution 194(III), "The Palestine Question". December 11, 1948.

15. U.N. General Assembly Resolution 302(IV), "Assistance to Palestine Refugees." December 8, 1949.

16. U.N., "Report of the Commissioner-General of the UNRWAPRNE 1 July 1988–30 June 1989." A/44/13, 1989, pp. 6–13; "Report of the C-G . . . 1 July 1982–30 June, 1983." A/38/13, 1983, p. 1.

17. UNRWA, "UNRWA: Past, Present and Future: A Briefing Document." (Vienna: UNRWA, 1986). p. viii; U.N., "Report of the Commissioner-General of the UNRWAPRNE 1 July 1988–30 June 1989." A/44/13 1989, pp. 28–30.

18. Author's interviews, officials of the UNRWA Division of External Relations, May 1986.

19. The contributions are raised annually at a "pledging conference" held in conjunction with the meeting of the U.N. General Assembly (and the sixth [political] committee which deals with UNRWA).

20. Author's interviews, UNRWA headquarters staff, May 1986.

21. UNRWA, "Summary of the Medium Term Plan for the period 1987–1989" (Vienna: UNRWA, 1986).

22. Author's interviews, UNRWA official, New York, August 1987.

23. This was particularly stressed in an interview with former Commissioner-General of UNRWA Sir John Rennie, who served in that position as well as in the position of Deputy C-G in the late 1960s and into the middle-1970s.

24. UNGA Resolution 302.

25. Economic Survey Mission. . . . , 1949. For description of negotiations over the water plans themselves, see David Stuligross, "The Johnston Negotiations, 1953–55: Arab-Israeli Cooperation?" Senior Honors Thesis, Department of Government, Oberlin College, April 1987.

26. Because of the political commitments underlined by UNGA resolution 194, programs for assisting the refugees could not be called resettlement. Except for a small number of people who were given assistance to set up small business activities in Iraq, on conditions that they take themselves off of UNRWA relief rolls, the self-support activities were called "reintegration" projects. The connotation of the term is interesting. The refugees were "de–integrated" from the regional economy by virtue of their dispossession, and assistance activities would "reintegrate" them economically without prejudicing their claim to repatriation or compensation. This would theoretically entail a separation of economic from political or territorial activities.

27. UNRWA, "UNRWA Experience with Works Projects and Self-Support

Programmes: An Historical Summary (1950–62)." *UNRWA Reviews: A Background Information Series* 5 (Beirut: UNRWA, 1962).

28. Vicky Randall and Robin Theobald, *Political Change and Underdevelopment: A Critical Introduction to Third World Politics.* (Durham, N.C.: Duke University Press, 1985), ch. 1 and 2.
29. Author's interview, former Commissioner-General of UNRWA Mr. John Davis, September 1985.
30. Operational Report of the American Friends Service Committee, February 1950, Appendix I: Suggested Policy for Refugee Educational Program.
31. UNRWA, "UNRWA: A Brief History 1950–1982" (Vienna: UNRWA, undated). pp. 113–148.
32. Author's interviews, UNESCO/UNRWA teacher training program officials. Amman Jordan, July 1984.
33. Avi Plascov, *The Palestinian Refugees in Jordan, 1948–57* (London: Frank Cass, 1981), pp. 143–145.
34. According to UNRWA officials.
35. According to UNRWA officials in the Gaza Strip.
36. Author's interviews, UNRWA officials in Vienna and the fields, February–May 1986.
37. "The Medical Program. . . . The most remarkable fact about the medical story is the absence of any large scale epidemic where there was every right to expect devastating outbreaks. . . ." Letter from Colin Bell to AFSC headquarters (Philadelphia), "Brief Report on AFSC Operation under UNRPR in Gaza Strip in Southern Palestine." August 29, 1949, p. 8.
38. Author's interviews, UNRWA employees in education and health divisions, Jordan and the West Bank, 1986.
39. AFSC archives: several internal memos, December 1949.
40. Annual Reports of the Commissioners-General; author's interviews with former senior Palestinian UNRWA employees, West Bank and Amman.
41. B. E. Harrell–Bond, *Imposing Aid: Emergency Assistance to Refugees.* (New York: Oxford University Press, 1986) pp. 124–127.
42. UNRWA, "The Problem of the Rectification of the UNRWA Relief Rolls (1950–1962)." *Background Information Series* 6 (Beirut: UNRWA, 1962); for a discussion of similar problems in the context of emergency aid to Ugandan refugees in 1980s Sudan, see Harrell-Bond, chapter 3.
43. Author's interviews with current and former senior UNRWA officials, 1986.
44. UNRWA Relief Services Instruction No. 2/83: paragraph 7.1–7.3. (November 1983).
45. U.N. Treaty Series, Vol. 620, p. 183, No. 8955. "UNRWAPNE and Israel: Exchange of Letters Constituting a Provisional Agreement Concerning Assistance to Palestinian Refugees." Jerusalem, June 14, 1967. Registered *ex officio* January 31, 1968.
46. Author's interviews. The annual Commissioner-General's Report always

includes a section on relations with the host governments, including problems experienced with them. Israeli officials complain that the reports are out of context; UNRWA officials note that they have the same reporting responsibility in the other fields of operation.

47. Report of the C-G of UNRWAPNE 1 July 1968–30 June 1969. UNGA XXIV Supp. 14 (A/7614).
48. U.N. Security Council, "Report Submitted to the Security Council by the Secretary-General in Accordance with Resolution 605 (1987). S/19433. January 21, 1988. Also reprinted in *Journal of Palestine Studies,* Vol. 17(1):66–79.
49. U.N. Security Council, "Report Submitted. . . ." pp. 10, 12–13.
50. U.N. Security Council, "Report Submitted. . . ." p. 13.
51. UNRWA, "Paper for Informal Meeting with Governments in Vienna February 29–March 1 1988: UNRWA Operations in Gaza and the West Bank." Draft of February 19, 1988, p. 4.
52. UN, "Report of the Commissioner-General of the UNRWAPRNE July 1, 1988–June 30, 1989." A/44/13, 1989, Parts VI.C. and D.
53. UNRWA internal document INT/4/5, May 29, 1989: Background Note, "Refugee Affairs Officers."
54. UNRWA, International Job Description: Legal Officer (undated).

11

STRUCTURALISM AND ITS CRITICS: RECENT PROGRESS IN INTERNATIONAL RELATIONS THEORY

Stephan Haggard

The last decade of international relations theorizing has been an exciting one. Kenneth Waltz's *Theory of International Politics* challenged virtually the entire field for "reductionism" and sparked a debate over international "structure" not seen since the attempts to extend systems theory to international relations in the 1960s.[1] Robert Gilpin, Stephen Krasner, and David Lake extended "structural realism" to international political economy.[2] Robert Keohane responded to the neorealist critique through an "institutionalist" synthesis of realist and liberal insights.[3] Keohane grounded his institutionalism on realist premises, however, including the presumption of international anarchy in which states are the dominant actors and an emphasis on the international "game" over subsystemic forces.

Others, such as Hayward Alker, Richard Ashley, Alexander Wendt, John Ruggie, and Friedrich Kratochwil, responded more critically to the realist revival.[4] These writers drew insights from contemporary sociological and legal theory to offer a contending, "reflective"[5] research program that paid greater attention to rules and norms. Writers in the world-systems, dependency, and interdependence traditions continued to articulate a view of the international system that gave *economic* structures greater weight.[6] Despite their many differences, these dissidents shared one important theoretical preoccupation with the neorealists: all sought to locate features of the international order that could be used in an explanatory way.

The intellectual origins of the new structuralism are diverse, but spring from two related theoretical impulses. The first is a dissatisfaction with theories that focus on the characteristics of individual "units." Waltzian neorealism was above all a response to "reductionist" theories of foreign policy. World-systems theory challenged comparative politics and sociology for treating nation-states as isolated entities rather than as components of a larger whole. The "reflective" research program offered a more recursive and open-ended conception of structure. Nonetheless, it sought to identify *common* norms, principles, and knowledge that oriented action across states. The second theoretical goal of the structuralist program was to conceptualize external constraints more rigorously. Rather than treating the international environment as a parameter, structural analysis used characteristics of the international system to explain other characteristics of the system, such as its stability or openness, as well as the behavior of individual states.

The purpose of this paper is different from that of the others in this volume. I am interested not in progress in international relations, but in progress in international relations *theory*, and particularly in assessing the current vogue of "systemic" and "structuralist" thinking. Elaborating criteria for measuring intellectual progress is difficult, since the schools of thought in the current debate begin from very different epistemological and even ontological starting points. In the first section, I explore some of these difficulties. I argue that social science cannot be wholly subsumed under a naturalistic philosophy of science. Nonetheless, gauging progress still demands that new theories demonstrate their competence against competing alternatives by accounting for new empirical data.

In the following three sections, I explore the strengths and weaknesses of structural explanation in three research programs: neorealism, the literature on international economic structures, and the "reflective" alternatives. Viewed dialectically, these structural research programs have been broadly progressive in forcing the consideration of variables that previous analyses neglected. There have been two costs to the new structuralisms, however. First, structure has proved to be a weak predictor of state action and has had to be " supplemented," often in an *ad hoc* way, with nonsystemic explanations. The result is a growing split between "high theory" of the systemic variety and the study of foreign policy on the other. The fifth section explores this split in more detail by analyzing the claim that the systemic level of analysis deserves some priority in constructing theories of international relations. These arguments can be reduced to a *methodological* injunction against ignoring the possible weight of systemic factors. A second difficulty with structural theory is particularly salient to a discussion of progress in world politics. International-structural theories are, by their very nature, poorly equipped to explain systemic change. In the concluding section, I examine several recent efforts at explaining systemic change, comparing economic models to the cognitive-evolutionary approach pioneered by Ernst Haas.

METATHEORY, THEORY, AND METHOD: GAUGING THEORETICAL PROGRESS

Recent debates on neorealism have been couched largely in metatheoretical terms. Metatheory is the discussion of fundamentals: the definition of basic concepts, ideas about how those concepts are interrelated, and particularly the epistemological and ontological suppositions that underpin inquiry. Examples of metatheoretical debate include how to conceptualize the international system and the validity of a naturalistic epistemology for the social sciences. *Theory*, by contrast, is *explanatory*. Explanation demands not simply the elaboration of broad *categories* of concepts, but the definition and operationalization of variables; the clear specification of the hypothesized relationship among them, including formalization where appropriate; and clear statement of the domain of conditions under which the hypothesized relationships are likely to obtain.

The metatheoretical cast to the recent debate over neorealism has allowed the protagonists to avoid specifying the *scope* of their claims. It is undeniably true that the distribution of capabilities influences the conduct of diplomacy and that shared knowledge influences behavior, but these claims are not illuminating unless it is specified *when* these factors matter, *how much* they explain, and over *what range* of outcomes. Any *generalized* claim for the theoretical priority of structure—or any other explanatory variable for that matter—is not sustainable. Apparently, metatheoretical debates may be resolvable through the elaboration and testing of contending hypotheses and explanations.

These concerns might appear to reflect a commitment to a naturalistic epistemology. The definition of theory offered here does not reduce the study of international relations to the quest for predictive nomological statements, however. First, it is not clear that generalization *should* be the sole aim of the study of international relations. This fundamentally normative claim is often asserted but is rarely successfully defended. Useful analysis may also be elaborated within an ideographic or comparative-historical framework that eschews lawlike propositions, or is at least modest about their scope. Second, it is not clear that IR theory *has* generated powerful predictive theory. As Alexander Field cautions, "it is not sufficient [for explanation] that the initial conditions of the model be consistent with the outcomes to be explained. They must also be inconsistent with other outcomes not observed."[7] There are, to my knowledge, no theories in international relations that pass this stringent test. Finally, there are reasons to believe that for a certain range of outcomes, such as those affected strongly by the evolution of new substantive knowledge, lawlike statements are impossible in principle.

If a naturalistic conception of explanation is rejected, there is still need for criteria against which the validity of contending truth claims can be measured. This is difficult across paradigms, when fundamental differences exist about what constitutes "explanation." Nonetheless, theories and research programs may be considered "progressive" when *they account for new facts and/or anomalies not accounted for by previous or contending theories and research programs.*[8]

THE CORE DEBATE: THE NEO-REALIST CONCEPT OF STRUCTURE

The success of the new structuralisms in meeting this test may be explored by examining three competing conceptions of structure that have appeared in recent literature.[9] The first, associated with neorealism, conceives of structure as an external constraint on the behavior of rational, optimizing agents. Once structural conditions are identified with sufficient precision, behavior can be predicted with little or no reference either to the internal politics and decision-making processes of states or to the cognitive processes of individuals; McKeown calls this the "structuralist bet."[10]

How is the neorealist concept of structure derived? The "organizing principle" of anarchy played a central role in Kenneth Waltz's first book, *Man, the State and War*.[11] Despite Waltz's claims, anarchy alone did no better than human nature in predicting war; like human nature, it was but a permissive condition. To generate more determinate predictions, Waltz followed the realist tradition, rooting his conception of structure in the distribution of national capabilities. This raised a quite similar problem, however. Asymmetries in power, like anarchy, are a perennial characteristic of international politics, and thus can produce explanations of only a broadly permissive sort.

The answer to this problem was found in the *number* of great powers in the system. The theoretical underpinnings of Waltz's major claims rest on the differences between bipolar and multipolar systems. A similar logic is visible in the literature on "hegemony," in which the key distinction is between systems dominated by one power and posthegemonic or transitional systems with several competing economic powers.

Inferring interests and actions from the distribution of capabilities demands, first, that there is some unambiguous way to assess the distribution of capabilities, and second, that a restricted set of outcomes results from that distribution.[12] Unlike other exercises in correlation, however, the delineation and measurement of the independent variable, "structure," is likely to be somewhat arbitrary. This was clear in the debate over bipolarity and multipolarity in the late 1960s and early 1970s[13] and is visible in the literature on "hegemonic stability" as well.[14] David Lake, who has offered one of the more refined versions of the theory, defines international structure within the trade area on the basis of two variables: the country's relative productivity and its share of world trade.[15] Broadly, these measures seek to explain both the *willingness* to pursue free trade and the *capacity* to do so. But Lake finds that hegemonic structures do not lead necessarily to free trade outcomes. Nor does the absence of a hegemon necessarily mean the inability to achieve a liberal outcome. At best, the structure sets a set of broad constraints and incentives, the "reading" of which is subject to conflicting domestic interpretations.[16] A number of critics have noted that the 1970s and 1980s provide at best ambiguous support for the predictions of hegemonic stability theory.[17] To account for anomalies, structural theories of trade policy have amended their accounts with domestic variables, or reverted in an *ad hoc* way to "lags" between international structural change and domestic policy adaptations.[18]

Neorealists are not always clear about the *mechanisms* through which structure operates to produce the predicted outcome. Waltz mixes a Darwinian metaphor under which superior strategies are "naturally selected" with an informal model of constrained optimizing behavior under which strategy is dictated by structure. It is not clear, however, that the market metaphor yields determinate predictions about state behavior.[19] Firm behavior under conditions of oligopoly, the structure most parallel to great power competition, is notoriously difficult to predict. Under a number of plausible assumptions, strategic interactions among oligopolists do not yield stable equilibria. For example, collusion and price leadership are as much a product of oligopolistic markets as price wars.

These theoretical difficulties arise because of the effort to avoid an investigation of actor preferences. Despite Waltz's references to microeconomic models, neorealism differs in this regard from game theory. Writing the payoff matrix for a game involves three steps: specifying informational assumptions; specifying the actors' choice set, or the range of possible actions; and specifying the preferences of the actors over those outcomes. The nature of the game therefore depends critically on actor preferences and strategies, nonstructural factors. For the neorealists, by contrast, different actors placed in the same structure will behave the same *regardless of their preferences*. This is only possible under highly restrictive assumptions about the likely distribution of actor preferences, *and* where those preferences produce relatively unambiguous choices. Neorealists solve the problem of actor preferences by underlining the ubiquitous interest in survival, but it is doubtful whether the survival preference alone will, in any particular case, predict a clear and stable equilibrium.

These problems can be seen by examining the most powerful of Waltz's claims: that great powers in a bipolar system will balance one another, resulting in a "stable" system. This insight says much about why Soviet–American relations changed so sharply between 1945 and 1950 and about underlying continuities in superpower relations. On the other hand, the prediction of "balancing" is consistent with a wide range of behaviors, from mutual postures of minimal deterrence to arms races and intense competition in the periphery. Thucydides reminds us that bipolar systems can even result in systemic war, casting into doubt the central claim that bipolar systems are stable. The stability of the present system may not be a function of the distribution of power at all, but of other factors, such as the presence of nuclear weapons.

The two major schools of thought on the mechanics of hegemonic leadership have faced similar difficulties in moving from structure to outcomes.[20] The "malign" view sees the hegemon providing coercive leadership. The hegemon enforces regime rules that are in its interest with positive and negative sanctions and extracts payment from smaller states to maintain the regime. In addition to the problem of deducing a hegemon's interests from its power position, there is no theoretical reason that hegemons would choose to behave in a coercive way, unless it is assumed that all differentials in power are fully exploited. This assumption sits poorly with historical fact. The United States *tolerated* derogations from liberal norms in the first two postwar decades, when its relative power was at its peak. Only when U.S. power *eroded* did it insist on reciprocity.

The benign view of hegemony begins with the Olsonian theory of public goods and argues that the hegemon is likely to constitute a "privileged group" for which the cost of supplying public goods is less than the benefit received. As Snidal points out, however, there is nothing in the theory of collective action that suggests that a single actor is required to provide public goods.[21] If a privileged subgroup exists such that each member benefits from providing the good even without cooperation from other members, the public good will be provided. Unless a hegemon is defined in a circular fashion as a state that has an interest in the provision of public goods, it is theoretically possible that a "hegemonic" state would *not* have the incentive to provide public goods. This was precisely Kindleberger's point in his classic study of the Depression; the United States was hegemonic, but for domestic political reasons was unwilling to take on leadership functions.[22] Again, the costs of not specifying actor preferences are clear.

It is plausible, however, that individual incentives to shirk on contributions to the provision of public goods will increase as the size of the privileged subgroup increases. Institutionalists have pointed out that international regimes can mitigate this effect by increasing the transparency of state action and ensuring compliance.[23] It is inadequate to respond that international regimes are only "mediating" or "intervening" variables between international structure and national policies. If the institutionalists are correct, the effect of structure can be wholly offset by this "intervening" variable![24]

The strength of the neorealist conception of structure lies in the simplicity of its assumptions, its parsimony, and the attention it focuses on the external constraints on state action. The claims that the theory generates tend to be broad, however, such as the "tendency" of major powers to "balance," and must therefore be supplemented with more refined theories. Some predictions, however, simply fit poorly with empirical fact, such as those linking hegemonic decline with changes in regimes. These problems stem largely from the difficulties of deducing preferences from structural position. The assumption of rational, maximizing behavior makes sense, but can yield unstable or multiple equilibria. Prediction is difficult where optimal strategies are unclear or where actors are pursuing multiple roles.

ECONOMIC STRUCTURES AND WORLD POLITICS

For an important range of systemic outcomes and national policy choices, position in the international division of labor is likely to be a more powerful predictor than position in the state system. For some purposes it is useful to think of a whole country as having a "position" in the international economy that dictates its preferences and behavior. For example, the timing of industrialization separates economic late-comers from leaders, and resource endowment, comparative advantage, and patterns of economic specialization can be used to generate typologies of different types of national economies.[25] It is hard to escape the simple observation, however, that the international system is both a system of states *and* a world economy. To the extent that the world economy is integrated, nonstate actors —sectors, firms, workers—also have international positions that affect their interests, blurring the distinction between systemic and nonsystemic levels of analysis so central to structural realism. Indeed, this was the central insight of the interdependence literature.

The major analytic problem is to define the international economic structure in a theoretically useful way. The most ambitious effort of this sort has been the distinction between core and peripheral states, outlined first by dependency theorists, elaborated by Immanuel Wallerstein and his followers, and adopted by some realists, including most notably, Robert Gilpin.[26] The definition of core and periphery positions has been a consistent problem. Are they identified on the basis of particular types of economic activity or in terms of broader complexes of social and political, as well as economic phenomena? The first definition suffers from the fact that core activities at one time can become peripheral at another; textile production provides an example. The second way of distinguishing the two zones establishes barriers to strong explanation; the more components of the local social and political structure that are incorporated into the definition of structural position, the more difficult it is to deploy structure in an explanatory way.

The most consistent definition of structural position is based on the *relative returns* to economic activity to different positions within the "commodity chains" linking zones. "Economic activities of each and every commodity chain tend to become polarized into positions from which the pressure of competition has been transferred elsewhere (core-like activities) and positions to which such pressures have been transferred (peripheral activities)."[27] This observation provides the framework for two lines of theoretical and empirical inquiry.

The first has to do with the nature of the zones themselves, particularly showing how local social and political structures and the choices they produce are determined by position within transnational market exchanges.[28] The dependency and world-systems programs broke with previous studies in comparative politics and sociology in arguing for the importance of "locating" national developments within such a larger systemic context. Patterns of economic specialization had a powerful effect not only on discrete policy preferences and behaviors, but also on class structures, modes of labor control, and state forms. The advantage of such an approach is that it encourages deductive thinking. Actor preferences over a range of policy and institutional outcomes can be predicted on the basis of economic position.

This approach has by no means been limited to world-systems analysis, however, and it need not rest on a core–periphery conception of international economic structures. The basic mode of explanation is common to recent work on trade policy by Peter Gourevich, Helen Milner, David Lake, and Ronald Rogowski.[29] All seek to deduce policy preferences and outcomes from international market position. Gourevich defines "market position" in terms of competitiveness; Milner, on the basis of the extent of transnational trade and investment ties; Lake, on the basis of relative productivity; and Rogowski, on the basis of comparative advantage.

The strategy of deducing economic policy preferences from economic position is reasonable. Critics have expressed greater doubts when the model is extended to policy *outcomes*, or to larger social, institutional, and political structures.[30] In the "new wave" of writing on multinational corporations, for example, determinant conceptions of international constraint have given way to more indeterminate bargaining theories in which outcomes depend as much on variation in national political structures and capabilities as on the characteristics of international industries.[31] This line of work recognizes that once the structure is specified and preferences are identified, there is still need for a *political* theory that translates preferences into outcomes, whether nationally or in an international bargaining setting.

The "positive heuristic" of economic conceptions of structure has been to focus greater attention on the interaction between the state and economic systems. Much comparative politics and sociology has been rewritten as a result of world-systems insights on the effects of the world economy on national development. Writers outside the world-systems tradition have used other conceptions of international economic position to construct explanations of policy, particularly trade policy, social structure, and politics. These approaches all share the simple yet powerful insight that market position is an important determinant of preferences and behavior. Yet this insight immediately opens the door to the analysis of sub-state actors: sectors, firms, households. These theories must rest on some implicit theory of the domestic political process through which internationally dictated preferences are translated into state choices. As with neorealism, the predictions of the third image are heavily dependent on assumptions about the second.

THE "REFLECTIVE" ALTERNATIVE

The main challenge to both neorealist and economistic conceptions of structure has come from a diverse group of scholars advancing a "reflective" research program. These include John Ruggie, Friedrich Kratochwil, Richard Ashley, Hayward Alker, and Alexander Wendt. There is some question, however, whether it is justifiable to consider any of these theorists "structuralists." According to Wendt, the core of what he calls the "structurationist" program is precisely the "joining [of] agents and structures in a 'dialectical synthesis' that overcomes the subordination of one to the other."[32] This synthesis is achieved not by abandoning the international level of analysis, however, but by *expanding* the concept of "structure" to include not only a distribution of capabilities or a division of labor, but a system of constitutive and regulative *rules* or *principles* around which actors orient their behavior.[33] Constitutive rules are of the sort that *define* a social order or institution. They establish who has standing and what moves are "appropriate." Constitutive rules not only establish a common meaning structure, but define who the players are and even their capabilities. In this sense, constitutive rules provide an even deeper or prior layer of structure than the realist one. The state system itself, for example, rests on a principle of sovereignty that is "generative" of the constituent units. In addition to such basic constitutive rules, structurationists also note the importance of *regulative* or prescriptive rules. Regulative rules are backed by legitimate sanctions, and thus provide a theoretical link to the domain of power. Even in international politics, power cannot be treated as a raw observable, however; it is always tied to certain *purposes*.

The distance from neorealism could not be greater. In neorealistic models, power is ultimately a function of the capabilities of states, understood as resources. According to what Ashley calls a "competence" model, by contrast: "the power of an actor, and even its status as agent competent to act, is not in any sense reducible to the inherent qualities or possessions of a given entity. Rather, the power and status of an actor depends on and is limited by the conditions of its *recognition* within a community as a whole."[34] Thus, a balance-of-power system, for example, is not the resultant of states acting under the constraining influence of other states, but "emerges" on the basis of identifiable constitutive rules. Edward Gulick's study of the nineteenth-century European diplomatic system falls closer to this tradition than to contemporary realism.[35] Similarly, Ruggie's interpretation of the postwar economic system combines the importance of power with a common ideological presupposition he labels "embedded liberalism"; this presupposition, rather than power alone, defined the nature of American hegemony.[36]

It is in the importance of considering normative structures as a kind of "cause" of action that the "reflectivists" make their sharpest break with neorealism. Explanation involves uncovering the constitutive rules of the "game," and paying closer attention to the stated purposes of actors themselves. As Friedrich Kratochwil argues, again in sharp contrast to Waltzian neorealism, "to have 'explained' an action often means to have made intelligible the goals for the purpose of which it was undertaken."[37] This does not necessarily mean reversion to psychologism, however, *since the norms that shape actor preferences themselves constitute an investigable structure.* Actor behavior is neither "caused" by antecedent conditions nor explained by reference to the rationality of compliance given certain power or economic incentives; rather, it is the result of orienting behavior to legitimate and authoritative norms. Socialization and learning thus become the key mechanism linking structure with behavior.

There are two set of problems confronting the structurationist program; one is epistemological, the other concerns the appropriateness of such models to the international arena. Both Waltzian and economic conceptions of structure see actors as heavily constrained by position. The reflective tradition, by contrast, sees situational constraints as looser, in part because of the ability of individuals to redefine their interests on the basis of learning. Wendt, for example, argues that structuration theory is an "analytical" rather than a "substantive" theory: "it provides a conceptual framework or meta-theory for thinking about real world social systems but it does not tell us what particular kind of agents or what particular kind of structure to expect in any given concrete social system."[38] For Wendt, structural analysis is not causal, but "possibilistic," outlining the conditions that "allow" events to occur. Since these conditions are compatible with a wide range of outcomes, structural analysis must be supplemented with "historical" research that takes the "interests and causal powers of agents as given . . . and then attempt[s] to explain particular events by focusing on how these powers and interests are affected by the incentives facing actors.[39] Similarly, Ashley considers research into the "social, economic and environmental conditions" upon which a balance of power system rests to fall within the realm of a competence model of structure.[40] Such research would fit neatly into the terrain defined by traditional forms of inquiry. The very language of incentives, powers, interests, and conditions fits with a rationalist epistemology.

The underlying question dates to Kantian antinomies: how, or can, naturalistic and hermeneutic approaches to the social sciences be reconciled? Actors orient themselves toward rules, but this may or may not provide a powerful explanation of behavior, in part because of the role of unintended consequences. Human action is also correlated with various situational constraints. We may agree that "structure" should encompass both resources and rules. Unless we deny altogether the significance of material constraints on action, this still leaves as an open *empirical* question the relative weight of rules and resources in explaining patterns of action.

The second problem with the structurationist program is the appropriateness of its assumptions to an analysis of world politics, where there is a *prima facie* case for the *relative* weakness of rules. The neorealist program may go too far in denying the theoretical importance of institutions and shared norms. But the structurationists often make strong assumptions about the possibility of uncovering common constitutive rules. Hayward Alker, an important critic of realism, notes that "the" international system cannot be subsumed under realist theory, because it is characterized by competing, but simultaneously coexisting, organizational logics.[41] Yet a similar criticism can be leveled against the quest for a "generative logic" of the current system, particularly in the renewed interest in the principle of sovereignty.[42] The common constitutive rule of sovereignty is crucial in distinguishing the modern system from its predecessor and sets important limits on the possible. Yet it is not clear that this constitutive norm is shared as widely as structurationists believe. In addition, it is difficult to untangle the effect of the constitutive rule of sovereignty *given that it precisely legitimates and "generates" realist behavior*. The methodological conundrums here are quite obvious. A structurationist approach is likely to carry more explanatory weight in those more limited areas where some common normative structures exist than in those in which they are absent or extremely broad.

THE HEGEMONY OF STRUCTURAL EXPLANATION

One finding that emerges from this review is that structural conditions, however defined, are often found to be compatible with a variety of different outcomes. There are two ways out of this impasse. One is to continue within the structuralist program by refining the concept of structure to yield more powerful explanations. An equally plausible alternative is to examine in more detail the importance of nonstructural variables. One reason for the failure of this second alternative is the deleterious influence exercised by the concept of "levels of analysis" on the study of international politics.

Ever since Kenneth Waltz's *Man, the State and War*, the mainstream of international relations theory has been dominated by three methodological presuppositions: that there are clearly distinct "levels of analysis"; that the appropriate conception of international structure for understanding world politics is the distribution of power; and that systemic explanations should enjoy some priority.

The first two claims are indefensible. The "appropriate" disaggregation of the international system into "levels" can no more be fixed by fiat than can the appropriate disaggregation of any complex system. As Waltz's discussion makes clear, his "images" are not distinct and mutually exclusive "levels" or forms of explanation, but rather clusters of theories and variables, the boundaries between which are fuzzy. Waltz uses theories that postulate a link between human nature and war, for example, to define his "first image." These are shown to be bad theories. It does not follow, however, that all theories focusing on the individual are therefore to be discarded. There are other first image theories that have to do with cognitive processes, perception and misperception, and decision making, just as there are numerous "second-image" and "third-image" theories as well.

The advantages of one definition of structure are not likely to be established through metatheoretical debate. For some explanatory purposes, structure *à la* Waltz might be precisely what is called for. However, there are some purposes for which we may want to think of the international "structure" not in terms of the distribution of capabilities, but as the international division of labor or a system of rules. To criticize such conceptions of structure as "reductionist" is an example of the reigning confusion between metatheoretical and theoretical argument. The debate cannot be resolved by arguing over who has the correct *definition;* it can only be resolved by showing that one conception of structure has greater explanatory power than another over some specified set of outcomes.

The claim that structural explanations deserve some primacy demands closer scrutiny, because it has strongly influenced research and theory in international relations in recent years. On what grounds might such an argument be made? One is that systemic factors are *generally* more powerful than those operating at other levels of analysis. Because survival is at stake, external threats and constraints will be the most important determinants of national policy. Survival is not always at stake in international politics, however, and in any case, such a general claim for the *Primat der Aussenpolitik* cannot really be tested in a conclusive way; it constitutes only a *judgment* or *bias* about an extremely broad, complex, and inconclusive body of empirical tests.

A somewhat weaker form of the argument for the primacy of systemic theory is that it is necessarily more parsimonious. This depends on what is being explained, however. Since there is, at any given time, only one system, but numerous states, systemic theory is *necessarily* more parsimonious than subsystemic theory *for explaining systemic outcomes*. Even if we were to devise an extremely parsimonious unit level theory, it would not be as "compact" as an equally parsimonious systems-level theory because the former would have to contain an algorithm for aggregating its unit level insights across the units. But this claim does not hold for the explanation of the behavior of particular units or of the strategic interactions among them. There is no *a priori* reason to believe that a systemic explanation of state action will be less parsimonious than one that incorporates unit level variables. Game theory provides an example. It provides a relatively parsimonious theoretical structure, but one that hinges critically on actor preferences.

In any case, the claim for the superiority of a theory on the basis of its parsimony cannot stand alone. What use is a parsimonious theory that is wrong or that explains only a small portion of the variance? The issue, therefore, is not one of parsimony *per se* but of the trade-off between parsimony and explanatory power. One hesitates about buying a little additional explanation of the variance through a substantial loss of parsimony, although even here a case could be made for the superiority of the more complex theory if it was not simply the result of *ad hoc* amendations. In general, however, given the complexity of international phenomena, it is highly unlikely that we would get powerful predictions using theories that predict primarily from one variable alone. Indeed, we should probably be *suspicious* of highly parsimonious theories. The general point, however, is that there is no reason to grant priority to systemic theory on the basis of its parsimony alone, unless it can be proved also to have at least equal explanatory power.

A third reason for giving primacy to systemic theory is more prudential. It is quite possible that laboring away at the level of the individual units, the researcher might miss the importance of systemic variables in understanding the phenomena she is trying to explain. This criticism is raised by Waltz against "reductionists" and was at the heart of the dependency and world-systems critiques of modernization theory. The warning is stated nicely by Keohane in an overview of Europe's political economy in the 1970s:

> An international-level analysis . . . is therefore neither an alternative to studying domestic politics, nor a mere supplement to it—an afterthought in which "the international dimension" is introduced. On the contrary, it is a *precondition* for effective comparative analysis. Without a conception of the common external problems, pressures, and challenges facing European political economies in the 1970s and 1980s, we lack an analytical basis for identifying the role played by domestic interests and pressures in the various countries.[43]

It is important to underline that this is not a *theoretical* argument for the primacy of systemic theory. One could find, for example, that the states of Europe responded quite differently to "common external problems, pressures, and challenges"; this seems, in fact, to have been the case. Keohane's warning is an important one, but its basic message is no different from the methodological injunction about drawing spurious causal inferences.

The primacy given to systemic theory has as its correlate a relative lack of attention to theorizing about the interrelationship between international and domestic-level factors or how they would be reconciled or weighted within the confines of a more integrated theory. Recent debates about neorealism make little reference to the determinants of foreign policy. Waltz argues that such integration is unnecessary: "an international political theory does not imply or require a theory of foreign policy any more than a market theory implies or requires a theory of the firm."[44]

What is the domain of these two types of theory? Is international politics like a market in which many outcomes can be predicted on the basis of spare assumptions about the units, or is it, in fact, a choice system in which understanding actor preferences is critical? Despite his extensive criticism of reductionist theories, Waltz is quite candid, if only briefly, about the strong limitations on structural theory:

> Structurally we can describe and understand the pressures states are subject to. We cannot predict how they will react to the pressures without knowledge of their internal dispositions. A systems theory explains changes across systems, not within them, and yet international life within a given system is by no means all repetition. Important discontinuities occur. If they occur within a system that endures, their causes are found at the unit level.[45]

Waltz is suggesting that the domain of systemic theory is relatively narrow. First, it is not the case that regularized patterns of behavior *within* a given system are *necessarily* best explained by systemic properties; they may also be equally well explained by subsystemic ones. For example, Michael Doyle has offered a parsimonious, subsystemic theory that democratic republics do not engage each other in war.[46] Yet even if we admit that systemic theory is likely to offer a parsimonious explanation for changes or variations across systems, or for continuities within them, *any variation in the behavior of similarly situated states within a given system cannot be explained by reference to the system.* Though formulated with reference to neorealism, Waltz' observation can logically be extended to other structural theories as well. These caveats are particularly troublesome for world-systems theory, because such disparate states and class structures are grouped within each of the three categories of core, periphery, and semiperiphery. Similarly, the constitutive rule of sovereignty "constrains" states only in comparison to the premodern system or to some counterfactual system in which the sovereignty norm is attenuated.

A similar split between foreign policy and international politics can be traced within the field of international political economy in the last decade. The fundamental observation driving Peter Katzenstein's *Between Power and Plenty* was that similarly situated states responded differently to external constraints as a result of variations in domestic structures.[47] Katzenstein might be faulted for not adequately exploring the differences in structural position among the advanced industrial states, but his basic insight resulted in an important branching within the field of international political economy. One strand moved toward the explanation of *systemic* outcomes. Robert Keohane's *After Hegemony*, Kenneth Oye's *Cooperation Under Anarchy*, and the literature on international regimes and cooperation are exemplary of this tradition.[48] A second strand followed Katzenstein's lead and sought to explore the domestic bases of foreign economic policy.[49]

The observations by Waltz and Katzenstein suggest the limits on structure as an explanatory variable. It is also salutary to note that many apparently "systemic" outcomes are in fact *aggregations* of unit-level characteristics or the result of *strategic interaction* among states. Strategic interactions, which include diplomatic exchanges and bargaining, are amenable to game-theoretic treatment, which, as I have argued, is quite distinct in its theoretical foundations from structural theory. The sharp division Waltz seeks to draw between international politics and foreign policy is thus artificial. For example, a stable system is equivalent to one in which no individual state has the incentive to challenge the status quo. There are asymmetries in the level of interdependence that might be seen to constitute an economic structure, but the level of interdependence in the system as a whole is equal to the sum of the levels of interdependence of individual countries. International rules are established through bargaining, and their reach is transnational, yet compliance hinges on domestic incentives and decision. All these systemic outcomes may, indeed, have systemic explanations, yet it is wrong to assume that they constitute characteristics of the system that cannot in principle be disaggregated.

Work within the realist tradition routinely departs from the rigid adherence to structure-level variables. An example is Steven Walt's rich and insightful study on *The Origins of Alliances*.[50] Walt notes that a pure balance-of-power theory of alliances would predict that alliances form against the strongest state or coalition. Walt rejects this theory, not only for its predictive weakness, but because of the need to "account for the other factors that statesmen consider when deciding with whom to ally."[51] Unlike Waltz, Walt explicitly incorporates both descriptive accuracy and an analysis of preferences into his criteria for good theory. In opposition to pure balance-of-power theory, Walt proposes that states tend to balance and ally not against power *per se* but against threat. This is a perfectly reasonable assertion, but it is important to underline that it is not a *systemic* one.

The concept of threat is highly elastic, and Walt offers no clear independent measure of it. Nonetheless Walt does suggest a number of factors that will affect threat levels. These include aggregate power, geographic proximity, offensive capability, and aggressive intentions. We know from Walt's premise that power alone cannot predict threat; it was precisely for that reason that the concept of threat was preferred to power. Along similar lines, proximity alone is unlikely to generate threat, and even "offensive power," a function of force structures, is likely to be indeterminate. This leaves aggressive intent as the most important variable in the equation, since it is only in the presence of aggressive intent that threats materialize; intent is a *necessary* condition for threat. If we are to avoid the unhelpful claim that states constitute threats when they behave in a threatening fashion, it is necessary to examine the perception of "aggressive intent" on the part of the *target* state. This in turn demands an examination of psychology, information processing, and domestic politics and allows for the possibility that states may balance against "threats" that do not exist. Even with this complex definition of threat, Walt still finds that ideological variables also matter in determining the range of alliance possibilities and that states may not balance threats under a number of conditions, including the unavailability of allies, particular weakness, or where there is clarity about the outcome of a pending conflict.

The central theoretical purpose of Walt's book is to test the proposition that states are more likely to balance against threats than bandwagon with them. His finding about the prevalence of balancing is an extremely important one, but to assess the utility of his modified realist framework it is equally important to know whether *either* of these *external* explanations of alliance behavior work as well as *domestic* or *transnational* ones. The core, neorealist version of balance-of-threat theory appears to work best under realist conditions; that is, crises or situations of external military threat. Of the thirty Middle East alliances against regional threats that Walt identifies, at least twenty included "threats" to *domestic* political legitimacy. These emanated from transnational movements and ideologies, facilitated by the linguistic integration of the region. It is of course possible to incorporate variables such as these under the heading of "threat." [52] Once the concept of threat is augmented to include domestic political concerns, the implicit claim to the priority of *external* conditions in determining alliance behavior is weakened and alternative domestic political explanations of foreign policy come to the fore. For example, it could be argued that in the absence of strong security concerns, political elites will pursue alliance strategies that maximize their *internal* political support.

The analysis in this section suggests that the dominance of systemic forms of explanation is unwarranted and must be considered primarily as a methodological injunction. Unfortunately, the preoccupation with systemic theory has led to a division of the field into those studying "international" phenomena, such as cooperation, regimes, alliance behavior or stability, and those studying foreign policy. This divorce was encouraged by systemic theorists, who argued, quite rightly, that international context could swamp the causal importance of the unit level variables on which students of foreign policy tended to focus their attention. In the study of foreign policy, though, the Janus-faced nature of the state is clearly revealed. On the one hand, it is rooted in the international system; on the other hand, it is simultaneously bound by domestic constraints. As Walt's study suggests, the methodological injunction of the structuralists can thus also be directed at them: convincing tests of systemic theories of foreign policy must show their superiority to second-image alternatives.

EXPLAINING STRUCTURAL CHANGE

At the beginning of this essay, I suggested two general problems confronting structural theory. The first had to do with the "looseness of fit" between structural conditions and outcomes, which I attributed to the neglect of "second-image" variables, including the preferences of actors. The second limitation on the new structuralisms concerns the explanation of change. Structural theory can explain change *across* systems in the sense of accounting for differences in outcomes that result from changes of or differences in structure. But the comparative advantage of structural approaches is in explaining *recurrent* behavior: "within a system, a [structural] theory explains recurrences and repetition, not change."[53] It is perhaps unfair to chastise a theory for not explaining what it does not purport to explain. Nonetheless, structural theories must look to subsystemic processes and domestic-level variables to explain change, including those most important changes of the system itself that establish new structural parameters.

Given differences in how *system* and *structure* are defined, one would expect to find a plethora of theories of systemic change. Surprisingly, however, three general types of theories dominate a small literature. The most common approach is economic and explains systemic change as the result of "disequilibria" resulting from the uneven nature of economic growth. The second theory focuses on exogenous changes in the relative costs or prices facing major powers. These changes, in turn, provide incentives for "system-changing" behavior. A final approach, which fits more neatly with the "reflective" research program, gives weight to autonomous changes in ideas and the evolution of new knowledge. All these approaches must revert to assumptions or implicit theories about domestic choice processes in order to be successful.

Uneven Development and Change

The most prevalent theory of structural change in international politics begins with the observation that economic growth in the world system has historically been *uneven*. This approach is common to realism in the balance-of-power tradition, world-systems theory, and the literature on hegemonic cycles in world politics.[54] The reasons for this unevenness involve both systemic factors and differences across countries and regions in their endowments, institutions, and technologies. In *U.S. Power and the Multinational Corporation*, Robert Gilpin stresses a systemic factor: cycles of concentration and diffusion of technology.[55] Technology tends to diffuse away from the innovating center over time, creating new opportunities for competitors. Unless great powers are capable of maintaining constant levels of innovation, their relative position vis-à-vis other states in the system will decline as competitors absorb existing technologies and challenge the hegemon's monopoly. Maintaining constant innovation is difficult, however, in part because major innovations appear to cluster in long cycles.[56] Even were such a clustering not observable, however, it is easier to apply a backlog of existing technologies than it is to create new ones. As a result, the "poor get rich and the rich slow down."[57]

These systemic processes are supplemented by variations in politics and institutions that also affect comparative levels of technological innovation, and more broadly, growth. Quite apart from the diffusion of technology, Kuznets, Chenery, and others have noted the s-shaped pattern that characterizes national growth trajectories: slow at first, then accelerating, before entering a period of "mature" growth at slower rates.[58] The reasons for this are still not well understood but include the one-time effect of shifting labor out of lower-productivity agriculture into manufacturing and increasing political pressures over time for consumption that squeeze savings and investment.

For realists, uneven economic growth translates directly into a change in structure if new great powers emerge or old ones decline. These structural changes, in turn, affect rules and individual state behavior. This second theoretical step is accomplished by assuming that the system as a whole is in some sort of "equilibrium"; there is a stable "fit" between the distribution of power and patterns of domination, incentives to aggression, and international rules. The change in the distribution of capabilities results in a "disequilibrium" at time t_2. As power is diffused, the costs of maintaining political dominance rise, there are new incentives to resist hegemonic domination or to act as aggressor, and pressures emerge to change rules in line with the interests of rising powers. In Gilpin's words, "If the disequilibrium in the international system is not resolved then the system will be changed and a new equilibrium reflecting the distribution of power will be established."[59]

What does this mean concretely? For theorists in the realist tradition, uneven development and the rise of new powers are linked to changing patterns of threat and alliance, which can in turn lead to war. A. J. P. Taylor and Paul Kennedy have offered similar accounts along these lines of the international–structural context prior to World War I.[60] For world-systems theorists, uneven development helps explain both the incorporation of new zones into the world economy and the shifting position of different states *within* the core-periphery structure. For theorists of hegemonic stability, the hegemon's decline can result in anything from a weakening of international regimes to general war.

These claims are sweepingly indeterminate. First, at the level of the system itself, Gilpin suggests that the disequilibrium can be resolved *within* the confines of the existing system; thus, we are not even certain whether hegemonic decline means a change *within* the system or *of* the system. Shifting from the level of system structure to the behavior of the hegemon itself, Gilpin lists a variety of possible responses to decline, from rejuvenation, to various types of retrenchment, to military defense of hegemonic prerogatives, all with sharply different implications.

There is no doubt that changing economic capabilities result in changing power position; this is true almost by definition. But pure power analysis yields little without assumptions or knowledge about actor interests. There is, for example, no clear theory of how rising powers will be accommodated. History yields examples of peaceful accommodation, as well as those in which hegemonic wars resulted from power "disequilibria." Great Britain accommodated the expansion of the United States in the Western Hemisphere in the late nineteenth century but could not accommodate the rise of Germany. In sum, the theory of uneven development points to an important source of parametric change and to crucial constraints on hegemonic power, but does not provide convincing arguments about how such changes are linked to political behavior.

Changes in Relative Costs and Incentives to System-Changing Behavior

In *War and Change in World Politics*, Gilpin also outlines a subtly different theory of systemic change that does not have recourse to the problematic concept of systemic equilibrium. This theory rests on an expected utility model and argues that a "state will attempt to change the international system if the expected benefits exceed the expected costs, i.e., if there is an expected net gain."[61] These change efforts, such as territorial, political, and economic expansion, will continue until their marginal costs and marginal benefits are equated. A similar argument has been made by Bruce Bueno de Mesquita in his expected utility theory of war initiation. Despite its statement in functional form, Robert Keohane's theory of regime compliance can also be posed in an expected utility framework. Powerful states will comply with regimes where they expect net benefits from them, discounted over some time horizon.[62]

In this form, the theory is static and does not offer an account of when expected utility for systemic change will be positive; it simply notes that states will seek to change the system if it is profitable and they are able to do so. But the theory may also be stated in a dynamic form. This demands identifying those factors that *alter* the cost–benefit calculus facing individual states and thus account for *changes* in their behavior. If this is done, systemic or institutional change can be endogenized.

This relative cost theory of change might be seen as simply a more general statement of the theory of uneven development. As Gilpin notes, the "critical significance of the differential growth of power among states is that it alters the cost of changing the international system and therefore the incentives for changing the international system."[63] But changes in the distribution of power are not the only factors that affect the incentives to "system-changing" behavior. Innovations in transport and communication, economic changes that result in economies of scale, and changes in military technology can all affect the incentives facing states. The literatures on the properties of offense- and defense-dominant systems and on the effects of technological innovation on stability fit within this broad theoretical framework.[64] In addition, there are a number of domestic changes that will affect the cost–benefit calculus, including any changes that increase or decrease the state's ability to extract resources.

These variegated observations do not constitute a single theory, but they do add up to a rich and variegated research program. The comparative cost framework promises an avenue for integrating the effects of both domestic and international political and economic changes on great power behavior, and thus captures the link between levels of analysis that structural realism ignores. It is worthwhile stating one important caveat about the ability of such a theory to explain changes in international institutions and rules, however.

Adopting the comparative-cost model to understanding institutional change demands the following premises and steps. First, changes in relative prices affect the *preferences* of key actors in predictable ways. Second, there are firm expectations about how a particular institutional change will affect actor interests; this defines the preferred institutional framework. Finally, it must be possible to explain the institutional change as the vector of the simultaneous efforts of a number of actors seeking different systemic changes. The first step is a reasonable one. The third presents a number of well-known problems.

The second step, however, presents difficulties for a comparative-cost approach to institutional change. These rest on problems of uncertainty and have been noted by Alexander Field in his penetrating critique of the North and Thomas model of institutional innovation in early modern Europe. Field argues that "there is no reason to assume that there are unique overhead costs associated with every set of rules, overhead costs independent of the length of time that set has prevailed, and, if the individual rule is part of an overall set of rules, the permanence of other elements of the institutional structure."[65] This means that neither the analyst nor the actors themselves can be sure about the costs and benefits associated with launching a particular institutional change. "Reformers" predicting gains from a change in the system will be pitted against "conservatives" fearing that the change will prove costly. Such debates are common prior to the initiation of major wars. How they are resolved is a function of domestic political, organizational, and decision-making structures. Once again, as with the model of "uneven development," the basic theory leaves indeterminacies in its prediction of a path of change that can only be resolved through reference to domestic decision-making processes.

Ideas and Change: The Contribution of Ernst Haas

As I argued in the previous section, the "reflective" research program maintains a healthy ambivalence toward the determinant conceptions of structure advanced by neorealists and world-systems theorists. Since *The Uniting of Europe*, Ernst Haas's work has reflected this ambivalence. The reasons have to do with the conception of the international system Haas and his neofunctionalist followers favored, the types of explanation they adopted, and the focus on change itself. Neofunctionalism was characteristic of what Hedley Bull labeled the Grotian middle ground between a Hobbesian view of international politics and Kantian cosmopolitanism.[66] The neofunctionalists parted company with the realists in the relative weight they gave to *organizational* factors in international life. Direct lines of descent can be traced from Haas through the literature on transnational relations to the current work on regimes and the "new" international institutionalism. Haas always included in his conception of the international system not simply structures of power and exchange or the policies of autonomously interacting "units," but the network of organizations and rules that institutionalize international life.

Epistemologically, Haas and the neofunctionalists were uncomfortable with strongly causal models of human behavior and shunned power as an explanation. This followed in part from the importance given to the role of international institutions. Unlike the spontaneous order of an anarchic system in which unintended consequences play an important role, organization results from *conscious design*. Power could not be conceived as a pregiven structure, because power could be *created* through institutional innovation. The rejection of a strong determinism also resulted from the focus on change *processes* and open or emergent systems that could not be specified through an identifiable end point. This was particularly true of the study of regional integration, the central empirical puzzle around which neofunctionalism coalesced.

If international structural determinism was rejected, how was systemic change to be explained? Here Haas' thinking underwent an evolution. In *The Uniting of Europe*,[67] pluralist models of politics were extended to the process of integration by examining the transnational coalitions favoring a united Europe. This early formulation of neofunctionalism had an important dynamic component: the concept of "spillover." The hypothesis of spillover was that steps toward organizational integration in one issue-area had feedback effects on the interests of actors and pushed them toward integration in other, related areas. Interests were not fixed, but changed as a result of the benefits yielded by the integration process itself.

Revisions in this scheme were not long in coming. The study of integration efforts in other regions naturally drew attention to those "background conditions" that were conducive to integration in Europe but served to block it elsewhere: structure mattered more than was initially thought.[68] De Gaulle's manufacture of a crisis for the European Community in the mid-1960s led Stanley Hoffmann to underline the reversibility of any community-building efforts and the kind of negative spillover in which attempts to move the integration process forward produced new *skepticism* about future efforts.[69] By 1971, Philippe Schmitter was identifying a host of other processes, including spill-back, muddle-about, and spill-around. These were signs not of progress but of theoretical disarray.[70]

A key problem was that explanations and outcomes were indistinguishable. Attention was being given to "process variables" as a form of explanation, though regional integration *itself* was nothing if not a process. The leverage that had been gained by the interest-based model of *The Uniting of Europe* and the strong hypothesis of spillover was being dissipated, and in 1975 Haas recognized as much in a monograph entitled *The Obsolescence of Regional Integration Theory.*[71] This proved a beginning as much as an end, however. By openly scrapping the assumption that authority would gradually be transferred to higher units and the confining focus on regional integration, Haas opened the door to the study of looser forms of issue-specific international organization that extended beyond any particular region or organization. The literature on regimes was born.

In an important series of articles written between 1974 and 1980, Haas began to explore more thoroughly the relationship between the nature of scientific knowledge and political purposes, on the one hand, and international-organizational form, on the other.[72] This focus was partly a response to neoidealists who believed that scientific knowledge or evolutionary imperatives could successfully legitimate ambitious international regulatory regimes. Haas rightly pointed out that this depended not on science but on actor purposes. How could these be investigated in a rigorous way? A return to the inductive, interest-based model of cooperation in *The Uniting of Europe* was not satisfactory. Haas had long argued that "interests" were not static; the hypothesis of spill-over rested on the fact that interests changed as a result of international cooperative processes. But rather than focusing on the way *organization* altered interests, Haas now turned to the more general question of how *knowledge and learning* affected actor interests. Scientific experts, economic agents, and politicians interacted and allied in pursuit of their interests, but they also reached consensus on theories and information that transcended ideological cleavages and redefined interests. Although Haas disagreed with the functionalist idea that new knowledge "demanded" more holistic problem-solving structures, he agreed that interdepen-

dence and expanding knowledge would delegitimate purely national, or decentralized solutions to economic, technological, and
environmental problems. And even if interdependence and new
knowledge did *not* reduce the importance of purely national responses, these responses might nonetheless be explained by changing knowledge; knowledge could operate to explain either new levels
and forms of cooperation or the behavior of individual "units."

The key problem was how to unpack "knowledge" so that it
could be causally linked to different organizational forms. The answer was to focus on two variables: the degree of, or trend toward,
consensus that existed about technical knowledge; and whether the
goals of politicians were narrow and static or "interconnected and
expanding." The intersection of these two variables produced four
"cognitive styles." There were, once again, important problems of
aggregation that were inevitable with such a "bottom-up" theory of
change. Predictions became difficult, for example, when cognitive
styles clashed. These problems were not wholly solved, but a set of
different linkage strategies and organizational forms was associated
with the "dominance" of a particular cognitive style in a particular
negotiating context.

One of the most interesting elements of Haas' scheme concerns
the role of power, and demonstrates clearly the difference between
the "reflective" and realist research programs. For Haas, power is
not of constant importance; rather, its significance depends on cognitive style. Put differently, *realist conditions are themselves the result of
cognitive stances that are subject to change.* "Structure" does not produce
actor purposes and knowledge, but the other way around:

> The type of systems theory I find useful features the inductive method in
> the construction of reality and uses the perceptions of actions of concrete
> human beings in grappling with reality as its main data. Such systems are
> assumed "open" in the sense that they do not tend, by definition, toward
> a given state, such as equilibrium. They are "constructed" in the sense
> that the theorist considers them as heuristic approximations rather than
> networks of determinative "laws" constraining choice.[73]

In the 1980s, Haas' thinking underwent another subtle change,
one echoed in the views of Emanuel Adler in his contribution to this
volume. This view, which Haas identified as "evolutionary epistemology," went far beyond his previous work in its ambition and
scope, but also mirrored some of the difficulties with the "reflective"

research program. First, the boundaries between changes in scientific knowledge and changes in international organizational form were blurred. The study of regimes became a vehicle for a broader exercise, "a way of understanding the interactions of *homo politicus* with nature and with culture. . . . The study of regimes illustrates the range of past and future choices about international collaboration in a context of changing self-understanding."[74] Second, a key component of this "changing self-understanding" was social scientific knowledge *about regime change itself.* Waltzian realism misleadingly posited for itself a detached Archimedean point from which international change could be viewed but was then forced to smuggle in prescriptions that had little grounding within the context of a deterministic theory. Haas, and the reflective program more generally, always raised the uncomfortable question of the purpose of the social scientific enterprise itself.

Haas' close interweaving of the growth of scientific knowledge and of changes in cooperation, and his evolutionary epistemology served to underscore the reflexive nature of political systems, but also created new theoretical difficulties. Evolutionary epistemology is a theory of knowledge, but the evolutionary nature of knowledge also serves for Haas as a key force behind the development and change in international regimes. Was a *theory* of how knowledge evolved necessary in order to use knowledge as an explanatory variable in examining cooperation?

The appeal to an evolutionary epistemology injected a dynamic component into the cognitive approach. But the observation that knowledge evolves does not, in itself, solve the critical problem of the *political* processes through which the selection of ideas takes place. What allows some knowledge to be selected while other knowledge withers politically? Put differently, how do we conceptualize the relationship between knowledge and power? Haas adopts an uneasy resolution in which "mechanistic" constraints operate, but are subject to redefinition and change on the basis of new knowledge. Adler, in his contribution to this volume, suggests the beginnings of a theory in which institutions become "carriers" of particular bodies of knowledge. Both underscore the central point of this essay. In constructing a viable theory of international politics, there is no escaping the need for a theory of the state and how domestic political interests and institutions interact to generate "national" choices.

CONCLUSION

How much progress has really been made? Do we really have a deeper understanding of the forces shaping international politics than Morgenthau, Carr, or Thucydides? Has structuralism added anything? The answer is yes. The new structuralisms introduced new vigor into international relations theory. Over the longer term, however, the unintended consequences of structural theory may prove more important than the fact that its objectives have been realized. Viewed from the perspective of the sociology of knowledge and progress within the discipline, the role of structural theory has been to open up new vistas and opportunities for nonsystemic theories. Structural and systemic theories, particularly neorealist theory, sought to define a comparative area of competence separate from the study of international diplomatic and economic processes, foreign policy, and comparative politics, economics, and sociology. This effort had numerous shortcomings. Structural realism has been forced to return again and again to how constraints are perceived and processed by different domestic political structures, decision-making, and cognitive processes. Strategic interactions and actor preferences mattered as much as or more than structure in determining how states behaved. From its origins in Wallerstein's work, world-systems theory exhibited a curious gap between somewhat grandiose theoretical pretensions and the fascinating empirical work that emerged by grappling with the relationship between domestic development and position in the international division of labor. More flexible conceptualizations of international economic structure have generated interesting new theory based on actors' locations in the market. These approaches succeed in large part because they join the international and domestic levels of analysis.

The reflective program represents the most interesting frontier for international relations research. "Reflectivists" were always comfortable building structures out of actor purposes, and thus maintained closer contact with domestic political, ideological, and cognitive processes. With the decline of the hegemony of structuralism, perhaps the field of international relations theory will spend greater time with that crucial "unit" that has been blackboxed for so long, the state, and less with abstractions such as system and structure that have yielded less than they promised. The return to domestic factors will also serve an even more important purpose. By introducing politics and choice more squarely into its analysis, the field of international relations theory might reduce its lofty distance from the rough and tumble world of foreign policy with which we are all ultimately concerned.

ENDNOTES

My thanks to James Caporaso, Sheila Grader, Stanley Hoffmann, John Ikenberry, Lisa Martin, Helen Milner, Andrew Moravcsik, Joe Nye, Robert Powell, and Steve Walt for their comments on earlier drafts of this paper and to Eunjie Kahn for research assistance. My thanks in particular to Emanuel Adler, who saved me from some particularly serious errors. This essay is dedicated to Ernst Haas, who bears no responsibility for its content beyond his shaping influence as a teacher.

1. Kenneth N. Waltz, *Theory of International Politics* (Reading, Mass.: Addison-Wesley, 1979).
2. Robert Gilpin, *War and Change in International Politics* (New York: Cambridge University Press, 1981); Stephen D. Krasner, *Structural Conflict: The Third World Against Global Liberalism* (Berkeley: University of California Press, 1985); David Lake, *Power, Protection, and Free Trade* (Ithaca, N.Y.: Cornell University Press, 1988).
3. Robert Keohane, *After Hegemony: Cooperation and Discord in the World Political Economy* (Princeton, N.J.: Princeton University Press, 1984).
4. See John Gerard Ruggie, "Continuity and Transformation in the World Polity: Toward a Neorealist Synthesis," Robert Cox, "Social Forces, States and World Orders: Beyond International Relations Theory", and Richard Ashley, "The Poverty of Neorealism," in Robert Keohane, ed., *Neorealism and Its Critics* (New York: Columbia University Press, 1986); Alexander E. Wendt, "The Agent-Structure Problem in International Relations Theory," *International Organization* (Summer 1987); 41(3):335–370; John Ruggie and Friedrich Kratochwil, "International Organization: A State of the Art on the Art of the State." *International Organization* (Autumn 1986), 40(4):753–776; Hayward Alker, "Dialectical Foundations of Global Disparities," *International Studies Quarterly* (March 1981), 25:69–98, and "The Presumption of Anarchy in World Politics," ms., Massachusetts Institute of Technology, 1986; Friedrich Kratochwil, *Norms, Rules and Decisions* (New York: Columbia University Press, 1989).
5. Robert Keohane used the term *reflective* in "International Institutions: Two Approaches," *International Studies Quarterly* (December 1988), 32(4):379–396.
6. For general statements of the world-systems conception of structure, see Immanuel Wallerstein, *The Modern World System* (New York: Academic

Press, 1974); Christopher Chase-Dunn and Richard Rubinson, "Toward a Structural Perspective on the World-System," *Politics and Society* (1977), 7(4):453–476; Giovanni Arrighi and Jessica Drangel, "The Stratification of the World Economy: An Exploration of the Semi-peripheral Zone," *Review* (Summer 1986), 10(1):9–74.

7. Alexander James Field, "On the Explanation of Rules Using Rational Choice Models," *Journal of Economic Issues* (March 1979), 13(1):51.

8. Imre Lakatos, "Falsification and the Methodology of Scientific Research Programmes," in Lakatos and Alan Musgrave, eds., *Criticism and the Growth of Knowledge* (New York: Cambridge University Press, 1970), pp. 118–119.

9. See also Wendt, "The Agent-Structure Problem."

10. Timothy J. McKeown, "The Limitations of Structural Theories of Commercial Policy," *International Organization* (Winter 1986), 40(1):43.

11. Kenneth Waltz, *Man, the State and War* (New York: Columbia University Press, 1959).

12. These problems are discussed in James Caporaso and Stephan Haggard, "Power in the International Political Economy," in Richard Stoll and Michael D. Ward, eds., *Power in World Politics* (Boulder, Colo.: Lynne Rienner, 1989).

13. On the effects of bipolarity and multipolarity, see Kenneth Waltz, "The Stability of a Bipolar World," *Daedalus* (Summer 1964), 93:881–909; Karl W. Deutsch, "Multipolar Power Systems and International Stability," *World Politics* (April 1964), 16:390–406; Richard Rosecrance, "Bipolarity, Multipolarity, and the Future," *Journal of Conflict Resolution* (September 1966), 10:314–327.

14. For reviews of the hegemonic stability literature, see Duncan Snidal, "Limits of Hegemonic Stability Theory," *International Organization* (Summer 1985), 39:579–614; Stephan Haggard and Beth Simmons, "Theories of International Regimes," *International Organization* (Summer 1987), 41(3):491–517.

15. David Lake, "Beneath the Commerce of Nations: A Theory of International Economic Structures," *International Studies Quarterly* (June 1984), 28:143–170.

16. Lake, *Power, Protection, and Free Trade.*

17. See Robert Keohane, "Theory of Hegemonic Stability and Changes in International Economic Regimes, 1967–1977," in Ole Holsti, ed., *Change in the International System* (Boulder, Colo.: Westview, 1980); Helen Milner, *Resisting Protectionism* (Princeton, N.J.: Princeton University Press, 1988); David Yoffie, *Power and Protectionism* (New York: Columbia University Press, 1985); and Judith Goldstein, "Ideas, Institutions and American Trade Policy," *International Organization* (Winter 1988), 42(1):179–218.

18. Stephen Krasner resorts to such lags in his "State Power and the Structure of International Trade," *World Politics* (April 1976), 28:317–347.

19. See Helen Milner, "Anarchy and Interdependence," paper prepared for

the Annual Meeting of the American Political Science Association, Washington, Sept. 1–4, 1988. See also Gilpin, *War and Change*, pp. 90–93.

20. The following draws on Haggard and Simmons, "Theories of International Regimes." The distinction between "benign" and "malign" conceptions is Snidal's.

21. Snidal, "Limits of Hegemonic Stability Theory."

22. Charles Kindleberger, *The World in Depression, 1929–1939* (Berkeley: University of California Press, 1973).

23. Ken Oye, "Explaining Cooperation Under Anarchy: Hypotheses and Strategies," *World Politics* (October 1985), 38:1–24.

24. See the introductory and concluding pieces in Stephen D. Krasner, ed., *International Regimes* (Ithaca, N.Y.: Cornell University Press, 1983).

25. See Ronald Rogowski, "Political Cleavages and Changing Exposure to Trade," *American Political Science Review* (December 1987), 81(4):1121–1138.

26. See Andre Gunder Frank, *Latin America: Underdevelopment or Revolution?* (New York: Monthly Review Press, 1969); Robert Gilpin, *The Political Economy of International Relations* (Princeton, N.J.: Princeton University Press, 1988).

27. Arrighi and Drangel, "The Stratification of the World Economy," p. 17.

28. See Robert Brenner's Marxist critique of Wallerstein, "The Origins of Capitalist Development: A Critique of Neo-Smithian Marxism," *New Left Review* (1977), 104:25–92.

29. Milner, *Resisting Protectionism*; Peter Gourevich, *Politics in Hard Times* (Ithaca, N.Y.: Cornell University Press, 1987); Rogowski, "Political Cleavages"; Lake, *Power, Protection, and Free Trade*.

30. This criticism is developed by Theda Skocpol, "Wallerstein's World Capitalist System: A Theoretical and Historical Critique," *American Journal of Sociology* (March 1977), 82(5):175–190.

31. Stephan Haggard, "The Political Economy of Foreign Direct Investment in Latin America," *Latin American Research Review* (1989), Vol. 29, No. 1.

32. Wendt, "The Agent-Structure Problem, p. 356. Wendt draws on Roy Bhaskar, *The Possibility of Naturalism* (Brighton, England: Harvester Press, 1979) for his epistemological claims, and makes reference to Pierre Bourdieu, *Outline of a Theory of Practice* (New York: Cambridge University Press, 1977), but it appears that the central ideas of his structurationist project are contained in Anthony Giddens's *The Constitution of Society: Outline of a Theory of Structuration* (Berkeley: University of California Press, 1984). There are, in fact, important differences between Bourdieu and Giddens, particularly in Giddens's emphasis on rules.

33. See Kratochwil, *Norms, Rules and Decisions*, ch. 2.

34. Ashley, "The Poverty of Neorealism," p. 291.

35. Edward Gulick, *Europe's Classical Balance of Power* (New York: W. W. Norton, 1955), particularly ch. 1–3.

36. John Ruggie, "International Regimes, Transactions and Change: Embed-

ded Liberalism in the Postwar Economic Order," in Krasner, ed., *International Regimes*.

37. Kratochwil, *Norms, Rules and Decisions*, p. 24.
38. Wendt, "The Agent-Structure Problem," p. 355.
39. Ibid., pp. 363–364.
40. Ashley, "The Poverty of Neorealism," p. 294.
41. Alker, "Dialectical Foundations."
42. On sovereignty as a constitutive norm, see Ruggie, "Towards a Neo-Realist Synethsis"; Ashley, "The Poverty of Neorealism"; Stephen Krasner, "Sovereignty: An Institutional Perspective," *Comparative Political Studies* (April 1988), 21(1):67.
43. Robert Keohane, "The World Political Economy and the Crisis of Embedded Liberalism," in John H. Goldthorpe, ed., *Order and Conflict in Contemporary Capitalism* (Oxford: Clarendon Press, 1984), p. 16.
44. Waltz, *Theory*, p. 72.
45. Ibid., p. 71.
46. Michael Doyle, "Liberalism and World Politics," *American Political Science Review* (December 1986), 80(4):1151–1170.
47. Peter Katzenstein, ed., *Between Power and Plenty* (Madison: University of Wisconsin Press, 1978).
48. Keohane, *After Hegemony*; Oye, "Explaining Cooperation Under Anarchy."
49. Others in this tradition include Peter Gourevitch, *Politics in Hard Times* (Ithaca, N.Y.: Cornell University Press, 1986); John Zysman, *Governments, Markets and Growth* (Ithaca, N.Y.: Cornell University Press, 1983); and the new wave of dependency theorists, including particularly Peter Evans, *Dependent Development: The Alliance of Multinational, State and Local Capital in Brazil* (Princeton, N.J.: Princeton University Press, 1979).
50. Steven Walt, *The Origins of Alliances* (Ithaca, N.Y.: Cornell University Press, 1988).
51. Ibid., p. 21.
52. Ibid., pp. 263–264.
53. Waltz, *Theory*, p. 69.
54. On hegemonic cycles, see Robert Gilpin, *War and Change in World Politics* (Cambridge: Cambridge University Press, 1981).
55. Robert Gilpin, *U.S. Power and the Multinational Corporation* (New York: Basic Books, 1975). Gilpin generalizes from Ray Vernon, "International Investment and International Trade in the Product Cycle," *Quarterly Journal of Economics* (1966), 80:190–207.
56. A comprehensive statement on the long-cycle literature is that by Joshua Goldstein, *Long Cycles* (New Haven: Yale University Press, 1988).
57. W. Rostow, *Why the Poor Get Rich and the Rich Slow Down* (Austin: University of Texas Press, 1980).
58. On the s-shaped pattern of national growth, see Simon Kuznets, *Modern Economic Growth* (New Haven: Yale University Press, 1966); Hollis Che-

nery and Moises Syrquin, *Patterns of Development: 1950–1970* (New York: Oxford University Press for the World Bank, 1975).

59. Robert Gilpin, *War and Change*.
60. A. J. P. Taylor, *The Struggle for Mastery in Europe: 1848–1914* (Oxford: Clarendon Press, 1954), ch. 1; Paul M. Kennedy, "The First World War and the International Power System," *International Security* (Summer 1984), 9(1):7–40.
61. Gilpin, *War and Change*, p. 50.
62. Bruce Bueno de Mesquita, *The War Trap* (New Haven: Yale University Press, 1981); Keohane, *After Hegemony*, ch. 6.
63. Gilpin, *War and Change*, p. 95.
64. See, for example, Robert Jervis, "Cooperation Under the Security Dilemma," *World Politics* (1978), Vol. 30. No. 2; Jack S. Levy, "The Offensive/Defensive Balance in Military Technology: A Theoretical and Historical Analysis," *International Studies Quarterly* (1984), Vol. 28, No. 2.
65. Alexander Field, "The Problem with Neoclassical Institutional Economics: A Critique with Special Reference to the North/Thomas Model of Pre-1500 Europe," *Explorations in Economic History* (1981), Vol. 18, p. 186.
66. Hedley Bull, *The Anarchical Society* (New York: Columbia University Press, 1977), ch. 2.
67. Ernst Haas, *The Uniting of Europe* (Stanford, Calif.: Stanford University Press, 1958), which was revealingly subtitled "Political, Social, and Economic Forces."
68. See, for example, Joseph Nye, *Peace in Parts* (Boston: Little, Brown, 1971).
69. Stanley Hoffmann, "Obstinate or Obsolete; The Fate of the Nation State and the Case of Europe," in Joseph Nye, ed., *International Regionalism* (Boston: Little, Brown, 1968).
70. See Philippe Schmitter, "A Revised Theory of Regional Integration in Lindberg and Scheingold, eds., *Regional Integration: Theory and Research* (Cambridge, Mass.: Harvard University Press, 1971). See also Ernst Haas, "The Study of Regional Integration: Reflections on the Joy and Anguish of Pretheorizing," *International Organization* (1970), 24(4):607–646.
71. Ernst Haas, *The Obsolescence of Regional Integration Theory* (Berkeley: Institute of International Studies, 1975).
72. This had been a theme before but became more pronounced in an important series of articles from the mid-1970s, particularly "Turbulent Fields and the Study of Regional Integration," *International Organization* (Spring 1976), 30(2):173–212; "Is There a Hole in the Whole?" *International Organization* (Summer 1975), 29(3): 827–876; and *The Obsolescence of Regional Integration Theory*.
73. Haas, "Is There a Hole in the Whole?" p. 837.
74. Ernst B. Haas, "Words Can Hurt You; or Who Said What to Whom About Regimes?" in Stephen Krasner, ed., *International Regimes* (Ithaca, N.Y.: Cornell University Press, 1983), p. 24.

12

TOWARD A THEORY OF PROGRESS IN INTERNATIONAL RELATIONS

Beverly Crawford

I believe one has to abandon the idea of global, massive progress that is valid for all societies. . . . I think one can speak of progress with a little "p," and in the plural. In certain epochs in certain places of the earth certain progresses have occurred, which have probably been paid for by regression in other domains.　　　　　　　　　　　　　　　　　—Claude Lévi-Strauss[1]

A sea change is under way in international relations. The Cold War security system has collapsed and Communist regimes in Central and Eastern Europe have crumbled. Rising international interdependence and revolutionary developments in science and technology have given birth to new global forces at a less visible level: the nuclear and information "revolutions," the evolution of an integrated international food system, a dramatic increase in cross-border pollution and the globalization of production and investment, to name but a few. Because the post-war era between 1945–1990 was one of relative peace, these economic, social, and environmental changes have assumed a political dynamic of their own, and are now central to political debates in international relations. Scholars have asked whether these new developments would transform the fundamental nature of international politics. Would they lead to new modes of cooperation or would they create new opportunities for conflict? Would these developments be a boon to peace, plenty, and welfare? Or would they provide increased incentives for war, inequality, and suffering?

In practice, political elites, in their efforts to harness these forces to make policy choice, have legitimated their decisions with arguments about progress. Indeed, the ideology of progress guides national policy and sets the context for the programs of international organizations. Nuclear energy, foreign aid, technology transfer—all have been touted as the keys to national and global prosperity and even peace. But in fact, we have seen that "progressive" programs like these and others often consolidate both national and international elite power with little residual benefit for the population at large. At times these programs have even been harmful. Although the last decade of the twentieth century opens with the "progressive" forces of democracy on the march, it is also witnessing the birth of governments weakened by economic disintegration, ethnic strife and political polarization, ripe for domination and exploitation. Scholars, then, have had cause for skepticism about where these new developments are taking us.

This project was intended to bridge the gap between the claims of political leaders, their proclamations in international fora, and current concerns of international relations scholarship. We began by developing a set of techniques to assess international change. The standard that guided our collective assessment was the idea of progress. We expressed that idea as a concern for the protection and promotion of human interests in international relations. We launched the project because we believe that an attempt to define progress carefully and think about it systematically can spark new ways of questioning the direction of international change. Despite the obvious and inherent difficulties of this task, it represents an effort to join scholarly analysis with our hopes for the future in order to understand more clearly what we have observed.

As the book now draws to a close, we can assess the success of our efforts. Have the essays assembled here deepened our understanding of the international conditions that might promote human interests? Are there common themes in our approaches and analytical strategies that can help us identify signs of progress in international relations? In the pages to come, I will pull together the arguments and lessons we have learned from our separate inquiries in order to move toward a theory of progress in international relations. I begin by reflecting on two objections to the themes we have introduced here. I then outline a set of conditions and processes culled from the essays that hold the promise of international progress. I conclude by pointing to future research topics that must be pursued if we are to achieve a fuller understanding of how international relations shape human interests.

CONCERN WITH PROGRESS

There are two fundamental objections to a concern with progress in international relations. First, the concept of progress itself has fallen into disrepute among scholars.[2] The very idea of progress evokes a picture of inexorable movement forward and change for the better. The idea is anchored in the faith that the expansion of science and technology, on the other hand, and the growth of reason, on the other, would provide solutions to problems of scarcity and security in increasingly differentiated, interdependent, and adaptive societies. According to the Enlightenment view of Progress, solutions to problems of scarcity and security would stimulate the development of responsive, efficient, and moral social institutions, which in turn would spread material welfare and political justice. The concomitant growth of scientific knowledge and responsive, highly developed social institutions would lead to a common interest in peace, justice, and welfare, which would improve the human condition.[3] This eighteenth-century evolutionary idea of progress was the driving force behind the literature on "development" and "modernization" after World War II.[4] Unfortunately, however, this picture of progress as incremental advance was not commensurate with the actual historical process of social change.

This Enlightenment picture of progress was also behind the "internationalist" view of change in international relations that emerged in the interwar years and was a propelling intellectual force behind the founding of the United Nations. Internationalists believed that knowledge of the destructiveness of modern weaponry as evidenced in two world wars inevitably led to the conclusion that war was no longer a "rational" instrument of national policy. As rational actors, enlightened politicians would seek military security and economic development by promoting international interdependence, law, and organization. This hope was dashed, however, with the onset of the Cold War. In both East and West, internationalism became a weapon in the struggle against the adversary and his opposing ideology, and the old forces of nationalism in world politics continued to prevail.[5]

In raising again the question of international progress, we depart from both the Enlightenment philosophy and the internationalist tradition. From both of these perspectives, progress was a "package" in which means and ends were fused together, becoming indistinguishable. As we argued at the outset, this was a "maximalist" view of progress. According to this view, scientific discovery and technological innovation were inherently "good" and their fruits would automatically enhance the quality of life for all. International cooperation and the growth of international institutions were desirable ends in themselves, for they were thought actually to embody a brighter future for all of humanity.

Most of the contributors to this volume have rejected this "maximalist approach, opting for a "minimalist" perspective. We do not believe that the achievement of human interests is in any way automatic or assured. We have thus steered clear of prescriptions for progressive change. We see progress in small changes—less war, misery, and human rights violations, rather than looking for a transformation of international relations that would usher in world peace, prosperity, and justice. Most important, the essays in this volume "unpack" the concept of progress, both conceptually and empirically. We argue for analytic distinctions between the *means* by which human interests are best achieved and the *ends*—security, welfare, and human rights. We call this a distinction between "instrumental" and "substantive" progress.

The advent of nuclear weapons exposes this weakness in the Enlightenment "package" of progress. Their appearance on the world scene challenges the Enlightenment view that scientific and technological advance are necessarily "progressive." Instead, science and technology are powerful instruments whose effects are indeterminate: nuclear technology can be used either to enhance security or to destroy the world. Security in superpower relations is best achieved by technological developments that would discourage the first use of nuclear weapons. But those developments are rapidly moving us in the opposite direction. Thus, they cannot be instruments of even "minimal" progress. Technological innovation can never be viewed as a progressive end in itself. Solutions to some problems create even greater ones. Expanding scientific and technical knowledge not only can be a boon to peace and plenty but can lead to pollution, war, and political repression. Acting together, states can work to solve problems of security, poverty, and injustice. But the institutions that embody international cooperation can also be wasteful and impotent and do not necessarily reduce international insecurity. Indeed, the old solutions to problems of security, welfare, and human rights are fraught with problems and need to be reexamined. We must discard the Enlightenment approach to Progress, begin to separate means from ends, and be vigilant about our own "ideologies" of progress. We must not rest easy with technological and institutional "fixes" to the problems we find most pressing.

The second objection to our concern with progress in international relations focuses not on the *idea* of progress itself but on the dim prospects for its achievement in the international arena. Many realists writing in the "structual" tradition of international relations scholarship[6] argue that the international system is the realm of recurrence, repetition, competition among the strong, and domination of the weak. Promotion of human interests may be possible within some states, but will not result from interaction among them. International anarchy obstructs progress in international relations and thus constrains hope for widespread improvement in the human condition. Thus, the international system is not the appropriate arena in which to consider the question of progress as we have defined it.[7] Three causes contribute to this dreary outlook: (1) the absence of central authority over states; (2) a lack of universally shared values, rights, and obligations in the international system; and (3) the inequality of states' capabilities.[8] Each of these characteristics of anarchy arrests the promotion of human interests in a somewhat different way.

First, in the absence of central authority the national interest in preserving autonomy and freedom of action are the dominant motivations for state action. Since states cannot appeal to a higher authority for protection, they must help themselves in order to secure the survival of populations within their territories. To protect themselves they maximize their power and military might. As Hans Morgenthau has written, states' interests in the international system are defined as power.[9] In amassing power, however, states threaten others. Barring disarmament, a sense of security for some individuals can only be purchased with the insecurity of others. Thus arises the "security dilemma" whose most devastating effect is the "unsolved problem of war."[10] In this environment the quest for security breeds insecurity; military budgets sap productive resources that are the essence of economic growth and welfare; militarized societies squelch human rights.

Second, structural realists argue that the lack of shared meanings, values, rights, and obligations among states thwarts the formation of universal community at the international level. The concept of "natural rights" has vanished, for states are sovereign over the definition of rights and obligations within their territories.[11] If the lack of a central authority over states implies the subordination of the larger "global good" to their selfish concerns, then a lack of shared values implies that the "global good" or even "human interests" can never be consensually defined. One state's view of progress may be experienced as another's domination. What one group of states upholds as human rights another group denounces as bourgeois values. The fundamental drive for national power obstructs the formation of international community.

It is the third aspect of anarchy, structural realists remind us, that is the most problematic in the achievement of progress in international relations. The fact that states, in the absence of central authority, are unequal in their capabilities provides incentives for domination, increased competition for power resources, and the "progress" of some at the expense of others. This inequality of capabilities among states has intensified since the industrial revolution.[12] Whereas the first characteristic of anarchy—the lack of a central authority over states—explains why cooperation among state elites to achieve mutual interests is difficult, this third characteristic predicts that enduring conflicts of interest and values will obstruct any universal attempts to protect human interests. Under anarchy, states perceive others' power increase as their own loss. Thus, it is often the "imperialism of great power"[13] rather than the realization of human interest that dominates international outcomes. Raymond Aron observed that the "international system has always been oligarchical (or hierarchic) in that, without civil society, rights depend largely on might.[14] Might permits those most powerful to impose their ideological preferences and vision of "world order" upon others. When international cooperation arises, it often tends to further the interests and goals of the strong and increase the vulnerability of the weak. Efforts to reduce their vulnerability are rebuffed by the powerful who defend the systems of interaction that they have created.[15] If Thucydides' statement "the strong do what they can and the weak suffer what they must" is still true, the prospects for progress as increased security, welfare, and rights for individuals in international relations appear dim indeed. The best we can hope for is a distribution of capabilities among states that will temporarily stabilize the international balance of power.[16]

Some realist observers are sanguine about these prospects. Indeed, they would argue that the anarchic system is "progressive" from both a statist and a systemic perspective in that it allows maximum state autonomy, freedom of action, and the decentralization of power. The "unsolved problem of war" may be a blessing in disguise. As Stanley Hoffman has observed, the "terror of war drags people to the good." It forces states to minimize violence, moderate demands, and settle disputes peacefully if possible.[17] Further, some argue that it is not the interaction of states' policies that will promote human rights for individuals but rather those individuals' own struggle for their rights within the boundaries of the nation-state. Human rights are promoted not by forces external to the state but by the struggle of those whose rights have been denied.[18] Indeed, if political actors try to engineer international "progress," they may distract themselves from a more crucial focus on their own national interest, thus decreasing their own security and prosperity. Indeed, the idea of progress itself with its faith in technology, rationality, a pliable environment, the stability of international cooperation, and an informed public as a guide to foreign policy may actually diminish both national and international security!

In sum, structural realists conceptualize states' interests in the international system as static and self-interested in ways that exclude and offend others. They argue that the anarchic international condition defines states' primary *interest* as survival. It is the quest for survival that shapes state goals in international relations. Those goals are the accumulation of power and wealth as the *means* to guarantee state perpetuity. A narrow national interest defined this way by statesmen almost certainly ensures that the promotion of human interests in international relations will be weak and thin.

Despite the plausibility of these claims, I believe that their widespread acceptance has unnecessarily silenced a concern with human interests in world politics. This volume has focused on a set of issues that demonstrate that human interests are increasingly affected by international relations. Whether those interests thrive or wither is of both theoretical significance and empirical import. All of the authors in this volume would agree that the anarchic condition constrains even the minimal promotion and protection of human interests in international relations. None, however, argue that anarchy and its requirement that states pursue their national interests will necessarily have the effects that structural realists predict. Instead, most of the contributors here have turned to a "minimalist" conception of progress that incorporates a healthy respect for the persistence of the state system. This minimalist approach has led us to ask *not* how human interests can come to replace national interests, but rather how national interests can come to incorporate a respect for the needs of individuals across borders. If we agree that the pursuit of national interests will persist in international relations, it would seem that those interests must be redefined by the actors themselves for the achievement of minimal international progress.

INTEREST REDEFINITION

In the beginning pages of this book we argued that three changes in world politics have reduced the necessity for most state actors to focus their goals, objectives, and strategies *primarily* on their interest in survival. In the seventeenth century, states established a set of authoritative rules to guide their interaction and order their relations. In principle if not in practice, these rules embodied the potential of reducing their fear for survival in relations with other states. Moderate modern realists have argued that over time, these rules have been increasingly incorporated into diplomatic practice.[19] Terry Nardin argued that, "What makes the state system a permanent society of states, as distinguished from either a ruleless anarchy or a temporary alliance of like-minded sovereigns, is *toleration by its associates of one another's independent existence* within an authoritative framework of common rules."[20] Even the father of modern realist thinking, Hans Morgenthau, saw in diplomacy a peace-preserving and community-building process. The three attributes of anarchy described earlier were not assumed to be immutable, and the system was not static. The external behavior of states conformed more to a "satisficing" than a maximizing model as states increasingly restrained their behavior in respect for one another's claims for independence.[21] Furthermore, the foreign policy decisions of state actors were not rigidly determined by an anarchic structure. Within certain changing constraints, choice was possible.

These observations are based on the recognition of a second event in international relations history: the triumph of sovereignty.[22] Beginning in the eighteenth century, states joined together to oppose universal pretentions of one state over others. In the nineteenth century, the rules of the balance-of-power system placed limitations on the exercise of power and use of force by states of relatively equal capabilities. In the twentieth century, another important shift took place in the diplomatic principles guiding state interaction. Whereas in the nineteenth century, the principle of great-power primacy—the third attribute of anarchy—still guided diplomacy of both large and small states, the principle of sovereign equality guided diplomacy in the twentieth century.[23] Colonialism and tributary status were rejected, and even small, weak states were accorded juridical equality in the international system. Although large states have continued to exercise their dominance, the rise of this principle further undermined the legitimacy of outcomes based on their demands.

Ironically, it is this principle of sovereignty which informed the creation of international institutions in the postwar era whose norms, rules, and procedures were constructed to contrain member states' powerful unilateral actions. Witness the current effort to "anchor" a sovereign and unified Germany within the European Community and within a broader security system. Multilateral institutions provide the means by which members of the international community protect their own sovereignty by minimizing others' power.

As much a result of these developments as the expansion of their own military forces, few states worry that other states will swallow them up. With a few notable and important exceptions, territorial conquest is quite out of fashion. Particularly in the postwar period, as Tim McKeown has noted, the "death rate" for states has been very low.[24] Decolonization demonstrated that new states could survive in the international system with very little power and wealth. Power, wealth, and national security are still dominant goals, but the point here is that the link between those goals and the interest they were originally formulated to protect—*survival* of the nation-state in the face of territorial conquest—is now frail. And it continues to wither as territorial conquests decline.

The dramatic rise in international interdependence in the postwar period is the third event in international relations history undermining the old narrow definition of the national interest. International relations literature in the functional and neofunctional tradition argued that, as a result of increasing domestic social mobilization and rising international interdependence, an interest in welfare has emerged to create new state goals in international relations.[25] As a result, states began to redefine their "national interest" and develop a more complex set of instruments to achieve their goals.[26] Ernst Haas was a central pioneer of this tradition.[27] He argued throughout his work that political actors have expanded their goals to include economic cooperation, institution building, and economic development in *other* states in the interest of their own national welfare. Building on his work, many contributors here have elaborated on this theme. They suggest that by triggering a reevaluation of national interests among decision-making elites, interdependence can mute each of the three effects of anarchy discussed earlier, thus paving the way for the promotion of human interests.

First, perceptions of interdependence can change decision makers' calculations about the usefulness of unilateral action in states' international relations. If the "myopic pursuit of self-interest" would result in the loss of future benefits of an interdependent relationship, states may calculate that the ultimate self-interest lies in cooperative behavior, either to obtain benefits or to avoid costs that cannot be achieved through unilateral action. The first attribute of anarchy— self-help—is thus modified.[28]

Second, interdependence, even among a small number of states and their decision-making elites, can create shared values, meanings, rights, and obligations. Common values and perceptions greatly encourage cooperation, and they are generally embedded in the norms of international regimes. For example, the norm of reciprocity has been highlighted in the literature on international cooperation.[29] If this norm is shared, then states must also arrive at a consensus on the *meaning* of cooperation and defection within their interaction. Thus, a wider set of shared meanings may arise in order to bolster the reciprocity norm. To the extent that interests consist of core values, states' interests are continually redefined in the process of reaching these agreements with others. The emergence of shared values that may result from long-term interdependent relationships among states may not exactly create community, but it can mute the effects of anarchy's second attribute.

The attenuating effect of interdependence on the third aspect of anarchy is more difficult to discern. Can international interdependence really invite states to redefine their interests in ways that can mitigate the effects of unequal power relationships in international relations? It can be argued that interdependence as mutual dependence between states is rare in international politics; relationships of independence and dependence are the norm. Those who are more powerful are more independent. Less powerful, dependent states become even more vulnerable in their relationships with powerful states. It has been fashionable to argue that "hegemonic stability" could guarantee cooperation in an international order in which violence could be reduced and prosperity could be increased.[30] But usually if cooperation arises, it will further the goals of those most powerful, for they have the resources of compensation and coercion to alter the behavior of weaker states. They can impose their norms on others. Therefore, it may be misleading to speak of shared norms among unequal powers. And cooperation must be carefully differentiated from compliance. Furthermore, more powerful states can easily defect from a previous agreement whenever they like because sanctions fail in the face of their power. And weaker states may hesitate to impose sanctions out of the fear that the powerful will retaliate. The existence of hegemonic power is no guarantee that the order it creates can foster progress as we have defined it.

We do not deny that power plays a central role in relations among states or that powerful states can obstruct efforts to promote human interests when they wish. Nor do we believe that progress depends on diminishing the role of power. What we argue is that interdependence can modify the calculations by which states choose to exercise their power and that under conditions of complex interdependence, power can be exercised to promote human interests. Jack Donnelly's essay here, for example, shows how perceptions of "moral interdependence" led the United States to use its power in the postwar period to implement international human rights programs in Latin America through the creation and maintenance of human rights regimes.

The point here is that *within* the anarchic condition, interdependence can pave the way for a redefinition of states' interests in ways that can embrace human interests. In many ways all the essays here reinforce the conclusion that under conditions of interdependence, states can no longer "help" themselves in important areas of public policy—areas ranging from the choice of macroeconomic instruments to environmental policy. Unilateral policies are no longer as useful as they once might have been, even for powerful states. Interests are increasingly "shared" and common goals are hammered out in multilateral fora.

These facts have changed the scope of legitimate state activities. For example, Kudrle and Lenway's essay here traces the process by which two states gave up some activities once within their sovereign control in exchange for perceived welfare benefits. Those states, however, fell short of handing over their sovereignty to a supranational agency. The point is that the emergence of new interests does not mean that the sovereignty norm itself has vanished or that states are no longer the universally accepted final political authority within a given territory. It does not mean that new political institutions will come to replace the state sovereign authorities or that states will not exercise power and force to get their way. Indeed, John Ruggie's essay argues that sovereignty in international regimes was strengthened relative to the pre–World War II period through the norm of embedded liberalism. I simply mean to suggest that because state survival as it was originally conceptualized is no longer as much at stake as it once was, national interests are in the process of being redefined by state actors themselves. Redefining interests does not mean relinquishing interests.

Finally, the fact of interdependence and even the redefinition of interests that can result does not mean the automatic promotion of human interests. Interdependence can also lead to war, conflict, exploitation, and injustice. The strong can grab its benefits and leave the weak empty-handed. Transnational activity can expand the gap between elites and masses within states.[31] Interdependence and interest redefinition, then, may only be necessary and not sufficient conditions for progress. I suggest later that the sufficient conditions include actor learning and the incorporation of restraint, obligation, and empathy into policy choice.

LEARNING

In this volume we have been specifically concerned with this *process* of interest redefinition. The essays here describe that process as "actor learning."[32] By learning, I mean two things: (1) the use of technical, theoretical, or experiential knowledge to alter either causative or ethical beliefs that underlie the previous definition of the national interest and the goals flowing from that definition, and (2) changes in reasoning processes, from short-term calculations toward more reflection on the long-term and widespread effects of policy decisions. *How* actors learn about the effects of their interdependent relationships with others concerns me here. Defined this way, learning means actor recognition of interdependence that triggers a more complex understanding of how issues are linked and how causes, effects, means, and ends are connected. This "complex" learning involves a shift in policy objectives.[33]

How do we known when decision makers learn? Our authors here look for learning in the use of scientific and technical knowledge in policy choice, experiences in implementation that result in redirecting policy, shifts in the programs of international organizations, changes in negotiating positions, changes in declared positions on various international issues, and changes in values, expectations, and attitudes. Certainly it can be argued that these concrete changes can result from forces other than actor learning. Revolutionary governments can come to power and reverse previous policies. States can always threaten and coerce others to change their foreign policies, activities, and bargaining positions. As I discuss in more detail later, however, these are not the *only* or even the most important sources of policy change.

Nonetheless, even if we can demonstrate that learning has occurred, we cannot predict actual policy outcomes with precision. Some learning will result in more "holistic" policies and some will result in scaled-down policies. For example, Emanuel Adler suggests that learning among international arms control negotiators resulted in policies that linked arms control efforts with environmental concerns, a move toward a more "holistic" policy. Ben Schiff's essay describes the process of organizational learning by which UNRWA scaled down its objectives in the face of political conflict over large-scale programs. Rather than let the organization stagnate, UNRWA shifted its primary focus away from large-scale infrastructure "works" projects toward economic empowerment of individual Palestinians through education.

Why would interdependence lead to learning? Certainly the fact of interdependence does not necessarily lead to a change in beliefs or an altering of reasoning processes. Nor does it automatically lead to a redefinition of national interests that would include human interests. In fact, many realists argue that if interdependence remains low among significant actors in the international system, conflict among them could be *minimized*, and individual welfare could be achieved through self-reliance.[34] The theme that we emphasize in this volume, however, is that interdependence can spark new political forces and patterns of acting that create disappointment in previous policies and influences the calculation of interests and goals. Of the many forces which trigger learning, our essays focus on two: experts and negotiations.

In the first place, governments have come to cope with international interdependence through expanding their use of "experts" in the policy formulation process. Expert knowledge of cause–effect relationships is believed necessary to effective policy. The use of scientific and technical expertise as a basis for foreign policy decisions may uncover new interests that were previously unknown. Interests are thus redefined as these new actors achieve new power in both the domestic political process and in international negotiations.

For example, Peter Haas shows how in the midst of the environmental crises in the early 1970s, government policymakers called in national marine scientists to help define the scope of pollution problems. Scientists from the countries in the Med region formed transnational linkages with one another and began to teach government officials about ecological cycles. This knowledge helped them better understand the many environmental consequences of policy decisions and helped them to appreciate how their policies affected other countries. As a consequence, they began to anticipate the ecological effects of their industrial policies and reformulate their policy preferences accordingly. Similarly, in their study of the U.S.–Canadian Free Trade Agreement, Kudrle and Lenway show how influential studies by "experts" in Canada, and to a lesser extent in the United States, altered prevailing beliefs about the relationship between trade protection and prosperity. The shift in elite opinion to a consensual belief that free trade would increase prosperity paved the way for negotiations to begin.

Second, states learn to redefine their interests through the process of bargaining with other states. Both the use of expertise as an "intellectual aid" to negotiations and the political process of exchanging concessions can contribute to this redefinition and recalculation. Again, Haas' essay shows how the use of technical information within negotiations contributed a more complex level of understanding on the part of negotiators about how policies of industrial development and cross-border pollution were linked together in a cause–effect relationship. This knowledge contributed to a convergence of concerns among states in the Med region to reduce pollution. In the same way, trading concessions in negotiations led to a mutual recognition of common interests. With this recognition, bluffs and threats were reduced, and bargainers came to a convergence of bargaining positions.

PROGRESS AND INTEREST REDEFINITION

Neither the use of technical expertise nor the bargaining process itself will lead to "progressive" learning unless human interests as we have defined them are promoted or protected. Just as interdependence can create greater gaps between rich and poor countries or as benefits of interdependent relationships can accrue to elites in both weak and strong nations at the expense of the poor, experts can train state decision makers in more effective modes of social repression, and states can negotiate to cooperate in order to oppress and exploit others.

The point here is that learning unharnessed to values opens the way for its own misuse. The preceding definition of learning in no way implies that learning on the part of decision-making elites can necessarily "make things better" or will result in even the most minimal promotion of human interests. How, then, can we conceptualize progressive learning? Adler's concept of cognitive evolution is intended to paint a picture of progressive learning that embraces a conscious self-reflective historical process of value change and interest redefinition. In other words, the concept of cognitive evolution describes collective learning that "sticks" because it is "backed by enough power to make people set aside competing ideas and beliefs."

The process of learning discussed earlier is a more immediate one, which can or cannot lead to cognitive evolution. Learning become internationally progressive when the historical self-reflective process of value change promotes human interests beyond one's own national boundaries.

In this volume we have purposely examined issues in which the processes outlined earlier could indeed lead to a promotion of human interests. I suggest that interdependence, interest redefinition, and learning are the necessary conditions under which security, welfare, and human rights for individuals can be promoted and protected in international relations. The next step, then, will be to outline more precisely the sufficient conditions for international progress. What kinds of policies and programs would signal a change in the definition of the national interest to include human interests, and what are the conditions under which those policies might come about?

Adler, Crawford, and Donnelly argued that it is difficult to measure progress by looking at overall changes in the number of wars and level of violent conflict, by counting the number of people in poverty, or by assessing changes in overall human rights violations. An alternative strategy involves looking at how states redefine and pursue the national interest in their international relations. If decision makers learn to think about their interests in ways that promote human interests and formulate policies accordingly, important conditions for progress in international relations are achieved. If we pursue this second strategy, we need a conceptualization of interest redefinition that conforms to our minimalist approach to progress. Robert O. Keohane makes useful distinctions among different ways states experience their interests relative to others, which he calls "instrumental, situational, and empathetic interdependence of interests."[35] I draw on these distinctions to explore how decision makers can recalculate their national interests to include human interests. I suggest that a "progressive" definition of the national interest will include principles of restraint, obligation, or empathy. It is to these three concepts that the discussion now turns.

Restraint

First, recognition of interdependence may lead decision makers to take into account the negative reactions of other states to the harmful effects of their own policies and, as a result, introduce new policies of *restraint*. This results from what Keohane calls the "instrumental interdependence of interests" and what Adler calls an awareness of limits, i.e., of what cannot be achieved in the international arena without having to pay for it with war, poverty, or human rights violations. [36]

Under what conditions will states exercise restraint? Recognizing that interdependence can lead to interference and harm, states come to see it as their responsibility to limit and restrain acts that may harm others as being in their interest. Policies based on the promotion of self-interest are thus defined in ways that avoid hurting others in the process of reaching self-interested goals. This is simply because harm can lead to retaliation. Here the road of prudential action is being traveled. Policy is defined in terms of constraints and limits on behavior if retaliation for harm is expected. This necessity for restraint arising from interdependence, for example, is what leads to cooperation among states to protect the environment or stabilize nuclear deterrence. Here state behavior is characterized by calculations of interest that take into account reactions of other states and thus possible long-term and widespread consequences of policy choice. Such calculations promote human interests when they enhance security and the quality of life for individuals.

Certainly a simple power model of policy change can often explain why states restrain themselves. State actors constantly put pressure on one another to bridle their actions. [37] Throughout the Cold War era, for example, the United States pressured its allies to cut their trade with the Soviet Union. The Soviet Union, in turn twisted its allies' arms to restrict contact with the West. The United States has pressured Third World nations to stop nationalizing U.S. corporations on their territory. And those nations have exercised restraint in doing so.

In the cases examined in this volume, however, restraint involved much more than a response to pressure. It resulted from learning and the redefinition of policy goals. It is these new triggers for restraint that may signal progress in international relations. Kudrle and Lenway show that as Canada's investments in the United States expanded, the Canadian government became less willing to restrict U.S. investments in Canada. Canadian elites argued that the government should be treating foreign investment as it wished its own investment to be treated. As a result of new knowledge about this interdependence, those elites developed an "awareness of limits"— of what they could not achieve without having to pay for it. Similarly, Peter Haas' essay traces the processes by which states in the Med region initiated policies of restraint. Those who were harmed by cross-border pollution began to protest, and transnational scientists provided new information to state elites about the ecological effects of their economic policies. Both the expert studies and international pressures led to a recognition that international cooperation was needed to manage the negative environmental effects of domestic industrial policies. Haas argues that the "national interest" was then redefined to include wider regional or systemic effects.

Certainly the Soviet Union's exercise of restraint in the face of the East European democratic revolutions of 1989 illustrate the argument. The consequences of repression in the face of rising protests were demonstrated to Gorbachev and East European Communist leaders in the June 1989 massacre of protesting Chinese students in Tienanmen Square. For Gorbachev, the massive bloodshed that would surely result from a continuation of the Brezhnev Doctrine was an intolerable consequence. In the conceptual terms used here, Gorbachev had developed an awareness of the limits of continued repression. He no doubt calculated that any loss of Soviet security which might result when the East European satellites spun away from the Soviet orbit was outweighed by the political and economic liability which he could abandon if he simply let them go. The Gorbachev era witnessed a dramatic redefinition of the Soviet national interest to include restraint in both security policy and diplomatic relations.

Obligation

Second, under conditions of interdependence, state actors may recalculate their interests to include others' welfare in their own policy calculations. This is what Keohane calls "situationally interdependent interests." Here obligations to others guide policy choice. This means that self-interest is understood to include an interest in the welfare of others.[38] Or to state it another way, responsibility to one's own welfare is defined as responsibility to others. Unlike restraint, obligations are expressed as an extension rather than a limitation of action.

Our essays suggest that the direct concern with others' welfare is triggered by perceptions of *dependence* within interdependent relationships. That is, policymakers in one state recognize that their welfare is dependent upon the welfare of others. They also recognize that they can formulate and implement policies that will increase the welfare of other states. For example, according to John Ruggie's analysis, the Generalized System of Preferences (GSP) represents a policy change triggered by this kind of interdependence recognition.[39] U.S. central decision makers perceived that the realization of U.S. interests was dependent on the stability of the international trading system. The GSP was an effort to avoid destabilization that was bound to appear when individual European countries granted selected trade preferences to LDCs. Thus, the GSP can be interpreted as a policy change that incorporated U.S. calculations of self-interested obligation toward the Third World.

Ben Schiff's discussion of UNRWA's activities on behalf of Palestinian refugees can be explained in much the same way. He argues that present commitment to UNRWA stems from a recognition that to terminate UNRWA's services would create a political explosion in the Middle East that would jeopardize those status quo states who view global stability as central to their national interest. These examples illustrate that powerful states are more likely to include obligations than to include restraint in their international relations, if their interests are more far-flung and systemically defined. The OECD countries, for example, have recognized an obligation to provide economic aid to the fledgling democracies of Eastern Europe. The obligation arises not only because the West had urged such a change for forty years, but also because domestic instability in Eastern Europe could lead to a military crisis and could result in a return to power of the forces of reaction.

Empathy

Finally, decision makers may make policy calculations that take into account others' welfare, security, and human rights that are only tenuously related to calculations of their own self-interest. Here empathy enters into states' policy calculations. This is what Keohane calls an "empathetic definition of interests." By empathy I mean that states derive benefits from others' welfare without a tangible effect on their own. Action is taken out of an experience of connection with other individuals rather than their experience of separation by national boundaries. Thus, as a basis for policy calculation, it deviates most radically from our expectations about policy derived from either the structural realist or even more moderate assessments of the effects of international anarchy on national policy.

What are the conditions under which empathy can arise? Does the recognition of interdependence and learning invoke empathy as a basis for policy? I would suggest that empathy springs from two sources. First, it arises out of a recognition of what Jack Donnelly calls "moral interdependence," rather than from material connections or a commitment to legal or ethical principles. Second, empathy can arise under conditions of "value convergence." Those individuals who share similar core values may tend to be more empathetic toward one another.

Human beings do not seem to possess "natural" empathy for others in the abstract, but empathy may arise as interdependent connections are created and recognized and when increasing channels of communication are established.[40] Empathy, however, is distinguished from restraint and obligation because it does not come to life out of fear of retaliation or a recognition of dependence. Rather, it arises out of a sense of solidarity and awareness of connections between people. When empathy is factored into policy calculations, policy choice is not affected by rules of reciprocity.[41] Empathy arises at the emotional and experiential rather than the cognitive level of awareness; it arises from a firsthand experience of connection and identification with the other rather than from an intellectual understanding of the effects of interdependence.[42] As a result, responsibility and obligation to others are defined as an *extension* rather than a limitation of action—an act of care rather than restraint of aggression or the self-interested extension of benefits. For example, pressure on South Africa to abolish the apartheid system may result from an empathetic definition of interests on the part of democratic states or their citizens.

In this volume, essays by Schiff, and Kudrle and Lenway suggest the possibility of empathy in international relations. Schiff's essay shows that empathy clearly entered into the original policy calculations of states in their creation of UNRWA despite the later shift toward obligation discussed earlier. The organization, whose members are nation-states and whose funding comes from voluntary donations, is committed to the promotion of the economic and social rights of the Palestinian refugees. The commitment was forged despite the fact that members continued to disagree about other matters in the Middle East. Kudrle and Lenway suggest that empathetic considerations came into play in the U.S.–Canadian Free Trade Agreement. U.S. empathy with Canadian autonomy fears led the United States to permit Canada to restrict U.S. cultural imports into Canada. In the end, the United States gave up some prosperity to alleviate fears of Canadian loss of cultural autonomy.

BETTER PROBLEMS AS A SIGN OF PROGRESS

Interdependence recognition, learning, and the redefinition of interests to incorporate policies of restraint, obligation, and empathy are still simply *means* to achieve the promotion of human interests, not indicators of *substantive* progress. How, then, can we know that these paths actually lead to the promotion of security, welfare, and human rights for individuals? Elites might learn, but their learning need not necessarily result in new definitions of the national interest that embrace human interests. They may behave with restraint, obligation, or empathy toward one another; human interests may or may not be served.

What we know for certain is that we will never be free from the problems that inhibit maximum security, welfare, and human rights. New problems arise to replace the old. Current problems can only arise from old solutions. Decision makers are constantly balancing the problem they are solving with the one they are creating. The problem of elite "brain drain" from the Third World is a result of expanded educational opportunities for Third World people. The problem of unemployment in Africa and Latin America results partly from investment in capital-intensive industry intended to promote economic growth and welfare. Thus, to look only at policy solutions as indicators of progress may be shortsighted and misleading. Our essays suggest that substantive progress is identified not by the present solutions but by broader historical criteria by which we can measure today's problems against the problems of an earlier period.

Are today's problems preferable to (i.e., less harmful than) those of the past?[43]

A focus on "better problems" is consistent with the minimalist approach to progress introduced in the early pages of this book. In contrast, the maximalist focuses on *solutions* to problems of war, poverty, and injustice, believing that such solutions provide a guarantee of progress. To argue that policy and program "solutions" to problems indicate progress in and of themselves is arrogant because such an argument implies that the formulators somehow had perfect knowledge that the policy's future consequences would not be harmful.

A focus on "better problems" is more humble and less determinist in its recognition that today's solutions can bring either better or worse problems in the future. Such a focus is consistent with the view of Claude Lévi-Strauss expressed in his observation that began this essay: "certain progresses must be paid for by regression in other domains." Progress—even minimalist progress—creates problems and even regressions. If we are concerned with assessing the impact of international change on human interests, it is incumbent upon us to assess whether those problems are better or worse than the ones that came before.

Most of the essays in this volume make judgments about what constitutes a "better problem." For example, Donnelly's essay reminds us that human rights practices have always been the concern of nation-states. The problem is that deeply entrenched sovereignty and nonintervention norms obstruct outside efforts to stop a state's human rights abuses. Without a central authority over states there is little international capability to enforce a change in the abuser's policy. Nonetheless, in the postwar period, as a direct result of the international consensus on the universal obligation to prevent human rights abuses, both governments and publics seem unwilling to treat those crimes as a legitimate right of national governments. The way states treat individuals within their territories has become the concern of citizens and governments in foreign countries, and, taken together, the existence of human rights regimes indicates a commitment to uphold those obligations. Communication advances have facilitated the flow of ideas about human rights and have thus increased "intersocietal sensitivity" to human rights issues.[44]

Because of its increasing visibility, state torture of individuals, for example, has become an international scandal and has actually lost its place in the legitimation of state power. Thanks to the normative force of the Universal Declaration of Human Rights and the activity of organizations like Amnesty International, the view that responsibility toward others stops at national boundaries has broken down.[45] The spread of knowledge and change in attitudes about human rights have altered the context within which policy decisions have been made, both for states that are violators of human rights and for states that have the power to pressure those violators. In this context it is harder for states to pursue policies with blatant disregard for minimal individual rights. Before World War II, the problem of international human rights could be defined as a lack of knowledge about human rights abuses in individual states. With communication advances and the emergence of "moral interdependence," those problems have found tentative solutions. Now the problem is one of global enforcement of human rights norms in individual states. We can probably agree that today's problems are preferable.

According to the criteria of "better problems," we may see similar signs of progress in other issue areas. For example, although the number of refugees worldwide continues to grow, increasing attention is given to their basic human needs. In the nineteenth century, no political body—national or international—existed that could guarantee the rights of stateless persons. Before World War II, there was little commitment to the economic and social rights of refugees. But today both the commitment and the international bodies exist. And as Schiff argues, the efforts of one of those bodies, UNRWA, have been successful. Palestinian refugees are still stateless. But their basic health problems have been solved and life expectancies extended. Education is available and educational programs are effective. The refugee problems persist and peace is as elusive now as it always was. Increased international commitment to upholding refugee rights, however, means that some basic human needs are being met that were not met earlier. Schiff argues that the problem is a "better" one.

Similarly, Haas' essay argues that in the Med region, the problem of marine pollution and the near death of the Mediterranean Sea has been replaced by problems of how best to coordinate policy, how to maintain the transnational alliance between marine scientists, and how to keep UNEP financially afloat. Kudrle and Lenway restate in their essay the classical liberal argument that today's problems of dispute settlement and increasing import competition in both Canada and the United States are better than the problem of aggregate welfare reduction in the absence of free trade.

Needless to say, there will always be controversy about what constitutes a "better problem." Some will say, "it depends on where you look." Others will say, "it depends on what you mean by 'better.' " Still others will say, "it depends on what you mean by 'problem.' " Those who reject all market solutions to welfare problems will disagree with Kudrle and Lenway's argument. Those who argue that UNRWA is part of an unacceptable status quo and that international services to refugees create dependence and passivity rather than self-sufficiency and political organization will disagree with Schiff. Those who claim that international agreements for environmental protection obstruct the realization of Third World development goals will disagree with Haas. Those who argue that the forces of international capitalism are in bed with the forces of bourgeois democracy, providing new centers of threat to Third World socialist democracies, will disagree with Schmitter.

Nonetheless, if we are concerned with assessing progress in international relations, we must make judgments, weighing past problems against present ones, always keeping in mind human interests as our standard of measurement. We must debate one another's definition of "better problems," or "worse problems." We must question ourselves and each other about the evidence we draw on to support our claims. We must be conscious of our level of analysis and the distinction between minimalist and maximalist definitions of progress. This volume is an invitation to begin those debates.

FUTURE RESEARCH

In pulling together the many things the essays here have had to say about progress in international relations, it becomes obvious that we need clearer conceptualizations of the processes by which human interests can be promoted in international relations. We need better ways of characterizing the process of learning, and clearer ways of measuring interest redefinition. We need to search out the sources of interest definition. How are interests formed? By whom? We need further studies that use these concepts to explain the lack of progress, stagnation, and regress, as well as progress itself.

We clearly need to probe further the sources of learning and change, particularly the changing domestic political coalitions that result from interdependence. The central impetus for actor learning discussed in our empirical essays here is technical expertise. Haas' essay also emphasized learning through negotiation. We might also add that transnational movements can trigger learning on the part of decision-making elites. The anti-apartheid movement in the United States and in Western Europe, for example, pushed their governments and their corporations to reduce economic involvement in South Africa. That pressure resulted in the incorporation of a concern for human interests in both corporate and government policies.[46] Adler suggests the importance of crisis as a trigger for change. Increasing recognition of environmental crises, for example, is pushing environmental issues to the top of the policy agenda in industrialized states.

First, we need more empirical studies on the role of transnational actors in the promotion of human interests. Transnational actors and informed publics provide channels of *both* information and political pressure that may be felt by central decision makers. Keohane and Nye have suggested, however, that because gaps between rich and poor are present everywhere and because transnational activity is unevenly distributed, its benefits have accrued to elites in rich, powerful countries at the expense of the poor. Transnationalism can increase the gap between elites and masses within states, as elites are "absorbed within transnational networks."[47] There is certainly evidence that transnational activity can be an obstacle to the promotion of human interests.

Nonetheless there are important aspects of transnational relations that provide incentives to states to pursue policies that promote security, welfare, and human rights, both at home and abroad. First, transnational links can provide more information to decision makers. As Peter Haas points out here, this was very important in the Med Plan. Second, transnational links can stimulate domestic political coalitions. As Donald Warwick has observed, "transnational participation may have its greatest impact on foreign policy through its effects on the climate of public opinion.[48] Take, for example, the organized protest against nuclear weapons that has grown in the West and has also spread to the East. Organized interest groups may also put direct pressure on governments to pursue policies that promote human interests. Private voluntary organizations also pursue transnational activities that promote human interests. The work of Amnesty International or Americas Watch provides an important example. Through each of these channels, governments receive information and experience pressure that may lead to cognitive change, recalculation of interests, and a redefinition of policy problems

Second, careful studies of the role of crisis can reward our efforts to understand the forces that lead to interest redefinition. Many of the essays here note that it often takes a crisis to invest experts and negotiators with the power to influence national policy. None of our essays, however, carefully probes the connections between crisis and learning. They do suggest, however, that crises provide decision-makers with immediate awareness about the failure of old policies, and provoke a search for redefinitions of the policy problem. Crises in security, human rights, food, energy, trade, and the environment have all led to a recalculation of how national interests could best be served. For example, Donnelly suggests that the Universal Declaration of Human Rights in 1948 was a direct response to the "crisis" of Hitler and World War II. And Haas argues that the near death of the Mediterranean Sea advertised the environmental problems associated with industrial development in the first place. Attention was necessary to mobilize new domestic and international political resources for environmental protection. Kudrle and Lenway posit that Canadians pushed for the Free Trade Agreement in the face of a perceived crisis of economic decline. These essays all suggest that crises have led to the search for new solutions to problems arising within interdependent relationships.[49]

Finally, we need studies that are sensitive to the contingent nature of international change. All the essays here share a concern with the specified historical and political context in which the empirical cases are located. We have made a distinction here between two roads to progress, the prudential and the functionalist roads. Whether one or the other is traveled depends on geopolitical factors, the strength of particular domestic political and transnational coalitions, the issue at stake, and the way that issue is conceptualized by political actors. A sensitivity to context is essential so that we do not dismiss the "road" when progress is not achieved in a specific case; some roads to progress are only appropriate in some circumstances. Thus, Schiff stresses that UNRWA's success is dependent on the historical circumstances of its creation. U.N. involvement was a direct result of its participation in the creation of the state of Israel and the resultant dispossession of Palestinians. It is highly unlikely that the United Nations will face a similar situation in the future; in another geopolitical and historical setting, different forces will shape the way international commitment to refugee rights will find institutional expression.

Essays by Donnelly and Kudrle and Lenway underscore the importance of the historical and geopolitical contexts in which progress was achieved. For Donnelly, the crisis of Hitler, and the hegemony of the United States led to a near universal demand for human rights regimes in the postwar period and undercut the legitimacy of those who might oppose their creation. Such conditions no longer exist; in the absence of another empathy-invoking crisis and a willing hegemon, it is unlikely that such a strong normative consensus could again emerge, except in an area where strong cultural homogeneity existed. A normative consensus built on a cultural community permits states to put into practice a national commitment to human rights and to give up important activities earlier associated with their sovereignty. In the absence of national commitment and cultural community or hegemony, state sovereignty prevents the growth of human rights regimes beyond the promotional "stage." Similarly, for Kudrle and Lenway, the U.S.–Canadian Free Trade Agreement would not have been constructed in the absence of U.S. hegemonic decline and severe economic difficulties in Canada.

In sum, this volume is dedicated achieving a careful joining of analyses of change and the protection and promotion of human interests. It has been our intention not to confuse analysis and values but rather to link them carefully together. Equally important has been our commitment not to sacrifice one for the other. We must develop a better understanding of the forces of international change, an understanding that is not diminished or distorted by our vision of how things *ought* to be. At the same time, however, we must not dismiss that vision. If we do, our inquiries into the nature of change lose all relevance.

important contribution to my thinking about empathy. See Waltraud Herbstrith, *Edith Stein: A Biography* (New York: Harper & Row, 1971), p. 81. See also Alice Miller, *The Drama of the Gifted Child* (New York: Basic Books, 1981) and Carol Gilligan, *In a Different Voice* (Cambridge, Mass.: Harvard University Press, 1982).

43. This question is posed by Aaron Wildavsky, "Progress and Public Policy," in Almond, Chodorow, and Pearce, eds., *Progress and Its Discontents*, p. 373.
44. Joseph S. Nye, Jr., and Robert O. Keohane, "Transnational Relations and World Politics: A Conclusion," p. 376.
45. For an excellent analysis of this development see Edward Peters, *Torture* (London: Basil Blackwell, 1985).
46. This argument is made by Pearl-Alice Marsh in "Grass Roots Statecraft: Popular Challenges to U.S. Foreign Policy in the Third World," a paper presented at the International Conference on State, Society and Social Movements in Africa, Institute of Developing Countries, University of Warsaw, Poland, March 26–29, 1990.
47. Nye and Keohane, "Transnational Relations and World Politics: A Conclusion," p. 388.
48. Donald P. Warwick, "Transnational Participation and International Peace," in Keohane and Nye, *Transnational Relations and World Politics*, p. 320.
49. Two points must be made here about the role of crisis in political change: first, crises are triggers for action, but they do not determine what kind of action will be taken. Second, the designation of many events as "crises" is a social naming action; that is, events are only crises relative to a certain set of interests or world views.

ENDNOTES

1. Interview with James M. Markham, reported in *The New York Times,* December 21, 1987, p. 11.
2. See Gabriel A. Almond, Mervin Chodorow, and Roy Harvey Pearce, eds., *Progress and Its Discontents* (Berkeley: University of California Press, 1982); and Robert Nisbet, *History of the Idea of Progress* (New York: Basic Books, 1980), ch. 9.
3. Gabriel A. Almond, Mervin Chodorow, and Roy Harvey Pearce, "Introduction," pp. 1–15, and Nannerl O. Keohane, "The Enlightenment Idea of Progress Revisited," pp. 21–40, in Almond, Chodorow, and Pearce, eds., *Progress and Its Discontents*.
4. For a critique of this literature see, for example, Charles Tilly, *Big Structures, Large Processes, Huge Comparisons* (New York: Russell Sage Foundation, 1984), pp. 33–56. See also Crawford Young, "Ideas of Progress in the Third World," in Almond, Chodorow, and Pearce, eds., *Progress and Its Discontents*, pp. 83–105.
5. See Thomas L. Hughes, "The Twilight of Internationalism," *Foreign Policy* (Winter 1985–1986), 61:25–48.
6. The most influential argument for a structural perspective is Kenneth Waltz, *Theory of International Politics* (Reading, Mass.: Addison-Wesley, 1979).
7. For example, see Martin Wright, "Why Is There No International Theory?" in Herbert Butterfield and Martin Wright, eds., *Diplomatic Investigations*. (Cambridge, Mass.: Harvard University Press, 1966), p. 26.
8. See Leo Gross, "The Peace of Westphalia, 1646–1948," in Richard A. Falk and Wolfram H. Hanrieder, eds., *International Law and Organization* (Philadelphia: J. B. Lippincott, 1968), pp. 45–67, and John Gerard Ruggie, "Continuity and Transformation in the World Polity: Toward a Neorealist Synthesis," *World Politics*, (January 1983), 35(2):261–286.
9. Hans Morgenthau, *Politics Among Nations*, 6th ed. (New York: Alfred A. Knopf, 1985), pp. 10–11.
10. Robert Gilpin, *War and Change in International Politics* (Cambridge: Cambridge University Press, 1981), p. 7.
11. See John Gerard Ruggie, "Continuity and Transformation in the World Polity: Toward a Neorealist Synthesis" *World Politics* (January 1983), 35(2):275–279.
12. See Robert Tucker, *The Inequality of Nations*, (N.Y.: Basic Books, 1977), p. 3, and Stephen D. Krasner, *Structural Conflict* (Berkeley: University of California Press, 1985), p. 33.
13. Waltz, *Theory of International Politics*, p. 34.
14. Raymond Aron, *Progress and Disillusion: The Dialectics of Modern Society* (New York: Praeger, 1968), p. 160. See also E. H. Carr, *The Twenty Years' Crisis, 1919–1939* (New York: Harper & Row) p. 169 (First published by Macmillan & Co. 1939).
15. Krasner, *Structural Conflict*, pp. 1–31.

16. Realists disagree among themselves about what configuration of capabilities would constitute a stable distribution of power. Where Gilpin argues, for example, that hegemonic power provides the most stability, Waltz argues that a bipolar balance is more stable, and others argue that a multipolar system of five powers is the most stable. See, for example, Gilpin, *War and Change in International Politics*; Waltz, *Theory of International Relations*; Morton A. Kaplan, *System and Process in International Politics* (New York: Wiley, 1964); and Gordan A. Craig and Alexander L. George, *Force and Statecraft: Diplomatic Problems of Our Time* (New York: Oxford University Press, 1983), ch. 3.

17. Stanley Hoffman, *Duties Beyond Borders* (Syracuse, N.Y.: Syracuse University Press, 1981), pp. 45–93. On the state system as a progressive force see also Stephen D. Krasner, "Sovereignty: An Institutional Perspective," unpublished manuscript, March 13, 1987.

18. Michael Walzer, *Just and Unjust Wars* (New York: Basic Books, 1977), pp. 87–91.

19. Hedley Bull has observed that most states, at most times, pay some respect to the basic rules of coexistence in international society. See Hedley Bull, *The Anarchical Society* (New York: Columbia University Press, 1977), p. 13.

20. Terry Nardin, *Law, Morality and the Relations of States* (Princeton, N.J.: Princeton University Press, 1983), p. 115.

21. See Keohane, *After Hegemony*, pp. 112–113.

22. On the triumph of sovereignty see Krasner, *Structural Conflict*, pp. 73–75.

23. On the norm of "great power primacy," see Max Weber, "The Prestige and Power of the Great Powers" in H. H. Gerth and C. Wright Mills, *From Max Weber: Essays in Sociology* (New York: Oxford University Press, 1958), pp. 159–162).

24. On the low death rate of states and the implications for international relations theory see Timothy J. McKeown, "The Limitations of 'Structural' Theories of Commercial Policy," *International Organization* (Winter, 1986), 40(1):53.

25. See Karl J. Holsti, *The Dividing Discipline* (Winchester, Mass.: Allen & Unwin, 1985).

26. The central weakness of the functional and neofunctional tradition was the view that international institutions would come to replace national political authority. Both perspectives were informed by Weber's theory of social change. Weber had shown how capitalism's demand for rational calculations required high levels of certainty and predictability in increasingly interdependent social systems. Stability was created by the emergence of rational-bureaucratic nation-states and society's dependence on legitimate central authority. Karl Deutsch, Ernst Haas, and others saw the possibility for a similar process to emerge as states interacted in international relations. The next stage in the "progress" of international relations would be transformation of anarchy through the creation of

legitimate superordinate authorities over states to create and ensure order and stability among them. For an overview of this literature see Stephen Genco, "Integration Theory and System Change in Western Europe: The Neglected Role of Systems Transformation Episodes," in Oli R. Holsti, Randolph M. Siverson, and Alexander L. George, *Change in the International System.* (Boulder, Colo.: Westview, 1980), pp. 55–80.

27. See Ernst B. Haas, *The Uniting of Europe: Political, Social, and Economic Forces, 1950–1957* (Stanford, Calif.: Stanford University Press, 1958) and *Beyond the Nation-State: Functionalism and International Organization* (Stanford, Calif.: Stanford University Press, 1970).

28. See Duncan Snidal, "The Limits of Hegemonic Stability Theory," *International Organization*, (Autumn 1985), 39(4):593–594 and Robert O. Keohane, *After Hegemony* (Princeton, N.J.: Princeton University Press, 1984), p. 121.

29. See Robert O. Keohane, "Reciprocity in International Relations, " *International Organization* (Winter 1986), pp. 1–27.

30. See Keohane, *After Hegemony*, pp. 32–46.

31. Nye and Keohane, "Transnational Relations and World Politics: A Conclusion," in Robert O. Keohane and Joseph S. Nye, Jr., *Transnational Relations and World Politics* (Cambridge, Mass.: Harvard University Press, 1971), p. 388.

32. For two recent efforts to explore the role of actor learning in international politics see Ernst B. Haas, "Why Collaborate? Issue-Linkage and International Regimes," *World Politics* (April 1980), Vol. 32, No. 2, and Joseph S. Nye, Jr., "Nuclear Learning and U.S.–Soviet Security Regimes," (Summer 1987), Vol. 41, No. 3.

33. On the distinction between complex and simple learning see Nye, "Nuclear Learning," p. 380. See also Lloyd Etheredge, "Governmental Learning: An Overview," in Samuel L. Long, ed., *Handbook of Political Behavior*, vol. 2 (New York: Plenum, 1981), pp. 76–77.

34. See, for example, Kenneth Waltz, *Theory of International Politics*, and Stephen Krasner, *Structural Conflict*.

35. Robert O. Keohane, *After Hegemony*, pp. 122–123.

36. I am thankful to Emanuel Adler for this formulation.

37. See Joseph Nye, "Nuclear Learning," pp. 378–379.

38. Robert Axelrod, *The Evolution of Cooperation* (New York: Basic Books, 1984), p. 7

39. John Gerard Ruggie, "Political Structure and Change in the International Economic Order: The North–South Dimension," in Ruggie, ed., *The Antinomies of Interdependence: National Welfare and the International Division of Labor* (New York: Columbia University Press, 1983), pp. 451–454.

40. See Tucker, *Inequality of Nations*, pp. 151–152.

41. Even the notion of "diffuse reciprocity" would not apply. See Robert O. Keohane, "Reciprocity in International Relations," *International Organization* (Winter 1986), Vol. 40, No. 1.

42. The work of Edith Stein, Alice Miller, and Carol Gilligan have made an

Contributors

Emanuel Adler is Senior Lecturer of Political Science at the Hebrew University of Jerusalem.

Michael Brenner is Professor of international Affairs at the University of Pittsburgh

Beverly Crawford is Visiting Assistant Professor in the Political Economy of Industrial Societies Program, University of California at Berkeley.

Jack Donnelly is Associate Professor of Political Science at the University of North Carolina at Chapel Hill

Peter M. Haas is Assistant Professor of Political Science at the University of Massachusetts

Stephan Haggard is Associate Professor of Government at Harvard University

Robert T. Kudrle is Professor of Public Affairs at the Hubert Humphrey Institute of Public Affairs and Director of the Freeman Center for International Economic Policy, University of Minnesota

Stefanie Ann Lenway is Associate Professor of Strategic Management and Organization at the Curtis Carlson School of Management, University of Minnesota

John Gerard Ruggie is Director of the University of California Institute on Global Conflict and Cooperation and Professor of International Relations and Pacific Studies at the University of California, San Diego

Benjamin N. Schiff is Associate Professor of Government at Oberlin College

Philippe C. Schmitter is Professor of Political Science and Director of the Center for European Studies, Stanford University

INDEX

Commission on the Status of Women, 343
Committee Against Torture, 342
Committee on the Elimination of Racial Discrimination, 341-42
Common security (season), 30, 134-37, 148-52, 162, 164
Common understandings, 157; in seasons of peace, 138
Communication, 18; and seasons of peace, 30, 134
Communism, 72, 438
Community, 448; human need for identification with, 236-37; and regime norms, 333; universal, 443
Community of interest, 175
Competence model, 413, 415
Complementarity principle, 76
Complex interdependence, 21-23, 24, 27; in Latin America, 101, 102, 103; and seasons of peace, 134
Compliance, 420; in European human rights regime, 331-32, 333-34; "good faith," 329; with Med Plan, 288-89, 303; with regime norms, 329; voluntary, 333, 334, 336
Compliance evaluation, in global human rights regime, 319-21
Concentration, cycles of, 423-24
Concepts, evolution of, 47, 49
Concert (season), 30, 135, 137-38, 164
Conference on Security and Cooperation in Europe (CSCE), 163
Confidentiality: in investigation of human rights violations, 321-22
Conflict: anarchy and, 6; expectations and, 143-44; reduction of, 451, 453
Conflict resolution, 5, 9, 26; in bilateral negotiations, 237; in Canada-U.S. FTA, 246-47, 250, 253, 255-58, 261-62; supranational, 91
Congress of Vienna (1815), 163, 164
Consciousness raising, in cognitive evolution, 185
Consensus, 57, 58, 299; regarding acquisition of nuclear weapons, 193; epistemic communities and, 65; on human rights, 32, 318; in human rights regimes, 336, 337, 349; regarding nonproliferation, 186, 187; regime, 181, 186; regarding technical knowledge, 430; regarding values, 359
Conservatism, institutional, 183, 184, 186

Conventions, in environmental protection, 279-82, 280-81*t*
Constraints, 404, 414, 415, 419-20, 432; on human rights regimes, 350; institutional, 145; to progress in international security, 156-60
Continuity, patterns of, in international economic order, 201, 208-26
Control: in evolutionary epistemology, 48; illusion of, 170*n*62
Convention against Torture and Other Cruel, Inhuman or Degrading Treatment or Punishment, 342
Conventional war(s), 131, 132, 140
Convention for the Protection of Human Rights and Fundamental Freedoms, 330, 331, 332
Convention on Genocide, 324, 342, 348
Convention on the Elimination of Discrimination Against Women, 343
Convention on the Political Rights of Women, 343
Convertibility, 210, 212
Cooper, Richard, 204, 211, 213
Cooperation, 52; distinct from integration, 113-14; economic, 447; efficacy expectations of, 145-46; Latin America, 107, 108; mutual benefits available through, 329
Cooperation, international, 22, 30, 441, 442, 443, 454; democratization and, 108-13; efficacy expectations of, 153; in environment, 275, 287, 288, 295, 455; hegemonic stability in, 448; impact of expectations on, 143-44; as indicator of progress, 8-9; interdependence and, 23; knowledge in, 431; in Latin America, 113, 117-21; moral value of, 41*n*9; in nation-state system, 265; in new economic order, 73-74; and nuclear nonproliferation, 35-36; and nuclear technology, 178-80, 182-84, 185-86; regime type and, 91, 92, 93, 94, 97; and seasons of peace, 137, 143, 151; science/technology and, 17-18, 19; in security, 134, 154; between sovereign and egoist states, 167*n*19; *see also* Policy cooperation
Cooperation in Case of Emergency Oil Spills (U.S.-Mexico), 284
Cooperation Under Anarchy (Oye), 420
Coordination: and seasons of peace, 135, 138
Core-periphery (structure), 411, 419, 424